SELF-MADE MADNESS

To my Mother, Father, and Ami

Self-Made Madness

Rethinking Illness and Criminal Responsibility

EDWARD W. MITCHELL
University of Oxford, UK

ASHGATE

Published by
Ashgate Publishing Limited
Gower House
Croft Road
Aldershot
Hants GU11 3HR
England

Ashgate Publishing Company
Suite 420
101 Cherry Street
Burlington, VT 05401-4405
USA

Ashgate website: http://www.ashgate.com

British Library Cataloguing in Publication Data
Self-made madness : rethinking illness and criminal responsibility
1.Criminal liability 2.Mentally ill offenders - Legal status, laws, etc.
I.Title
345'.04'0874

Library of Congress Cataloging-in-Publication Data
Mitchell, Edward W., 1972-
Self-made madness : rethinking illness and criminal responsibility / Edward W. Mitchell.
p. cm.
Includes bibliographical references and index.
ISBN 0-7546-2332-7
1. Insanity--Jurisprudence. 2. Criminal liability. 3. People with mental disabilities and crime. 4. Mentally ill offenders--Mental health. 5. Criminals--Mental health. 6. Offenders with mental disabilities. I. Title.

RA1151.M527 20043
345'.04--dc22

2003056774

ISBN 0 7546 2332 7

Printed and bound in Great Britain by Athenaeum Press Ltd., Gateshead

Contents

List of Figures

List of Tables

Preface

> *Dear Sir, I was very interested to read about your report today in The Times. I myself am on anti-psychotic medication (Stelazine and others) and can readily sympathise with those people who don't take them...in fact I often do not take the medication. My main point is, I often feel that I might be violent and seriously harm or kill someone. My problem (as with many in your study) is that I sometimes drink a great deal, and then I have the greatest tendency to be aggressive...I have given up on [psychiatrists] entirely. With one very notable exception they have only been interested in manifest symptoms and medication (the so called 'medical model')...I have told various psychiatrists (including a forensic one) about my murderous thoughts, but as I say I don't think they think I will ever do it. I just hope they are right...In the meantime, I hope I can find some psychotherapy. Any advice you can give on this, I would be most grateful for.*
>
> Letter received by The Zito Trust,
> published in ZTMonitor, Issue 4, July 1998

This book describes and examines the notion that mentally disordered offenders may, to varying degrees, be responsible for the causation or exacerbation of their[1] own mental disorder and thus their concomitant criminal responsibility. Such a concept is denoted by the neologism 'meta-responsibility' ('responsibility for one's criminal responsibility'). Societal reactions to such blameworthiness for mental disorder are examined, through the lens of the insanity defence in particular.

This book does not pretend to be a definitive statement on the nature of mental disorder; it does not espouse a voluntaristic model to the exclusion of other models such as the medical model. As Slovenko (1995) points out, it is neither necessary nor advisable to adopt a single model for every possible situation. The proposition 'mentally disordered offenders cause their own mental disorder and therefore should be held accountable for their criminal responsibility' is not made during the course of this book, and no subscription on the part of the reader to such a proposition is required. Instead, we examine a question: 'What if we were to contrast accepted doctrine on the nature of mental disorder with a voluntaristic model? What effect would that have on criminal responsibility?' Even if the reader does not subscribe to such a voluntaristic model of mental disorder, it is hoped that he or she will find the manner in which the question is treated

---

[1] Where convenient, the pronouns *he, him,* and *his* are used generically (i.e. gender-neutrally) in contexts in which the grammatical form of the antecedent requires a singular pronoun.

satisfying, and the conclusions drawn appropriate ones given the research question in hand.

The meta-responsibility theory is a commonsensical one. The intuitiveness of the idea makes it a worthwhile object of study. That the mentally disordered can be easily conceived of as causing their own disorder (Chapter 1 shows that this has indeed been a major theme in the history of psychiatry) is precisely why, it is contended here, the idea of meta-responsibility impacts upon the processing of the mentally disordered in the criminal justice system[2] (and upon societal reactions towards the mentally disordered more generally). If such an idea was inconceivable – if the idea of meta-responsibility was so inherently complex and unobvious – then autonomy in illness (mental or otherwise) would remain largely theoretical, and the law could quite happily remain blind to the concept of meta-responsibility. There would be no mismatch between legal machinery and popular intuition.

However, it is contended that this mismatch in overt and covert acknowledgement is involved in many of the societal and legal difficulties that face the mentally disordered. If people (including the lay public, psychiatrists, lawyers, jurors and judges) intuitively take into account meta-responsibility, the law and societal zeigeist give them little or no chance to do so. This is perhaps the root cause of what Perlin (1994) refers to as pretextual decision-making and sanism: the processing and disposal of the mentally disordered (and particularly the mentally disordered offender) in a covert and discriminatory manner. Sanism (a process akin to racism or sexism) engenders such phenomena as incarceration for periods far longer than therapeutic concerns can justify as a 'punishment' for a successful insanity plea. Such disposals seem expressive of a 'barely concealed desire for retribution' towards mentally disordered criminals (Verdun-Jones, 1989: 23). Retribution for what? The theory of meta-responsibility developed here hopefully points the way to an answer.

The neologism 'meta-responsibility' would not have been introduced if it were not deemed necessary to service the concepts discussed in this book. The notion of causing one's own mental disorder and its concomitant effect on criminal responsibility – whilst perhaps a construct often used by society in the processing of mentally disordered offenders – has been so neglected as a research topic so as to leave it without even basic terminology.

---

[2] This study examines case and statutory Anglo-American criminal law. Where terms such as 'the criminal justice system' or 'the legal system' are used, this either refers to the general laws of the two jurisdictions (the United States and England and Wales), or it is made clear within the text (and/or index of cases in the bibliography) to which jurisdiction the case or reference is made (e.g. US State jurisdictions). Perhaps the most notable difference between the two major jurisdictions examined is the frequency of insanity defences; see *INFRA* note 1, Ch. 2. The meta-responsibility theory described in this study is perhaps most applicable to the US, where insanity defence usage is far higher and considerable public hostility exists towards the use of the defence (Appelbaum, 1994).

The ethical implications of introducing and researching the concept of meta-responsibility also need to be justified. The author has great interest in not seeing the mentally disordered face a further level of responsibility that might exacerbate their already problematic societal, clinical, and legal situation.

Instead, it is hoped that this research will challenge perceptions of the mentally disordered, particularly the low level of autonomy generally attributed to them that is responsible for much of their poor treatment in both criminal and civil law and in society more widely. The autonomy of mentally disordered persons promises to be a decisive factor in their fate with the proposal by the Richardson Committee[3] for a capacity test as the determinant of compulsion and coercion in treatment. The Committee reported that they believe capacity should have 'a central role within any future compulsory mental health structure'.

Furthermore, one of the central objects of enquiry of this book, medication non-compliance, has become a major concern to both the mental health field and society more generally over the last decade. Research shows not only that the non-medicated mentally disordered have a significantly elevated risk of violent offending (Mitchell, 1999a), but also that up to 70 per cent of psychiatric patients discharged from hospital become non-compliant within two years. Non-compliance has been shown to be a factor in the breakdown of care of over 50 per cent of mentally disordered persons who subsequently commit homicide (Howlett, 1998). The reaction of the press to such findings, and to policies such as Care in the Community, has thrown the situation of the mentally disordered into the centre of the political arena, with proposals for incarcerative/detentive approaches to care

---

[3] Department of Health (1999) *Review of the Mental Health Act 1983: Report of the Expert Committee*. London. HMSO. The Richardson Committee was charged by the UK Government to provide detailed proposals for the overhaul of the Mental Health Act (1983). A capacity test was proposed as the central criterion for compulsory detention/treatment, using the Law Commission definition of capacity under which compulsion may be justified if 'he or she is unable to make a decision based on the information relevant to the decision, including information about the reasonably foreseeable consequences of deciding one way or another or failing to make the decision' (p. 89). This study argues for a greater presumption of capacity, and that responsibility for decisions (or the failure to make them) rests, at least in part, upon the patient. It should be noted that the proposals for consultation presented by the Secretary of State for Health based on the Richardson Committee's report threw caution on the capacity model and proposed an alternative 'health and safety' model (Secretary of State for Health (1999) *Reform of the Mental Health Act 1983: Proposals for Consultation*, Cmnd. 4480. London: HMSO). Both models are compatible with a dominant theme in the call for change in UK mental health law: that of doing away with specific mental health legislation and introducing 'best interests' legislation (of the patient and community) common to both physical and mental disorder (e.g. Eastman and Peay, 1999). However, no author has yet proposed how such a theme of the integration of the physical and mental might be applied to the insanity defence (if indeed it *could be* applied to an exclusively mental defence).

being the predictable result.[4] Such a situation was paralleled in the United States with the outrage over the successful insanity defence of John Hinckley, President Reagan's would-be assassin (e.g. Appelbaum, 1994; Spring, 1998), with resultant restriction of the insanity defence and longer periods of detention for insanity acquittees. Through examining the autonomy of mentally disordered persons, apparently sanist societal reactions might become better informed.

There is one final aim to this book, and that is to contribute to the reconciliation of 'critical-psychiatric' approaches to mental disorder with the predominant medical or 'liberal-scientific' approach. Critical-psychiatric approaches, whilst seeming to have a great deal to offer the mental health field (particularly with regard to understanding the 'inner space' of patients; Ingleby, 1980: 10) were brushed aside by mainstream psychiatry after their brief rise to prominence in the 1960s and early 1970s. Attempting to impress the important elements of the former on the latter (and vice versa) does not, however, appear to be a futile aim, in spite of the widespread adoption of organic models in psychiatric research and therapy. Of the relation between medical and critical-psychiatric paradigms, Ingleby (1980: 26) states: 'Though the different paradigms are to a striking extent self-confirming and self-contained, they could logically be brought into some relation with each other…'. It is hoped that theses such as this help promote such relation, to the benefit of both paradigms and, perhaps more importantly, to the benefit of patients with which each is ultimately concerned.

With such aims in mind, the meta-responsibility theory is cast as a project in psychiatric and legal ethics, and to help understand why society and its criminal justice system treats the mentally disordered in the manner that they do. Furthermore, the experimental component of the study detailed in Part II demonstrates that considering meta-responsibility may actually improve the legal standing of the mentally disordered offender by reducing sanist decision-making with regard to recommended length of hospital detention. Whilst it has been previously proposed that there may be an autonomous component to mental disorder, this is the first piece of research to thoroughly examine such a component and apply a multi-disciplinary approach, particularly in the socio-legal implications of the notion of voluntaristic conceptions of mental disorder.

The structure of this book has been based largely on the need to examine fundamental background issues to the meta-responsibility theory. Part I of the book therefore details historical, legal, philosophical and clinical issues. Part II details the methodology of a large mock juror study designed to examine the meta-responsibility theory, with analyses of quantitative and qualitative data obtained from the study. This study examined the effect of manipulating information concerning a defendant's meta-responsibility on insanity defence verdicts in mock

---

[4] See, e.g. Home Office/Department of Health (1999) *Managing Dangerous People with Severe Personality Disorder: Proposals for Policy Development*. London: Home Office, recommending a detentive approach even in the absence of any index offence by the individual.

jurors (n=334). In addition, the study examined the effect of a meta-responsibility insanity test (MRIT: a test making provision for the mock jurors' evaluation of the defendant's meta-responsibility) in comparison to the McNaughton Rules (the traditional test for insanity in Anglo-American criminal law).

Chapter 1 introduces the meta-responsibility theory, and examines its relation to contemporary and historical conceptions of mental illness and notions of freewill and autonomy. The terms used in the book, most notably 'mental disorder' and 'mental illness', are also defined.

Chapter 2 introduces the insanity defence and examines the mismatch in the ability of the legal system to consider voluntarism in the incapacitating conditions of intoxication and automatism (in which the presence or absence of voluntarism in the incapacitating condition is central to the legal outcome) and insanity (in which the presence or absence of voluntarism is not considered). This chapter further examines how such a paradoxical mismatch has arisen: either a) through an autopoietic model of the relationship between law and psychiatry (an inability for the self-referential law to consider principles from psychiatry); or b) through the deliberate refusal of the law to consider meta-responsibility in insanity but not in other incapacitating conditions.

Chapter 3 builds on the introduction to the meta-responsibility theory in Chapter 1 by examining how mental disorder could be self-caused or exacerbated (i.e. voluntaristic, autogenous, or autonomous), with recourse to clinical models of medication non-compliance and the two 'critical-' or 'anti-' psychiatric models of mental disorder highlighting voluntarism: the existential phenomenological and social constructivist models. This chapter also examines the controversial notion of benefits of the mentally disordered state, a central tenet of the two voluntaristic models. Two types of meta-responsibility are delineated: consensual meta-responsibility (in which the individual consents to the generation or exacerbation of mental disorder through, for example, medication non-compliance due to medication side effects); and purposive meta-responsibility (in which the individual's actions are primarily directed toward the purposive goal of generating or exacerbating mental disorder).

Chapter 4 examines the notion that the ostensibly therapeutic/sympathetic insanity disposal is in fact punitive and retributive, and examines the constructs of sanism and pretextual decision-making in light of the meta-responsibility theory. This chapter posits that the treacherous passage that the mentally disordered offender faces through the criminal justice system is due, at least in part, to covert feelings amongst society and the criminal justice system that individuals may be culpable for mental disorder (and hence meta-responsible). Harsh insanity disposals punish meta-responsibility in the absence of any other societal or legally acceptable means of reflecting culpability for disorder.

Chapter 5 examines psychological and legal research that has a bearing on the meta-responsibility theory, particularly that derived from social psychological and socio-legal frameworks, and from the mock juror research genre that is used as the methodology in the experimental work detailed in Part II of the book.

Chapter 6 details the methodology of such a mock juror study, conducted to examine the effect of meta-responsibility information on mock juror decision-making. Previous mock juror research with a methodological bearing on the present study is examined. The research design used factorial manipulations of meta-responsibility information within insanity defence case vignettes (a between-subjects design), with subjects being asked to reach a verdict (guilty/NGRI – Not Guilty by Reason of Insanity), make disposal recommendations, etc. The vignette was embedded within a survey instrument eliciting attitudinal responses to issues concerning the vignette and other areas of interest with regard to the insanity defence.

Chapter 7 details the quantitative analysis of results of the experiment, which suggest that meta-responsibility is an important construct in decision-making with regard to insanity defence cases, and that a meta-responsibility insanity test allowing mock jurors to consider meta-responsibility has, under certain conditions, a significant effect on verdict and disposal outcomes (particularly the ability to reduce the length of hospital disposals).

Chapter 8 discusses the quantitative experimental results, with reference to the qualitative data derived from subjects' reasons for their verdicts.

Chapter 9 concludes the overall study and enquires whether the meta-responsibility theory is a viable birth; it examines methodological limitations of the mock juror study, and suggests possibilities and directions for future related research within the area of psychiatry and law.

The appendices contain each factorial version of the case-vignette and the measuring instrument used in the experimental research, as well as selected journal papers published during the course of this doctoral research.

Whilst this book espouses and examines voluntaristic models of mental disorder, it does not hold that mental disorder is simply 'self-caused'. Instead, it suggests that there is a continuum of autonomy to be found in all mental disorder, with some patients having a greater capacity for self-regulation than others. While advocating a change in legal, clinical and societal provision for considering meta-responsibility, it does not espouse punishment of those found to be meta-responsible as a respectable goal (indeed, it is contended that this is the current position taken by society and the criminal justice system and that it is an inherently *sanist* solution to dealing with mentally disordered offenders). In short, considerable effort has been made to deal with the issues surrounding culpability for mental disorder in as sympathetic a manner as possible.

Acknowledgements

The thesis upon which this book was based was written whilst a doctoral student at Cambridge University Institute of Criminology and a visiting research fellow at Harvard Medical School.

In Cambridge I was funded by the Trinity Hall Nightingale Scholarship. I am therefore much indebted to Trinity Hall and the Nightingale family. Whilst at Harvard, I was generously supported by Fulbright and Wingate Scholarships.

In Cambridge, the assistance given by Loraine Gelsthorpe was crucial to my research. I am also thankful to David Thomas, Donald West, David Farrington and Nigel Walker.

Tom Gutheil and Harold Bursztajn were kind enough to invite me to Harvard and supervise my research there. Help was given by Mike Commons, Jennifer Radden, Margery Gans, and other members of the Program in Psychiatry and Law.

The following also provided advice and assistance: Joanna Shapland, John Crichton, Anthony Colombo, Alec Buchanan, Norm Finkel, Michael Perlin, Jeff Schaler, and Karen Terry. Nigel Shackleford and Jean Bushell arranged access to NGRI files at the Home Office.

Some elements of this book appeared as an article in the *Journal of Forensic Psychiatry*. I am grateful to anonymous reviewers for their comments.

I am indebted to Thomas Szasz for his help, advice, and hospitality. Finally, but most importantly, this book would not have been possible without the untiring assistance and friendship of my doctoral supervisor in Cambridge, Adrian Grounds.

List of Abbreviations

-2LL	-2 Log Likelihood
ALI	American Law Institute
APD	Antisocial Personality Disorder
CAR	Capacity Activation Responsibility
CDR	Capacity Development Responsibility
CMR	Consensual Meta-responsibility
DOM	Disability of Mind
DSM (IV)	Diagnostic and Statistical Manual of Mental Disorders *(with edition number)*
EP	Existential Phenomenological (model of mental disorder)
GBMI	Guilty But Mentally Ill
ICD (10)	International Classification of Diseases *(with edition number)*
IDRA	Insanity Defence Reform Act
KMO	Kaiser-Meyer-Olkin (test of sampling adequacy)
LS	Liberal-scientific (model of mental disorder)
MDO	Mentally Disordered Offender
MHA	Mental Health Act
MHRT	Mental Health Review Tribunal
MR	Meta-responsibility
MRIT	Meta-responsibility Insanity Test
NGRI	Not Guilty by Reason of Insanity
NGRIs	Persons found Not Guilty by Reason of Insanity
NMR	No Meta-responsibility
OCS	Ordinary Common Sense
PCA	Principal Component Analysis
PMR	Purposive Meta-responsibility
PPD	Psychopathic Personality Disorder
PSRB	Psychiatric Security Review Board
PTSD	Post-traumatic Stress Disorder
QSJ	Quasisubjective Insanity Test
RSU	Regional Secure Unit
SC	Social Constructivist (model of mental disorder)
SES	Socio-economic status
WHO	World Health Organization

Notation of factors within case vignettes and tables:

Diagnosis:

D	Depression
P	Personality disorder
S	Schizophrenia

Type of Meta-responsibility:

CMR	Consensual meta-responsibility
NMR	No meta-responsibility
PMR	Purposive meta-responsibility

Type of Insanity Test:

MN	McNaughton insanity test
MR	Meta-responsibility insanity test (MRIT)

The case vignette denoted by S>PMR>MR therefore described the defendant as schizophrenic, having purposive meta-responsibility, and required subjects to render a verdict using the meta-responsibility insanity test.

Notation denoting questions and attitudinal measures in the measuring instrument:

ABOLISH	The insanity defence should be abolished
AFFECTED	Tom's illness affected his ability to look after himself (e.g. take medication) and resist getting more ill
CAREFUL	Tom should have been more careful in taking his medication
CAUSED	Tom caused his own illness
CENSOR	Censorship of films and magazines is necessary to uphold moral standards
COGEAT	Mental illness is caused by learning from others with similarly strange and bizarre behaviour
COGTREAT	Mental illness should be treated by showing patients the proper way to act and think
CRIMRATE	The insanity defence doesn't affect the crime rate
DANGER	The insanity defence allows dangerous people out on the streets
DEATHPEN	For some crimes, the death penalty is the most appropriate sentence
DUTY	Tom has a duty to take responsibility for his own illness
ENTTREAT	Insane defendants are entitled to treatment
FAIRSHAR	Ordinary people do not get their fair share of the nation's wealth
FAULT	Tom made his illness worse through his own fault
FREE#	Out of every 100 defendants found Not Guilty by Reason of Insanity, how many go free immediately?

HARDTIME	Judges and juries have a hard time telling whether defendants are really sane or insane
HARSH	In general, the courts deal too harshly with criminals
HOSP#	How many are sent to mental hospital?
HOSPSTAY	If defendants are sent to a mental hospital, how long do they stay there on average?
ILLEVID	Illegally obtained evidence should not be admissible in court even if that evidence is the only way of obtaining a conviction
INSAPUN	Even if people are insane, we should punish them if they break the law
INSAPUN2	Insane people should be punished for their crimes just like everyone else
JUSTIFY	The insanity defence is sometimes justified
KILLED	Tom killed his wife because of his illness
LAWOBEY	The law should always be obeyed, even if a particular law is wrong
LAWRICH	There is one law for the rich and one for the poor
LEGTECH	Too many guilty persons escape punishment because of legal technicalities
LIKED	Tom liked being ill
LOOPHOLE	The insanity plea is a loophole that allows too many guilty people to go free
MANEMPL	Management will always try to get the better of employees if it gets the chance
MDEXP	Please rate the amount of experience you think you have of mental disorder (e.g. personally suffered from it, friends/family suffered from it, etc.)
MDINFORM	Do you think you are well informed about mental disorder and mental disorder issues?
MDTESTIF	Psychiatrists should testify about a defendant's medical condition in insanity trials
MEDAET	Mental illness is caused by medical problems such as chemical imbalance in the brain
MEDTREAT	Mental illness should be treated through the use of medical drugs
MESSAGE	The insanity defence sends a message to criminals that they can get away with crime
NECESSAR	The insanity defence is a necessary part of our legal system
NGRI#	Out of every 100 defendants who plead insanity, how many are actually found Not Guilty by Reason of Insanity?
OBEYAUTH	Schools should teach children to obey authority
PLEAD#	Out of every 100 defendants who are charged with a crime, how many do you think plead Not Guilty by Reason of Insanity?
PSYAET	Mental illness is caused by a number of social stresses such as money worries
PSYCH$$$	If psychiatrists are paid enough, they will say anything about a defendant's sanity

PSYTREAT	Mental illness should be treated by producing a more comfortable and less stressful society
PUNWORK	Punishment doesn't work on the insane
REALYMAD	Most people found Not Guilty by Reason of Insanity are really insane
REDIST	The Government should redistribute income from the better-off to those who are less well off
REFORM	The insanity defence needs a lot of reform
RELSAFE	I'm confident that people found Not Guilty by Reason of Insanity are only released when it's safe to do so
RESISTED	Tom should have resisted his illness more
RESPBRIT	Young people today don't have enough respect for traditional British values
RICHDEF	The insanity defence is mainly a rich person's defence
STIFFER	People who break the law should be given stiffer sentences
TREATPUN	The insane should be treated rather than punished if they commit crime
UNDSTOOD	Tom understood that he was ill
WRONGPUN	It is wrong to punish insane people who break the law

Notation denoting factor score variables emerging from principal component analysis or other data analysis:

+

CCHANGE	Measure of Tom's degree of character change pre- to post-illness
FBEATRAP	Measure of support for notion of insanity defendants 'beating the rap'
FCOG	Measure of ascription to the cognitive-behavioural model
FLEFRIGH	Measure of left-wing atttidues
FLEGCONC	Measure of concern about legal aspects of the insanity defence
FLIBAUTH	Measure of authoritarian attitudes
FMDKNOW	Measure of subject's self-reported knowledge and experience concerning mental disorder
FMED	Measure of ascription to the medical model of mental disorder
FMEDCONC	Measure of support for medical involvement in the insanity defence and associated disposal
FMR	Measure of appraisal of Tom as meta-responsible
FNGRISUP	Measure of support for the insanity defence
FPROD	Measure of Tom's behaviour appraised as product of his illness
FPSY	Measure of ascription to the psychosocial model of mental disorder
FPUNISH	Measure of support for punishing the insane

PART I
AN INTRODUCTION TO THE THEORY OF META-RESPONSIBILITY

Chapter 1

Introduction: Nomenclative, Philosophical, and Historical Issues

Much Madness is divinest Sense
To a discerning Eye

Emily Dickinson, No. 435

When the wife of F. Scott Fitzgerald became mentally disordered, he wrote of her predicament to his daughter, Frances:

> How strange to have failed as a social creature – even criminals do not fail that way – they are the law's 'Loyal Opposition,' so to speak. But the insane are always mere guests on earth, eternal strangers carrying around broken decalogues that they cannot read (Turnbull, 1963: 63).

How fascinating would Fitzgerald have found the double failure of being both insane *and* a criminal. Such individuals will never be afforded the status of 'Loyal Opposition' – they have long proven a theoretical and practical thorn in the side of the law and criminal justice system. If they are an opposition of sorts, they are certainly one that does not play by the standard rules of the game. Even Fitzgerald's peculiar genius may have had difficulty in turning the insane criminal's double failure into worthy poetry.

This book examines one rule of the game to which the mentally disordered are not subject: that players are to be held responsible for their actions. Such a rule may be waived when, for example, a mentally disordered person 'acts out' on a hospital ward or behaves oddly in public. The attribution in such cases by the medical profession or society is usually that the person's actions were the result of putative illness, and not the sort of actions that the pre-morbid person in question would have performed; their behaviour that transgresses social norms can thus be 'excused'. Such attributions have long been given legitimacy in criminal law, through provision for the excuse of behaviour that transgresses *legal* norms. Ever since the birth of ancient legal systems, the presumption that we all know and understand the law and its relationship to our actions (and thus the presumption of responsibility[1] for those actions) has been suspended for some mentally disordered

---

[1] Hart (1968) delineates four major types of responsibility: 1) causal responsibility (for

defendants (e.g. Walker, 1968). Anglo-American criminal law, through requiring both a legal transgression *(actus reus)* and concomitant criminal intent *(mens rea)* for the commission of a crime, has traditionally made provision for total or partial exculpation of the otherwise criminal acts of the insane.

Specific provision for such exculpation in English law is exemplified by the seldom-used defence of insanity, embodied by the rules laid out during the furore over the murder acquittal of Daniel McNaughton[2] in 1843, which have remained the corner-posts of Anglo-American legal tests of insanity:

> Everyone is to be presumed sane and to possess a sufficient degree of reason to be responsible for their crimes until the contrary is proved...to establish a defence on the ground of insanity, it must be clearly proved that, at the time of committing the act, the party accused was labouring under such a defect of reason from disease of the mind, as to not know the nature and quality of the act he was doing, or if he did know it, that he did not know that what he was doing was wrong (*Daniel McNaughton's Case*;[3] cited in West and Walk, 1977: 75).

A protracted debate surrounding the utility of the McNaughton Rules as a test of legal insanity has resulted in stalemate between The Rules' supporters and critics, both tacitly agreeing that The Rules indeed fail to provide an adequate test, but are perhaps better than all alternatives tried thus far (see Chapter 2). This study proposes a new motion to the debate: that the mentally disordered should only enjoy their privileged position within the criminal justice system if the incapacity which grants them exemption from the rules of the game is not of their own making. Avoidance of criminal responsibility should therefore be inextricably linked with non-culpability for mental disorder. If the mentally disordered are in some way responsible for their own disorder, then they should also be held responsible for any actions committed whilst under 'its influence' (as is the drunken offender for having responsibility for his drunkenness). The purpose of this book is to examine such a notion and to examine its effect on criminal responsibility and socio-legal reactions to the insane. To accept the notion would

---

causing an outcome); 2) role responsibility (duties arising from a particular role); 3) capacity responsibility (cognitive or volitional control); and 4) liability responsibility (for consequences of acts or omissions). The latter is bifurcated into legal liability and moral liability. Chapter 5 discusses the relevance of different types of responsibility to meta-responsibility, particularly capacity responsibility and liability responsibility.

[2] Different authors have used different spellings of Daniel McNaughton's name. Slovenko (1995) lists 12 spellings. The spelling used in the present study is based in accordance with the appraisal of West and Walk (1977) and the present author's examination of one of his surviving signatures.

However, see also Moran (1981) who through his appraisal of a different signature uses 'McNaughtan'.

[3] Daniel McNaughton's Case (1843), 10 C. & F. 200.

result in mentally disordered offenders having a certain level of responsibility for their criminal responsibility. This 'responsibility for responsibility' is henceforth denoted by the neologism 'meta-responsibility'.[4]

There is no intention to question the excusatory power of madness *per se* in this book. The excusatory power of mental disorder is taken as a given, whether as a 'moral intuition' as Radden (1985: 6) calls it, or as embedded in criminal law codification or case law in almost every legal jurisdiction[5] (from Ancient Hebrewic law[6] through present-day Anglo-American law). Such conceptions of insanity generally rely on either or both components of Aristotelian excuse: ignorance and compulsion.[7] Attempts to change such deeply embedded notions have been far from efficacious;[8] that 'madness mitigates blame for wrongdoing' (Radden, 1985: 7) seems to be a deeply ingrained societal principle[9] (however, as Chapter 4 shows,

---

[4] From *meta-* 'arising subsequently to', 'dealing with ulterior problems'; and *responsibility* 'morally accountable for one's actions; capable of rational conduct' (both OED). Hyphenation of the meta- prefix is common where stylistically useful: hence *metaphysics* but *meta-analysis* and *meta-responsibility* rather than *metaanalysis* and *metaresponsibility*. The need for the neologism arises due to inadequate language to service the concept of meta-responsibility. Previous research into the notion of causing one's own mental disorder have used the following terms: culpable mental disorder and advertence (Mitchell, 1986), responsibility for one's mental instability (Finkel and Slobogin, 1995), risking madness (Slodov, 1989), capacity development/activation responsibility (Alicke and Davis, 1990), disability of mind (Fingarette and Hasse, 1979), and autogenic mental disorder (Szasz, 1997). All these terms refer to blameworthiness for developing a mental disorder, and not to the effect of culpable mental disorder on concomitant criminal responsibility. Perhaps the closest any term comes to meta-responsibility is that of Robinson (1985) – causing the conditions of one's own defence.

[5] See e.g. Buchanan (2000); Walker (1985).

[6] Ancient Hebrewic law stated that 'It is an illness to knock against a deaf, mute, an imbecile, or a minor: he that wounds them is culpable, but if they wound others they are not culpable' (Hermann, 1983: 18).

[7] Nichomachean Ethics (Aristotle, 1955).

[8] Particularly in the US. The Insanity Defense Reform Act of 1984 attempted to restrict the defence's scope and usage after public and political outrage after the Hinckley trial, in which President Reagan's would-be assassin, John Hinckley, successfully pled insanity (see Appelbaum, 1994). The Act urged a return to a restrictive version of McNaughton; a neo-conservative attempt to drown the 'liberal' American Law Institute (ALI) standard (American Law Institute, 1962), which by 1980 had been adopted in 50 per cent of states and all federal circuit courts. The results have been predictably unsuccessful; Simon (1967) showed that type of insanity test makes little difference to verdict outcomes. See generally LaFond and Durham (1992).

[9] Although in the UK the absence of the death penalty removes some of the *raison d'être* for the defence of insanity, it still persists, suggesting exculpation of the mentally disordered is a more ingrained principle than simply as a means to avoid capital punishment. As Morris (1982) states:

whilst madness may mitigate blame for wrongdoing, society may exact blame and retribution in other ways). This is not to minimize the argument as to whether madness should mitigate blame for wrongdoing (e.g. Morris, 1982; Szasz, 1997), but merely to say that society, the legal profession, and the medical profession generally believe that madness offers some sort of excuse for otherwise unacceptable behaviour and/or cognition.

This study does, however, introduce the theory of meta-responsibility as a further 'moral intuition', and thus questions Radden's other assumption; that 'madness is not blameworthy'.[10] It is, however, first necessary to examine what is

---

> Historically, the special defence of insanity made good sense in relation to capital crimes…but even perfervid advocates of capital punishment do not favour the execution of the mentally ill…one is left, therefore, with a sense that the special defence is a genuflection to a deep-seated moral sense that the mentally ill lack freedom of choice to do good or ill and, therefore, that blame should not be imputed to them for their otherwise criminal acts (p. 504-505).

[10] There is a further, more distal mechanism, by which one could be said to be the foundation of one's own madness, and that is through the longitudinal development of one's character or personality. This point is particularly pertinent when examining the criminal responsibility (and meta-responsibility) of the personality disordered offender, who is not necessarily seen as suffering from an illness and hence more responsible for criminal acts. Rudnick and Levy (1994: 416) refer to this as the 'status solution' to the argument concerning the criminal responsibility of personality disordered persons. It is clear that there is an unwritten general presumption within society and the law that that we are responsible for our characters. Else we would be unable to praise the person 'whose generous nature makes him help people', or indeed to blame or punish the 'evil' person; their actions would simply be products of their characters, and if the foundation and development of their characters were outside their control then they would be not responsible for any resultant actions. As Elliot (1996) states:

> If a person's action results, at least in some weak sense, from his character, and if his character is a product of conditions largely outside his control, then to hold him responsible for this action seems unjust (p. 68).

Responsibility for character has troubled philosophers since Aristotle's initial formulation of the principle:

> But perhaps a man is the kind of man not to take care. Still they are themselves by their slack lives responsible for becoming of that kind, and they are themselves responsible for being unjust or self-indulgent, in that they cheat or spend their time in drinking-bouts and the like; for it is activities exercised on particular objects that make the corresponding character. This is plain from the case of people training for any contest or action; they practice the activity the whole time. Now not to know that it is from the exercise of activities on particular objects that states of character are produced is the mark of a thoroughly senseless person (Aristotle; cited in Elliot, 1996: 30).

Aristotle sees responsibility for character as relevant to culpability; responsibility for negative traits may be an aggravating factor in terms of blame and punishment (see Intoxication, Chapter 2):

> They punish the offender for his very ignorance, if he is thought responsible for it; e.g. penalties are doubled for committing an offense in a state of drunkenness because the source of the action lay in the agent himself; he was capable of not getting drunk, and his drunkenness was the cause of his ignorance...so too was it at first open to the unjust and licentious persons not to become such, and therefore they are voluntarily what they are...Nobody would criticize a person who is blind by nature or as a result of disease or injury – he would more likely be an object of pity – but anyone would blame a person whose blindness is due to heavy drinking or some other self-indulgence (Aristotle; cited in Sherlock, 1984: 488).

Responsibility for character has also troubled more applied academic endeavours such as criminology. In Hirschi's model of self-control (Gottfedson and Hirschi, 1990; Wiebe and Hirschi, 1997), building on observations made by the Gluecks over 50 years ago, data is presented suggesting that the strongest correlates of delinquency are not amorality and impulsivity, but lack of diligence, interest and care in schoolwork, laziness, and inattention. Delinquency is thus thought to *precede* personality development. Similarly, Laub and Sampson (1994) present data suggesting that adult criminality is associated with childhood misbehaviour (e.g. truancy, drinking, etc.), independently of IQ, SES and ethnicity. Perhaps risk for mental disorder in adulthood is similarly associated with lack of diligence in childhood – low self-control may also apply to the development of mental health problems, as well as to the commission of criminal acts whilst mentally disordered. Reznek (1997) maintains that a principal reason why we exculpate the insane (adding to the Aristotelian cognitive and volitional reasons of ignorance and compulsion) is 'character change' (p. 11) – that madness causes changes in moral character that in turn affect responsibility. The converse of Reznek's thesis might be argued: that moral character may in turn affect the genesis and expression of mental disorder, and that, in deference to Aristotle, our characters are the products of our actions. As Szasz (1963) realises, the self is not something one finds; it is instead something one creates.

Such conceptions of mental disorder echo both 'moral' causes of madness (e.g. 'the moral causes include...gusts of violent passion...indulgence in grief...erroneous views of religion...[and] the degradation of pride'; Shelford, 1833; cited in Fingarette, 1972: 21), Laing's conception of the psychotic state as one of *metanoia* or atonement (Burston, 1996), and the notion of mental disorder as residual rule breaking, suggesting it might be precipitated by a personality type unafraid to break rules (Chadwick, 1997). The schizotypal personality (Raine, Lencz and Mednick, 1995) is prone to the development of schizophrenia and itself encompasses some aspects of that disorder. Schizotypal personality disorder (Cluster A personality disorder, diagnostic code 301.22) has the essential features of a pervasive pattern of social and interpersonal deficits marked by acute discomfort and reduced capacity for close relationships as well as perceptual distortions and eccentricities of behaviour. Of course, the inclusion of such a 'personality type' in DSM-IV brings it within the realm of the liberal-scientific model (in spite of some schizotypal traits being cast as beneficial rather than disabling by some researchers, e.g. Claridge, 1985) and therefore largely abdicates personal responsibility in direct contradiction to Aristotelian conceptions

meant by mental disorder, and to examine historical and contemporary perspectives on culpability for mental disorder. To use Fitzgerald's language, only then is it possible to examine the proposition that the mentally disordered may have broken their own decalogues, and hence bear responsibility for their inability to read and obey the Ten Commandments.

1.1 On Mental Disorder and Mental Illness

To understand how a person could be responsible for mental disorder, it is necessary to describe what is meant by mental disorder. Clearly, someone who did not subscribe to any objective phenomenon of mental disorder would also have difficulty subscribing to the notion that someone could be held responsible for its genesis or exacerbation in the first instance.

For the purposes of this book, the following terms are used interchangeably: mental illness, mental disorder (the term favoured by the 4th Edition of American Psychiatric Association's Diagnostic and Statistical Manual of Mental Disorders [DSM-IV]; APA 1994), psychiatric illness, psychiatric disorder, etc. Madness is a term generally reserved for historical or popular contexts. Such terms in any guise have long provided a pregnant topic of definitional and nosological debate. At least three parties have interest in such debate: 1) society (where there is a popular need to explain 'crazy behaviour' and label individuals 'mad' to beware the self and others);[11] 2) the legal professions (where mental disorder has a bearing on the making of laws or the processing of mentally disordered individuals within civil or criminal justice systems); and 3) the medical profession (the identification of signs

---

of personality and character. It is such concepts as responsibility for character that would need to be examined in a detailed analysis of meta-responsibility in personality disordered offenders. However, except for this brief discussion, the concept of madness being precipitated by character for which we have responsibility will not be further examined; the philosophical arguments required to substantiate such a notion and apply it to criminal law are far beyond the scope and central interest of this study. Suffice it to say, however, if disorder was to a certain extent caused by our characters for which we have responsibility, it would provide another limb of meta-responsibility (consensual *or* purposive; see Chapter 3).

[11] Folk interest in nosology no doubt emerges because 'since antiquity mental illness has been defined by experts but discovered by laymen' (MacDonald, 1981: 113). Matthews (1999) characterises popular opinion of mad people thus:

> Mad people are thought of as different from the rest of us, out of touch with reality as most of us conceive of it. They are seen as liable to engage in anti-social behaviour, for which they are not (or are not fully) responsible (p. 47).

Such a folk definition of madness *includes* diminished responsibility for acts as central to the definition. This has obvious implications for meta-responsibility that eschews the immediate assumption of diminished responsibility.

and symptoms of mental disorder as a collection of clinical syndromes within psychiatry, and therapeutic response to such syndromes).

The characteristic essence of mental disorder – that which seems to transcend the nosological and explanatory needs of each of the interested parties – is that it constitutes a disturbance of mental function, notable for its magnitude or temporal persistence. To describe it as a deviation from mental health engenders value judgment, but it must clearly constitute a departure from normative notions of a reasonable standard of psychological functioning (Veatch, 1982). Exactly whose normative notion is another question; Lewis (1955: 110) criticizes the World Health Organization's definition of health ('a state of complete physical, mental and social well-being and not merely the absence of disease and infirmity') by equating it to a state of perfection 'such as was enjoyed perhaps by archangels and by Adam before the fall' (p. 110). Szasz (1960) applies such notions to disorders of mental health:

> In the case of physical illness, the norm is the structural and functional integrity of the human body. Thus although the desirability of physical health, as such, is an ethical value, what health is can be stated in anatomical and physiological terms. What is the norm deviation from which is regarded as mental illness? (Szasz, 1960; cited in Clare, 1980: 28).

Few can physically or mentally measure up to the WHO definition of health; that we are all mad to a greater or lesser degree (Connolly, 1830; Laing, 1967) may thus be a disturbing proposition, but hardly a contentious one. More contentious is the degree of behavioural or psychic deviation required for an ascription of madness as morbidity. To qualify as either mental or physical disorder a significant impairment must exist. In the case of mental disorder, the quantity or quality of such impairment must not be 'so narrow as to set at liberty half the patients at Bethlem or the Bicêtre...[or] so loose and capacious as to give a strait waistcoat to half the world' (Good; cited in Clare, 1980: 14). Whilst gauging such quantity or quality clearly provides the locus of the value judgment, Szasz's argument is hardly controversial in the light of counter-arguments by, amongst others, Sedgwick (1973) who argues that all diagnoses, whether of mental or physical disorder, require a value judgment on the diagnostic agent's behalf.

Szasz (1961) uses the value-judgment hypothesis to argue that the concept of mental disorder has no objective referent – that it is an ontological red herring, so to speak. His view holds that crazy behaviour *is* mental disorder (or 'crazy is as crazy does'); there is no entity of schizophrenia, only persons whose behaviour appears to others of the quality to render a 'diagnosis' of schizophrenia. This would not trouble the meta-responsibility theory any more than it has troubled theoretical and clinical psychiatry more generally, were it not that this study borrows from Szasz and Laing's social constructivist and existential phenomenological models in examining voluntaristic characteristics of mental disorder (see Chapter 3). It is important, therefore, not to fall foul of the logical fallacy that the meta-responsibility theory involves the central tenet of self-causation or self-exacerbation of a condition that does *not exist*.

The meta-responsibility theory does not fall foul of such fallacious reasoning, because it does not require an ascription to the ontological and epistemological components of such theories (e.g. that mental disorder is a myth); it only requires the elements of those authors' theories that posit an autogenous, autonomous, or advertent component to the cognitions, behaviour, etc. that we generally term mental disorder. These are indeed among the theoretical elements that 'post-anti-psychiatric' literature has emphasized (e.g. Sedgwick, 1973; Moore, 1975, 1984; Bentall, 1990; Boyle, 1990; Thomas, 1997; Veatch, 1997), without becoming embroiled in arguments about the epistemological referent of mental disorder, the philosophy of linguistics, and the nature of psychiatric coercion and control.

Szasz's objection to the notion of mental disorder as *illness* (or indeed the use of the term 'mental illness') is of greater importance to the meta-responsibility theory. The analogy between mental and physical illness is, this study contends, responsible for much of the removal of individual culpability for mental disorder. The illness label makes presuppositions about the aetiology of mental disorder and its relationship to symptomatology. The phrase 'mental illness' brings psychic or behavioural deviation within the realm of the liberal-scientific model of illness (see below), an ascription made along ideological as well as scientific dimensions, and one very different from autonomous models that this study examines. Its usage is therefore declined here except to elaborate the metaphor or to preserve others' usage. However, this study does not adopt linguistic idiosyncrasies and abandon the mental disorder concept altogether, referring to 'problems of living' or some other deformation of language that brings with it as much ontological baggage as does the phrase 'mental disorder' in the first instance.

Whilst cautious about using the term 'illness' when describing behavioural or psychic deviations, this study does not accept Szasz's more basal argument that mental disorder is a phrase without referent; *a myth*. If it were, we could happily ignore the theory of meta-responsibility. As Moore (1984) states:

> There is a disturbing tendency to regard complicated legal issues, notably the proper place of mental illness in various legal tests (of insanity in criminal trials, of incompetency to perform various legal acts or to stand trial, the tests for civil commitment), as solved by the new truth that mental illness is but a myth anyway (p. 155).

This study does not adopt such an easy solution. Even if mental disorder refers only to crazy behaviour, it is still a phrase with a referent. A referent for the label 'mental disorder' is evident in a folk definition, e.g. a failure to meet the criteria for mental health given by Karl Menninger:

> Let us define mental health as the adjustment of human beings to the world and to each other with a maximum of effectiveness and happiness. Not just efficiency, or just contentment, – or the grace of obeying the rules of the game cheerfully. It is all of these together. It is the ability to maintain an even temper, an alert intelligence, socially considerate behaviour, and a happy disposition. This, I think, is a healthy mind (Menninger, 1930; cited in Boorse, 1976: 70).

Where mental disorder is not given a folk or legal definition, it is a concept bound to a medical diagnosis. DSM-IV defines mental disorder as:

> ...a clinically significant behavioural or psychological syndrome or pattern that occurs in an individual and that is associated with present distress (e.g. a painful symptom) or disability (i.e. impairment in one or more areas of functioning) or with a significantly increased risk of suffering death, pain, disability, or an important loss of freedom. In addition, this syndrome or pattern must not be merely an expectable and culturally sanctioned response to a particular event, for example, the death of a loved one. Whatever its original cause, it must currently be considered a manifestation of a behavioural, psychological, or biological dysfunction in the individual. Neither deviant behaviour (e.g. political, religious, or sexual) nor conflicts that are primarily between the individual and society are mental disorders unless the deviance or conflict is a symptom of a dysfunction in the individual... (APA, 1994: xxi-xxii).

The DSM arranges nosology around a multi-axial system consisting of five axes designed to facilitate systematic evaluation of the mentally disordered individual: I) Clinical disorders and other conditions that may be a focus of clinical attention; II) Personality disorders and mental retardation; III) General medical conditions; IV) Psychosocial and environmental problems; and V) Global assessment of functioning. The term mental disorder is generally reserved for those disorders constituting the first axis. Although the neurotic/psychotic distinction has been dropped from DSM-IV, it is still a widely used distinction with substantial utility (Stevens and Price, 1996). Such a nosological system distinguishes: organic (somatic) psychoses (e.g. Alzheimer's dementia); functional or other psychoses (e.g. schizophrenia, affective psychosis); and neurotic disorders (those without a demonstrable organic basis, e.g. depressive disorders, anxiety, obsessive-compulsive disorder). Axis II includes the personality disorders (maladaptive behavioural patterns distinguished by no pre-morbid/morbid course).

Legal definitions of mental disorder tend to be couched in general terms, no doubt because the legal system finds its object of enquiry (competency, volition, criminal responsibility, disposal, etc.) concerned with *symptoms* of mental disorder rather than disorder *per se* (being schizophrenic is not a criminal offence, whereas assaulting another under the influence of delusions [which often happen to be associated with other signs and symptoms that collectively make up the clinical syndrome of schizophrenia] *is*). As Gerard (1999: 67) states, 'The law is not in the business of creating illnesses and diseases'.[12] The Mental Health Act 1983 thus

---

[12] *Mutatis mutandis*, nor should the medical profession be in the business of creating defects of reason or diseases of the mind. DSM-IV states:

fails to provide any strict definition, 'contenting itself with a list of synonymous expressions' (Matthews, 1999: 48). S.1(2) of the Mental Health Act 1983 states that:

> 'Mental disorder' means mental illness, arrested or incomplete development of mind, psychopathic disorder and any other disability of mind and 'mentally disordered' shall be construed accordingly.

The 'catch-all' phraseology of 'any other disability of mind' (Eastman and Peay, 1999: 4) is tempered by the provision in S.1(3) of the Act, which states that 'promiscuity or other immoral conduct, sexual deviancy or dependence on alcohol or drugs' are alone not enough to warrant a 'legal diagnosis' of mental disorder. The current definition is, however, interpreted as including DSM-IV Axis II personality disorders (see below) such as antisocial personality disorder (APD) which is a term used interchangeably with its anglicized linguistic variant, psychopathic personality disorder (PPD).

In spite of folk, medical and legal systems finding differential utility in offering strict definitions of mental disorder, all three are traditionally concerned with three main classes of disorder: the schizophrenias, mood disorders (of which the exemplar is major depressive disorder), and personality disorders (of which the exemplar is antisocial personality disorder). These three types of disorders provide the focus for the mock juror experimental research detailed in Chapters 6, 7 and 8.

1.2 The Liberal-Scientific Conception of Mental Disorder

The meta-responsibility theory relies on a level of autonomy, autogeny or advertence in mental disorder to hold an individual responsible for his or her criminal responsibility. It is clear, however, that current psychiatric conceptions of mental disorder rarely provide for such responsibility. This, it is contended, is largely due to psychiatry's adoption of the liberal-scientific model of mental disorder.

> It is to be understood that inclusion here [in DSM-IV], for clinical and research purposes, of a diagnostic category such as Pathological Gambling or Pedophilia does not imply that the condition meets legal or other nonmedical criteria for what constitutes mental disease, mental disorder, or mental disability. The clinical and scientific considerations involved in categorization of these conditions as mental disorders may not be wholly relevant to legal judgments, for example, that take into account such issues as individual responsibility (APA, 1994: xxvii).

However, this study, like that of Halleck (1988), argues that individual responsibility should also be a *clinical* as well as a *legal* term, and that abdication of responsibility in the clinical sense (i.e. responsibility for disorder or illness) should impact upon responsibility in the legal sense.

Psychiatry has had a different historical trajectory to other areas of medicine, but began to converge as a result of the positivism and Enlightenment thought of the eighteenth century (see below), being established as a professional speciality within clinical medicine by the mid-nineteenth century. The assimilation of psychiatry within clinical medicine was principally characterized by the former's adoption of the liberal-scientific conception of the object of its enquiry (Busfield, 1986) which portrays mental disorder as the product of a 'diathesis-stress' interaction in the manner of 'physical' disease; that is, as a product of interaction between individual and/or environmental pathology.

The liberal-scientific or 'ethicomedical model' (Edwards, 1997: 102) engenders that not only should psychiatry turn to science in its quest for the aetiology and treatment of mental disorder, but also that it is a more *liberal* or humane approach than any alternative model. As such, the model is of greater scope than other models popular in current psychiatric thought through its addition of an ideological element: that the role of the psychiatrist is to facilitate recovery of the mentally disordered, that he is best able to facilitate that recovery, and that the development of his skills in research, diagnosis and treatment will be best serviced by study of medical science. The medical model, and a sub-model, the disease (organic) model, lack this specifically ideological component but are subsumed within (and tend to be described interchangeably with) the liberal-scientific model.

The most notable element of all liberal-scientific models is their removal of the patient's responsibility for assuming the sick role, instead transferring that responsibility onto the disorder itself; health cannot therefore be restored through an act of will or decision. This is the first of four 'Postulates' (Parsons, 1951) which might be said to treat the patient as an 'ideological pea' in a liberal-scientific 'pod'. The notion central to the postulates is that assumption of the illness role is a deviance, subject to a negative moral or social evaluation. The sick are exempted from some (or all) social responsibilities, according to severity of illness (Postulate II); are expected to desire health and 'to want to get better' (Postulate III); and are expected to seek appropriate medical care and cooperate with such care (Postulate IV). Entitlement to the sick role is limited by the locus of disturbance: disturbances of particular obligations (e.g. crime or disloyalty) are distinct from disturbances of the person (e.g. illness or immorality). Thus, Veatch (1997: 114) states that 'A sinner or criminal or morally irresponsible person would be seen as deficient in character to the extent that he has brought on his condition; the person in the sick role is not…it seems clear that one of the primary functions of the sick role is to remove culpability'.

Here, Veatch betrays the functional aspect of a model: it is not merely an instrument to view, interpret, and understand a part of the universe of phenomena. A decision to exclude or include a certain phenomenon with respect to a model may be made more along ideological/instrumental rather than scientific/theoretical dimensions; inclusion or exclusion may impact upon, as well as serve to explain, the phenomenon in question. Thus a diagnosis, in the liberal-scientific tradition, brings with it more than simple descriptive utility:

> The 'diagnosis'...may state no more than a resemblance of the symptoms and signs to a previously recognized pattern: but more usually it makes a statement about aetiology; about a microscopic or macroscopic anatomical abnormality, about a disorder of function, about a specific deficiency or about a biochemical or chromosomal abnormality (Scadding, 1967: 879).

Laing extends this false descriptive/prescriptive dichotomy even to the observation of simple signs or symptoms upon which the diagnostic process rests:

> A 'sign' or 'symptom' of a disease is actually a theory about a disease we are trying to describe...'a description' of a disease is not a simple description of a reality because calling something a disease is already part of a theory of accounting for it (Laing; in Mullan, 1995: 112-113).

There is clearly utility in the application of a particular model; phenomena can be fitted to models as well as models to phenomena. Inclusion of mental disorder within the liberal-scientific model may have the utility of placating our 'moral intuition' that 'madness is not blameworthy' (Radden, 1985). This is not to say that the liberal-scientific conception of mental disorder exists *only* for this reason (putative organic geneses are likely to be of greater importance), but that such inclusion placates our moral intuition that madness is not blameworthy is, at the very least, a useful concomitant. In the same manner, Charcot's emphasis on the similarity between conversion hysteria and traditional conceptions of physical disease was 'not a matter of scientific deliberation, but was rather motivated by humanitarian efforts (on behalf of the suffering hysterics) and professionalistic ambitions (on behalf of psychiatry as an expanding medical enterprise)' (Svensson, 1995: 16). Other psychiatric nosological interventions have had similar effects, perhaps the most notable of which was Kreapelin's grouping together of three conditions that described what had until that time been regarded as socially undesirable behaviour (*catatonia*, *hebephrenia* and *vesanica typica*) into the single 'disease' of *dementia praecox* (subsequently renamed schizophrenia by Bleuler; Szasz, 1974).

One of the major consequences of the transformation of social deviancies into medical deviancies is the forbiddance of voluntaristic analyses. This removal of culpability is most pertinent in the disease model (a sub-model of the liberal-scientific and medical models), which has, in the second half of the twentieth century, ascended as the predominant model applied to research into, and therapeutic response toward, mental disorder. It is the application of the disease model to mental disorder, in combination with an insanity test that also subscribes to such a model, which has secured the exclusion of any consideration of meta-responsibility of mentally disordered offenders. However, as the next section shows, status as disease should not be inextricably linked with exclusion of voluntarism and culpability, and hence should not automatically exclude consideration of meta-responsibility.

1.3 The Disease Model of Mental Disorder and the Exclusion of Voluntarism

Perhaps the major characteristic that has secured mental disorder's inclusion within the liberal-scientific model is its putative organic genesis, affording it the status of disease in the manner of physical disease. The disease model holds that mental disorder is an illness like any other illness; that mental disorder is characterized by structural as well as functional abnormality. Such a neo-Cartesian approach considers disorders of the brain and disorders of the mind to be equivalent (Fenwick, 1993). The disease model thus holds, for example, that the apparently unintelligible behaviour of the schizophrenic is caused by (ultimately, if not presently) demonstrable brain pathology (e.g. Kandel, 1991).

There is now much good evidence that mental disorders, particularly somatic and functional psychoses, are associated with pathology of the brain. Hippocrates was amongst the first to advance a somatogenic hypothesis of mental disorder in the fifth century BC:

> Madness comes from [the brain's] moistness. When the brain is abnormally moist, of necessity it moves, and when it moves neither sight nor hearing are still, but we see or hear now one thing and now another, and the tongue speaks in accordance with the things seen and heard on any occasion. But all the time a brain is still, a man can think properly (Hippocrates; cited in Kandel, Schwartz and Jessell, 1991: iii).

Recent biological psychiatric research associates a number of biological abnormalities with schizophrenia as predisposing, triggering or functionally-modulating factors (e.g. Kandel, 1991; Reverley and Deakin, 1999). Those receiving greatest attention are: 1) neuroanatomical and neuromorphological abnormalities such as hippocampal neuronal loss, cortical atrophy, and enlargement of cerebral ventricles; 2) abnormal neurotransmitter function in mesolimbic and mesocortical pathways of monoamines (particularly dopamine), peptides and amino acids; and 3) chromosomal abnormalities and genetic influences (as indicated by genetic linkage and inheritance studies).

However, this predominance of somatogenic hypotheses of the aetiology of mental disorder is tempered by the relationship between organicity and culpability; specifically, that the first does not negate the latter. This is historically evident in the case of syphilitic infection which, in spite of its discovered organic basis, hardly secured sympathy from the medical profession due to its sexually transmitted cause in an age emphasising abstinence. Similarly, the biological abnormality involved in lung cancer from cigarette smoking does not exclude an analysis of the culpable nature of the condition or, as Turner-Warwick (1994: 530) phrases it 'contempt for God's good gifts [of the human lung]'.[13] Other clearly

---

[13] Smokers tend to be regarded as addicts, much like alcoholics. Smoking behaviour (as well as, of course, diseases *caused by* smoking, e.g. lung cancer) has been recast into a disease falling under the auspices of the liberal-scientific model:

organic conditions may also be subjected to an analysis in terms of culpability: coronary heart disease, mountain sickness, decompression sickness in SCUBA divers, broken teeth sustained after starting a fight, or even a fractured hip from falling off an inadequately secured ladder. Another example might be halitosis (bad breath); although we may know of the condition's organic origin (bacterial waste products) we cannot forestall an attribution that the person might clean their teeth more diligently or at least suck a mint (halitosis has the property of potential impact upon others, as do insanity, intoxication and automatism [see Chapter 2], instigating a search for whether the precipitating condition is culpable or not). As Szasz (1997) states, in many cases a conclusively demonstrated biological basis for mental disorder may actually *strengthen* a culpable analysis where prevention, intervention and cure are available (as is increasingly the case with psychiatric conditions). Veatch (1997) goes even further, extending the analysis to physical disorders:

> Exposure to bacteria may be wilful, through failure to observe sanitary and inoculation procedures known or thought to be effective...Genetic counselling and screening is moving rapidly to make even genetic disease a culpable event albeit culpable at the parental level (p. 115).

Veatch believes that Western societies, where freewill and personal autonomy are prized societal values, will move toward two culpable conceptions of illness: those culpable at the individual level where there is a failure of personal preventative action or intervention, and those culpable at the national level where medical bodies fail to provide adequate scientific explanation and cure. An example of the latter might be serious organic diseases such as cystic fibrosis for which a genetic basis is not understood and diagnosis cannot be made prenatally. Whilst Mitchell (1986) asserts that 'the disease model of non-judgmental, amoral maladies is founded on the example of tuberculosis, rubella, epilepsy, malaria and pneumonia, which are generally not caused by the diseased person' (p. 276), even such diseases are now at least partly culpable (for many living in post-industrial Western societies) due to immunisation, hygiene, sanitation, and pharmacotherapy. In any case, it is clearly as fallacious an argument to say that a demonstrable

---

> Anti-smoking propagandists define the behaviour of smokers as if it were some kind of epileptic seizure. Their attempts to absolve people of responsibility for their behaviour are the obvious consequence...[but] there's a difference between what smoking does to a person's body and how smoke gets into his body (Schaler, 1997: 1).

Smokers cannot thus be overtly censured when their behaviour impacts upon others (through annoyance or the health risks of passive smoking) as their behaviour falls within a liberal-scientific model. However, common sense dictates that smokers are able to stop smoking if they truly try – they are merely morally weak (quite literally have no 'will power').

organic basis banishes a mental disorder to the realm of the non-voluntary as it is to say that a lack of such demonstrable organicity means the condition is not an illness in the first instance (Szasz [1997] argues this latter proposition).

Whatever the future holds for the organic and voluntaristic conceptions of illness, the notion that organicity negates culpability for a condition is well entrenched in Western society:

> The relationship between organicity and non-voluntariness is important. There is quite clearly an association between a belief in organicity and non-voluntariness. If behaviour is 'in the chemistry', we are convinced it is not in the control of the will...but there are enough instances...of behaviour which is organic yet culpable, that the correlation is not perfect (Veatch, 1997: 120).

Perhaps more importantly, there appears to be a willingness amongst society at large to see mental disorder as an illness even in the *absence* of any consensus of organicity of origin:

> ...lay respondents wish to confer the benefits of the 'sick' role on the schizophrenic patient without necessarily agreeing that the disorder has an organic origin (Furnham and Bower, 1992: 206).

Moore (1975) applies similar arguments – that of conferring benefits (such as the sick role) on the mentally disordered in spite of lack of evidence of the organicity of their condition (and an organic connection between that condition and supposedly contingent behaviour) – to the offer of legal excuse:

> ...the reason it has been a century's-old and fundamental feature of our collective conscience that the mentally ill, who cause injurious results, are nonetheless not morally blameworthy is because...one who is mentally ill is not as rational as the rest of us...since mental illness negates our assumption of rationality, we do not hold the mentally ill responsible...our intuitive feeling that the mentally ill should not be blamed (and...excused from criminal liability) thus survives any insights about category mistakes lawyers or others might make in thinking of mental disease as a mechanical cause (Moore, 1975: 1483).

If such an argument (upon which Radden [1985] bases her analysis of madness as unreason) is injurious to Szasz's core assumption that lack of demonstrable pathology entails criminal liability, it does not defeat a core assumption of the meta-responsibility theory: that *culpable conditions* (characterized by organicity or otherwise) should entail criminal liability. Such culpability in the meta-responsibility theory has little to do with organicity; we have seen how organic conditions can be culpable and those without such organicity can be nonculpable. If we accept Moore's and Radden's arguments that we should excuse mentally disordered persons because madness is unreason, we can still subject such *unreason* to an analysis in terms of culpability (madness *may* entail unreason, *but* is this madness that entails unreason voluntaristic?). However, Moore and Radden fail to note that insanity tests do not rest on a criterion of unreason; but rather on criteria of cognitive defects caused by disease of the mind.

If unreason is our *raison d'être* for exculpation, we are doing something very different to what our insanity tests tell us to do.

Whilst we may or may not excuse on the basis of organicity, it is clear that lack of culpability is very much dependent on the inclusion of the excusing condition in the liberal-scientific model (such inclusion itself, as shown above, may be made more along pretextual and ideological lines than those based on organicity). However, we have also seen that such inclusion should not exclude an analysis of the condition in terms of freewill or voluntarism.

1.4 Freewill and Determinism in the Liberal-Scientific Model

Why does the liberal-scientific model remove culpability? The liberal-scientific model views illness as something that 'happens to us' rather than something we 'do' (Szasz, 1997; Elliot, 1996). Again, this study does not intend to examine whether mentally disordered offenders can do otherwise than they do, but instead questions whether the mental disorder that excuses their acts *itself* lies within the realm of practical freedom or metaphysical libertarianism. It would be inappropriate, indeed impossible, to attempt to characterize and propose a solution in this study to the freewill debate, but instead it will suffice to say that the liberal-scientific model removes sickness from such a realm by removing the assumption of the sick role from the collective set of actions that are indeed one's own; the ill person has no liberty to do otherwise than be ill. To follow the argument to its conclusion requires subscription to sickness as a form of hard determinism: that is, the 'behaviour' of being ill is brought about by constitutional and environmental factors, and the individual contributes nothing to it. The same would be true of any acts, criminal or otherwise, which arise as a product of illness.

Veatch (1997) delineates four sub-system theories of determinism: organic, psychological, social and cultural sub-systems. Deviant behaviour may be subjected to a freewill/determinism analysis using one of these sub-systems as a primary reference point. Organic determinism is represented by, for example, the disease model. Psychological determinisms are represented by, for example, Skinnerian behaviourism which proffers that a certain response is determined by a particular stimulus reinforcement history. Social determinisms are represented by notions that behaviour is effectuated by the socio-economic world, e.g. poor upbringing causes delinquency. Cultural determinism sees behaviour as predestined, e.g. within a religious framework or due to logical laws. Mental disorder has been subjected to extensive deterministic analysis with regard to all four subsystems, perhaps best represented by the dopaminergic hypothesis of schizophrenia (organic determinism), behavioural models of addiction or phobias (psychological determinism), social causes of schizophrenia, e.g. labelling theory (social determinism), and mental disorder as God's punishment (cultural determinism).

A further four sub-systems guide our analysis with regard to the primary reference point: the behavioural stage (the manner in which the deviancy is manifested, e.g. organic or social symptoms); the response stage (e.g. organic or psychosocial therapy); the proximal cause stage (e.g. an immediate psychological need to engage in the deviancy); and the ultimate cause stage (e.g. an underlying organic mechanism causing engagement in the deviancy). The greater the incidence of organicity at each of these stages, the more the deviancy will be evaluated as being not of the person's will.

Aristotle realized, however, that although illness is susceptible to analysis in terms of organic determinism, the *antecedent conditions* to the illness (equivalent to Veatch's ultimate cause sub-system analysis) may not be so privileged. He phrased the argument in terms of inability to act rightly:

> He [cannot] stop being unjust...no more than a sick man can become healthy, even though (it may be) his sickness is voluntary, being the result of incontinent living and disobeying his doctors. There was a time when it was open to him not to be ill; but when he had once thrown away his chance, it was gone; just as when one has let go of a stone, it is too late to get it back – but the agent was responsible for throwing it, because the origin of the action was in himself (Aristotle, 1955: 92).

It is clear that the use of an illness model to explain a deviance makes presuppositions about aetiology, and therefore the *cause* of the deviance (Scadding, 1967; Laing, 1995). It is, however, fallacious to *excuse* behaviour on the basis of such causal accounts. Morse (1994: 159) addresses 'the fundamental conceptual error in forensic psychiatry and psychology – the notion that if a behaviour is caused or a causal account can be given, then the behaviour is fully or partially excused'. Morse applies the error to a theory of action to show that the acts of mentally disordered offenders should not necessarily be excused as they are not compelled; but why should such an analysis be only applied to *acts* resulting from 'ill-health' and not the ill-health *itself*? As stated above, research into mental disorder has uncovered an array of candidates for causes of mental disorder; but this does not entail that disorder should be *excused* (i.e. automatically subject the patient/disorder to Parsons' Postulate I) as causal accounts do not in themselves entail non-voluntariness or negation of freewill. From a philosophical viewpoint, causation is not equivalent to determinism (nor, *vice versa*, is absence of causation indicative of agency or freewill). Whilst such concepts are familiar to the philosophy of action (e.g. Moore, 1993), they do not seem to impact significantly upon clinical medicine or psychiatry.

In spite of such a fallacy, it is clear that mental disorder (and increasingly deviance more generally, e.g. medical conceptions of crime; Raine, 1993) is rightly or wrongly understood within a deterministic framework. This has the effect of forestalling any attribution of meta-responsibility, as determined phenomena (including mental disorder) cannot be subjected to a voluntaristic analysis. It was not, however, always so. The next section of this study shows that the inclusion of madness within a liberal-scientific framework has been a comparatively recent development.

1.5 Historical Notions of Autonomy in Mental Disorder

In the pre-classical age described by Michel Foucault (1967) in *Madness and Civilisation*, the culpability attached to leprosy and subsequently to mental disorder conspired to create a barely watered-down parody of the world described in Samuel Butler's *Erewhon* (1872/1970). Butler wryly cleaves the association of illness with absence of culpability, creating a world in which illness is punished whereas crime is medicalized:

> [I]f a man falls into ill health, or catches any disorder, or fails bodily in any way before he is seventy years old he is tried before a jury...and if convicted is held up to public scorn and sentenced more or less severely as the case may be. There are subdivisions of illness into crimes and misdemeanours as with offences amongst ourselves – a man being punished very severely for serious illness, while failure of eyes or hearing in one over sixty-five who has had good health hitherto is dealt with by fine only, or imprisonment in default of payment. But if a man forges a cheque, or sets his house on fire, or robs with violence from the person, or does any other such things as are criminal in our own country, he is either taken to a hospital and most carefully tended at the public expense...he is suffering from a severe fit of immorality...I should add that under certain circumstances poverty and ill luck are also considered criminal (Butler 1872/1970: 107).

As far back as the seventh century, Italian law treated both madness and leprosy as culpable conditions:

> If it happens that after a girl or woman has been betrothed she becomes leprous or mad or blind in both eyes, then her betrothed husband shall receive back his property and he shall not be required to take her to wife against his will. And he shall not be guilty in this event because *it did not occur on account of his neglect but on account of her weighty sins and resulting illness* (Robinson, 1996: 51 [italics added], from edict 180 decreed by the Duke of Brescia, Rothair, from his 338 Edicts).

During the Middle Ages, madness was viewed as God's punishment for sin (Neaman, 1975). The fifteenth century *Malleus Mallificarum* asserted that deprivation of reason was the injurious work of the devil. However, such supernatural aetiologies did not mean the afflicted were blameless:

> The belief in the freewill of man is here [in the *Malleus*] brought to its most terrifying, although most preposterous, conclusion. Man, whatever he does, even if he succumbs to an illness which perverts his perceptions, imagination, and intellectual functions, does it of his own free will; he voluntarily bows to the wishes of the Evil One. The devil does not lure and trap man; man chooses to succumb to the devil and he must be held responsible for this free choice. He must be punished; he must be eliminated from the community (Zilboorg, 1935; in Szasz, 1961: 184).

If one of the goals of punishing criminals is to protect against societal anxiety that the force of good might not triumph against the force of evil (Perlin, 1996), then it is hardly surprising that the mentally disordered (who, by the seventeenth century, were variously recipients of God's own punishment, witches, demonic progeny, and agents of the devil) provided an ideal outlet for the venting of such anxieties through their punishment. Indeed, treatment for insanity during the seventeenth century consisted largely of pseudo-therapeutic punishment:

> Furious Mad-men are sooner, and more certainly cured by punishments, and hard usage, in a strait room...Bloodletting, Vomits, or very strong Purges, and boldly and rashly given are most often convenient...let the diet be slender and not delicate, their clothing coarse, their beds hard, and their handling severe and rigid (Willis, 1680; in Busfield, 1986: 168).

Whilst such pseudo-therapeutic punishment withered toward the end of the eighteenth century, its replacement was 'moral' treatment, which Foucault (1967) asserts was merely a continuation of the judgment and condemnation of the mentally disordered:

> Madness escaped from the arbitrary only in order to enter a kind of endless trial for which the asylum furnished simultaneously police, magistrates, and torturers (Foucault, 1967: 269).

This judgment of mental patients in practice was backed by the prevailing aetiological theories of the day, which arose from (and in turn, informed) a grossly inaccurate human anatomy. For example, women who succumbed to mental disorder were seen as morally too lax. Morality was portrayed onto physical dimensions: their frail fibres, like overtightened strings on a violin, would resonate too strongly their passions, affections and imaginations. To Foucault, this made the mad both more innocent and more *guilty*: more innocent because such pathology caused the individual to swiftly drown in a sea of disease, but more guilty because the patient had 'cultivated all too complacently'[14] these precipitating factors. Here we see the underpinnings of an autogenous or autonomous model of mental disorder; that the control of its aetiology or symptomatology lies with the patient. Indeed, 'eighteenth century therapeutics tried to persuade the madman of his madness in order to release him from it...treating madness in its arrogance rather than treating it in its aberration'.[15] The conceptualization of madness as unreason suggests error on the part of the insane in their failure to rationalize their disease: 'a rational hold over madness is always possible and necessary, to the very degree that madness is non-reason'.[16]

---

[14] Foucault (1967: 157).
[15] *IBID* at 264.
[16] *IBID* at 107.

The 'new' moral treatment, like the torture and terror that chronologically preceded it, was designed to infuse the mentally disordered with a sense of responsibility for their 'disease':

> The natural tendency of such treatment is, to degrade the mind of the patient, and to make him indifferent to those moral feelings. Which, under judicious direction and encouragement, are found capable, in no small degree, to strengthen the power of *self-restraint*; and which render the resort to coercion, in many cases, unnecessary (Tuke (1813); cited in Busfield, 1986: 212; italics added).

The cohabitation of the mentally disordered and criminals, spendthrifts, blasphemers and libertines in the same institution underlined the sentiment of mental disorder as a crime or deviance.[17] Here we see a radical departure from the maxim of Roman law (attributed to Aurelius) that 'madness is its own punishment' (*furiosis furore ipso punitur*). Central to this departure was the notion that punishment can have therapeutic value. If both the cause (and the iniquity) of insanity is moral weakness such as idleness, then work and punishment prove of therapeutic and remedial value. Foucault himself acknowledged the parallel between the treatment of the insane and the criminal:

> The asylum of the age of positivism...is not a free realm of observation, diagnosis, and therapeutics; it is a judicial space where one is accused, judged and condemned, and from which one is never released except...by remorse (Foucault, 1967: 269).

Although authors such as Radden (1985) see Foucault as describing a transition away from moral blame to a medical model, it might be argued that moral blame never died, and indeed became *associated* with certain elements of the 'new' medicine (through the moral treatment and consequent covert judgement of mentally disordered persons). The *overt* association between the medical model and morality was lost during the nineteenth century, at the beginning of which Pinel described the 'mentally sick' as:

> Far from being guilty persons who merit punishment, are...people whose miserable state deserves all the consideration due to suffering humanity (Pinel, 1806/1962; cited in Radden, 1985: 7).

With Pinel's assertion comes the shift from the autogenous/autonomous model to the liberal-scientific model. In spite of the association of morality and the medical model being broken, the two did not cease to coexist. It is argued in Chapter 4 that a thread connecting the liberal-scientific model with morality has remained (that in spite of viewing the mentally disordered as 'ill' we may still

---

[17] Contemporary echoes of such provision surface, for example, in Article 5(1)(e) of the European Convention on Human Rights which lumps together alcoholics, vagrants and people of 'unsound mind' (Heginbotham and Elson, 1999: 66).

believe there is an autogenous element to their behaviour) and it is this association that is responsible for sanism and pretextual decision-making with regard to the mentally disordered offender. The thread was certainly intact in 1833 when Shelford wrote that madness is indeed disease, but diseases are a product of morality:

> Insanity is essentially a bodily disease, and the moral causes operate in producing it, as they do in other complaints...The moral causes include those emotions which are conceived to originate from the mind itself, and which, from their excess, tend to distort the natural feelings; or, from their repeated accessions, and over-strained indulgence, at length overthrow the barriers of reason and established opinion: such are the gusts of violent passion, and the protracted indulgence of grief; the terror impressed by erroneous views of religion; the degradation of pride; disappointment in love; and sudden fright...The moral cause, therefore, is always the remote cause; the physical, the proximate, or that state of the cerebral functions which immediately preceded the peculiar action denominated maniacal (Shelford, 1833; cited in Fingarette, 1972: 21).

By the twentieth century, the focus of the culpability of the mentally disordered had moved from the cause of their illness to the effect in terms of negative economic and social contribution:

> ...one wholesome function of the Lunacy and Mental Deficiency Acts is the segregation from the public of those who, by reason of mental disorder or defect, impair the social machine by their inefficiency as citizens (Lord, 1927; cited in Barham and Barnes, 1999: 135).

Although this new-found preoccupation with the moral *effects* of morbidity (rather then precipitating *causes*) had seemingly spun the thread connecting morality and the medical model so fine as to be almost imperceptible, Foucault (1967: 269) states 'For a long time to come, and to our own day at least, [madness] is imprisoned in a moral world'. In spite of this, autogeny and morality in mental disorder would find little overt mention in psychiatry for the next 150 years, until the critical- and anti-psychiatric formulations of the 1960s and 1970s (discussed in Chapter 3).

1.6 Concluding Overview

The purpose of this chapter has been to present the theory of meta-responsibility and its relation to historical and contemporary conceptions of mental disorder. In particular, we have examined the effects of locating mental disorder within a liberal-scientific framework. These include removal of culpability for disorder (Parsons' Postulate I), which has the effect of placating our moral intuition that madness is not blameworthy. This contrasts with the voluntaristic model of mental disorder that entails culpability for disorder and hence responsibility for criminal responsibility (meta-responsibility).

If mental disorder and concomitant criminal responsibility can be subjected to an analysis in terms of voluntarism, before such an analysis can be made it is appropriate to examine insanity law, as the insanity defence is where the excusatory power of mental disorder is at its keenest and most pertinent to the theory of meta-responsibility. It will become apparent that the liberal-scientific/McNaughton combination has been instrumental not only in removing culpability for acts committed *whilst* mentally disordered, but also in forestalling any analysis of culpability *for* that disorder in the first instance. Chapter 2 thus examines the insanity defence (in which the law is blind to meta-responsibility), and two other incapacitating conditions – intoxication and automatism – in which it will be seen that the criminal law *does* consider the individual's responsibility for causing the condition and hence his criminal responsibility.

Chapter 2

Meta-responsibility in Insanity and Other Legally Incapacitating Conditions

I do not suppose that, when a drunkard reasons with himself upon his vice, he is once out of five hundred times affected by the dangers that he runs through his brutish, physical insensibility; neither had I, long as I had considered my position, made enough allowance for the complete moral insensibility and insensate readiness to evil which were the leading characters of Edward Hyde.

Robert Louis Stevenson, Dr. Jekyll and Mr. Hyde

This chapter introduces the insanity defence and examines Anglo-American criminal law's consideration of voluntarism (and meta-responsibility) in three major classes of incapacity that may excuse responsibility or mitigate punishment for a criminal act: intoxication, automatism, and insanity. It will be seen that the law considers meta-responsibility in the first two incapacitating conditions, but not in insanity. The illogicality and inconsistency of considering meta-responsibility in only two of the three incapacitating conditions is considered, as well as how such a state of affairs might have arisen.

2.1 Insanity

The insanity defence constitutes an ostensibly remarkable, albeit infrequent,[1] act of altruism afforded to those who 'don't know any better' because of their mental

---

[1] Infrequency of use should not be conflated with lack of importance:

> Because this defense is raised in fewer than 2% of all criminal trials, and is successful in fewer than 10% of those cases, it has been referred to by at least one writer of note as a 'no consequence' issue. But if infrequency of occurrence causes an issue to be of no consequence, the same might be said of accidents at nuclear power plants...we know that is not so (Spring, 1998: 188).

Exculpating the insane appears to be a deeply-rooted endeavour fundamental to societal principles of individual responsibility and autonomy (Moore, 1975; Perlin, 1996); The Royal Commission on Capital Punishment 1949-1953 Cmd. No. 8932 (1953) stated that:

> ...it has for centuries been recognised that, if a person was, at the time of his unlawful act, mentally so disordered that it would be unreasonable to impute guilt to him, he ought not to be held liable...views have changed and opinions have differed...about the standards to be applied in deciding whether an individual should be exempted from criminal responsibility....but the principle has been accepted without question (p. 98).

Rubin J. stated in *United States v. Lyons* (1984), 739 F.2d 994 that the insanity defence is a reflection of the 'fundamental moral principles of the criminal law'. If the insanity defence is clearly of importance far beyond a paltry legal showing; the question we should perhaps be asking is 'Why is the usage of the insanity defence so low?'. In England and Wales data on successful insanity acquittals (only) is available, showing a mean of only 3.5 successful cases occurring annually between 1975 and 1988 (extrapolated from the data of Mackay, 1990).

However, between 1991 and 1996 an average of 8.8 successful insanity pleas occurred per annum (Mackay and Kearns, 1999). This increase in usage is unsurprising given an increased range of disposals, including absolute discharge, made available under the Criminal Procedure (Insanity and Unfitness to Plead) Act 1991 and the protection given to patient interests offered by the possibility of regular application for release by a Mental Health Review Tribunal (MHRT) under the Mental Health Act 1983. The Criminal Procedure (Insanity) Act 1964 (under which Mackay's [1990] sample fell) discouraged insanity defence usage, as a successful plea resulted in indefinite commitment to a mental hospital. Insanity defence usage in England and Wales may further rise due to a) recently implemented provisions in the Crime (Sentences) Act 1997 which allow courts to order a prison sentence with a direction for immediate transfer to hospital (a hybrid disposal bound to be seen as highly undesirable by most defendants and their lawyers who face a Hobson's choice with regard to pleading insanity or facing a hybrid disposal); and b) the introduction of a life sentence upon conviction for a second serious offence in the Crime (Sentences) Act 1997 (under which remit mentally disordered offenders also fall); a plea of diminished responsibility [DR] to a charge of murder (or a reliance upon mitigatory psychiatric factors in sentencing) will not avail the offender, as DR is still a 'guilty' finding (instead defendants will be forced to gamble on an 'all or nothing' insanity plea in an attempt to avoid a life sentence).

Insanity defence use is far more frequent in the US (Perlin, 1994), although still less than one per cent of defendants charged with a serious crime prior to the Insanity Defence Reform Act (1984) were found NGRI (Pasewark and McGinley, 1985). However, in some states insanity acquittees occupy over 50 per cent of long-term psychiatric hospital beds (insanity acquittees in Missouri numbered 797 in 1992; Linhorst and Dirks-Linhorst, 1997). Such figures had long been a major concern to the public and lawmakers, the final straw being the insanity acquittal of President Reagan's attempted assassin, John Hinckley, which resulted in the 1984 Insanity Defence Reform Act (IDRA) (see Finkel, 1989). In the hearings for the IDRA, Representative Coughlin stated 'nothing less than the credibility of our Federal justice system [is] at stake' (Perlin, 1994: 17). It is clear that the importance of

disorder. Through relieving a few such individuals of criminal responsibility, we reaffirm the ideal that the majority will be held responsible and not privileged by such special provision (Miller and Radelet, 1993). As Platt and Diamond (1965) remark:

> The criminal law of England and the United States, from its earliest systematisation in the middle of the thirteenth century until the present day, has always considered insanity as a mitigating or exculpating factor which exempts the accused from punishment (p. 356).

The mechanism by which such exemption has been traditionally granted is one borne from the bifurcation of criminal components: that to commit a crime an individual must not only commit a criminal act (*actus reus*) but also have intended to commit such an act (*mens rea*). This bifurcation was cited as far back as Henrici de Bracton's thirteenth century text, '*On the Laws and Customs of England*' – 'a crime is not committed unless the will to harm be present' (Walker, 1968: 39), although the excusatory power of mental disorder clearly predates such a formulation. Bracton's formulation of the *mens rea* doctrine undoubtedly grew out of his ecclesiastical training, which emphasized moral guilt (that conduct should be blameworthy in both the eyes of God and man) rather than strict liability.

If mental disorder conspires to negate *mens rea*: that is, by constituting a disease of the mind which caused a defect of reason interfering with the actor's ability to know the nature and quality of the act or that it was wrong, then no crime has been committed (only an *actus reus*), and the defendant should be relieved of criminal responsibility. Such conceptions of disease of the mind, defect of reason, etc. are legal terms, and as such the test of insanity is a legal test rather than a clinical one. Whilst courtroom enquiry into the defendant's sanity or otherwise is likely to be informed by psychiatric testimony (indeed, the evidence of two psychiatrists is required for the court to consider a special verdict under the Criminal Procedure [Insanity and Unfitness to Plead] Act 1991), 'ultimate issue' testimony by clinicians concerning the defendant's *legal* insanity is both prohibited by the law (insanity is to be left to legal fact finders) and represents a violation of the clinician's professional ethics (clinicians are not qualified to diagnose jurisprudential diseases of the mind just as the law is unable to diagnose psychiatric disorders; Ogloff, 1996).[2] Bracton's use of the terms 'sense' and 'reason' (which could not possibly be considered clinical terms) provides a precursor to such legal tests:

---

the insanity defence extends far beyond a paltry showing in England and Wales, and this justifies its use as the spindle about which the thread of meta-responsibility is spun. As Perlin (1985: 863) states, the defence is 'the raw nerve at the cutting edge of psychiatry and law'.

[2] See *SUPRA* note 12, Ch.1.

> But what shall be said of the madman who has no reason, and of the lunatic and the raving, or of the child, or if he who labours in a severe illness drowns himself, it is asked whether he commits a felony against himself. It seems that they do not, nor do they forfeit their inheritance or their chattels, because they lack sense and reason and can no more do wrong or commit a felony than a brute animal (*brutum animal*), since they are not far [from being] brutes (*brutis*), according to what can be seen in the minor; if he kills someone whilst under age, he will not suffer judgment (Bracton; cited in Hermann, 1983: 23-24).

Edward Coke, in his sixteenth century text, '*Institutes of the Laws of England*',[3] furthered Bracton's 'wild beast' test through the maxim 'no felony or murder can be committed without a felonious intent or purpose' (cited in Hermann, 1983; 24). Coke proposed three classes of persons lacking such intent or purpose (due to being *non compus mentis*): the idiot (who from birth suffers the infirmity of lack of reasoning); the person who by sickness, grief or accident loses memory and understanding; and the lunatic, who is *non compos* during the times he is in absence of his mental faculties. Importantly for the meta-responsibility theory, he also distinguished a fourth class whom, although *non compos*, could *not* be excused: the person who by his own vicious act deprives himself of memory and understanding, as in voluntary drunkenness (Hermann, 1983). Indeed, drunkenness was viewed as an *aggravating* rather than *mitigatory* circumstance at trial.

Sir Matthew Hale, in his '*History of Pleas of the Crown*' (1736), further differentiated the incapacity of persons who lack either understanding or liberty of the will (and by doing so provided a precursor for volitional or irresistible impulse tests of insanity): idiocy, insanity (*dementia accidentalis vel adcentita*), and drunkenness (*dementia affectata*). He also distinguished a quantitative dimension of exculpating insanity: partial (*quod hoc vel illud insanire*), or total. To exculpate, Hale believed understanding should be reduced at least to the level of a fourteen year old child.

A theatrical parade of high-profile English eighteenth and nineteenth century insanity trials laid the foundation for the modern Anglo-American insanity defence: *Rex v. Arnold* (1723)[4] ('to be exempted from punishment: it must be a man that is totally deprived of his understanding and memory, and doth not know what he is doing, no more than an infant, than a brute, or a wild beast'); *Rex v. Hadfield* (1800)[5] ('If a man is in a deranged state of mind at the time, he is not criminally answerable for his acts'); *Reg. v. Oxford* (1840)[6] ('The question is, whether the prisoner was labouring under that species of insanity which satisfies you that he was quite unaware of the nature, character, and consequences of the act he was committing, or in other words, whether he was under the influence of a diseased mind, and was really unconscious at the time he was committing the act,

---

[3] Coke (1719).

[4] *Rex v. Arnold* (1723), 16 How St. Tr. 684.

[5] *Rex v. Hadfield* (1800), 27 How. St. Tr. 1281.

[6] *Reg. v. Oxford* (1840), 9 C. & P. 525.

that it was a crime'); and finally *Daniel McNaughton's Case* (1843)[7] from which the eponymous rules take their name. The Rules have weathered attacks from the judiciary, academics, and public sentiment for over 150 years and still constitute the test of insanity in English law.[8] The McNaughton Rules became assimilated into US case law (and added a volitional or 'irresistible impulse' limb) with the decision in *Parsons v. Alabama* (1886)[9] ('If there be either incapacity to distinguish between right and wrong as to the particular act, or delusions as to the act, or inability to refrain from doing the act, there is no responsibility'). The swings and roundabouts of US case and statutory law have since provided a number of further insanity tests[10] (most notably those used in the cases of *State of New Hampshire v. Pike* (1869),[11] *Durham v. United States* (1954),[12] and the test stipulated in the ALI Model Penal Code),[13] but the Insanity Defence Reform Act 1984 returned most US jurisdictions to a restrictive McNaughton-style cognitive test[14] (which provides a defence if the defendant 'as a result of a severe mental disease or defect was unable to appreciate the nature and quality or the wrongfulness of his acts').[15] Such a test was confirmed in the case of *United States v. Lyons* (1984).[16]

English law makes provision for the prosecution to raise evidence of insanity, and for the judge to raise the issue and put it to the jury provided there is evidence embracing all the relevant considerations in the McNaughton Rules e.g. *R v. Thomas* (1996).[17] The 'defence' is therefore unusual in that it may be raised by

---

[7] See SUPRA note 3, Ch. 1.

[8] For the wording of The Rules, see the introduction to Chapter 1.

[9] *Parsons v. Alabama* (1886), 2 So. 854.

[10] See INFRA note 28, Ch. 2.

[11] *State of New Hampshire v. Pike* (1869), 49 NH 399.

[12] *Durham v. United States* (1954), 214 F.2d 862.

[13] See INFRA note 25.

[14] See INFRA note 28.

[15] Insanity Defense Reform Act 1984 18 USC s 20(a); cited in Mackay (1995: 113). California adopted a 'conjunctive' McNaughton style test which requires that the defendant 'was incapable of knowing or understanding the nature and quality of his act *and* of distinguishing right from wrong at the time of the offence' (California Penal Code (Supp 1987) s 25(b); cited in Mackay, 1995: 114). Alaska restricted its test to the first limb of the McNaughton Rules, whilst Montana, Idaho, and Utah abolished a specific insanity defence, reducing questions about the defendant's mental state to an evidentiary question concerning the presence of *mens rea*. About two-thirds of states with an existing insanity plea place the burden of proof on the defendant, usually to demonstrate his insanity by a preponderance of the evidence (Federal law and Arizona require that the proof be 'by clear and convincing evidence'; Mackay, 1995: 117). In addition, 12 states enacted provision for a finding of 'Guilty But Mentally Ill'; see INFRA note 28.

[16] See SUPRA note 1.

[17] *R v. Thomas* (1996), 2 BMLR 120. Of the 48 US jurisdictions that allow the insanity defence, seventeen permit the defence to be imposed over the objections of defendants (Miller, Olin, Johnson *et al.*, 1996).

either defence or prosecution. The prosecution may request the court to consider a special verdict if the defendant puts his sanity at issue, e.g. if the defendant raises a plea of diminished responsibility or automatism. In such cases, the prosecution bears the burden to prove the defendant's insanity beyond reasonable doubt, e.g. *R v. Podola* [1959].[18] Where the issue is raised by the defence, the burden of proof lies with the defendant to prove his insanity on the balance of probabilities. Furthermore, Section 1(1) of the Criminal Procedure (Insanity and Unfitness to Plead) Act 1991 specifies that 'A jury shall not return a special verdict under section two of the Trial of Lunatics Act 1883 (acquittal on ground of insanity) except on the written or oral evidence of two or more registered medical practitioners at least one of whom is duly approved'. This requirement, along with that of the issue being put to the jury by the judge, seems to restrict much of the discretion of the jury to render a finding of insanity in the courtroom. Such requirements do not usurp the principle that 'although the medical evidence will be crucial to [the jury's] decision, it is not for doctors to decide the issue but for the jury to decide it on the basis of their evidence' (Allen, 1991: 108). The tightening of procedural matters does, however, place limitations on the type and extent of such evidence that the jury will be allowed to hear and consider. In the US, the Insanity Defence Reform Act 1984 has had similar effects.

Whilst the type and extent of evidence concerning insanity that is admissible in court has been a subject of debate for as long as the defence of insanity has existed, a more recent development in UK and European law has placed a further constraint upon the range of conditions that may be raised as evidence of insanity. Such constraints arise through the potential *consequence* of an insanity finding, namely detention in psychiatric facilities, rather than due to exigencies of the defence *per se.* Article 5(1)(e) of the European Convention on Human Rights (as adopted into English law by the Human Rights Act 2000) specifies that involuntary psychiatric detention must rely on the person being of 'unsound mind' for his right to liberty and security of person to be removed. The court in *Winterwerp v. The Netherlands* [1979][19] established that:

> ...except in emergency cases, *the individual concerned should not be deprived of his liberty unless he has been reliably shown to be of 'unsound mind'*. The very nature of what has to be established before the competent national authority – that is, a true mental disorder, calls for *objective medical expertise*. Further *the mental disorder must be of a kind or degree warranting compulsory confinement.* What is more, *the validity of continued confinement depends upon the persistence of such a disorder* [italics added].

Sutherland and Gearty (1992) realized the incompatibility between such a ruling and those in diabetic, somnambulism, and epilepsy cases in which the incapacitating condition either cannot be deemed to constitute unsoundness of

[18] *R v. Podola* [1959] 3 All ER 418.
[19] *Winterwerp v. The Netherlands* [1979] 2 EHRR 387.

mind, or fails to warrant confinement due to its failure to persist after the criminal episode or trial:[20]

> While it remains open for the prosecution to force the defence of insanity upon defendants falling within the outmoded McNaghten *[sic]* rules, eventually one of our sleep-walking, epileptic or diabetic 'insane' charged with murder will find him – or herself facing mandatory commitment, notwithstanding the 1991 Act. If so, the chance of an application to Strasbourg would present itself. An adverse judgment by the European Court may eventually be the final straw that compels the Government to rid itself and us of the McNaghten Rules (p. 424).

The matter recently bothered UK courts in the case of *AG v. Prior* (2001)[21] leading the bailiff of Jersey, Sir Philip Bailache, to wrestle with what constituted insanity under the Criminal Justice (Insane Persons) (Jersey) Law 1964. He concluded that:

> The McNaghten *[sic]* Rules do not form part of the law of Jersey and do not therefore at first blush provide the answer to the question of the meaning of 'insanity' in the Criminal Justice (Insane Persons) (Jersey) Law 1964... It is not necessary for me to decide whether the McNaghten Rules are in compliance with the requirements of the European Convention on Human Rights. It is, however, strongly arguable that their adoption in this jurisdiction, particularly in the absence of legislation equivalent to the 1991 Act, would involve a breach of Article 5 of the Convention... I should therefore adopt a definition of 'insanity' which is consistent with the evidence given to the Royal Commissioners in 1846, compliant with Convention rights under the Human Rights (Jersey) Law 2000, and appropriate to the state of medical knowledge in the 21st century...I prefer, and I respectfully adopt, a definition suggested by Professor R. D. Mackay. I therefore hold that a person is insane within the meaning of Article 2 of the Criminal Justice (Insane Persons) (Jersey) Law 1964 if, at the time of the commission of the offence, his unsoundness of mind affected his criminal behaviour to such a substantial degree that the jury consider that he ought not to be found criminally responsible...This test will permit objective medical evidence of a defendant's unsoundness of mind to be given in the sense required by Convention jurisprudence while retaining a clear causal link between the offence and the mental disorder. It will also cater for defects of volition. I do not believe that the heavens will fall in as a result of this ruling.

This remarkable ruling was deemed sufficient by *The Times* newspaper to run the headline 'INSANITY DEFENCE SET TO BE SCRAPPED', under which it stated that:

---

[20] See *INFRA* notes 24 and 32 for a discussion of such cases and insane versus non-insane automatism.

[21] *AG v. Prior* (2001), (Unreported, Royal Court of Jersey Judgment No. 2001/035, 9th February).

> THE defence of insanity under English law, used for more than 150 years, is expected to be scrapped after a judge ruled that it breaches the Human Rights Act.
>
> A judge in Jersey said that the so-called McNaghten *[sic]* rules – which courts use to decide if offenders are insane – breach article five of the Act which guarantees the right to liberty. It is believed that a similar challenge would succeed in England and Wales and lawyers predict that ministers are likely to review the law.
>
> The ruling was made in a case at the Royal Court of Jersey by Sir Philip Bailhache, the Bailiff. He recommends a test which draws on medical evidence on the defendant's state of mind yet retains a causal link between the offence and the mental disorder.
>
> Conor Gearty, a human rights specialist, and Professor of Law at King's College London, welcomed the ruling. He said: 'Hopefully officials will take this ruling as a stimulus to review the law.' He said the rules had been applied in an arbitrary way and had been criticised for decades (*The Times*, 14th Feb 2001, p. 4).

Whether the new test does indeed become adopted in England and Wales it provides a unique opportunity for the law to not only comply with human rights law, but also to comply with commonsensical notions of justice and introduce a clause for the consideration of meta-responsibility, which is not of course represented in the new 'Mackay Rules'.

Whilst such recent legal conundrums have brought general dissatisfaction with the McNaughton Rules to a head, exculpation on the grounds of mental illness had been a subject of fierce debate as a legal, ethical and philosophical conundrum long before the birth of Daniel McNaughton. His legacy, in the form of the McNaughton Rules, has only served to fuel such debate. Two traditional forms of objection to The Rules may be distinguished: 1) The Rules are inappropriate because there is no need for a legal test of insanity (e.g. Halpern, 1977; N. Morris, 1982; Szasz, 1997); or 2) there is a need for a legal test of insanity, but The Rules do not provide it (Schopp, 1991; G. Morris, 1975). In the former case, the defence is often criticized as a ruse to allow supposedly mentally disordered defendants to escape punishment;[22] other authors deem it redundant in that the legal system may reflect sympathy and mitigation in sentencing or disposal, or by allowing other

---

[22] For example, the following is part of the preface to a book entitled 'Beating the Insanity Defence: Denying the License to Kill':

> This book...is designed to help prosecutors beat the mental defense and the defendant's expert witness...This endeavour is necessary since the defense very often is a hoax, enabling the guilty defendant to be set free. Once successful with the defense, the defendant may have the equivalent of a free pass to commit further crimes (Nissman, Barnes and Alpert, 1980: viii).

general defences (e.g. duress, necessity etc.).[23] Where The Rules are deemed to provide an insufficient test of legal insanity, they are usually criticized along the following dimensions: 1) they are based on the faulty supposition that conduct is mediated purely by cognition, and take no account of volitional or affective components; and 2) they are riddled with definitional ambiguities, particularly the terms 'defect of reason', 'disease of the mind',[24] 'nature and quality', 'know',[25] and 'wrong'.[26]

The arguments are well rehearsed[27] and may be found in most textbooks on law and psychiatry or historical accounts of the insanity defence (e.g. Walker, 1968; Robinson, 1996); they will not be examined in detail here.[28] Instead, as

---

[23] For example, Finkel's quasisubjective insanity defence in Chapter 5 (based on *justificatory* rather than *exculpatory* principles; Finkel and Slobogin, 1995).

[24] Devlin J., in the case of *R v. Kemp* [1957] 1 Q.B. 399, defined the 'mind' as the mental faculties of reason, memory and understanding. Insanity could therefore include any defect of the above brought about, for example, by arterio-sclerosis (a condition which, with relevance to the present argument, might constitute a condition for which the sufferer has at least partial culpability). A similar stance was adopted by the House of Lords decision in the case of *R v. Sullivan* [1984] A.C. 156, concerning the unconscious violence of an epileptic in the post-ictal stage of *grand mal*, where the McNaughton Rules applied because:

> ... if the effect of a disease was to impair so severely as to have either of the consequences referred to in the latter part of The Rules, it mattered not whether the impairment was organic, as in epilepsy, or functional, or whether the impairment was permanent or was transient and intermittent, provided that it subsisted at the time of the commission of the act.

[25] The American Law Institute (1962) Model Penal Code test and the University of Virginia Institute of Law, Psychiatry and Public Policy test ('The Bonnie Rule'; Bonnie, 1983) both substitute 'know' with the less constrictive 'appreciate'.

[26] The McNaughton judges referred to *legal* wrong in their formulation of The Rules, which would tend to presuppose an appreciation that the act was also morally wrong. However, more recently it has been questioned whether a defendant may know his act is contrary to law but not morally wrong (as in the case of a psychotic person believing he must steal an object to save the world); see Radden (1985).

[27] Perlin (1994: 81) offers the following quotes in derision of the test from various sources: 'untrustworthy', a 'facade', 'absolutist', an illustration of 'a fiction being a fetish', 'an absurd dictum which has long been discredited by medical science', 'outmoded and unrealistic', based on 'an entirely obsolete and misleading conception' and 'bearing little relation to the truths of mental life'.

[28] Some objections have been addressed in major reformulations of the criteria for being judged Not Guilty by Reason of Insanity: The Royal Commission on Capital Punishment (1953) (an unlawful act is excused if 'at the time of the act the accused was suffering from disease of the mind [or mental deficiency] to such a degree that he ought not to be held responsible'); Durham formula (1957) (*Durham v. United States* (1954), 214 F.2d 862 'the accused is not criminally responsible if his unlawful act was the product of mental disease or mental defect'); American Law Institute Model Penal Code (ALI, 1962) ('the defendant, as a result of mental disease or mental defect, lacked substantial capacity either to appreciate

described in Chapter 1, this study highlights a new objection to the traditional insanity defence: the self-causation of mental disorder and its concomitant effect on criminal responsibility.[29]

---

the criminality of his conduct, or to conform his conduct to the requirements of the law'); Butler Committee (1975) ('the defendant did the act but lacked *mens rea*, being mentally disordered at the time <u>or</u> the defendant was able to form intentions and carry them out but at the time of the offence was suffering from severe mental illness or severe mental handicap'); The Law Commission (1989) Draft Criminal Code for England and Wales ('The defendant is acquitted of an offence only because, by reason of evidence of mental disorder...it is found that he acted or may have acted in a state of automatism, or without the fault required for the offence, or believing that an exempting circumstance existed; <u>and</u> it is proved on the balance of probabilities that he was suffering from mental disorder at the time of the act').

Modifications have, however, been largely trivial (e.g. replacing McNaughton's 'know' with 'appreciate') and retained the core product of the McNaughton wording: that the test for being pronounced NGRI is essentially a cognitive one (a 'right-wrong' test). The revolution in *Durham* and ALI in which a volitional prong emerged has now been largely negated by the decision in *Brawner v. United States* (1972), 471 F.2d 969 (in which Judge David Bazelon abandoned his own *Durham* decision), the Insanity Defence Reform Act (1984) urging a return to '*status quo ante* 1843: the year of...McNaughton' (Perlin, 1994: 25), and the Guilty But Mentally Ill (GBMI) verdict (both of which revert to a more restrictive McNaughton style test and shift the burden of proof to the defendant; Spring, 1998). However, the American Psychiatric Association (1982) argues that a control element would be redundant anyway:

> Most psychotic persons who fail a volitional test for insanity will also fail a cognitive-type test when such a test is applied to their behaviour, thus rendering the volitional test superfluous in judging them (APA, 1982; cited in Edwards, 1997: 502).

In any case, it might be argued that changes to the core elements of any insanity test are pointless, as mock juror experiments (e.g. Simon, 1967; Finkel and Slobogin, 1995) show different wordings of the insanity test to have little effect on verdict outcome. This study, whilst urging provision for the consideration of meta-responsibility (and introducing a meta-responsibility insanity test in Part II), does not attempt such futile tampering with the core concepts of the test, instead introducing the peripheral principle of meta-responsibility.

[29] The meta-responsibility theory is also relevant to the much more commonly used mitigatory principle of diminished responsibility for murder, and to unfitness to plead (of which there were 125 findings in the UK from 1992-1996; Mackay and Kearns, 2000). This study, however, discusses the meta-responsibility theory in relation to insanity, particularly because of the status of insanity as a 'flagship' defence (see SUPRA note 1). However, Verdun-Jones (1989) suggests that the consideration of mental illness in determining criminal responsibility is moot with the near demise of the insanity defence in modern English law; it is far more commonly considered by the court in the case of disposal, e.g. hospital order under s.37 MHA 1983 or under a plea of diminished responsibility (murder to manslaughter) under s.2(1) of the Homicide Act 1957, which is satisfied if the defence can establish:

As seen in the McNaughton Rules, the substantive test of insanity does not concern itself with the aetiology of the 'defect of reason' or 'disease of the mind'; all that has to be proved is that one existed at the time of the offence and that it caused cognitive impairment amounting to unawareness of the nature and quality of the act, or the knowledge that the act was wrong. If this is proved, the defendant bears no legal culpability for the act (through supposed absence of *mens rea*) and should be acquitted. What, however, are we to do with the defendant who fulfils the criterion for being found Not Guilty by Reason of Insanity (NGRI), but whose mental disorder was in some way his own fault? Common sense dictates that such a defendant might not be allowed to rely on a mental condition defence to excuse his act, as the condition upon which he relies is of his own making (the mentally disordered offender thus bears some responsibility for his level of criminal responsibility or meta-responsibility).

Should mentally disordered offenders be held culpable for their mental disorder and offences committed 'under its influence' to the degree that the disorder has an autogenous component? Whilst literature attests to mentally disordered offenders being both 'mad' and 'bad' (e.g. Radden, 1985; Schopp, 1991; Moore, 1993; Reznek, 1997; McSherry, 1999) this literature generally focuses on the ability of the offender to *avoid committing the offence* in question, rather than whether the offender was able to *avoid the disorder* of which the offence was supposedly a product. 'Badness', therefore, is considered only as a contributory factor to the crime itself, and not a contributory factor to the *disorder that preceded the crime*. The meta-responsibility theory abandons the traditional mad/bad dichotomy and acknowledges that whilst defendants may be both mad and bad, madness may be an offspring of badness.[30]

In Foucault's (1967) pre-classical age, meta-responsibility would have scarcely raised an eyebrow, as mental disorder was seen as a product of 'badness'

> ...he was suffering from such abnormality of mind (whether arising from a condition of arrested or retarded development of mind or any inherent causes or induced by disease or injury) as substantially impaired his mental responsibility for his acts and omissions in doing or being party to the killing.

In *R v. Byrne* [1960] 2 QB 396 Lord Parker CJ described the abnormality test as 'a state of mind so different from that of ordinary human beings that the reasonable man would term it abnormal'. It is thought to encompass both transient states *and* volitional impairment where the offender could not have resisted an impulse without substantial difficulty.

Verdun-Jones' eulogy on the demise of the consideration of mental disorder in determining criminal responsibility may, however, be premature due to the increased use of the insanity defence in recent years (see *SUPRA* note 1).

[30] In Chapter 1, this notion was examined with regard to 'physical' disorder, where 'bad' behaviour (i.e. that subject to a negative societal value-judgment, e.g. failure to be vaccinated) could lead to disease. Whilst mental disorder differs in terms of quality and quantity of autogeneity/voluntarism, it is clear that subscription to the liberal-scientific conception (i.e. equating 'mental' disorder with 'physical' disorder) cannot automatically exclude a voluntaristic analysis.

and therefore culpable. Modern Anglo-American criminal law, however, is quite clear that it does not wish to attach culpability to mental disorder or any other sort of disorder; in the case of *Robinson v. California* (1962),[31] enquiring whether drug addiction was a crime, the court heard:

> It is unlikely that any State at this moment in history would attempt to make it a criminal offence for a person to be mentally ill, or a leper, or to be afflicted with a venereal disease...Even one day in prison would be cruel and unusual punishment for the 'crime' of having a common cold.

It will be argued in Chapter 4, however, that the consideration of mental disorder in modern Anglo-American criminal law (and in society more generally) is not as far removed as we should like to think from the manner in which Erewhonians treat physical disorder (see Chapter 1). In terms of overt statutory or legal definition, however, it is clear that insanity tests do not impute culpability for the aetiology of the defect of reason or disease of the mind. The only consideration given to the aetiology of an incapacitating condition that might eventually support a defence of insanity arises when the law has to decide whether automatic behaviour supports a defence of insane or non-insane automatism (on the basis of an endogenous or exogenous cause).[32] Mackay (1995: 168) states that 'surely it is

---

[31] *Robinson v. California* (1962), 370 U.S 660.

[32] Such enquiries into the aetiology of automatic behaviour are not strictly enquiries into the *culpability* of the condition, but rather enquire as to which defence the incapacity supports. A blow sustained to the head and somnambulism may both lead the defendant to commit a criminal act, but in spite of the former having an aetiology external to the individual and the latter an internal cause, both are presumed by the law to be fault exclusionary (i.e. are not induced by the individual so afflicted). Whilst findings of both insane and non-insane automatism lead to an acquittal, the latter is not likely to lead to post-trial committal due to its presumed transient cause, whereas the former (if it arises as a result of a disease of the mind) may be deemed supportive of a defence of insanity with appropriate disposal. Thus in the cases of *Quick* [1973] Q.B. 910 (involving a hypoglycaemic diabetic coma caused by failure to ingest food after taking insulin), *Hennessey* [1989] 2 All ER 9 (involving a hyperglycaemic diabetic coma due to failure to ingest insulin), and *Sullivan* [1984] AC 156 (involving an epileptic seizure), the defendants preferred to plead guilty after the trial judges rejected their pleas of automatism and stated the only defence available to them would be one of insanity (see INFRA note 55 discussing why courts are likely to prefer an insanity plea to one of automatism). Defence fears as to the consequences of being forced to plead insanity may be allayed by the provisions in the Criminal Procedure (Insanity and Unfitness to Plead) Act 1991 that does not mandate automatic post-trial detention for persons successful with an insanity defence (apart from those whose crime is murder; see INFRA note 13, Ch. 4). However, it is clear that the *locus*, but not necessarily the *culpability* of the incapacity is taken into account during such enquiry.

The situation is made more complex by the Court of Appeal's quashing of the conviction in the case of *Quick* – Lawton LJ deemed that the defendant's condition had been due to an external cause (insulin injection) and the defence of automatism should have been left to the jury. This suggests that the diabetic whose coma is due to excessive insulin

time...to reconsider the blanket exclusion of fault once the insanity defence is raised'.[33]

Insanity is unique amongst incapacitating conditions in this respect. In the other two incapacitating conditions commonly considered by the criminal law – intoxication and automatism – consideration is given to the defendant's responsibility for causing or contributing to the incapacity. Not all incapacitating conditions are thus smothered under the blanket exclusion of fault. The characteristic peculiar to these three species of incapacity is their likelihood of impacting upon others. It might be argued that all voluntaristic incapacities impact upon others to a certain degree, e.g. the draining of limited healthcare resources in the case of lung cancer caused by smoking (or even the distress of the smoker's family at potential and actual bereavement). Lung cancer, however, does not give occasion to commit criminal acts, as may intoxication, automatism, and insanity. Matthews (1999) characterizes mental disorders as differing fundamentally from physical illness in this respect: 'someone who is physically ill suffers him- or herself, and any harm caused to others (e.g. through infection) is contingent' (p. 54). This is not true of intoxication and automatism, which, like insanity, may give rise to criminal acts, but which differ from insanity in that the criminal law considers the autogeneity and voluntarism of the conditions.

2.2 Intoxication

Intoxication, for the purposes of the criminal law, is divided into that which is involuntary and that which is voluntary. In the terms of the present study, involuntary intoxication, due to its lack of autogeneity (i.e. lying outside of the collection of actions which are 'one's own') does not give rise to meta-responsibility. This is not true of voluntary intoxication.

---

secreted by the pancreas is insane, whereas the diabetic whose coma arises due to excessive insulin by injection is not. The blanket exclusion of fault remains, however, as the court in *Bailey* [1983] 1 WLR 760 deemed it unacceptable to impute prior fault to diabetics who fail to regulate their blood sugar (be it due to either an internal or an external cause). Such cases further demonstrate that the law *may* enquire into the aetiology of an incapacity that lies within the realm of the liberal-scientific model, even in the absence of proper ascription of culpability. It is clear that mental disorder caused/exacerbated by medication non-compliance as a source of meta-responsibility (see Chapter 3) would be deemed *internal* in origin and therefore still relevant to the insanity defence.

[33] The blanket exclusion of fault does not apply to *all* legal enquiries into responsibility for psychiatric illness. It is possible, for example, for a patient being treated for depression to be held responsible for his own problems and subsequent death by suicide where a wrongful death suit is brought against a psychiatrist, through contributory negligence (e.g. *Hobart v. Shin* (1998), Ill. Sup. Ct., WL 884567). The court's task in such cases is to find the proportion to which the patient contributed to his death through negligence (e.g. from medication non-compliance) *versus* the proportion of that contribution which could rightly be attributed to the physician.

Involuntary intoxication parallels traditional notions of insanity in that the incapacitating condition is outside the individual's sphere of control. Evidence of involuntary intoxication may be used to support a denial of *mens rea* in offences of specific intent (e.g. murder) or basic intent (e.g. manslaughter, assault).[34] However, unless the effect of the intoxicant was to negate *mens rea*, involuntary intoxication cannot provide a defence, e.g. *Davies* [1983].[35] Where intoxication is involuntary (e.g. where a drink has been 'spiked' or the defendant has been 'slipped a Mickey Finn') but the defendant is proved to have formed the specific *mens rea* for the offence, mitigation of sentence is the likely result, e.g. *Kingston* (1994).[36] Involuntary intoxication may also cover situations where a defendant has taken a prescribed drug non-recklessly, and could not have foreseen the resultant incapacity.[37] The principle has also been extended to cases involving 'pathological intoxication'.[38]

---

[34] The complex principle of distinguishing between crimes of specific and basic intent was introduced by Lord Birkenhead in *DPP v. Beard* [1920] AC 479 in which he stated that:

> Where a specific intent is an essential element of the offence, evidence of a state of drunkenness rendering the accused incapable of forming such an intent should be taken into consideration in order to determine whether he had in fact formed the intent necessary to constitute the particular crime.

The principle has now been given a meaning which Lord Birkenhead probably never intended: offences of specific intent are those to which intoxication may negate *mens rea*, whereas intoxication is irrelevant to those of basic intent. It is thought that crimes of specific intent require proof of a purposive element, and may not therefore be committed recklessly. Offences of specific intent include murder, burglary, robbery, wounding or causing grievous bodily harm with intent. Crimes of basic intent include rape, manslaughter, criminal damage, malicious wounding or inflicting grievous bodily harm, and offences based on assault.

[35] *Davies* [1983] Crim. LR 741.

[36] *Kingston* (1994), 99 Cr. App. R. 286.

[37] *See R v. Hardie* [1984] 3 All ER 848 where it was found that:

> There was no evidence that it was known to the appellant or even generally known that the taking of valium in the quantity taken would be liable to render a person aggressive or incapable of appreciating risks to others or have other side effects such that its self administration would itself have an element of recklessness.

[38] The ALI Model Penal Code §2.08 (5)(c) makes provision for where an actor's intoxication is 'pathological' (Tiffany and Tiffany, 1990) where it is 'grossly excessive in degree, given the amount of intoxicant, to which the actor does not know he is susceptible'. Such a principle may be applied to mental disorder where, for example, the defendant could not have appreciated that his disorder might have the consequences that it did (see Chapter 3).

Voluntary intoxication is not so likely to elicit the law's sympathy. Voluntary intoxication may only support a denial of *mens rea* in offences of specific intent, but if *mens rea* can be proved it matters not that the defendant would not have committed the offence when sober. In such a case, the defendant has been *reckless*[39] in the act of becoming intoxicated; he has effectively *created the conditions of his own defence*.[40] For example, in *DPP v. Majewski* (1977)[41] (in which the defendant struck a police officer under the influence of barbiturates, amphetamines and alcohol), Lord Elwyn Jones described the principle of self-causation:

---

[39] The term recklessness has been as great a source of legal speculation as the specific/basic intent distinction. For some offences such as murder, intention must be proved to establish criminal liability. For most offences, however, intention *or* recklessness constitutes sufficient *mens rea*. Recklessness may be roughly defined as taking an unjustifiable risk, the consequences of which the defendant as a reasonable man foresaw or should have foreseen. In *Cunningham* [1957] 2 QB 396 a subjective meaning was given to recklessness: the accused would only be reckless where he had recognized the possibility of the prohibited consequence occurring. This type of recklessness is often referred to as 'Cunningham Recklessness'. However, in *Caldwell* [1982] AC 341, Lord Diplock redefined recklessness in objective terms: the test of 'Caldwell Recklessness' thus finds the defendant reckless if he *ought* to have foreseen the consequences of his act/omission; there is no requirement that he *did* foresee any prohibited consequences. See generally Mackay (1995), for a discussion of the type of recklessness involved in self-induced incapacity.

In *Elliot v. C (a minor)* [1983] WLR 939, mental illness was deemed irrelevant to the application of *Caldwell* (objective) recklessness. Such a (paradoxical) judgment of expecting the mentally disordered to behave and think like a reasonable man is inconsistent with the judgments in *Bowen* [1996] Crim. LR 577 (mental disorder is relevant to the second [objective] limb of the test in duress) and *Ahluwalia* [1992] 4 All ER 889 (mental disorder is relevant to the second [objective] limb in provocation). It seems the mentally disordered may be held to the standard of the reasonable man (or not) in the absence of any guiding principle.

[40] See Ashworth (1975: 102) 'an accused should not be permitted to rely on an incapacitating condition which arose through his own fault'; Robinson (1985: 33) 'An actor may be culpable as to causing the ultimate offense when he causes the disability…or when he fails to terminate or at least to make allowance for a pre-existing disability'. A number of other defences is subject to the consideration of culpability as to the defence-causing conditions, e.g. 'heat of passion' defences. For passion to provide any level of excuse or mitigation, 'the anger…must itself be formed under circumstances in which the actor cannot be fairly blamed for his anger' (Dressler, 1982; cited in Mitchell, 1986: 290). Likewise, provocation, duress, and self-defence: a person should not be able to rely on the defence of duress if forced to commit criminal acts at gunpoint by a terrorist organisation, if he is a high-ranking member of that organisation who sanctioned the policy of kidnapping persons and forcing them to commit criminal acts at gunpoint; he would have effectively created the conditions of his own defence.

[41] *DPP v. Majewski* [1977] AC 443.

> If a man of his own volition takes a substance which causes him to cast off the restraints of reason and conscience, no wrong is done to him by holding him answerable criminally for any injury he may do while in that condition. His course of conduct in reducing himself by drugs and drink to that condition in my view supplies the evidence of *mens rea*, of guilty mind certainly sufficient for crimes of basic intent. It is a reckless course of conduct and recklessness is enough to constitute the necessary *mens rea* in assault cases.

This judgment has been interpreted by Lord Diplock in *R v. Caldwell* (1981)[42] that self-induced intoxication is not a defence to any crime in which recklessness is enough to constitute the requisite *mens rea*.

Where the defendant has made a mistake whilst intoxicated this will only avail him where he pleads justification[43] (e.g. self-defence); where he pleads an excusatory defence (e.g. duress or provocation) he is expected to exercise the self-control and judgment of a reasonable man. However, the self-causation inherent in such offences does not appear to hold true for an abnormality of mind or insanity *caused by* intoxication; in *Davis* (1881),[44] Stephen J stated that:

> …drunkenness is one thing and diseases to which drunkenness leads are different things; and if a man by drunkenness brings on a state of disease which causes such a degree of madness, even for a time, which would have relieved him from responsibility if it had been caused in any other way, then he would not be criminally responsible.

The judgment in *Davis* has particular relevance to meta-responsibility. It seems the law is willing to recognize the voluntarism of a condition where that condition falls short of an illness (e.g. intoxication), but when the condition crosses the line into the realm of the liberal-scientific model and becomes an illness (e.g. mental disorder *caused by* intoxication), it becomes subject to the blanket exclusion of fault. This strengthens our analysis that meta-responsibility is tied inextricably to the medical status of an incapacity. Even diabetes and epilepsy cases (e.g. *Hennessey*, *Quick*, and *Sullivan)*,[45] in which the incapacity will still likely be present during and after trial, have been subject to a blanket exclusion of fault as confirmed in the case of *Bailey*.[46] In such cases, the aetiology of the condition producing the automatic behaviour has been examined (and thus its

---

[42] *R v. Caldwell* [1981] 1 All ER 961.

[43] A defendant pleading a justificatory defence accepts responsibility for the act in question but purports that no wrong was done, e.g. injuring an attacker. Excusatory defences do *not* purport that no wrong was done, but instead abdicate (partially or fully) culpability for this wrong (Austin, 1970; Katz, 1987) e.g. administering a fatal dose of medicine due to it being incorrectly labelled. For a discussion of psychiatric explanations as excuses, see Walker (1985) or Buchanan (2000).

[44] *Davis* (1881), 14 Cox CC 563.

[45] See *SUPRA* note 32.

[46] See *SUPRA* note 32.

status as a medical incapacity rather than a mere transient condition), but even where the court has recognized the self-induced nature of the automatism, ascription of prior fault has not followed (as in the case of *Davis*).[47]

The origins of the fault-exclusionary position may be found in the writings of Hale.[48] Hale, like the decision in *Davis*, was not concerned with meta-responsibility. Hale's *dementia affectata* ('induced witlessness') equates to modern English law's notion of insanity caused by intoxication. Walker (1968) underlines the exclusion of fault inherent in Hale's 'induced witlessness':

> If heavy drinking had caused 'an habitual or fixed phrenzy' he should be treated by the law as if it were involuntarily contracted – a principle that was to save several Victorian alcoholics from the gallows (p. 39).

The fault-exclusionary position of Hale (and expressed in *Davis*) conflicts with the doctrine of prior fault of *Majewski*: that a person should not be allowed to rely on an exculpatory condition where he has deliberately or negligently brought about that condition (Ashworth, 1975; Robinson, 1985). The effective difference between the two conditions is that one receives a liberal-scientific classification (e.g. Korsakoff's psychosis from thiamine deficiency caused by alcoholism); the other does not (intoxication as a result of drinking alcohol). Both, however, involve prior fault. The long-term psychoactive substance user or alcoholic (with a potentially greater level of prior fault) may thus paradoxically find himself eligible for excuse or mitigation if he suffers from a secondary mental disorder as a result of his substance use or alcoholism, whereas the 'short-term' user (i.e. the intoxicated) will not. As Kermani and Castaneda (1996: 1) state, '[the U.S.] legal system inclines toward the view that the use of alcohol or other substances involves an element of choice and therefore would not amount to a legal insanity defence if the substance abuser commits a crime whilst intoxicated'. The factor that appears to be important to the legal system is whether the substance has caused an 'illness' or 'disease'.[49] Intoxication does not qualify as a disease of the mind and thus is not supportive of an insanity test; for that, repeated use has to lead to illness.

As in the analysis presented in the present study, Weinstock (1999) compares the 'moral capacities' of intoxicated individuals versus those who become mentally disordered through medication non-compliance, and concludes that there is no major qualitative or quantitative difference in the capacities of the two classes: both know the potential consequences of ingesting or failing to ingest the particular substance (alcohol or medication); the only difference is that one involves an action and one an omission (which are equivalent in terms of

---

[47] See *SUPRA* note 32.

[48] See *SUPRA* section 2.1.

[49] Although see *SUPRA* note 32 which discusses the law's consideration of the aetiology (but not culpability) of conditions falling within a 'disease framework' that are induced by ingestion or failure to ingest substances such as food or insulin.

recklessness). In the language of the present study, both would have a similar level of meta-responsibility, which throws suspicion on the fault exclusionary position of insanity. Of course, it may be argued against Weinstock that neither the person who ingests alcohol nor the person who fails to ingest medication realize the potential consequences of their acts or omissions; however, the law of insanity and the law of intoxication will still be disparate, as intoxication then inappropriately considers voluntarism (and therefore wrongly imputes meta-responsibility) whereas insanity (quite rightly) does not. There is an obvious discrepancy between the two areas of criminal law, whether we believe insight into possible consequences is a necessary condition for culpability or not.

Whatever the inconsistencies between legal provision for considering voluntarism in insanity and intoxication, they are also apparent between insanity and automatism.

2.3 Automatism

In *Bratty v. A-G for Northern Ireland* (1963)[50] (involving the defendant's strangulation of a girl whilst apparently in a psychomotor epileptic seizure), Lord Denning defined automatism as:

> …an act which is done by the muscles without any control of the mind, such as a spasm, a reflex action or a convulsion; or an act done by a person who is not conscious of what he is doing, such as an act done whilst suffering from concussion or sleep walking.

Automatism becomes relevant to meta-responsibility where it is self-induced (through something that the accused has done or failed to do). However, case law in the area of automatism is more piecemeal than that in the area of intoxication; sometimes the voluntarism of a condition negates culpability; sometimes it does not. The most common example of voluntarism in automatism is probably that of automatic acts committed after ingestion of alcohol or prohibited drugs; as with intoxication such a defence will not succeed where the offence is one of basic intent. In *Bailey* (1983),[51] Griffiths LJ ruled that self-induced automatism through hypoglycaemic coma (induced after the diabetic defendant failed to take food after an insulin injection) provided a defence to offences of basic intent, where the diabetic *did not appreciate* the risk of becoming aggressive or uncontrollable after such an omission.[52] Other diabetics have had more difficulty with pleading

---

[50] *Bratty v. A-G for Nothern Ireland* [1963] AC 386.

[51] See *SUPRA* note 32.

[52] The court in *Bailey* stated that diabetics should not necessarily be presumed to appreciate such a risk:

automatism: in *Quick* (1973)[53] and *Hennessey* (1989),[54] both defendants changed their pleas to guilty rather than be forced to plead insanity after their diabetic comas were deemed to constitute a disease of the mind.[55] However, in *Hennessey*, the defendant failed to regulate his blood sugar due to an episode of stress, anxiety and depression. The role of emotion and mental disorder in interfering with both foresight and insight is therefore of utmost importance to the self-causation of mental disorder. The relevance of insight into mental disorder will be discussed further in Chapter 3 (*Hennessey* is perhaps an example of disorder-mediated meta-responsibility; also see Chapter 3).

On the other hand, self-causation is implicitly referred to in *Kay v. Butterworth* (1945)[56] and used to impute culpability, where the defendant was convicted of driving without due care and attention after driving into a group of soldiers while asleep at the wheel. Humphreys J ruled that it was of no importance that he was not conscious of his actions when the offence was committed, as *he should have ceased driving when he realized he was becoming drowsy*. It could of course be argued that the driver's drowsiness affected his insight into being drowsy in the first instance; that drowsiness affects processes of attention and diligence, and thus affects one's very ability to realize that one is becoming drowsy. Such a situation parallels psychiatric conceptions of mental disorder in which disorders themselves (particularly psychotic disorders) are often seen as affecting insight into disorder, thus preventing imputation of liability to the defendant/patient for management of the disorder, and hence forbidding attribution of culpability for acts arising from that disorder. *Kay v. Butterworth* again underlines the considerable dissonance between the legal positions on insanity and other incapacities of legal interest.

> It is common knowledge that those who take alcohol to excess or certain sorts of drugs may become aggressive or do dangerous or unpredictable things...But the same cannot be said, without more, of a man who fails to take food after an insulin injection. If he does appreciate that such a failure may lead to aggressive, unpredictable and uncontrolled conduct and he nevertheless deliberately runs the risk or otherwise regards it, this will amount to recklessness. But we certainly do not think that it is common knowledge, even among diabetics, that such is a consequence of a failure to take food.

This principle seems to encompass *Cunningham* rather than *Caldwell* recklessness (Mackay, 1995; see *SUPRA* note 39).

[53] See *SUPRA* note 32.

[54] See *SUPRA* note 32.

[55] Where the insanity defence is forcibly imposed this may be a means of covert punishment (see Chapter 4); an insanity acquittal is likely to result in a lengthy period of hospitalization unlike automatism defences which are associated with immediate release (cases such as *Jones v. United States* (1983), 463 U.S. 354 give constitutional backing to lengthy post-trial committal for insanity acquittees, sanctioning detention for a period potentially longer than the maximum sentence had the defendant been found guilty).

[56] *Kay v. Butterworth* (1945), 173 LT 191.

A converse (fault-exclusionary) decision emerged in the Kentucky case of *Fain v. Commonwealth* (1879),[57] in which a defendant offered an involuntary act defence claiming he suffered from a sleep disorder causing violent acts on waking:

> If the prisoner is and has been afflicted in the manner claimed, and knew, as he no doubt did, his propensity to do acts of violence when aroused from sleep, he was guilty of a grave breach of social duty in going to sleep in the public room of a hotel with a deadly weapon on his person, and merits, for that reckless disregard of the safety of others, some degree of punishment, but we know of no law under which he can be punished…the mere fact that he had the weapon on his person and went to sleep with it there did no injury to any one, he cannot be punished for that.

This unusual position acknowledges the legality of the defence-causing condition (sleeping with a deadly weapon), and because of this does not then impute culpability for the offence through denying an automatism defence (in spite of the defendant's recklessness). Whilst the principle of somnambulism negating criminal responsibility has a respectable history ('Where the defendant has attacked another during sleep, there is generally no doubt that he is not responsible in law...'; Glanville Williams, cited in *Salzman v. United States* (1968), 405 F.2d 358), there is an equally respectable history of imputing prior fault to the defendant's conduct if it is deemed reckless (as in the case of *Kay v. Butterworth*). The next section shows how *Fain* bears striking similarity to the position on insanity; being insane is, like going to sleep with a deadly weapon, not itself illegal. This legality is then conflated with exclusion of fault; a conflation dissonant with commonsense notions of justice and piecemeal legal provision for the other incapacities described in this chapter.

2.4 The Blanket Exclusion of Fault in Insanity

This chapter has examined the legally incapacitating conditions of insanity, intoxication and automatism, and shown that self-causation of the incapacity is considered to a greater or lesser degree in the latter two conditions, but not the former. The insanity test used in English law makes no provision for the consideration of self-causation. And yet if the law is indeed 'the trailing edge of public morality' (Heginbotham and Elson, 1999: 59), then commonsense notions of justice dictate that the three incapacitating conditions be brought into line. As Robinson (1985) points out:

---

[57] *Fain v. Commonwealth* (1879), 78 Ky. 183.

...every jurisdiction considers an actor's causing his own defence for some defences, and every jurisdiction thus acknowledges that such causing-one's-defence can be relevant to the actor's liability. If it is relevant when an actor causes one defence, why is it not equally relevant when he causes another? (p. 24).

Such concepts were not lost upon legal commentators of the nineteenth century, who showed greater regard for the concept of meta-responsibility. As Fitzjames Stephen wrote in his *History of the Criminal Law*, in attempting to codify an irresistible impulse test of insanity:

> If it is not, it ought to be the Law of England that no act is a crime if the person who does it is at the time...prevented either by defective mental power or by any disease affecting his mind from controlling his own conduct, *unless the absence of the power of control has been produced by his own default* (Stephen, 1883; cited in Finkel, 1988: 31).[58]

Stephen's maxim is essentially a meta-responsibility insanity test (a meta-responsibility test is experimentally tested in Part II of this book), which makes provision for the consideration of voluntarism/autonomy of the condition used as a defence. Combined with a consideration of a disorder's severity (which would seem to be an essential component of any insanity test), Stephen's maxim would be represented graphically by Figure 2.1.

If the heuristic represented in Figure 2.1 is actually used by judge and jury in the courtroom, then it is certainly not considered in the substantive insanity test. The McNaughton Rules make provision for considering the x-axis of Figure 2.1 only: level of autonomy in mental disorder (the y-axis) is irrelevant to the determination of criminal responsibility. Why has this anomalous state of affairs between insanity and other incapacitating conditions arisen?

[58] Here, Stephen articulates the notion of 'Capacity development responsibility' (CDR) over one hundred years before Alicke and Davis (1990); see Chapter 5. Robinson (1980), from his analysis of pre-McNaughton insanity case law finds that 'disease is and always has been a permissible ground of forgiveness so long as it is not wilfully imposed by the actor on himself'.

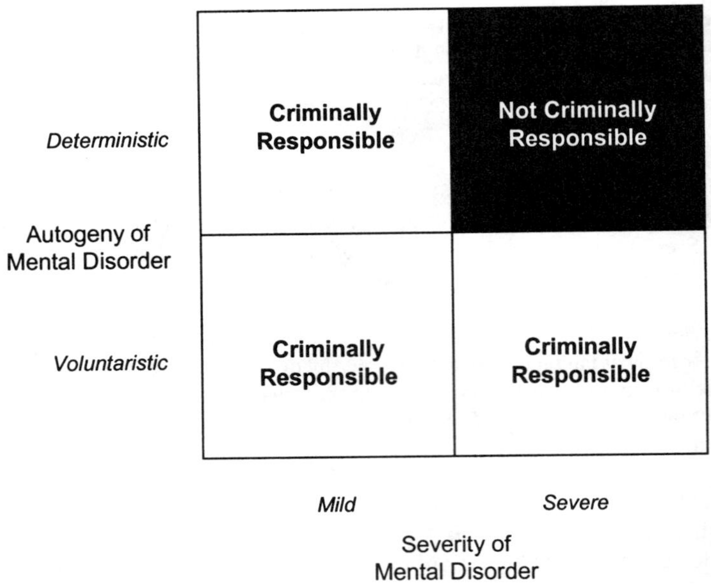

Figure 2.1 The relationship between autogeny (self-causation), severity of mental disorder, and criminal responsibility (adapted from Ogloff, 1996)[59]

2.5 The Law's Inability to Consider Meta-responsibility in Insanity: Autopoiesis or Obstinacy?

Two analyses of the law's ignorance of meta-responsibility in insanity may be offered: active and passive ignorance. Active ignorance would involve the law's deliberate refusal to consider meta-responsibility in insanity. Passive ignorance would merely proffer the law to have no insight into its anomalous position. An autopoietic model of the relationship between psychiatry and law might provide a clue to the source of such passive ignorance. Teubner (1993), for example, argues

---

[59] Ogloff's (1996) paper used Freewill → Determinism as the *y* axis and was intended to demonstrate that psychopathy does not obey the legal rule that the more severe the disorder, the less likely it is that the individual will be found criminally responsible. Such a *y* axis is concerned with the *effects* of illness upon criminal behaviour, rather than the *cause* of the illness itself (with which we are concerned here). In contrast, the legal concept of insanity is an 'either/or' phenomenon; whilst there may be shades of grey in clinical severity of mental disorder, the law's position is black or white: the quantity or quality of the disease of the mind and consequent defect of reason will EITHER reach a threshold to render a special verdict OR the defendant will be found criminally responsible.

that the law is inherently self-referential and thus *cannot* (rather than *does not*) consider scientific reality. Inconsistency between psychiatry and law (and moreover within different legal fields such as intoxication and insanity law, particularly the law's ignorance of meta-responsibility in the latter) would simply be part and parcel of this autopoiesis.

It does not seem that passive ignorance on the part of the law can be substantiated. Firstly, legal processes *do* take into account much from mental health sciences; Eastman and Peay (1999: 21), for example, note the 'dominance of tribunals [Mental Health Review Tribunals] by the clinical model'. Secondly, the law's anomalous position is consonant, rather than dissonant, to established (yet, this study argues, equally anomalous) scientific opinion on mental disorder, which itself excludes voluntaristic analyses through locating mental disorder within the liberal-scientific model (see Chapter 1).[60]

Therefore, the notion that scientific disciplines fail to influence a self-referential legal system (i.e. autopoiesis) does not necessarily substantiate the law's passive ignorance in the case of meta-responsibility. The law does not shy away from psychiatric opinion in a manner that the autopoietic model predicts; indeed, the Mental Health Act's reluctance to offer strict definitions of the mental disorders falling under its remit (see Chapter 1) suggests it is quite comfortable with deferring such matters to psychiatric opinion ('definitional power under the Act rests on clinical judgment'; Eastman and Peay, 1999: 4). Where, however, there are likely to be considerable public policy or financial implications of deferring to psychiatric opinion (as in incapacity to consent to informal admission to hospital in the case of *L v. Bournewood* [1998][61] entailing formal admission of all incapacious patients), the law is likely to intervene (hence the Court of Appeals' reversal of the *Bournewood* finding).

In a similar vein, whilst no consideration of a person's role in the genesis or exacerbation of disorder is required by the insanity defence, mental health law does not shy away from detaining those likely to develop or exacerbate mental disorder through their own actions. Blom-Cooper, Hally and Murphy (1995) argue that it is unnecessary to wait for a psychotic condition to reoccur for a patient to fall under a detention order if it could be demonstrated that the patient had previously become psychotic upon cessation of medication (and the patient was again refusing medication). This suggests that active symptomatology is not required for a patient

---

[60] See generally Slodov (1989) and Moore (1985). Slodov (1989: 279) underlines the relationship between the McNaughton Rules and the medical model (particularly Parson's Postulate One): 'By providing an insanity defense where a mental disease or defect renders the actor incapable of exercising reasoned choice or subverts volition such that conduct no longer reflects individual will, we are acknowledging that the presence of certain mental diseases can render one a mere agent of his illness'.

[61] *L v. Bournewood Community NHS Trust, ex parte L (Secretary of State and Others Intervening)* [1998] 3 All ER 289 (HL).

to fall under the auspices of the MHA.[62] Thus it is recognized by mental health law, but not by the criminal law, that a patient's actions can have the effect of generating or exacerbating mental disorder.

However, consonance between the psychiatric and legal positions of the fault-exclusionary nature of mental disorder is certainly not enough to prove that the law has actively ignored its own anomaly. More persuasive evidence is provided where the law has *deliberately* chosen to ignore a voluntaristic analysis of insanity, for example in the case of *Davis*.[63] Where it is recognized that insanity may be brought about by the defendant's own actions, he will be 'relieved...from responsibility [as] if it had been caused in any other way'.[64] American appellate cases such as *State v. Maik* (1972)[65] confirm such a principle: where insanity is at issue, the court will not consider the aetiology of the disease of the mind. Whilst statutory provision is available to consider such causation in a very few American jurisdictions,[66] the only causal process considered is that of voluntary intoxication bringing about insanity in appellate cases.[67] Even if the legal machinery is available, then it is not being utilized as it might be.

Very occasionally, the issue of culpable mental disorder has received explicit mention in the courtroom (Slodov, 1989), being compared on at least one occasion to the law on intoxication. The defendant in *State v. McLeary* (1979)[68] had been taking medication for schizophrenia for eleven years, but became non-compliant three or four days before wresting a handgun from a park ranger. The trial court convicted the defendant, suggesting the theory of meta-responsibility in its reasoning:

> ...there is a distinction between insanity and insanity that can be controlled. This may simply be the reverse of the law that applies where one induces his own 'insanity', by becoming intoxicated and thereby engaging in wrongful behaviour.

---

[62] This interpretation is confirmed in *R v. MHRT for South Thames Region, ex parte Smith* (1998), (unreported QBD).

[63] *Davis*; see *SUPRA* note 44.

[64] *IBID.*

[65] *State v. Maik* (1972, 60 N.J. 203). This case affirms the reluctance of the courts to investigate the aetiology of the excusing condition: '[It is] unlikely that the enquiry would be useful, for when...the acute psychosis could equally be triggered by some other stress, known or unknown, which the defendant could not handle, a medical opinion as to what did in fact precipitate the psychosis is not apt to rise above a speculation among mere possibilities' (Slodov, 1989).

[66] See e.g. P.R. Laws Ann. Tit. 33, § 3154 (1983) ('Transitory mental unsoundness caused purposefully does not excuse criminal liability'); Wash. Rev. Code Ann.§ 10.77.010(7) (Supp. 1984-1985) ('No condition of mind proximately induced by the voluntary act of a person charged with a crime shall constitute "insanity"').

[67] See e.g. *United States v. Henderson* (1982), 680 F.2d 659; *United States v. Burnim* (1978) 576 F.2d 236 (insanity caused by voluntary intoxication is no defence).

[68] *State v. McLeary*, No. CR49471 (C.P. Cuyahoga City, Ohio Nov. 19, 1979), reversed No. CR42116 (Ohio Ct. App. 8th Dist. Nov 20 1980).

> Here this defendant had the training, the experience, the opportunity and the medication with which to control his behaviour...he chose not to do that and, thereby, placed himself in the position where he was liable to engage in anti-social and, indeed, criminal behaviour.

The appellate court, however, reversed the decision because the *defendant had proved his insanity by a preponderance of evidence.*

In the case of *R v. Thomas* (1996),[69] the judge put the issue of insanity to the jury where the defendant was charged with robbery and burglary whilst suffering from hypomania aggravated by alcohol. It seems, therefore, that the principle of meta-responsibility cannot be considered without explicit legislative reform in the insanity defence. Cases such as *Thomas* and *McLeary* appear to substantiate the law as actively complicit in bringing about its anomalous position, due to the inextricable link between legal insanity and the liberal-scientific model of mental disorder examined in Chapter 1. Just as psychiatry is reluctant to consider the autogeneity of the conditions under its remit, so is the law when such conditions come to its attention through the commission of criminal acts. It seems that the blanket exclusion of fault 'trickles down' from psychiatric opinion to the legal opinion. To argue properly for the consideration of meta-responsibility in a legal context, then, it is first necessary to examine voluntarism in mental disorder in a *psychiatric* context. This will be done in Chapter 3.

2.6 Concluding Overview

It appears that the law is willing to take into account potential or actual genesis/exacerbation of an incapacitating condition by the self where intoxication and automatism are concerned (and in situations such as contributory negligence and involuntary detention on psychiatric grounds), but unwilling to do so in the offer of an insanity defence. This position is contradictory to commonsense notions of justice and to internal consistency within criminal law. The law is clearly not blind to notions of genesis or exacerbation of mental disorder, but does not in any case consider the construct of meta-responsibility in the substantive insanity test. This ignorance of meta-responsibility cannot be explained by simple recourse to an autopoietic relationship between psychiatry and law, due to the clear influence of the former on the latter (e.g. in MHRTs). A *political* reason why the law fails to consider meta-responsibility is discussed in Chapter 4: that the law achieves its ends concerning those pleading insanity *without* overt recourse to

---

[69] See *SUPRA* note 17. The Court of Appeal overturned the conviction on the grounds that the judge should not have put the issue of insanity to the jury. This was, however, because the defence argued that the defendant was so drunk that she could not have formed the specific intent necessary (and not because of culpably induced defence conditions); the judge had therefore confused the defences of *mens rea* and insanity.

meta-responsibility, through the process of covert punishment of insanity acquittees.

Whether the reader thinks the law's inability to consider meta-responsibility in insanity is a grave inadequacy or not will depend upon whether that reader believes that mental disorder can *actually* be generated or exacerbated by the self. Chapter 3 is therefore devoted to a voluntaristic analysis of mental disorder and the delineation of two types of meta-responsibility: *consensual* meta-responsibility (under which the patient *consents* to the generation or exacerbation of mental disorder through the pursuit of sensual appetites); and *purposive* meta-responsibility (under which the patient's behaviour and cognition are *purposefully* directed to the goal of generation or exacerbation of mental disorder).

Chapter 3

Consensual and Purposive Meta-responsibility

It was very much like being mad, only it was worse because one was aware of it.

Joseph Conrad, The Secret Sharer

That wild madness that's only calm to comprehend itself.

Herman Melville, Moby Dick

The meta-responsibility theory presented in this chapter is based upon two possible variants of autogeny in mental disorder, which may be loosely delineated as those acts and omissions relating to the genesis or exacerbation of mental disorder that are *consensual*, and those that are *purposive*. The former type of act or omission (consensual) is derived broadly from the liberal-scientific model discussed in Chapter 1, and the latter (purposive) from social constructivist (SC) and existential phenomenological (EP) models of mental disorder. The SC and EP models are often cast as antithetic to the liberal-scientific model, but this chapter emphasizes their complementary characteristics.

The acts or omissions leading to consensual meta-responsibility are reasonably intuitive and will be recognized by most practitioners involved in the care of psychiatric patients. However, the notion of purposive meta-responsibility (due to its reliance on components of the SC and EP models) will be considerably more alien to those subscribing to the liberal-scientific conception of mental disorder. This study wishes to extract from these models core issues relating to the nature of voluntarism, without subscribing to the peripheral socio-political and radical psychiatric elements that were largely responsible for their demise. It is worth reiterating that the use of such models is not to denigrate or exclude liberal-scientific conceptions of mental disorder,[1] but instead to explore potential generation or exacerbation of mental disorder by the self. The use of these models to inform the present investigation into autonomy, autogeny, and the self-causation

[1] As stated, to criticize medical conceptions of mental disorder is beyond the aims and scope of this study. For contemporary critiques of the medical model of mental disorder, see Barney (1994), Breggin (1991), Brown (1990), Kovel (1988) and Sarbin (1991).

of mental disorder does not require subscription to anti-psychiatric frameworks of thought.

Indeed, the effect of following the EP and SC models to their logical conclusion (total responsibility, even for the mentally disordered) is to argue for the abolition of the insanity defence (e.g. Szasz, 1997).[2] It is a consequence of not 'believing' in mental disorder – claiming that it is a social construction and that an objective phenomenon of mental disorder cannot be epistemologically supported – that one cannot also believe mental disorder provides an excuse for actions. Total ascription to the social constructivist model therefore defeats any notion of responsibility for criminal responsibility, as under an extreme implementation of the model there is no such thing as criminal responsibility in the first instance. Szasz (personal communication) has thus asked whether the notion of meta-responsibility is illogical, as one cannot be responsible for a disorder *that does not exist!* This is, however, to ignore the tenets and purposes of the present analysis which does not wish a) to abandon the liberal-scientific conception of mental disorder (but instead to embellish its applicability to criminal responsibility through the addition of the conception of autogenous mental disorder); or b) to examine whether mentally disordered offenders can do otherwise than they do, in terms of their criminal acts. The object of the present study is instead to assess the effect on criminal responsibility of voluntaristic conceptions of *mental disorder* (not voluntaristic conceptions of *criminal acts*). To do this does not require us to follow the SC or EP models to their logical conclusion, or even require any level of ascription to mental disorder as a social construction.

3.1 Consensual Meta-responsibility

In consensual meta-responsibility, it is not the goal of the person to generate or exacerbate mental disorder, but through the pursuit of sensual appetites (e.g. a wish to be free of psychiatric medication and its side-effects or a wish to drink excessive alcohol/use narcotic substances) the patient *consents* to the genesis or exacerbation of mental disorder. The archetypal example is that of medication non-compliance due to medication side-effects (in which the sensual experience pursued might be the experience of not having a dry mouth, nausea, disruption of libidinal function, etc.).

The notion of consenting to certain (sometimes undesirable) events in the pursuit of sensual appetites is illustrated by the following example. In the pursuit

---

[2] Szasz (1997) contends that the *mens rea* of the mentally disordered offender is as intact as that of the 'normal' offender – if not more so; exculpation under an insanity defence that places an emphasis on *mens rea* cannot therefore be supported. Even in the absence of conscious intention or *mens rea*, acts may still be culpable; see Cohen (1996) who uses Freudian theory to assert that the criminal law should take account of 'the possibility that seemingly unintentional acts, are, in fact, generated by the deliberations unconscious of the mind' (p. 511).

of satisfying the sensual appetite of hunger, I may decide to cook a meal and exhibit behaviour designed to satisfy that sensual appetite (i.e. cook). Cooking the meal generates dirty dishes and washing-up, although that is certainly not the primary purpose of the exercise. I do not *want* to generate washing-up, but *consent* to doing so rather than give up my purposes and the means I have chosen to satisfy my sensual appetite. Consent does not imply that the 'side-effect' (washing-up or mental disorder) is *consciously* chosen (or indeed enters consciousness at all; Kenny, 1978). It is a consequence of cooking that washing-up will be generated, and none of us would be surprised to find we have washing-up to do after cooking, in spite of not having given it much (or any) thought at the outset.

Consensual meta-responsibility is relevant to problems of clinical management, e.g. non-compliance with medication or medical instructions, failing to attend outpatient appointments, etc. It thus takes its theoretical basis from the liberal-scientific model, particularly Parsons' Postulates III and IV (that the sick are expected to desire health, to seek appropriate medical care, and to comply with such care). The clinically undesirable consequences (e.g. medication non-compliance or ignorance of physician instructions) and concomitant generation/exacerbation of mental disorder are consented to in the patient's pursuit of the primary sensual experience (e.g. being free of pharmacological effects or perceived physician control).

3.2 Medication Non-compliance as Consensual Meta-responsibility

Medication non-compliance is examined here as an example of consensual meta-responsibility, particularly within the context of the schizophrenias (the disorders most likely to be considered for eligibility for an insanity defence; MacKay and Kearns, 1999). Blackwell (1976) defines non-compliance as 'failure to enter a treatment program, premature termination of therapy, and incomplete implementation of instructions, including prescriptions' (p. 513). Non-compliance features in all realms of medical treatment; Gomes and Maia (1998) note that 40 per cent of epileptic patients in their study reported non-compliance with anti-epileptic medication in the previous week. Buchanan (1996) asserts that psychiatric patients are no more, or less, compliant with medication regimes than other classes of medical patients (approximately one third of the patients in Buchanan's sample was non-compliant two years after leaving a general adult psychiatry ward). Young, Zonana and Shepler (1986), in a meta-analysis of reports of non-compliance, find a median default rate of 41 per cent for schizophrenic outpatients on oral neuroleptic medication, with values ranging from 10-76 per cent. Johnson (1984) notes that 80 per cent of episodes of non-compliance are associated with relapse in schizophrenic persons thereto in remission.

Whilst medication default rates may be no higher for psychiatric patients than other classes of patients, the potential effects of medication default upon the self and others differs fundamentally between the two classes (through the potential of mental disorder to give rise to criminal acts and hence impact on others; see

Chapter 1), which brings with it a greater responsibility for control of the condition in the former group.[3] As one psychiatrist states:

> I do maintain that even for seemingly regressed or floridly psychotic patients, there is at least a kernel of willpower, lurking somewhere in the nether regions of their minds and amid the maelstrom of thought and emotion, which can be employed constructively to counter their deviant impulses. No doubt it may require significant effort for patients to master and channel these impulses, but this does not exonerate them from making a sustained effort to do so or from being receptive to outside therapeutic help (Ludwig, 1971; cited in Slodov, 1989; 301).

Similarly, Sherlock (1984) details the control available to the patient over his condition and the consequent effects on blame and punishment:

> Both in legal punishment and moral blame we have a deep seated sense that it is wrong to punish people for either acts they did not know were wrong or that they could not prevent themselves doing. In the last decade, however, developments in psychiatric medicine have rendered this seemingly uneventful conclusion increasingly questionable. The most significant of these developments is our increasing capacity to control most severe forms of mental illness with appropriate pharmacological treatment. Such a development carries with it a transfer of a measure of control over the presence of psychosis to the patient and out of the range of fate…in light of these advances in psychopharmacology it is no longer correct to assume in any given case that no one is responsible for this person developing acute psychotic symptoms… (p. 485).[4]

Howlett (1998), in his report commissioned by the Zito Trust, examined independent enquiry reports instituted after a homicide committed by a mentally disordered person. Twenty (57 per cent) of the reports cited medication non-compliance as a factor leading to the breakdown of care immediately prior to the homicide.

---

[3] See the following cases involving criminal acts committed temporally contiguously with medication non-compliance (Slodov, 1989): *United States v. Samuels* (1986), 810 F.2d 1052; *State v. Johnson* (1988), 753 P.2d 154; *People v. Chavez* (1981), 629 P.2d 1040; *Naidu v. Laird* (1988), 539 A. 2d 1064; *Hill v. State* (1978), 358 So.2d 190; *In re Noel* (1979), 601 P.2d 1152.

[4] Sherlock (1984), however, considers that only wilful cessation of medication should receive our blame and censure:

> …if the patient had knowingly and wilfully stopped taking his medication and had then relapsed into a manic state, would we not want to hold him responsible for being in a manic state and for the harms he commits while in that state? (p. 486).

3.2.1 The Role of Insight in Medication Non-compliance

Is non-compliance and concomitant generation or exacerbation of disorder sufficient for an ascription of meta-responsibility to the patient? If hay-fever gave rise to criminal acts, then it seems certain that those failing to take anti-histamines might be deemed meta-responsible. However, psychiatric opinion delineates a fundamental difference between hay-fever and mental disorder that appears to forestall an ascription of meta-responsibility in the latter: physical disorders such as hay-fever are generally not deemed to affect the ability of the afflicted to conform to Parsons' Postulates (such as seeking to get well i.e. take medication),[5] whereas mental disorder *does* interfere with such abilities. The rift between the *requirements* of Parsons' Postulates and the ability and volition of the mentally disordered to *conform* to those Postulates is generally seen to be a function of mental disorder itself; specifically, disruption of insight into the disorder. Such deficits interfere with the ability of the patient to recognize or understand the nature or severity of his illness, or even that he is ill at all. This lack of insight into disorder ostensibly discharges the duty of the patient to 'be a responsible patient'. If a patient is not responsible for any role in the management of his/her disorder, then it follows quite logically that he or she could not be found responsible for his or her criminal responsibility that is consequent upon any mismanagement of the disorder.

Lack of insight is generally seen to be a function of severity of psychopathology, whereby the more severely disordered are less likely to admit they are ill (Neumann, Walker, Weinstein and Cutshaw, 1997). Such a situation differs fundamentally from physical disorder in which the relationship between severity and awareness of illness is likely to be a positive one. In schizophrenic patients, lack of insight is generally seen as due to deficits in meta-representation caused by the disorder that remove the possibility of control and management of thinking (Frith, 1992). Bolton and Hill (1996: 43) generalize this 'disruption of self-knowledge' to all psychological disorders of clinical severity. If a person does not therefore concord with a physician that he or she is mentally ill (i.e. has insight), then that person cannot be expected to take medication prescribed by that physician (or even seek out such a physician in the first instance, as Parsons' Postulate IV entails). After all, one would not seek out and accept the recommendations of a gardener if one did not believe one had a garden. For

---

[5] Although see the Report of the Richardson Committee which proposes a capacity test for consent to treatment common to both physical and mental disorders (see SUPRA note 3, Preface). Situations may be envisaged where a physical disorder affects ability to make treatment decisions such as medication compliance, e.g. the effect of a brain tumour upon cognition and behaviour, emotional distress caused by a diagnosis of cancer, etc. Infectious diseases might also afford grounds for detention (e.g. quarantine). Matthews (1999) uses such examples to argue that the separation of mental and physical disorders in terms of specific mental health legislation cannot be justified; a principle that the Richardson Committee embraces.

example, in the study of Van Putten, Crumpton and Yale (1976: 1446), a patient who refused anti-psychotic medication stated that 'I don't need medication; there is nothing wrong with me'. Daniel McNaughton himself appeared to have considerable deficits of insight, as indexed by the testimony of one physician at his trial:

> I asked him if he had availed himself of medical advice? He replied, that physicians could be of no service to him; that if he took a ton of drugs it would be of no service to him; that in Glasgow he observed people in the streets pointing at him…(Dr. E.T. Monro; cited in Maeder, 1985: 28).

The psychiatric patient is, therefore, often seen as being faced by a vicious circle of medication non-compliance and disorder exacerbation: severe disorders engender medication non-compliance which engender disorder of greater severity. Such a cycle is enough to forestall any attribution of meta-responsibility, as the consensual meta-responsibility (in this case, medication non-compliance) does not arise from the recklessness, negligence, etc. of the patient, but rather is seen to be a *function of the patient's disorder*, for which he cannot be held responsible.

3.2.2 Should Lack of Insight Forestall an Attribution of Consensual Meta-responsibility?

Howlett's (1998) study cited lack of insight by the patient as a cause of medication non-compliance as a feature of 80 per cent of the homicide inquiry reports where such non-compliance was evident. If a straight *causal* relationship between lack of insight and medication non-compliance existed, then lack of insight would indeed be enough to rule out the issue of consensual meta-responsibility. Medication non-compliance could not provide the requisite source of culpability *for* disorder.

However, such a straight causal relationship cannot be substantiated. The first reason is that lack of insight cannot be deemed the sole cause of medication non-compliance. Howlett's (1998) study also cited medication side-effects as a cause of non-compliance in 85 per cent of cases in which it occurred, poor aftercare and supervision in 85 per cent, substance abuse in 65 per cent, poor communication with family and/or the patient in 55 per cent, and non-attendance by the patient at outpatient appointments in 50 per cent of cases.

Secondly, it appears that some schizophrenic persons *do* have insight. Chadwick (1993) states that deficits in meta-representation of the sort described by Frith (1992) only occur in Type II schizophrenic persons – those predominately suffering from negative symptoms, e.g. dysphoria and social withdrawal (Crow, 1980). Type I patients, suffering from a predominance of positive symptoms such as delusions/hallucinations, 'appear to have an ability to reflect on events and their own thoughts' (Chadwick, 1997: 248). It is patients with positive symptoms, particularly command hallucinations, who are most at risk of violent behaviour (Mitchell, 1999a).

Thirdly, Lysaker, Bell, Milstein *et al.* (1994) find that heightened levels of psychopathology do not negatively correlate with level of insight, casting suspicion upon the notion that those disorders deemed supportive of an insanity defence (i.e. those exhibiting severe psychopathology) are necessarily those that disrupt insight and hence the ability to comply with medication regimes. In any case, those found NGRI include persons with disorders that are generally deemed not to cause disruption of insight; for example, depression, alcohol/drug abuse, personality disorder, and post-traumatic stress disorder (Mackay, 1990; Mackay and Kearns, 1999).[6]

Fourthly, treatment refusal does *not* appear to be correlated with insight, cognitive function, satisfaction with treatment, age, time since onset of illness, and even treatment type (Eskey, 1958; Wing, Monck, Brown and Carstairs, 1964; MacPherson, Alexander and Jerrom, 1998). Van Putten *et al.* (1976: 1443) found that the only predictor of treatment refusal was a 'wish to be crazy'.[7]

Finally, the very concept of insight has been criticized as unmeaningful, having poor construct validity, and an amalgam of component dimensions (Beck-Sander, 1998).

If mental disorder *does* interfere with insight, medication-compliance, etc., then the meta-responsibility contingent upon the commission of a criminal act might be termed 'disorder-mediated meta-responsibility'. Disorder might be a mitigatory factor in assessing meta-responsibility in such a case.[8] Sherlock (1984:

---

[6] Of the 49 NGRIs in Mackay's (1990) sample, schizophrenia was diagnosed in 25, alcohol/drug abuse in five, depression in four, epilepsy in four, personality disorder in three, psychosis (unspecified) in three, hypomania in two and brain damage in two (one was classified as having an 'other' diagnosis). During the years 1987 to 1996, NGRIs exhibited the following diagnoses: schizophrenia in 23, acute/transient psychosis in five, hypomania in four, depressive/anxiety disorders in three, epilepsy/post-ictal state in three, sleepwalking in two, drug-induced psychosis in two, brain damage in one, and PTSD in one (Mackay and Kearns, 1999).

[7] This study is discussed below as an example of purposive meta-responsibility; the medication non-compliance in such a case appears to be goal-directed behaviour exhibited towards the primary goal of experiencing mental disorder.

[8] Incapacity caused by physical disease provides an example of disorder-mediated meta-responsibility. Tom develops a degenerative condition of the retina. His eyesight becomes worse over a period of a few years, but the change is sufficiently slow for him not to notice. Like all drivers, he receives a notice from the driving licensing agency reminding him to have a regular eyesight check. However, his eyesight has deteriorated to the point where he reads the number '2' as '5' in the sentence 'Licensed drivers should have an eyesight check-up once every 2 years'. As it is only two years since Tom's last check-up, he decides to leave the check-up for three years. A year later, his poor eyesight is responsible for his not seeing a small child in the road, who he knocks over. Would we be inclined to hold Tom responsible for knocking over the child? Two answers may be envisaged: a) Tom should have taken extra care to read the eyesight notice, and in any case should have realised that once every five years is too infrequent to be sure of good eyesight; or b) Tom was acting upon an illusory state of affairs brought about by the disorder of which his accident was a product (as in mental disorder). If we are inclined toward a), then even disorder-mediated meta-responsibility may provide a source of culpability.

495) lists classes of patients who might have disorder-mediated meta-responsibility: those who 'never get well enough to understand adequately their need for medication', those whose 'family will try to sustain medication compliance but this correspondingly reduces the individual's own responsibility for compliance or non-compliance', and those whose 'responsibility will be diminished but not eliminated by virtue of the fact that his medication only partially controls his illness'.

3.2.3 The Principle of Responsive Adjustment and Consensual Meta-responsibility

Perhaps the most important reason why lack of insight (and associated justification for medication non-compliance) should not be presumed in those pleading insanity is that medication non-compliance often occurs in the context of periods of lucidity (or at least during a period of adaptation to the defect). An example would be the patient who is judged well enough to be discharged from inpatient care and be responsible for his own medication regimen when mental disorder is in remission (often due to the effects of this medication). It is during these periods that insight might be expected to be full or at least greater than during the disordered state.

A patient discontinuing medication during such a period may have the benefit of insight (and hindsight) in his decision-making. Weinstock (1999) alludes to the meta-responsibilities of such patients:

> Many psychotic individuals...discontinue their medication, despite evidence on multiple occasions that their symptoms escalate whenever they do so...similarly most addicted individuals display denial and are certain that they can have just one more drink or use a substance yet maintain control, despite all past evidence to the contrary. The two situations are morally identical except for the negligible distinction that one involves taking a substance and the other involves stopping medication...to be consistent logically, both groups should be held responsible or not responsible for the same behaviours (conference abstracts, p. 194-195).

The mentally disordered patient may therefore have the opportunity to accrue evidence that his omission will have consequences to the self and others. It seems reasonable that a patient with such evidence who discontinues medication without significant cause (e.g. severe side-effects, extra-pyramidal symptoms, etc.) would be consensually meta-responsible if a criminal act results from mental disorder engendered by the non-compliance. Although Weinstock states that the moral capacities of the two groups (the addict and the non-compliant patient) are identical, it may be that a non-compliant patient is *more* responsible for his incapacity (and hence more meta-responsible) than the drinker who assaults someone without any evidence that his drinking would give rise to this situation, or the drug user without evidence of drug effects (see *R v. Hardie*).[9] The law

[9] *Supra* note 37, Ch. 2.

accommodates ability to accrue evidence through allowing the 'first time defence' of pathological intoxication,[10] and such a principle might be extended to the patient who stops his medication for the first time and commits a criminal act as a product of the concomitant relapse. This might apply only, however, where there was good evidence that the patient had not been warned of the possibilities of relapse due to medication non-compliance, or, if he had been warned, did not understand this instruction. Unfortunately, it seems that non-compliance often verges on the habitual, in spite of evidence accrued as to potential adverse effects. Examples were uncovered in the case-files of persons found Not Guilty by Reason of Insanity.[11] For example:

> Since [1983] [Patient W] has been admitted almost on a yearly basis for relapses in his illness occasioned by his habitual non-compliance with depot medication. Many of these relapses have been characterised by violent behaviour and bizarre grandiose delusions.
>
> [Patient X] has a history of psychiatric treatment. His offence was serious and the medical reports indicate he has been violent in the past. He does however respond to treatment and it is likely that his offences were committed while defaulting on medication.

Some NGRIs appeared in remission and to have the requisite insight to hold them consensually meta-responsible for any further offences:

> In the light of the seriousness of [Patient Y's] last offence he says that he has changed his attitude to medication and feels that he should receive it regularly and indefinitely.
>
> At the present time [Patient Z] is free of active symptoms of paranoid schizophrenia...he is compliant with medication and his therapeutic management

---

[10] See *SUPRA* note 38, Ch. 2.

[11] Used with permission. The author was kindly granted access to the case-files of all insanity acquittees and persons found unfit to plead in England and Wales at the Home Office Mental Health and Criminal Cases Unit and made a preliminary examination of the files *in situ*. These case-files contained information from various sources including court reports, MHRT reports, hospital records, newspaper cuttings, applications for escorted leave, etc. In agreement of the author and the Home Office, all data on the persons in these files was anonymized at the point of transcription. Whilst the material examined in these case-files was originally intended to provide a substantial component of the 'field work' of this study, it was felt that the time and space constraints of the doctoral thesis upon which this book is based could not accommodate the huge amount of qualitative information held in the case-files. However, the rarity of access to such information and the quality and quantity of material pertaining to meta-responsibility and more general issues present an invaluable research opportunity. Therefore, it was decided to leave detailed analysis of such material to a separate study but to present a small amount of information anecdotally where appropriate.

program. He has developed a partial insight into his mental illness and the need to take medication to prevent it from occurring.

This would be encouraging were it not for the ability of such patients to plead NGRI in the future. As an example of consensual meta-responsibility, consider the following extract from a letter sent by a US forensic psychiatrist:

> A case I recall is a good example of your MR [meta-responsibility]. I evaluated and treated someone who had been found not responsible due to mental illness (NGRI) of a burglary charge and a few other things, none too exciting. He had a *bona fide* bipolar disorder and was quite crazy when committing his crimes. In assessing him I found he had history of doing very well on medications. Every once in a while he would smoke marijuana. Shortly after that he would stop his meds and in a short time become manic. In his manic state he would commit crimes (again, usually nothing to get excited about). When I met him, it was his third NGRI. I wrote up my report for the court (as he was no longer showing any sign of MI when I evaluated him) saying I believed he could be released, but I hoped that in the future if he stopped his meds that he not be allowed to plead NGRI as his stopping the meds was a voluntary act with knowledge of the likely outcome.[12] But I doubt that would ever happen. Unfortunately, not all cases are as clear cut, but there is plenty of room for more consideration of MR (Anon., 1999, personal communication, used with permission).

Such cases probably make a significant contribution to the public perception of the insanity defence as a loophole.[13] Although these 'myths' (Perlin, 1996: 5) are based more on sanism and 'Ordinary Common Sense' (OCS; Perlin 1996: 16) than the appraisal of real cases (see Chapter 4), a putative basis in fact cannot be ignored as a contributory factor to the negative public (and even legal and academic) opinion surrounding the insanity defence.

Perhaps the reason why the above case seems so offensive to commonsense notions of justice is that it violates the Principle of Responsive Adjustment (PRA) (French, 1991a), a societal principle to which responsible agents are expected to adhere after a negatively appraised event occurs as a result of their acts or omissions:

> PRA captures the notion that, after an untoward event has happened, the person(s) who contributed to its occurrence is (are) expected to adopt certain courses of future action that will have the effect in his (their) future conduct of preventing repetitions (French, 1991a: 138).

Under the principle of consensual meta-responsibility governed by the PRA, a first episode of mental disorder differs in terms of moral obligation from future

---

[12] Such a recommendation, whilst comporting with commonsense notions of justice, may in fact be a violation of ethical codes (in this case that of the American Psychiatric Association), as it pertains to a legal judgment, not to a medical one.

[13] See *SUPRA* note 22, Ch. 2.

episodes. If insight is attained after the first episode, then medication non-compliance, etc. as to future episodes will violate the expectation of responsive adjustment and should therefore attract blame, rather than excuse. Take the example of a diabetic patient:

> A man might not be responsible for acquiring diabetes mellitus, but whether he becomes symptomatic depends on whether he takes insulin. Knowing that his symptoms depend on taking insulin, if he refuses to take insulin, becoming comatose at the wheel of his car and killing a cyclist, he *is* responsible (Reznek, 1991: 124).[14]

Although the diabetic in this example does not have previous experience of killing cyclists when non-compliant with insulin, he had both sufficient evidence and capacity to foresee that a negative event might occur because of his omission. He has still, in effect, violated the PRA. In legal terminology, he has certainly been subjectively reckless, and possibly objectively reckless.[15]

Sherlock (1984) details conditions under which the non-compliance can itself be justified, entailing exemption from the PRA:

> ...if the patient has no history of violence it may be reasonable to say that he has a valid justification for stopping his medication when it is ineffective in controlling his illness. Justification of non-compliance in such cases will therefore require a twofold showing: (1) that the medication really was ineffective or had serious side effects; and (2) that the patient had no history of violence that would suggest that he should be required to stay on his medication even if it was only minimally effective (p. 498).

However, it would not necessarily seem that the PRA has to rely upon personal experience of the effects of the act or omission; information is merely enough (see the example of Ulysses detailed in Chapter 9). Therefore, a non-offending schizophrenic patient having insight after a previous psychotic episode, may be told by a psychiatrist that failure to maintain medication could result in a further breakdown. He has no evidence that this might occur other than the psychiatrist's word. Would we hold him responsible if a future breakdown resulted in a criminal episode? Certainly, if we are inclined to hold the diabetic in the above example responsible. The two cases do not differ in a) the knowledge of likely consequences of the omission; or b) the ability to conform behaviour to the PRA to avoid such an omission and its consequences. In the language of the present study, both have a similar level of consensual meta-responsibility.

---

[14] See also Slodov (1989: 283): 'The non-compliant psychiatric offender has conceptually run a similar risk in deciding to discontinue medication that an epileptic runs in deciding to risk harm to others by not taking his medication. They each have an endogenous disorder that may be effectively controlled by medication'.

[15] See SUPRA note 39, Ch. 2, and *Kay v. Butterworth* at SUPRA note 56, Ch. 2.

Lehrman (1994) argues that release of NGRIs should be contingent upon responsive adjustment:

> Should insight also be required – full understanding, shared with caretakers, of the thought processes of the acquittee at the time of the crime in order to reduce the likelihood of his or her repeating it and to guarantee criminal responsibility if another crime is committed? (p. 1766).

Such a notion is opposed to that of Bloom and Williams (1994) who contend that release should depend only 'on current symptom expression of mental illness rather than on past criminal justice history' (cited in Lehrman, 1994: 1766). Conversely, a system involving the PRA may allow an initial NGRI plea, but acquittal or release would be conditional on an agreement of strict liability for any future criminal acts committed as a product of mental disorder. Medication non-compliance would not facilitate a second NGRI through virtue of being off medication and thus mentally disordered, allaying our discomfort concerning the NGRI burglar described above.[16] This would allay the concern of Slodov (1986), who states that a putative NGRI could 'get away with murder as many times as he is released from an institution' (p. 320).

3.2.4 Substance Abuse and Consensual Meta-responsibility

The example of the NGRI burglar also highlights the issue of co-morbidity; mental disorder in tandem with substance abuse. Substance abuse may comprise another element of consensual meta-responsibility, and its association with medication non-compliance to produce violent behaviour in severely mentally disordered individuals is well established (providing an even better predictor of violent behaviour than *past history* of violent behaviour; Swartz, Swanson, Hiday *et al.*, 1998).[17] Lindqvist's (1986) study of all persons committing homicide in Sweden

---

[16] Pasewark *et al.* (1982: 373) note that rearrest of NGRIs is confined to a core group of 'anti-social' NGRIs 'whose criminal history is interrupted only by the NGRI hospitalization'.

[17] It might be argued that patients would be immediately negligent or reckless upon medication refusal due to the established contribution of mental disorder on violence, in the same way that the effects of alcohol on facilitating antisocial and violent behaviour are well known and presumably constitute the foreknowledge component for recklessness through intoxication. The effects of mental disorder on violent behaviour (whether precipitated by medication non-compliance or otherwise) are to raise the prevalence of violence by approximately five times compared to those with no diagnosis (Swanson, Holzer, Ganju and Jono, 1990). A variety of empirical studies show mental disorder to elevate risk of violence and violent offending, as indexed by violence amongst the mentally disordered, and prevalence of mental disorder amongst the violent in samples drawn from prison populations, community studies, birth cohorts and hospital patients (Mitchell, 1999a). Furthermore, a large body of attitudinal literature shows widespread public sentiment that the mentally disordered pose a threat of violence (e.g. MacLean, 1969); although such

during 1970-1981 showed that 53 per cent were mentally disordered, of whom 38 per cent were co-morbid for alcoholism and/or substance abuse. Of the co-morbid, 85 per cent were intoxicated at the time of the homicide. Ward and Applin (1998) examined 17 reports into homicides by mentally disordered offenders and found that drink and/or drugs played a substantial role in 14 of them.

Howlett (1998) indicates both direct and indirect causal relationships between alcohol/substance abuse and non-compliance:

> Abuse of alcohol or drugs leads to an increase in non-compliance, in part because drugs and alcohol produce adverse side-effects when mixed with anti-psychotic medication. Drug and alcohol abuse also impacts negatively on compliance as it leads to a deterioration of the patient's mental health, which may increase non-compliance (p. 70).

The interaction between the co-morbid elements appears a particular source of concern for mental health professionals and features prominently in NGRI case-files. In a court report one forensic psychiatrist wrote 'it has been noted that when he drinks more alcohol he is more likely to talk about the SAS, his half brothers and other delusional ideas'. An application for escorted leave stated that:

> Alcohol does not appear to be a problem in itself although his breakdowns are characterized by an increase in alcohol consumption. He likes to smoke cannabis when he can get it.

As in Chapter 2 which highlighted the inconsistency of the criminal law subjecting substance and alcohol use to a voluntaristic analysis, but not insanity, so it seems that we should also examine voluntarism where substance or alcohol use provide a *source* of insanity, e.g. through medication non-compliance. Here we are left in the position of the offender having responsibility (through drug/alcohol use) for his responsibility (medication non-compliance) for his criminal responsibility: 'meta-meta-responsibility' (perhaps better termed second-order meta-responsibility). If the conditions that brought about his alcoholism or substance use were also within his voluntary control, such as to diminish adverse affect caused by gambling losses,[18] then we might provide an analysis in terms of third-order meta-responsibility. These meta-levels of responsibility become pertinent where we invoke a 'historical search' for the antecedent conditions of culpability (Finkel 1988; Finkel, 1995). The meta-responsibility theory can be extended to provide for *n*-level responsibility determinations with regard to a historical search, with third-order meta-responsibility determinations perhaps having a more tenuous

---

sentiment is rarely based on empirical evidence, presumably the mentally disordered are not immune to this opinion.

[18] Although the medicalization of gambling (as well as alcoholism and substance abuse) has recast it as a disorder, ostensibly excluding it from providing a source of meta-responsibility (due to its new-found association with the liberal-scientific model e.g. Comings, Rosenthal, Lesieur *et al.*, 1996).

relationship with criminal responsibility – than first-order ('simple') meta-responsibility. For the purposes of the present study, however, it is more appropriate and economical simply to refer to meta-responsibility, howsoever it might arise through the causal chain.

3.3 Purposive Meta-responsibility

What if the NGRI burglar in the above example had taken drugs and stopped his medication for the *very reason* of relapsing into mental disorder? In such an instance, mental disorder would constitute a primary goal. This entails a re-evaluation of our 'washing-up' example: would someone cook (or become non-compliant) for the very reason of generating what the rest of us consider to be an unwanted side-effect – washing-up (or mental disorder)? Whilst we might think of people who want to generate washing up as 'crazy', mental disorder may bring with it potential benefits. The SC and EP models characterize potential benefit in mental disorder, in contrast to the disease model that emphasizes the negative effect of mental disorder on the individual.

Purposive meta-responsibility differs from consensual meta-responsibility in that advertence is directed towards mental disorder itself: a *purposive* short- or long-term goal that is valued for its own sake (Kenny, 1978), rather than a mere 'side-effect' of the pursuit of some other goal. Purposes, like consents, need not always be present in one's mind while operative; for example, an intention to follow a particular career path (e.g. a marine biologist) is a long-term purpose affecting short-term behaviour (e.g. revising hard for biology exams), but will not always be present in the conscious mind (Kenny, 1978). Medication non-compliance becomes relevant to purposive meta-responsibility (rather than consensual meta-responsibility) where it arises not due to a desire to be drug free or avoid side-effects, but due to a preference for the mentally disordered state over 'cold psychiatric sobriety'.[19]

Does the source of medication non-compliance make any difference to the question of culpability? Is there any difference in the meta-responsibilities of the patient who stops medication to avoid side-effects and the patient who stops medication because he values the known effect of such cessation? The law certainly delineates between accidental incapacity and incapacities caused 'with aforethought' (as in the case of the 'Dutch courage' or 'grand schemer' defendant

[19] It is difficult to disentangle any preference amongst patients for the mentally disordered state *per se*, rather than simply a preference for the mentally disordered state *given their current life situation*. For example, mental disorder may lead to negative life events, e.g. spousal/family rifts, loss of employment, homelessness, psychiatric hospitalization, etc. Grandiose delusions, comforting voices, hypomanic activity, etc. may indeed provide relief from such a depressing reality. Whilst mental disorder may thus provide *subjective* benefit to the morbid patient, that patient may not *objectively* prefer mental disorder to his pre-morbid state.

who drinks or ingests substances for the primary goal of committing a criminal offence which he would not otherwise have the wherewithal to perform).[20] Mental disorder would not likely be generated or exacerbated with such an outcome in mind (which would satisfy an 'at fault *in order to*' recklessness test used in some US jurisdictions; Robinson, 1985), but mental disorder as a primary goal would certainly increase the likelihood of satisfying a subjective (or even objective) test of recklessness.[21] In such a case the primary consequences of the act or omission of generation or exacerbation could be foreseen (becoming mentally disordered), if not the secondary consequences (a potential criminal episode). Furthermore, it seems that purposive behaviour directed to the goal of mental disorder could not be used to counter attributions of meta-responsibility through a justification of reasons for non-compliance. This difference between consensual and purposive meta-responsibility would thus become especially pertinent in establishing a 'defence' to a 'charge' of meta-responsibility. As Sherlock (1984) states:

> Among the major variables associated with non-compliance in psychiatric settings are the relationship with the therapist, the attitude of the therapist toward drugs, the choice of therapy, the form and dosage of the medication, *secondary gains associated with the 'crazy' state, especially mania*, and finally side-effects. Intuitively, *it seems that only one of these, the desire to be crazy for secondary gains, can be forthrightly excluded from consideration as a possible justification for non-compliance* (p. 504; italics added).

Van Putten *et al.* (1976) examined such reasons for non-compliance in 29 habitual drug-refusers who discontinued medication on discharge (even though their psychosis was shown to be drug-responsive), and 30 drug-compliers who habitually returned for refills or depot anti-psychotic medication. Drug-refusers could not be distinguished from drug-compliers along the many dimensions thereto thought to constitute the reasons for non-compliance, e.g. side-effects, complexity of pharmacotherapy regime, social supervision, lack of insight, severity of illness, doctor's attitudes, or extrapyramidal symptoms.

Instead, the only variable on which the two groups differed on a discriminant analysis was that drug-refusers tended to relapse into an ego-syntonic grandiose psychosis shortly after discontinuing medication. When taking medication faithfully, they experienced dysphoric effects of depression and anxiety, as well as insight into their disorder. The authors concluded that a 'wish to be crazy' was responsible for choosing to discontinue medication: that is, through the positive reinforcing effects of a grandiose psychosis and absence of dysphoric symptoms, these patients avoided the unpleasant effects of drug-induced reality contact. Such patients spoke of 'being great composers', having 'billions', and being the 'greatest

---

[20] The girlfriend of one NGRI patient (contained in Home Office NGRI case-files), when asked if drinking was the cause of her boyfriend's behaviour stated 'Who needs a drink to become disturbed when you are already insane?'.

[21] See *SUPRA* note 39, Ch. 2.

aeronautical engineer in the world' (Van Putten *et al.*, 1976: 1446). The authors concluded that:

> The hard-core drug refusers resemble Elwood P. Dowd, the whimsical hero of the play 'Harvey'. When his psychiatrist urged him to struggle with reality, he responded, 'Doctor, I wrestled with it for forty years and I am happy to state that I finally won out over it' (p. 1446).

Hogarty, Goldberg and The Collaborative Study Group (1973) also suggested that one reason why 40 per cent of psychotic patients in their sample discontinued medication was a preference for a mental state in which the symptoms of schizophrenia are experienced, compared to a medicated state of sanity.

To examine why such a 'wish to be crazy' might originate, it is necessary to examine literature that attests to possible voluntarism and benefit in mental disorder. Much of this literature is derived from the social constructivist and existential phenomenological models of mental disorder.[22]

3.3.1 Voluntarism in the Social Constructivist (SC) and Existential Phenomenological (EP) Models of Mental Disorder

The social constructivist model (e.g. Szasz, 1961, 1973, 1997; Scheff, 1966) and existential phenomenological model (e.g. Laing, 1964, 1965, 1967, 1969; Laing and Cooper, 1964) grew out of critical-psychiatric thought of the late 1950s and 1960s. Both models placed a primacy on the individual's freewill and rejected the specific pathological constraints on behaviour that liberal-scientific models espouse. The two models differed dramatically from other models of mental disorder along four dimensions (Burston, 1996):[23] 1) the kinds of causal factors that impact upon human behaviour; 2) the locus of disordered thoughts, feelings, and behaviour (internal or external to the individual); 3) how psychological health and disorder are defined; and 4) what degree of active agency or responsiveness the models attribute to human beings. It is this last dimension that is of particular relevance to the present study. The EP model, in particular, emphasized the active agency of human beings, being influenced by the existential and phenomenological philosophy of Ludwig Binswanger, Maurice Merleau-Ponty, Martin Heidigger,

---

[22] The introduction to this chapter, and the section on mental disorder and mental illness in Chapter 1, justify and caution the use of these models. Some more recent critiques of the liberal-scientific model (e.g. Sedgwick, 1973; Boyle, 1990; Thomas, 1997; Veatch, 1997) have abandoned the extreme political and anti-psychiatric elements of such models, but often retained core principles, particularly the *contextual* analyses of mental disorder inherent in the existential phenomenological model (e.g. Ingleby, 1980; Pam, 1990).

[23] The models are: 1) the medical model; 2) the behaviourist model; 3) the cognitive or information processing model; 4) the psychoanalytic model; 5) the existential phenomenological model; and 6) the social constructivist model.

Edmund Husserl, Søren Kirkegaard and Jean-Paul Sartre. For Sartre (1943), freewill and hence total responsibility is an attribute and consequence of existence:

> ...I am without excuse; for from the instant of my upsurge into being, I carry the weight of the world by myself alone without anything or any person being able to lighten it...I am responsible for everything, in fact, except for my very responsibility, for I am not the foundation of my being. Therefore everything takes place as if I were compelled to be responsible...I find myself suddenly alone and without help, engaged in a world for which I bear the whole responsibility without being able, whatever I do, to tear myself away from this responsibility for an instant. *For I am responsible for my very desire of fleeing responsibilities* (p. 710; italics added).[24]

The social constructivist model, whilst similarly emphasising the primacy of freewill in human behaviour, took particular issue with the referent of the phrase mental disorder, deeming it to be a social construction referring to behaviour deviating from socially acceptable norms (see Chapter 1). The SC model is thus built upon the sociology of labelling theorists such as Howard Becker and Edwin Lemert, and the political philosophies and ethics of, for example, Thomas Hobbes and John Stuart Mill.

A common feature of the two models is their dramatic impact, through their emphasis on the primacy of freewill in behaviour (including mentally disordered behaviour), on the *responsibility* of the individual *for* that behaviour. In particular, both models view mental disorder as strategic, goal directed behaviour, designed to deal with the social world and the difficulties inherent to living within it (termed 'problems of living' by Szasz, 1961). As F. Scott Fitzgerald (1965: 52) stated of his wife's mental disorder, 'Growing up, and that, is a terribly hard thing to do. It is much easier to go from one childhood to another'. Fitzgerald's statement echoes Laing's observations on the defective patterns of communications in families, creating untenable social situations which engender mental disorder:

> Without exception, the experience and behaviour that gets labelled schizophrenic is a special strategy that a person invents in order to live in an unliveable situation (Laing, 1967: 114-115).

Sartre similarly viewed mental disorder as a strategic attempt to deal with impossible existences:

> I regard mental illness as the 'way out' that the free organism, in its total unity, invents in order to live though an intolerable situation (Sartre, in Laing and Cooper, 1964: 6).

Szasz (1961) appears to comport with such a view:

---

[24] See also the section on freewill and determinism in Chapter 1 (SUPRA section 1.4).

> It is possible for a person to use intrapersonal conflicts to avoid facing up to interpersonal and socio-political difficulties (p.71).

The American writer and physician Oliver Wendell Holmes had pre-empted such formulations by over a century: 'Insanity is often the logic of an accurate mind overtasked' (*Autocrat of the Breakfast Table*). The EP model espouses that mentally disordered behaviour becomes intelligible if we set it in what might be termed an 'ecological' context, i.e. in relation to the social environment and particularly the defective praxes and processes of socialization and existence engendered by the family (Laing, 1967). The EP and SC models' emphasis on the *active (invents, use, avoid;* see above*)* contrasts vividly with the passive language of previous psychoanalytic theories of human behaviour. Freudian theory, in particular, abdicates agency in the manner of the liberal-scientific model:

> ...his thoughts may well *go their own way* and *refuse* to be directed by his will. *They pursue* problems that are quite indifferent to him, but from which *he cannot get free*. Quite ludicrous tasks, too, are *imposed on him*, such as counting up the windows on the fronts of houses. And when he has performed simple actions such as posting a letter or turning off a gas jet, *he finds himself* a moment later doubting whether he has really done so...*he is unable* to fend off the idea that he has pushed a child under the wheels of a car (Freud, 1926/1991: 9; italics added).

Such passive accounts often differ from those given by patients, which often draw upon active, voluntaristic elements. The Nobel Laureate mathematician and economist, John Forbes Nash Jr., describing his own experiences of schizophrenia, believed that 'it was quite possible for a so-called schizophrenic to control both his delusions and his behaviour' (Nasar, 1998: 261). Indeed, when his son became schizophrenic, he stated that 'I don't think of my son...as entirely a sufferer. In part he is simply choosing to escape from the world'.[25] Exit from the schizophrenic state, to Nash, was made possible by recognizing and rejecting paranoid ideas, in the same way as a dieter becomes thin by recognizing and rejecting fatty food; Nash describes it as a constant, conscious struggle, involving the policing of one's thoughts, and believes that he willed his own recovery.[26] Radden (personal communication) refers to such processes as 'epistemic duties'. Such an idea comports with some data as to the efficacy of cognitive-behavioural

---

[25] Nasar (1998: 385).

[26] *IBID.* That exit from the schizophrenic state can be aversive is more widely acknowledged than the notion that entering the schizophrenic state may be attractive:

> Sensitivity can coexist with a recognition that disorder brings with it a conflict between the desire of the sufferer to be free of negative symptomatology, but still to retain control over when and how that alleviation occurs, for alleviation brings with it its own negative consequences (Caldicott, Conlan and Zigmond, 1999: 75).

intervention with deluded patients: that intervention can reduce ratings of preoccupation and conviction and even rid the patient of the delusion (Garety, 1992). Theories of 'willed recovery' are consonant with the analyses of Laing and Sartre, who 'construed the mad (or nearly mad) as an active agent in the creation and perpetuation of his own misery, who must choose, finally, to abandon his schizoid isolation in favour of authentic relatedness to others in order to regain his sanity' (Burston, 1996: 58).[27]

---

[27] Later, Laing's data on the pathological praxes and processes of families, and the parents' putative schizophrenogenic role, would seemingly cause him to 'absolve the young of responsibility for spiritual malaise' (Burston, 1996: 104). Indeed, madness had become 'an abortive attempt at self cure' (p. 227) – a self-directed therapeutic attempt to restructure a false self brought about by a defective social environment, through, for example, repeated exposure to double binds and other social processes described by Bateson and other researchers at the Palo Alto Research group (see e.g. Bateson, Jackson, Haley and Weakland, 1968). However, Laing never observed that dysfunctional communication, etc. within the family may be, at least in part, adaptation and effect of the schizophrenic member's disturbance, and not the other way around (e.g. Mishler, 1973). Such an observation would still impute culpability for disorder to the patient. As Burston (1996) states:

> If many patients appear to lack insight, decency, or self-restraint, it seems foolish to attribute their attitudes and actions solely to a lack of agency brought about through the connivance of others, particularly when so many of their acts and utterances have a strongly purposive character. We might as well suppose that their apparent lack of agency, or of any responsibility for their actions, is strictly a product of neurochemical defects (p. 247).

This latter objection might even be levelled at the social constructivist model; by positing that the schizophrenic's behaviour is merely an effect of labelling, defective social processes, problems of living, or prototypical attempts at communication (e.g. Szasz, 1961), we are effectively falling foul of merely another attempt at reductionism. We are positing a cause of behaviour (social lesion), and an effect (schizophrenic behaviour). Such an analysis, then, may not be totally alien to the medical model; it merely places the lesion external to the individual. The notion of purposive meta-responsibility, on the other hand, requires autonomous behaviour as its foundation.

The same is true of another 'advertent' model presented by Mitchell (1986). Mitchell considers that mental disorder may be advertent (and that such advertence may have a concomitant effect on criminal responsibility) in so much as it is 'in some part the result of rational, though excessive pursuit of psychological satisfactions' (p. 273). Mitchell offers scant supporting evidence for his theories, and that which he does offer centres around the statement of one supposedly psychotic prisoner who said 'My goal is to make myself as happy as I possibly can and to experience life to the fullest' (p. 275). Mitchell interprets the statement thus:

Jaspers (1963) offers an account by a patient lending credence to such voluntaristic notions:

> I believe I caused the illness myself. In my attempts to penetrate the other world I met its natural guardians, the embodiments of my own weaknesses and faults...I wanted to bring myself closer to the higher sources of life. I should have prepared myself for this over a longer period...since 'nectar' is not for mortal lips (p. 417-418).

Laing (1964) commented on this account that:

> It is as understandable that a man should undertake a journey into his own mind, and get confused and lost, as that he should discover a new ocean or explore a new continent (p. 3).

This emphasis on voluntarism and the active agency of individuals renders their behaviour outside the scope of the liberal-scientific realm and cannot therefore remove responsibility for that behaviour, as its foundation lies with the 'afflicted' individual. Such autogenous conceptions dictate that societal and legal blame should now fall upon the individual, as acts can no longer be attributed to a 'defect of reason' or 'disease of the mind':

> It is by claiming the mentally ill to be always autonomous, that is always free of specific (pathological) organic constraints and free to determine their own goals that Szasz excludes the mentally ill from the world of medicine and renders them always responsible (Laor, 1984: 32).

> The prisoner plainly wants to maximise enjoyment and to achieve that goal he rejects all restrictions including regard for others, concern for public opinion or worries about the future... [the] subject is not ill, although *he may be causing himself to develop an illness* (p. 275-276; italics added).

Mitchell sees his advertent model as fundamentally incompatible with the liberal-scientific model of mental disorder (in contrast to the present study) and maintains that 'the liberal (-scientific) hypothesis...does constitute a refutable theory' (p. 280). However, by advocating that the burden of proof should lie on the liberal-scientific theorist, he ostensibly discharges his own burden of proof. Similarly, by espousing such dubious points as 'laboratory animals can develop drug addictions as well as neurotic or psychotic responses...beliefs and self-awareness do not appear to be essential ingredients in the development of mental illness' (p. 285) he contradicts his other statements such as 'paranoia is, I believe, the result of an addiction to self-flattery' (p. 288). By his use of liberal-scientific terms such as illness, addiction, etc., Mitchell falls foul of that which he is trying to criticize; he is positing a non-voluntary cause and effect of mental disorder which themselves fit into a liberal-scientific framework, as do psychoanalytic and later Laingian formulations of mental disorder. Mitchell's model therefore does not inform our analysis of purposive meta-responsibility.

However, even if individuals *were* subject to the pathological constraints which the SC and EP models abandon, this would not necessarily abdicate responsibility for a condition and acts committed whilst supposedly under the influence of that condition (see Chapter 1). Indeed, Szasz (1997) advocates that if a putative biological basis for schizophrenia is ever proven,[28] the schizophrenic who commits a criminal act 'as a result of' his illness should be held *more* responsible than the mentally healthy for a particular crime, as he should have had foreknowledge that his incapacity might put him in that situation (and taken steps to avert the situation, e.g. through medication compliance). In the language of the present study, some conditions falling within the auspices of the liberal-scientific model may actually *increase* the levels of meta-responsibility of the mentally disordered offender, due to their disorder's presumed vulnerability to medical treatment (e.g. Sherlock, 1984).

The social constructivist and existential phenomenological models do therefore indicate the element of voluntarism that is required by the notion of purposive meta-responsibility. However, that mental disorder may have a voluntaristic element does not answer the question as to why someone would wish to court mental disorder purposively in the first instance. To do this some sort of subjective or objective benefit of the mentally disordered state must be posited. The notion of 'positive' mental disorder, or primary/secondary gains of the mentally disordered state, will be examined in the next section.

3.4 The Benefits of Being Mentally Disordered

Benefits accrued to those 'suffering' from mental disorder, if they occur at all, may be delineated into those specific to mental disorder, and those entailed by the status of mental disorder within the liberal-scientific model (this second class of benefits, or *secondary gains*, e.g. entitlement to the sick role, are also common to physical disorders). Benefits of mental disorder may therefore be bifurcated into those that are uniquely consequent upon being mentally disordered, and those that are simply consequent upon 'being ill'. The SC and EP models are again instructive with regard to both categories of benefit.

3.4.1 Benefits Specific to Mental Disorder (Primary Gains)

Certain physical diseases may confer some benefit upon the person they afflict, e.g. the immunity to malaria of persons with sickle-cell anaemia, the keener olfactory and auditory senses of the blind, or the poetic ability of some persons suffering

---

[28] The distinction between autonomous and liberal-scientific models may not always be clear cut. For example, Mitchell (1986: 227) asserts that 'genetic factors also affect the development of advertent illnesses...but biological variation is not behavioural imperative'.

from Wernicke's aphasia.[29] There would seem to be no *prima facie* reason why mental disorder (as understood within the liberal-scientific framework) should differ in potential gains. The notion that mental disorder may bring benefit to those traditionally thought as 'suffering' from it is, however, a controversial one, but one that has long been evident in literature, art and religion.

As far back as the sixteenth century, Erasmus had bifurcated the nature of insanity into that which was deterministic and hellish, and that which was autogenous and delightful:

> The nature of insanity is surely twofold. One kind is sent from hell by the vengeful furies whenever they let loose their snakes and assail the hearts of men with lust for war, insatiable thirst for gold, the disgrace of forbidden love, parricide, incest. The other is quite different, desirable above everything, and is known to come from me. It occurs whenever some happy mental aberration frees the soul from its anxious cares and at the same time restores it by the addition of manifold delights (Erasmus, 1509/1993: 59).

Erasmus' bifurcation echoes the words of the poet John Dryden: 'There is a pleasure sure, in being mad, which none but madmen know' *(The Spanish Friar)*. Such conceptions of a *positive*[30] or 'superphrenic' component to the experience of mental disorder (Karlsson, 1972) are apparent in Laing's (1969) formulation of schizophrenia which he saw as a valuable ethical and religious experience to which society reacts through psychiatry to impose violence and control over those it labels as mentally ill. Laing termed the 'schizophrenic journey' *metanoia* (μετανοια), a term used in the Greek New Testament for atonement (Burston, 1996). Indeed, increased quality and strength of religious experience seem to be a 'symptom' of schizophrenia often cited by former and current patients (and is a central theme of the personal accounts given below). The EP model also suggests other benefits to the mentally disordered that were identified in the discussion on

---

[29] Chadwick (1997) tells of how a serious hand injury facilitates long periods of writing without any pain in the phalanges from which he suffered before the injury. Sacks (1986) in *'The Man Who Mistook His Wife for a Hat'*, describes a fascinating array of benefits associated with neurological disorder. Sedgwick (1973) offers the example of a tribe in South America that not only considers infection by dyschromic spirochetosis as part of normal health, but that those without the associated skin discoloration are regarded as 'pathological' and indeed excluded from marriage (in Clare, 1980).

[30] The use of the term 'positive' in such contexts bears no relation to the traditional psychiatric use of the term with regard to positive symptoms of schizophrenia (delusions, hallucinations, word salad speech, etc.) experienced by peripheral or Type I patients (in comparison with the predominately 'negative' symptoms experienced by nuclear or Type II schizophrenic patients; Crow, 1980). Instead, the term positive is used here to denote that the subjective experience of mental disorder may provide benefit to the patient. It is clear that 'negative' symptoms can have a positive effect upon the patient, by causing withdrawal from a schizophrenogenic social environment, etc; and likewise 'positive' symptoms can be negatively evaluated or experienced by the patient.

voluntarism (see above); most notably allowing the self to deal with otherwise unliveable or aversive situations.[31]

Benefits arising from symptomatology in mental disorder appear to be specific to particular diagnoses, e.g. the energetic feeling associated with hypomania, the lack of fear and social inhibition associated with antisocial personality disorder, or the revelatory/mystical experiences sometimes associated with the schizophrenias. The affect created by the grandiose delusions of schizophrenia (and the avoidance of the dysphoria created by *not* having such delusions) has been identified in relation to the study of Van Putten *et al.* (1976) mentioned above.

Another potential benefit seems to be the effect on creativity and affect of bipolar depression and other psychotic disorders, of which there appears to be a high incidence in artists and writers (Storr, 1972). However, Jones (1999) notes a trade-off between such creativity and responsibility to the self and others:

> ...especially for artistic persons suffering from bipolar disorder, taking medication that will deprive them of the intense energies available during manic episodes may seem not worth the cost they will pay in lost artistic expression and achievement...yet not taking medication may exact what seems to others an even higher cost – sanity and possibly life itself (conference abstracts, p. 192).

The experiences of John Forbes Nash Jr. (Nasar, 1998) are again useful in providing some insight into the link between creativity, success and mental disorder. Nash enjoyed grandiose delusions ('I am the left foot of God on earth')[32] and felt a sense of loss when in remission ('The growing relevance and clarity of his thinking, which his doctor, wife and colleagues hailed as an improvement,

---

[31] Another model, more compatible with the liberal-scientific model than the SC or EP models, also suggests benefit in mental disorder. The evolutionary model of mental disorder (Stevens and Price, 1996) applies Darwinian evolutionary theory to the aetiology of mental disorder. Mental disorder is cast as a product of the ancient 'reptilian brain', increasing the evolutionary fitness of the individual and species. The model is particularly compatible with Jungian theory and the existence of archetypes in the phylogenetic psyche, as well as the ethological observations, particularly in primate society. The model removes the individual from the twenty-first century and relocates him in the environment of evolutionary adaptation (EEA) where mental disorder may have played a role in the survival of individuals and species, e.g. schizophrenia as an aid to 'group-splitting' or anorexia nervosa to promote food conservation. In modern times, such disorders have a vestigial quality similar to the human appendix.

Whilst the model suggests benefit in disorder, its emphasis on the locus of aetiology in the phylogeny of the individual, and its benefit to the species rather than the individual, makes it difficult to cast it as an autonomous model. However, it offers the proposition that liberal-scientific models should not exclude considerations of benefit (evolutionary or otherwise) to the individual or species.

[32] Nasar (1998: 275).

struck him as deterioration';[33] remissions were 'interludes of enforced rationality').[34] Indeed, Nash's periods of medication non-compliance arose as a reaction to such dysphoria:

> 'Why, when they were making you well, did you stop taking drugs?'
> 'If I take the drugs I stop hearing the voices'.[35]

In the following conversation, Nash, whilst languishing in mental hospital, is being questioned by a friend, Harvard Professor George Mackey:

> 'How could you, a mathematician, a man devoted to reason and logical proof...how could you believe that extraterrestrials are sending you messages? How could you believe that you are being recruited by aliens from outer space to save the world? How could you...?'
> '...Because...the ideas I had about supernatural beings came to me the same way that my mathematical ideas did. So I took them seriously'.[36]

Peter Chadwick, a former schizophrenic patient, has become an exponent of the 'schizophrenic credit' (Claridge, 1985) by which view some mentally disordered persons experience enhanced levels of functioning in some aspects of their existence.[37] Research has focused on: increased perceptual awareness (Cooper, Garside and Kay, 1976) as indexed by performance on stroop tasks/latent learning; increased ability at detecting facial deception (La Russo, 1978); and increased creativity (Storr, 1972), of which a wealth of anecdotal evidence exists concerning famous people who, usually posthumously, have been diagnosed as mentally disordered (including Darwin, Ruskin, Joyce, Wittgenstein, Einstein and Nietzsche).

Chadwick (1997) describes the positive side of his own psychotic episode and concomitant grandiose delusions:

> I was surely an agent of God, misunderstood, tormented, crucified yet redeemed and blissfully happy. My energy level rose, I hardly needed to eat and could walk for miles at high speed. At night I was 'at one' with the star-spangled sky; the universe and I were a unity. The beauty that is the cosmos was my beauty, in turn my beauty belonged to the world...from 'nothing and nobody' I became everything and everybody...my terminus was Nirvana (p. 177).

---

[33] *IBID* at 295.
[34] *IBID* at 295.
[35] *IBID* at 321.
[36] *IBID* at 11.
[37] Although, see *SUPRA* note 19 for a discussion of subjective/objective benefit to the mentally disordered state. Whilst certain symptoms of mental disorder may make the individual feel more creative/able, etc., the *objective* quality of the existence of mentally disordered persons and their output whilst mentally disordered is generally seen as of lesser quality than when healthy; i.e. mental disorder is seen as *objectively* disabling (Crumbaugh, 1968).

Psychosis might thus represent, for certain persons at certain times, a 'preferred reality' (Roberts, 1991: 19). Patients in Roberts' sample, when asked what their life without their delusions would be like, made statements such as:

> I would be shattered – I've devoted so much time and effort to it; £250 fines, five weeks in prison…if it's proved wrong what am I going to do? I'd be left with nothing (p. 27).

> I know I'm right…I'd be depressed…I'd be without any sense of communication with other people – but it could never happen really. I haven't got anything else really…there wouldn't be any reason to go on…(p.27).

Individuals may also derive benefit from personality disorders. Weibe (1997) presents data suggesting that psychopathic disorder may primarily represent the manifestation of a particular sexual strategy. Clinical and neuropsychological data comport with such a view (e.g. Raine, 1993); the psychopathic physiology and personality support short-term, low commitment, coercive sexual activities (through, for example, a lack of empathic autonomic reactions, and perseverance in goal directed strategies in the face of discouraging environmental circumstances, e.g. a hesitant sexual partner).[38] Others have also recognized a positive side to antisocial personality disorder:

> …people suffering from 'psychopathic disorder' rarely find themselves subject to civil commitment, which would be expected if the disorder were genuinely problematic for the individual. Perhaps the 'mythical' personality type – ruthless, cold, uncaring, and egocentric – actually benefits the entrepreneur (Peay, 1997: 689).

Ian Fleming's *James Bond* may not be the only person, fictional or otherwise, to reap the benefits of psychopathic behaviour. Gustafson (1996) presents an analysis of psychopathy as a manifestation of 'aberrant self-promotion'; many successful businessmen, politicians, entertainers, etc. may have psychopathic personalities, but find positive outlets for its expression. A level of psychopathy (perhaps failing to meet clinical criteria but prominent nonetheless) may thus prove to be a successful strategy in stepping on others in a bid to 'get to the top'.

3.4.2 Benefits General to Illness and the Assumption of the Sick-role (Secondary Gains)

A second category of benefits is afforded to the mentally disordered patient as a result of entitlement to the sick-role (in the same manner as 'physical' disorders). It is clear that diagnosis can even provide a source of positive experience for some

---

[38] Such a sexual strategy raises the question of differential benefits of mental disorder by gender.

people.[39] Chadwick (1997: 22) states of schizophrenia that '…it is well known that patients are even grateful for the diagnosis as it organizes their perception of their life's history and removes their feelings that that they are a morally "bad" person'. Peay (1997: 688) extends this analysis to mentally disordered offenders: 'offenders are prepared to be perceived as victims, even if they show greater reluctance to be labelled as "mentally disordered"…all of the ingredients are present to permit a restructuring of experiences as explanations or excuses'. It is perhaps easier to apply the liberal-scientific terms of determinism, genetics, upbringing, environment, biochemistry, life-stresses and disease to oneself, rather than the autonomous terms of strength, responsibility, morality, resistance, autonomy, restraint, and self-control.[40]

Ill people, through being patients in an age where illness is associated with a medical model, are able (to varying degrees) to adopt an illness- or sick- role; the person with a broken limb takes medical advice, elicits attention and sympathy, and is encouraged to renounce his normal lifestyle for a period of time (e.g. through avoidance of work responsibilities). Illness thus acts as an 'excuse', albeit usually only a temporary one:[41]

---

[39] Factitious disorders and malingering often appear to occur for this very purpose of diagnosis and concomitant sympathy. In common with the analysis of mental disorder presented here, they clearly have a voluntaristic component. However, such 'fake' disorders do not lie in the realm of the liberal-scientific model that is of central interest to this study, which is concerned with 'real disorders' that have a voluntaristic component. However, for a discussion of factitious disorders coming to the attention of the legal system, see Eisendrath (1996); for a discussion of malingering in insanity acquittees, see Gacono, Meloy, Sheppard *et al.* (1995). Factitious disorder has itself been medicalized (DSM-IV code: 300.16/19, with specifiers as to predominately psychological, physical or combined signs and symptoms). Malingering is listed in DSM-IV as an additional condition that may be a focus of clinical attention (V65.2). Conversion disorder is also listed in DSM-IV, but 'although the individual may derive secondary gain from the conversion symptom, unlike in Malingering or Factitious Disorder the symptoms are not intentionally produced to obtain the benefits' (APA, 1994: 454). However, through attempting (consciously or unconsciously) to bring one's problems within the realm of the liberal-scientific model, factitious disorders, malingering and conversion disorder provide excellent examples of the kinds of benefits accrued to those assuming the sick-role, and suggest further reasons why persons might indeed 'wish to be crazy'.

[40] Szasz (1997) believes that compulsory commitment may actually be a comfort to the mentally disordered patient, and in fact his ultimate aim. However, for the patient to recognize such a goal would be ego-dystonic and therefore most patients would object to their compulsory commitment to satisfy themselves that it is not their own doing.

[41] The excuse afforded by illness in post-modern Western society contrasts with the situation described in *Erewhon* (see Chapter 1) in which illness is associated with a *moral* model rather than a *liberal-scientific* one. It is clear that in such a society there is no benefit accrued to the ill (instead the consequences of illness are wholly negative). Such societies would no doubt see a much lower prevalence of factitious disorder, malingering and conversion disorder (see *SUPRA* note 39), and possibly mental disorder as well.

> It is part of our ethical belief system – that is, the rules by which we play the game of life – that we ought to feel sorry for sick people, and should try to be especially kind and helpful to them (Szasz, 1961: 129).

The mentally disordered offender finds himself in such a position: he is excused (to varying degrees) from rules that apply to the normal person (in this case, punishment due to a criminal act); he is overtly afforded sympathy from the legal system (although, as the next chapter shows, begrudgingly). Most of us recognize the excusatory power of illness: few cannot remember feigning illness to avoid sports lessons or maths tests at school. And, like the boy turning up with a sicknote from his mother, the mentally disordered offender who invokes the insanity defence presents the court with 'the ultimate sicknote' (usually backed by a team of psychiatrists). Indeed, the honesty of this excuse is often raised by those who see the insanity defence as a ruse to escape punishment (in spite of the literature attesting to the ability of psychiatrists to discriminate malingerers from the genuinely morbid, e.g. Rogers, 1988). Perhaps one of the most often heard phrases relying on the excusatory power of the liberal-scientific model (and also the one most often subjected to an analysis of the veracity of excuse, particularly with regard to the possibility of malingering) is 'Not now, I have a headache'.

Berglas and Jones (1978) have introduced the notion of 'self-handicapping' as a strategy to avoid dealing with anticipated failure. It is then possible to ascribe one's failure to succeed to this handicap, and to other people's bias or prejudice towards this handicap. Such a strategy may not only appease the ego in the event of failure, but also mitigate, excuse or justify in the eyes of others. Mental disorder might be used as such a 'self-handicapping' strategy; it certainly elicits sympathy or mitigation in the face of failure. However, the concepts of malingering or self-handicapping were medicalized by nineteenth century psychoanalytic conceptions of human behaviour, i.e. viewed as mental disorder *themselves* (or indicative of underlying mental disorder; Szasz, 1961). Such 'pretend illnesses' are represented in DSM-IV.[42] Szasz (1961) attempts to relocate malingering and 'mental illness' to the realm of the voluntary, recasting both as sign-using, rule-following and game-playing behaviour – a protolinguistic attempt to communicate problems of living:

> ...hysteria is (1) a form of nonverbal communication, making use of a special set of signs; (2) a system of rule-following behaviour, making use of the *rules of illness*, helplessness, and coercion; and (3) an interpersonal game characterized by, among other things, strategies of deceit to achieve the goal of domination and control (p. 10; italics added).

In Szasz's view the benefits afforded to the person under the reaction of the liberal-scientific model to his plight, play a predominant role in the cause and continuation of his illness (in fact, medically misinterpreted *protolinguistic*

---

[42] See *SUPRA* note 39.

communication). The insanity defence and other mental condition defences have extended the rules of illness from the medical to the legal.[43] The object of this study is to examine the effect of changing one of these rules of illness; the rule which states that illnesses have no voluntaristic component.

3.5 Concluding Overview

This chapter has examined two types of meta-responsibility (responsibility for criminal responsibility). The first type, consensual meta-responsibility, arises from the consent to genesis or exacerbation of mental disorder in the pursuit of sensual experiences, e.g. medication non-compliance because of a wish to be free of medication side-effects. The second type, purposive meta-responsibility, arises from a 'wish to be crazy' in which mental disorder is valued as a primary goal and behaviour/cognition is directed toward this goal (e.g. medication non-compliance, acquiescence in symptomatology). The counterintuitive notion of the 'wish to be crazy' has been examined though the lenses of the existential phenomenological and social constructivist models of mental disorder (which emphasize the primacy of voluntarism and freewill in human behaviour) and through certain benefits afforded by mental disorder and illness more generally.

What effect might the meta-responsibility theory have upon the treatment of mentally disordered offenders in the criminal justice system? Would considering the autogeneity or voluntarism in mental disorder ameliorate or exacerbate the socio-legal situation of the mentally disordered offender? It was noted in Chapter 1 that moral models of mental disorder were associated with inhumane and punitive treatment of the insane. Chapter 4 examines the present day insanity disposal as a contemporary equivalent of such punitive treatment, and that it is now a *function* of mental disorder being subject to the liberal-scientific/McNaughton combination. Chapter 4 therefore asks whether the meta-responsibility theory may be an advance in psychiatric and legal ethics, which paradoxically improves the situation of the mentally disordered in the criminal justice system and society more widely, through forestalling sanist/pretextual decision-making and covertly punitive disposals.

---

[43] One of the most dramatic examples of *legal* benefit derived from mental disorder comes from the Eighth Amendment of the US constitution which deems it unconstitutional for an 'insane' or 'unfit' person to be executed (Miller and Radelet, 1993); see *Ford v. Wainwright* (1986), 477 U.S. 699.

Chapter 4

Meta-responsibility and the Disposal of the Mentally Disordered Offender

Ye people of England: exult and be glad
For ye're now at the will of the merciless mad.
Why say ye that but authorities reign-
Crown, Commons, and Lords! – You omit the insane!
They're a privileg'd class, whom no statute controls
And their murderous charter exists in their souls.
Do they wish to spill blood-they have only to play
A few pranks-get asylum'd a month and a day-
Then heigh! to escape from the mad-doctor's keys,
And to pistol or stab whoever they please.

Thomas Campbell,
after the trial of Daniel McNaughton

The mentally disordered offender finds himself (or puts himself) in a difficult and unique legal and societal position. He has not only failed through being a criminal (as Fitzgerald would say), but has the additional failure of being insane. Yet this second failure, as Chapters 2 and 3 show, may bring him benefit. Perhaps the greatest benefit in principle that mental disorder can bring to the 'criminally insane' is the exclusion from punishment for otherwise criminal acts.

Society is thus left in a period of extreme dissonance with regard to the mentally disordered offender. On the one hand, it wishes to censure him for his failure in being a criminal. However, his second failure, that of being mad, paradoxically prevents or at least attenuates society's ability to do so, frustrating societal aims. A US opinion survey after the shooting of President Reagan by John Hinckley showed that 75 per cent of people advocated that the insane should be punished like other criminals (Perlin, 1989). However, as Chapter 2 shows, the criminal law sees exculpation of the insane as one of its fundamental principles. Those who fail singly may be punished; those who fail doubly may not. It is no surprise that such an odd state of affairs should bring about an even odder state of affairs with regard to the passage of the mentally disordered through the criminal justice system: that of covert punishment of the insane. If insanity acquittees are indeed 'the most despised and feared group in society' (Perlin, 1996: 22), it comes as little surprise that their disposal might be expressive of a 'barely concealed desire for retribution' (Verdun-Jones, 1989: 23).

Halleck (1986) summarises the rather sorry situation of the mentally disordered offender:

> We remain uncertain how to treat them. We are unwilling to leave them alone, yet most agencies seek to avoid responsibility for their care. We confine them to prisons and to prison-like hospitals where they are sometimes treated worse than other offenders. They almost always receive worse treatment than mental patients in public or private hospitals (p. 12).

4.1 Covert Punishment

Punishment of the mentally disordered, in spite of their special legal status, has long occurred both covertly *and* overtly. The mediaeval court of law was keenly concerned with the veracity of the excuse and the possibility that the apparent insanity before them was somehow brought about by the defendant's own actions. Walker (1968) describes how, when faced with a mute defendant who would not plead to a charge, the court gave him three warnings, then decided whether the defendant was mute by visitation of God or mute of malice. The former had a not guilty plea entered on their behalf, the latter were confined in a small cell and starved until death or the prisoner 'decided' to enter a plea ('*prison forte et dure*'). A more active countermeasure to suspicious incapacity was employed from 1406 by squashing the prisoner with increasing weights, until a plea was entered or he died ('*peine forte et dure*'). Those incapacious at trial, then, faced the possibility of *overt* punishment if the veracity of their excuse was closely examined.[1]

The similarity to the situation described in Butler's *Erewhon* (see Chapter 1) cannot be ignored. Punitive parallels going under the guise of medicine are not, and have never been, difficult to find. In 1859 John Stuart Mill realised that confinement in the asylum may be punishment by another name (note Mill's use of the term *silent*, i.e. covert):

> In former days when it was proposed to burn atheists, charitable people used to suggest putting them in the madhouse instead; it would be nothing now-a-days were we to see this done, and the doers applauding themselves, because, instead of persecuting for religion, they had adopted so humane and Christian a mode of treating these unfortunates, not without a *silent* satisfaction at their thereby having obtained their deserts (Mill; cited in Szasz, 1963: 91; italics added).

William Burroughs, in his psychedelic classic, *The Naked Lunch*, suggests the expansive possibilities for covert punishment ('necessities') *due to* (rather than *in*

---

[1] Voluntaristic mutism has been given disorder status in DSM-IV. *Selective* mutism (code: 313.23) was formerly (in previous editions of the DSM) known as *elective* mutism. It is clear that the simple addition of an 'S' serves to remove voluntaristic connotations of the previous nosology.

spite of) the medicalization of behaviour, in a scene where a psychiatrist talks to a patient suspected of homosexuality:[2]

> '...take the matter of *sexual deviation*...we regard it as a misfortune...a sickness...certainly nothing to be censured or uh sanctioned any more than say...tuberculosis...Yes,' he repeated firmly as if Carl had raised an objection... 'Tuberculosis. On the other hand you can readily see that *any* illness imposes certain, should we say *obligations*, certain *necessities* of a prophylactic nature on the authorities concerned with public health, such necessities to be imposed, needless to say, with a minimum of inconvenience and hardship to the unfortunate individual who has, through no fault of his own, become uh infected...That is to say, of course, the minimum hardship compatible with adequate protection of other individuals who are not so infected...' (Burroughs, 1959: 170; italics in original).

The insight of philosophers and writers such as Mill, Butler and Burroughs is made flesh in the current disposal system for insanity acquittees (if not the mentally disordered in general), particularly through the use of 'hospital as prison' (Peay, 1997: 689). Through detaining the insanity acquittee for a period of time often double to the sentence he would have received had he simply pleaded guilty to the charge and gone to jail (Morris, 1982; Perlin, 1994), he may be covertly punished for a) sentiment that he may cause the conditions of his own defence; and b) 'cheating' the legal system from exacting justice. In *Jones v. United States* (1983)[3] the Supreme Court facilitated automatic and indefinite detention of NGRIs, relaxing due process requirements for their confinement and release, further ruling it constitutional for hospital disposals to exceed the maximum prison sentence for the index offence. Some authors have therefore questioned whether detention is not the true purpose of the defence. Goldstein and Katz (1963: 868), for example, state that 'the insanity defense is not a defense, it is a device for triggering indeterminate restraint'.

In a recent speech in the House of Representatives concerning supervised day release for Hinckley, James Traficant Jr. summed up societal attitudes toward NGRIs: 'What is next, Mr. Speaker? White House tours? Disney World?...Hinckley should go to jail...we should throw away the keys' (Leonard, 1999: A1). It comes as little surprise that hospital may be used as a vehicle for the punishment of such persons, advocated by both society and their elected representatives.

---

[2] Burroughs' comparison of sexual deviation to tuberculosis echoes the statement of Mitchell (1986: 276): 'the disease model of non-judgmental, amoral maladies is founded on the example of tuberculosis, rubella, epilepsy, malaria and pneumonia, which are generally not caused by the diseased person'. See Chapter 1.

[3] *Jones v. United States* (1983), 463 U.S. 354. This judgment superseded that in *State v. Krol* (1975), 344 A. 2d 289, which stated: 'that the person to be committed has previously engaged in criminal acts is not a constitutionally acceptable basis for imposing upon him a substantially different standard or procedure for commitment'.

Hospital may thus be used as an alternative to prison to facilitate incapacitation and retribution. Grounds (1990) notes that s.47 transfers to hospital from prison may be as much indicative of a desire to protect the public[4] as a desire to ensure the patient receives appropriate care and attention. Grounds notes that one third of such transfers to Broadmoor hospital is made during the last month of sentence. Such last-minute transfers clearly have a pretextual basis. In the absence of any *legally* sanctioned method of extending prison sentences, a *medically* sanctioned method will suffice.

Dell and Robertson (1988), in their provocatively titled book, *Sentenced to Hospital*, find that personality disordered offenders in Broadmoor hospital are detained for periods *commensurate with the violence of their offence* rather than on the basis of assessed recovery. Furthermore, 45 per cent of psychotic patients at Broadmoor stated they would rather have gone to prison for determinacy of sentence. Only 28 per cent of psychotic patients and 23 per cent of personality disordered patients were thought by their doctors to need the maximum security that Broadmoor provides. It therefore seems sensible to ask whether hospital is not being used as prison. As Grounds (1987) states:

> Although in principle the hospital order is imposed to enable treatment, and carries an implicit promise of release when the patient's condition is improved...the reality is more complicated. In practice covert tariff considerations do apply for the psychopathic offender under a hospital order in a special hospital. Carefully veiled intimations of this occasionally emanate from the Home Office, and tariff considerations also colour our own clinical judgment although sometimes this is masked by our psychiatric vocabulary. I commonly hear from nursing colleagues the view that a particular individual who has committed a grave offence has *a long time to do* or that *his problems will take a long time to resolve* – the two notions are interchangeable (Grounds, 1987; in Dell and Robertson, 1988: 121; italics added).

Length of detention for insanity acquittees also seems to be better predicted by criminological rather than medical factors; Morris (1997) notes that the length of post-trial detention for US insanity acquittees is proportional to the *seriousness of the crime* rather than any need for therapy.

Of course, such findings may be explained without recourse to covert punishment if those committing more serious crimes are likely to be more severely mentally disordered, thus warranting lengthier post-acquittal detention purely on therapeutic grounds. Schanda, Felsberger, Topf *et al.* (1993) found, for example, a greater severity of psychopathology in NGRIs detained for longer periods. However, index offence was not recorded, and correlation does not indicate

[4] Bonta, Law and Hanson (1998) indicate psychopathology to be unrelated to recidivism, therefore such last-minute 'therapeutic' transfers rarely contribute to the protection of the public. The use of the phrase 'protecting the public' in such cases may be synonymous with punishment, retribution and incapacitation – means for which should be provided by prison, not hospital.

causation (or its direction) between length of detention and psychopathology; longer detention may *cause* a greater severity of psychopathology. Shah, Greenberg and Convit (1994) noted that level of functioning (including personal care skills, social acceptability and perceived aggression) was *better* in 62 NGRIs than civilly committed patients in a regional state hospital. Taken in context of the much longer time NGRIs are likely to spend in hospital than such control patients, this result suggests that assessed recovery is a criterion for release that is not applied equally between the two patient groups. In any case, longer detention of NGRIs on the basis of therapeutic concerns is difficult to justify; Fein (1984) suggests that the insanity acquittal may actually retard treatment.

The combination of the criminal and the medical conspires to create such anomalies. Morris (1982) states:

> When the two powers [criminal law power and mental health law power] are blended, the 'criminal-patient' may suffer from the worst of both worlds – imprisonment for what he did with duration of the imprisonment limited only by predictions of his continuing dangerousness (p. 479).

Morris' statement would be less disconcerting if predictions of dangerousness were particularly accurate; however, research suggests they are not (even the most optimistic researchers tend towards a conclusion of risk assessment having only a modestly better than chance predictive value, e.g. Mossman, 1994; Monahan, 1997). Furthermore, recent research suggests that detention of mentally disordered offenders on the grounds of psychopathology cannot be justified in terms of dangerousness/recidivism considerations. Bonta, Law and Hanson (1998) find psychopathology to be *unrelated* to recidivism for mentally disordered offenders; the predictors of recidivism were the same for both disordered and non-disordered offender samples. Similarly, Pasewark *et al.* (1982) find recidivism in insanity acquittees to be related to *prior* criminality rather than clinical factors, and that escaped insanity acquittees are no more likely to be rearrested for subsequent offences than those discharged with the sanction of hospital facilities.[5]

It seems the insanity acquittee cannot escape association with his or her crime in spite of being found *not guilty* of that crime.[6] In Oregon (with four times as

[5] Pasewark *et al.* (1982) found in their sample of 148 discharged or escaped NGRIs that 29 per cent were rearrested (average days out of hospital at time of study=1826; see Mitchell, 1999a for a critique of arrest rate studies). 22 per cent were rearrested for a felony offence. The rearrest rate did not vary by discharged (n=133) or escaped (n=15) status. That escapees did not have a higher rearrest rate further suggests that length of detention is not a function of treatment or dangerousness considerations.

[6] The inseparable connection between the insanity acquittee and his offence is made clear in statements such as that of the Parliamentary Under-Secretary of State for the Home Department (concerning a Bill amending the Police and Criminal Evidence Act 1984):

many insanity acquittees as the US state average), the state Psychiatric Security Review Board (PSRB) has jurisdiction over insanity acquittees throughout the *maximal sentence for their crimes* (Bloom and Williams, 1994).[7] Lehrman (1994: 1765) describes this as their 'insanity sentence'. The divestment of the criminal law, under which fewer and fewer individuals are subject to its sanctions (Kittrie, 1971), has perhaps led the legal system to search for new ways in which to impose its goals and vent its frustrated intent. Kittrie lists juveniles, the mentally ill, alcoholics, drug addicts and psychopaths as increasingly able to escape traditional legal sanctions. Punishment under the guise of therapy may represent the expression of such goals and frustrations toward the insanity acquittee. Few could contend that the true spirit of the Government White Paper concerning the review of the Mental Health Act 1959[8] flourishes:

> In making a hospital order the court is placing the patient in the hands of the doctors, foregoing any question of punishment and relinquishing from then onwards its own controls over them (p. 45).

As Potas (1982) states:

> To assume a hospital order is not punitive is to misconceive the object of this sanction. It shares with imprisonment the consequences of depriving an individual of his or her liberty. Like imprisonment it offers protection to the community by separating inmates from normal societal intercourse. Unlike imprisonment, however, the aim...is to provide...medical or psychiatric treatment...unfortunately, it is also here that the rights and liberties of individuals are at greatest risk (p. 13-14).

A provision in the Crime (Sentences) Act 1997 for courts to combine a prison sentence with a direction for immediate hospital transfer (the hybrid disposal order) makes the separation of the medical and criminal powers even more

---

> It will also allow DNA samples to be taken from offenders who were not convicted but were either found not guilty by reason of insanity or found unfit to plead...as a captive audience, so to speak, those offenders will be easy to identify and locate...For DNA sampling purposes, clause 2 will *ensure that such offenders will be treated as if they had been convicted of an offence* (House of Commons Hansard Debate, 24 January 1997, italics added).

[7] This system of jurisdiction over mentally disordered offenders is also evident in those found unfit to plead, where restoration of competency is a reasonable and probable goal (i.e. the accused is not an 'unrestorable incompetent'; Morris, 1982: 521). Indefinite detention of such persons has otherwise been ruled unconstitutional in the US case of *Jackson v. Indiana* (1971), 406 U.S. 715. In the UK, Mackay and Kearns (2000) note that 43.7 per cent of those found unfit to plead since 1992 were given restriction orders without limit of time.

[8] Department of Health and Social Security (1978). Review of the Mental Health Act 1959. Cmnd. 7320. London: HMSO.

tenuous,[9] although the hybrid order does at least have the potential to make therapy a *legal* (not a covertly *pretextual*) precursor to punishment.

The hybrid order also avoids the conundrum outlined in a comment to the Model Penal Code (American Law Insitute, 1962):

> What is involved specifically is the drawing of a line between the use of public agencies and public force to condemn the offender by conviction...and modes of disposition in which that ingredient is absent, even though restraint may be involved... the problem is to discriminate between the cases where a punitive-correctional disposition is appropriate and those in which a medical-custodial disposition is the only kind which the law should allow (Model Penal Code §4.01; cited in Morris, 1982: 503).

It seems that current systems of disposal are able to blend the medical-custodial with the punitive-correctional to the extent that the two become indistinguishable, except by the location in which each occurs (hospital or prison).

Those receiving punitive-correctional disposals after attempting to plead insanity face harsher treatment than those who did not try to 'beat the rap'. In a study by Callahan, McGreevy, Cirincione and Steadman (1992), those found Guilty But Mentally Ill (GBMI; i.e. established that they were mentally disordered but were found guilty anyway) received *longer* sentences than a control sample of defendants who simply pleaded guilty; mental disorder is certainly not a mitigating factor in such instances.[10] Indeed, Silver (1995) indicates that persons found *guilty* are more likely to be released without ever having been confined than persons acquitted by reason of insanity.[11] Morris (1982) in discussing the *retroactive*

---

[9] The 'hybrid order' was partly introduced to avoid judgments such as *Fleming* (1993), 14 Cr. App. R.(s) 151 in which an offender who had previously been released by a MHRT committed homicide and was given a life sentence in spite of a hospital bed being available. This contradicted the case of *Howell* (1985), 7 Cr. App. R.(s) 360 (prison sentences should not be made to circumvent MHRT release powers); although see *R v. Merseyside MHRT and Another ex p. K* [1990] 1 All ER 694 in which the court ruled a restricted patient could not be released even though currently he was not mentally disordered (decision justified on the basis of a possible mental condition relapse). Mackay (personal communication) indicates the hybrid order has only been used once up until July 1999.

[10] For a discussion of the GBMI verdict, see Mickenberg, 1987; Finkel, 1989a. The aggravating effect upon sentence of invoking the defence parallels the situation in the UK in which the introduction of supposedly mitigatory psychiatric information in a case can be used to impose a longer than usual sentence; see Solomka (1996) and the Lord Chief Justice's statement in the case of *Pate* [1987] Crim L. R. 645 (discussed below).

[11] The acquittal of Edward Oxford for the shooting of Queen Victoria (*Reg. v. Oxford*, see *SUPRA* note 6, Ch. 2) provides an example of the perils of an insanity acquittal compared to a conviction. Oxford spent 27 years in a hospital for the criminally insane, yet 'of the three young men who discharged pistols at Queen Victoria between the years 1840-1842, Oxford was the most severely punished, and he was the only one *not* convicted of a crime' (Moran, 1986: 171). Oxford's case is indeed an excellent illustration of 'how the verdict of insanity can be made to serve the interests of the prosecution...[Oxford's] confinement demonstrates

provisions in Illinois for the state to take control of the release of any NGRI acquitted of a felony, mandating indefinite commitment up to the maximum length of time that the defendant would have been required to serve,[12] mentions 'the façade of an acquittal' (p. 525).[13]

Perlin and Dorfman (1993) cast such findings as evidence of 'sanist' attitudes (attitudes driven by the same kind of irrational, unconscious and bias-driven stereotypes exhibited in racist and sexist decision-making, that privileges information supporting a conclusion that the fact-finder wishes to reach, but subordinates information attesting to an unacceptable conclusion). Perlin (1994) sees sanist attitudes as responsible for the origin and perpetuation of insanity defence 'myths', of which he delineates eight:[14]

1. The insanity defence is overused.
2. The insanity defence is limited to murder cases.
3. There is no risk to the defendant who pleads insanity.
4. NGRIs are quickly released from custody.
5. NGRIs spend much less time in custody than do convicted defendants.
6. Defendants who plead insanity are usually faking.

---

the punitive use of the insanity verdict...And it suggests a new and different perspective on that defence' (Moran, 1986: 189).

[12] Furthermore, the 'acquittee' can be civilly committed after the expiration of detention under this legislation.

[13] The only study to reject the idea of insanity disposal as 'the psychiatric equivalent of a life sentence' (Dell, 1983: 432) is that of Mackay (1990). In his sample (n=49) of NGRIs between 1974 and 1988, two patients were released immediately by the courts and one appealed successfully against the insanity decision. Of 26 patients sent to local hospitals and Regional Secure Units, ten were released within nine months (indicating that belief in Perlin's fourth insanity myth [see below] is not totally unfounded). However, patients sent to high security hospital were not so fortunate – 50 per cent were not be released by 1991 (including cases decided in 1975, 1976 and 1977). Although Peay (1997) sees this study as proving that defence fears about long-term disposal are misplaced, Mackay (1990) notes that most of the cases were not murder trials but other non-fatal offences against the person. Clearly, insanity acquittees may still spend a lot longer in custody than offenders pleading guilty to the same charge. Release without commitment was either contrary to law or due to a successful appeal against the special verdict. Mackay and Kearns (1999) note that since the 1991 Act, 52.2 per cent of insanity acquittees have received community disposals and that 'these disposals were not used solely for minor offences...supervision and treatment orders were used for charges of attempted murder, grievous bodily harm and robbery' (p. 724). However, the existence of the mandatory hospital order for murder and that 18 of 21 hospital order patients also received a restriction order (17 without limit of time) suggests that purely therapeutic concerns do not yet reign. Figures pertaining to exact detention lengths of insanity acquittees are, however, unavailable in the UK. Steadman, Monahan, Hartstone *et al.* (1982) estimate length of stay for insanity acquittees as 23.2 months in the US.

[14] Empirical research lending support to Perlin's (1996) myths is discussed in Chapters 6, 7 and 8; see generally Hans (1986).

7. Most insanity defence trials feature 'battles of the experts'.
8. Lawyers employ the defence - perhaps inappropriately - to 'beat the rap'.

In the courtroom, these myths are given life through what Perlin (1996: 16) terms 'Ordinary Common Sense' (OCS) decision-making. OCS decisions are made with little or no knowledge of the underlying psychological issues, instead focusing on intuitive superficial issues, e.g. the defendant's behaviour in court. In legal settings, Perlin contends, everyone becomes an expert on both normal and abnormal psychology. Everyone knows what mental illness 'is', what it 'looks like' and how 'it works'. The presumption of such knowledge, together with sanism, OCS, and the teleological acceptance of social science evidence combine to produce pretextual and meretricious decisions.

Peay (1997) summarizes the dilemma facing the legal system with regard to the mentally disordered offender:

> The conflict between jurisprudential logic, which may sanction punishment and treatment for the 'culpable' mentally disordered offender, and decades of a humanitarian response endorsing a common sense preference for treatment rather than punishment, ought to be reversed in favour of the former only where treatment can be demonstrated to be wholly inappropriate (p. 692).

It is strange that punishment is viewed as the alternative if treatment is demonstrated to be inappropriate. If insanity acquittees are to be truly held equivalent with the civilly committed, then punishment cannot be a viable alternative where treatment is demonstrated to be inefficacious or inappropriate. A civilly committed patient is not subject to punishment if treatment is deemed inappropriate!

The notion of treatment going under the guise of punishment is not exclusive to the insanity acquittee, but is instead a result of the affording of excuse to any who would abdicate responsibility for their acts (or have this responsibility abdicated on their behalf):

> Those who would attribute all criminal activity to social conditions or to psychological factors beyond the criminal's power generally opt for alternatives to punishment. We still, however, will want to separate the criminals from the non-afflicted, normal members of society, so mental wards and asylums would still have a role to play in the non-punishment society...the disease and not its symptoms would be the target of the therapy and the reasons for detention. There is certainly something very appealing in what sounds like a very humane way to handle criminal offenders. But insofar as *the techniques of the asylum may be indistinguishable from the prison*, the real difference between the two approaches comes down to a matter of the description of the social intentions. The reason it is not punishment is only because our intent is not to exact an eye for an eye; rather, *it is to treat the disease even if during the treatment an eye or two is lost* (French, 1991b: 8; italics added).

The point in exculpating the insane should not be to give them treatment (if it works), as this can be accomplished without an acquittal (through a hospital order).

It is instead to avoid the usual social consequences of a conviction: blame, punishment and retribution. To punish if treatment is deemed inappropriate is to fall into the trap of sanism and pretext. In reality, where the criminal justice system acknowledges mental disorder but does not recommend a therapeutic disposal, it is likely that little or no treatment for the condition exists, such as in the case of antisocial personality disorder.[15] Judges and juries find such conditions (which tend to be associated with appraisals of dangerousness) to be a source of concern in terms of public protection, so they may recommend longer than normal sentences without special rights to treatment or procedural safeguards to which, for example, discretionary life sentence prisoners are privy (Peay, 1997). Furthermore, the practice of extending discretionary life-sentences to mentally disordered offenders in England and Wales 'could be interpreted, particularly by the offenders themselves, as *increasing* punishment on those who are mentally disordered' (Verdun-Jones, 1989: 5). In the case of *Pate* (1987),[16] the Lord Chief Justice stated that:

> This man is plainly mentally ill and represents a danger to the public. We take the view that this is a case which merits life imprisonment by reason of its gravity.

Such practices are perhaps expressive of Mackie's (1985: 215) statement that we have an 'ingrained tendency to see wrong acts as calling for penalties' – what he terms the Rule of Retaliation – and it seems that not even Lord Chief Justices are immune from this rule even when faced with a 'plainly mentally ill' person before them.

As an interim summary, UK insanity law may be a redundant artefact of a basic human compassion, the need for which has long died out; a means of pardoning the insane, in order to avoid their execution (although this consideration is still relevant in other jurisdictions with the death-penalty). The defence still endures, however, because exculpating the insane for their crimes is (as stated in Chapter 2) a fundamental principle of most criminal justice systems, reaffirming the responsibility of the majority. Whilst the principle remains intact, the spirit does not, and the insanity acquittee faces covert (and, indeed, overt) punishment. Is this punishment directed at the mentally disordered offender simply part and parcel of predominantly negative societal attitudes held toward the mentally disordered in general (e.g. Goffman, 1963)? Before discussing the specific origin

---

[15] It is, however, a myth that psychopathic disorder cannot in some cases be treated successfully (see Garrido, Estaban and Molero, 1996, for a review of treatment efficacy in psychopathic disorder). Antidepressant medication is sometimes prescribed, especially for secondary symptoms; non-compliance with such medication provides the requisite source of meta-responsibility in the case vignettes used in the experimental component of this study detailed in Part II.

[16] See *SUPRA* note 10.

of covert punishment, then, it is helpful to examine the literature on stigma and lay theories of mental disorder.

4.2 Stigma: The Mentally 'Ill' Versus the Mentally 'Disordered'

Early research into the stigmatization of the mentally disordered tended towards the conclusion that 'old people and young people, highly educated people and people with little formal training – all tend to regard the mentally ill as relatively dangerous, dirty, unpredictable and worthless' (Nunnally, 1961: 51). Sociological studies of the 1960s (using attitudinal and social-distance measures) indicated that the public viewed the mentally disordered as unpredictable, potentially violent, criminal, threatening, and fear-provoking (Cumming and Cumming, 1957; Joint Commission on Mental Illness and Health, 1961; Star, 1955). Programmes designed to counter such societal conceptions have generally attempted to reduce stigma by educating professionals and the public in terms of the liberal-scientific model of mental disorder. The 'mad' have therefore been cast as mentally 'ill' (Rabkin, 1974).

Studies into the efficacy of such programmes may be bifurcated into those optimistic or pessimistic about their success (Colombo, 1997). Optimistic studies suggested that not only were the public able to identify certain signs and symptoms of mental illness, but that this ability was associated with greater care, understanding and lowered stigma (e.g. Flew, 1985). Pessimistic studies, such as those of Sarbin and Mancuso (1970; 1972), saw attempts to educate the public in terms of the medical model as ideological and inefficacious ('improper conduct is not disease'; Sarbin and Mancusco, 1972: 1), concluding that society still rejected and stigmatized those it labelled mentally ill. One particularly significant finding amongst these studies was that of Eker (1985), who found that the respondents in his study 'perceive mental illness more and...desire more social distance in organic cases (i.e. where the 'type of cause' is described as organic) than in the psychosocial cases' (p. 246). Such attitudes could be explained by a previous study by Star (1952: 23): 'fear, distrust, suspicion and apprehension [were] derived primarily from the assumption that the person could not really be cured'.[17]

---

[17] In contrast, friends and family of mentally disordered persons (and, indeed mentally disordered persons themselves) are highly accepting of illness models of the person's condition. This is not to say that illness models do not provide adequate accounts of the condition but it is important to underline the potential teleological acceptance of models in order to placate 'moral intuitions'. The alternative for friends and family is to face the possibility that the patient is a) the cause of his/her own condition and/or b) that they themselves may have a role to play in the situation of the patient as the EP and SC models espouse. As Jones (1996: 101) states, 'to accept a medical diagnosis may free people from debilitating feelings with regard to guilt and responsibility'. Jones also found that 'Theories of organic cause were more generally, from the families' point of view, the most "morally neutral"' (p. 101). Such theories also purge any blame from the individual for his condition.

Stigma, of course, is not unique to the mentally disordered. A further class of persons whose disorder is understood within the liberal-scientific framework yet who face negative societal and legal attitudes are alcoholics.[18] Whilst the 10th edition of the International Classification of Diseases (ICD-10) lists alcoholism as a mental illness (after the research of Jellinek, 1960), Peele (1989) posits that many people who regard alcoholism as a disease also see alcoholics as *morally weak* and *personally responsible for their illness*. Although it may be 'kinder' to alcoholics to subscribe to the disease model of their affliction, 'most people still believe that only certain (morally corrupt) individuals will develop drinking problems' (Baumeister, Heatheron and Tice, 1994: 145). The law has comported with such a view in cases such as *R v. Tandy* (1989)[19] in which the court recognized the defendant's crime was due to his alcoholism, but convicted him of murder as it deemed the defendant's first drink of the day had been voluntary (a pretextual justification to emphasize culpable causation whilst ostensibly leaving subscription to the disease model intact).

Other authors acknowledge no 'disease' process to alcoholism (e.g. Fingarette, 1988) viewing it as a disorder of volition and self-control. In the same way, whilst people may ostensibly subscribe to a disease model of mental disorder (Crocetti, Spiro and Siassi, 1971; Furnham and Bower, 1992), at a deeper level many believe the mentally ill are morally deviant and merely fail to exert self-

---

However, Fisher and Farina (1979) have found that giving individuals a genetic explanation for addiction leads them to use more alcohol and other drugs than those given a social-learning explanation. Baumeister, Heatherton and Tice (1994) interpret this as due to a feeling that they lack self-control. It might be hypothesised that organic/genetic explanations of mental disorder might similarly exacerbate the patient's condition through inducing feelings of a lack of self-control and the futility of responsibility for its management through, for example, medication compliance. Sherlock (1984) states that:

> A common feature of mental illness is that those who are afflicted with it often view themselves as 'helpless' cripples in need of more help and guidance than is either necessary or desirable. They use the 'sick role' to avoid responsibility for their own situation, an avoidance made easier because of 'role expectations' attached to the label 'mental illness' (p. 499).

[18] Alcoholism is a condition that, like insanity, may give rise to criminal episodes. Like mental disorder, alcoholism is often given the status of disease in criminological literature:

> Over 50 per cent of crimes involve alcohol and drug abuse. Recent studies have shown that alcoholism is a biological disease, related to the way in which the brain metabolises alcohol due to the presence or absence of 2,3-butanediol (Jeffery, del Carmen and White, 1985: 42).

[19] *R v. Tandy* [1989] 1 WLR 350.

control over their problems (Sarbin and Mancusco, 1972).[20] For example, Hall and Tucker (1985) found a societal belief that mental disturbances could be controlled by the avoidance of morbid thoughts (this view was more predominant amongst black than white respondents).

Stigma may thus be a *function* of subscription to the medical model. To cast mental disorder in a voluntaristic capacity may be to *reduce* stigma; the mentally disordered person, if mental disorder is voluntaristic, may be seen as 'curable' (albeit by the person himself); their behaviour would not then be viewed as due to a putative organic process invulnerable to lay understanding. Such a demystification of the condition of the mentally disordered is likely to be associated with a lowering of fear and rejection, and hence stigma. As Colombo (1997: 28) states, 'the mentally disordered offender may be less stigmatized if knowledge of the mental abnormality is more positively perceived'. Medical models do not appear to engender such positive perceptions (Eker, 1985).[21] Liberal-scientific conceptions of mental disorder may actually increase stigma, especially with regard to the criminal mentally disordered.

4.3 The Aetiology of Covert Punishment

It might seem that the insanity defence is a privilege afforded to the mentally disordered that contrasts with the otherwise negative attitudes and behaviour represented by their stigmatization. Whilst the insanity defence ostensibly appears to be expressive of societal sympathy toward the mentally disordered (see Chapters 1 and 2), this chapter has shown that the associated *insanity disposal* is anything but sympathetic. The mentally disordered offender faces even greater stigma than the mentally disordered more generally:

---

[20] Such a principle might also be derived from societal notions that people have responsibility for their emotions. For example, Spackman, Belcher and Sauls (1999) in examining the murder/manslaugher distinction by jurists, have investigated 'how jurists ascertain the relative intensity of an emotion, and how emotional intensity is incorporated into jurist's "folk theories" of attribution of responsibility of emotions' (conference paper, p. 2). It seems that if jurists have folk theories of responsibility for emotions, then they are also likely to have folk theories (not necessarily overt or entering consciousness) concerning responsibility *for* mental disorder, especially for those mental disorders which are seen as due to emotional disturbance (i.e. neurotic as opposed to psychotic).

[21] This analysis also suggests that the introduction of a capacity test common to mental and physical disorder (as proposed by the Richardson expert committee) will fail to achieve one of its stated aims: to reduce stigma by portraying the equivalence of physical and mental disorder (see *SUPRA* note 3, Preface).

> Public perceptions of the criminally insane are dominated by fear of the extreme danger they are seen as possessing, and this danger is substantially greater than that posed by former mental patients who have been shown in previous studies to be highly rejected and feared individuals themselves (Steadman and Cocozza, 1977: 527).

In spite of such negative stigmatization, the McNaughton/liberal-scientific combination forbids punishment of insanity acquittees. The insanity finding entails that the crime of the defendant was a product of an illness. To punish him for the crime would be therefore to punish him for being ill. The finding in *Robinson v. California*[22] stated that being ill is itself not illegal, and that legal systems do not wish to make it so. The insanity acquittee's avoidance of criminal responsibility and consequent punishment should not therefore constitute a transgression that would incur the wrath of society and the legal system and thus engender overt punishment.

Covert punishment is, however, a different matter. The analysis presented here suggests it is a product of the socio-legal view that mentally disordered offenders are not entirely blameless in their condition. Instead, like the alcoholic, they might be viewed as weak and corrupt individuals. Evidence from attitudinal studies indeed suggests that 'lay evaluations of the mentally ill are more in line with their view of the normal offender rather than the physically sick' (Colombo, 1997: 24). Mentally disordered offenders appear to be viewed by the public as more offender than mentally disordered.

Previous analyses of covert punishment of mentally disordered offenders (e.g. Perlin, 1994) have not accommodated this possible aetiological factor of covert punishment: that mentally disordered offenders are not seen as completely blameless for their disorder, and hence their avoidance of criminal responsibility cannot be justified. This is perhaps largely due to the paucity of empirical evidence suggesting that people view the mentally disordered as, at least in part, responsible for their disorder;[23] Radden (1985) suggests quite the opposite (the 'moral intuition' that 'madness is not blameworthy'). However, the similarities between present-day disposals of the mentally disordered offender (particularly the insanity acquittee) and their covert punishment during the height of the moral model of mental disorder (Foucault, 1967) make it difficult to ignore such a model as a possible explanation of covert punishment (see Chapter 1).

If there is a covert societal feeling that mentally disordered offenders are meta-responsible through the self-causation of mental disorder, society suffers

---

[22] *SUPRA* note 31, Ch. 2.

[23] The taboo nature of the notion of mental disorder being self-caused is in no small part a cause of such a paucity of attitudinal research. Colombo (1997) states:

> Questions found in research such as...'insanity is God's punishment for some sin' – are conspicuous by their absence from more recent studies (p. 19).

from an inability to openly reflect such a construct through the insanity defence and its disposal (due to the blanket exclusion of fault which the McNaughton/liberal-scientific combination conspires to weave). A consequence of such a notion is that sanist and covertly punishing behaviour should be forestalled (or at least reduced) if the criminal justice system is given the opportunity to reflect its opinion that the mentally disordered offender is culpable for his disorder (e.g. given a meta-responsibility insanity test, detailed in Part II).

The mentally disordered may therefore face stringent penalties, going under the guise of mercy, especially when they 'circumvent justice' by the use of the insanity plea, because they are at least partly seen as the architects of their own downfall, yet the locus of their disorder at the same time falls within the realm of the liberal-scientific model and thus forbids society to censure them. Insanity defence myths, espousing that insanity acquittees have in fact 'beaten the rap', arise as an attempt to satisfy such societal and medico-legal cognitive dissonance; by asserting the exact opposite to what is true, society may justify continued retribution against just that section of society it meanwhile claims to be so lenient towards. How indeed could insanity acquittees be described as 'beating the rap' if they were unfortunates at the mercy of a disease? Society clearly does not subscribe to Aurelius' maxim that 'madness is its own punishment' (see Chapter 1).[24] A more accurate maxim might be that offered by Cohen (1940):

> If the natural desire for vengeance is not met and satisfied by the orderly procedure of the criminal law we shall revert to the more bloody private vengeance of the feud and of the vendetta (p. 987).

The analogy of the boy turning up to games with a sicknote – another medical defence like that of insanity – is again helpful (see Chapter 3). The sports teacher may impose a menial and boring task such as blackboard cleaning or litter picking (a task often *designed* to be worse than the sports lesson itself), covertly 'exacting revenge' for the pupil's invoking the 'parental defence' (and discouraging him from invoking such a defence in the future). Such punishment cannot of course be visited upon the pupil *overtly* by the sports teacher – pupils cannot be given *detentions* for being ill (paralleling the *Robinson v. California*[25] finding in an educational setting), but they can be treated as if they *were* subject to detention (through being given boring, menial tasks). Similarly, insanity acquittees cannot be punished for illness, but they can be treated as if they were subject to punishment. As Perlin (1996) states:

---

[24] The maxim suggests that there is indeed something about madness which *should* require punishment.
[25] *SUPRA* note 31, Ch. 2.

> Although modern psychiatry and psychology illuminate many of the reasons why certain criminal defendants commit 'crazy' acts, we reject such psychodynamic explanations, both on personal and justice-system levels…most strikingly, we do this even when we are faced with incontrovertible evidence that the 'successful' use of an insanity defence can lead to significantly longer terms of punishment in significantly more punitive facilities than the individual would have been subjected to had he pled guilty or been found guilty after a trial (p. 11).

Lack of statutory provision for dealing with meta-responsibility may have forced society to deal with it in more covert and sinister means. This inability legitimately to consider aspects of meta-responsibility at trial may be the root cause of our 'vindictive resentment' to insanity acquittees (Perlin, 1994: 59). Where there *is* a clearly defined aetiology for a mental disorder, a 'true' insanity acquittal may occur (as the matter of meta-responsibility becomes moot). In such cases, there is no mismatch between the constructs for which the McNaughton Rules provide, and those invoked by judges and juries (and hence no frustration due to inability to consider or reflect in deliberation that the defendant is the architect of his or her downfall). Appelbaum, Jick, Grisso, *et al.* (1993) thus find that insanity defendants with post-traumatic stress disorder (PTSD) are less likely than other NGRIs to be detained after trial (PTSD is the only disorder in DSM-IV with a clearly defined non-culpable aetiology as a component of its diagnostic criteria). In the case of an insanity defendant with PTSD, there is no violation of the commonsensical notion that exemption from criminal responsibility (and concomitant blaming and punishment) should be inextricably linked with lack of culpability for the condition that brought about such exemption (as there is no culpability for disorder in the first instance). Conversely, those contributing to their own state are less likely to receive the sympathy of the law. Beaudoin, Hodgins and Lavoie (1993) show that schizophrenics found guilty were more likely to have been alcohol/drug abusers (i.e. meta-responsible) than schizophrenics found NGRI.[26]

The existence of grave stigma towards the mentally disordered and covert punishment of the mentally disordered offender in an age where mental disorder is very much understood within a medical model (e.g. D'Arcy and Brockman, 1977) suggest that the meta-responsibility theory (espousing voluntaristic analysis of the mentally disordered state) cannot substantially worsen the socio-legal situation of the mentally disordered. Instead, the meta-responsibility theory holds the potential

---

[26] Cirincione, Steadman and McGreevy (1995) investigated factors associated with an insanity acquittal versus a guilty finding using a sample of 8,138 defendants. A finding of NGRI was associated with: 1) being female; 2) being older than 20 years; 3) having a greater number of years of formal education; 4) being married; 5) being of white ethnic origin; 6) committing a violent crime other than murder (followed by murder and then other offences); 7) victimizing a person related to the defendant; 8) having no prior arrest history; 9) not having been previously incarcerated; 10) having a major mental illness (followed by other diagnoses and then no mental illness); and 11) having a previous history of hospitalization.

to allow society to reflect commonsensical notions of justice that are frustrated by the McNaughton/liberal-scientific combination, which may in turn reduce covert punishment.

4.4 Concluding Overview

This chapter has cast ostensibly therapeutic disposals as covertly punitive. It has been questioned how such covert punishment arises, given that mental disorder is understood within a liberal-scientific framework (as an illness), which should absolve the mentally disordered for acts committed as a result of such illness. However, the straight relationship between illness and excuse does not acknowledge a 'missing link' of socio-legal attitudes toward the meta-responsibility of the mentally disordered; attitudes frustrated by the insanity defence (which makes no provision for the consideration of meta-responsibility). This study contends that a mismatch between covert attitudes and overt legal provision for the determination of criminal responsibility gives rise to sanism, pretextuality and insanity defence myths that serve to placate our cognitive dissonance concerning the defence. Such attitudes (and the liberal-scientific model's inability to accommodate them) may help explain widespread stigma still attached to the mentally disordered more generally.

It is therefore suggested that the introduction of meta-responsibility into insanity defence law may paradoxically improve the miserable socio-legal situation of the mentally disordered. Chapter 5 will examine psychological and socio-legal research having a bearing on such a hypothesis and the meta-responsibility theory more generally.

Chapter 5

Psychological and Socio-legal Research with a Bearing on the Meta-responsibility Theory

I have been made to learn that the doom and burden of our life is bound forever on man's shoulders, and when the attempt is made to cast it off, it but returns upon us with more unfamiliar and awkward pressure.

Robert Louis Stevenson, Dr. Jekyll and Mr. Hyde

This chapter examines social psychological and socio-legal research with a bearing on meta-responsibility. Such research has typically examined: 1) how mock jurors react to information concerning culpability for incapacity; and 2) how such notions might be operationalized within the criminal law. The mock juror research genre provides the focus of this chapter as it is a mock juror study that constitutes the experimental work on the meta-responsibility theory detailed in Part II of this book (Chapters 6, 7 and 8).

5.1 Social-Psychological and Mock Juror Research

Research into causality and attribution theory (derived from both legal and social psychological frameworks; Hart and Honore, 1959; Heider, 1958) suggests that people are rarely held responsible for an event merely by a temporal or geographical contiguity with that event; an element of causal influence must exist for proper ascription of blame and responsibility. Feinberg's (1970) 'stain criterion' of causal attribution builds upon the traditional 'presence versus absence' causal models of Hume (1739/1978), Mill (1843/1967) and Kelley (1967). The stain criterion represents our desire to 'pin the blame' on an actor for a negative outcome as an expression of our indignation, as a method of retribution, or a 'stain' to beware the self and others of the actor.

Alicke (1992) presents evidence confirming the model's prediction that causal judgments may be conflated with ascriptions of blameworthiness; an actor is cited more frequently as the cause of an accident when his reason for speeding is to hide drugs than to hide a gift. Alicke (1992: 368) dubs this process 'culpable causation'.[1]

Ellsworth, Bukaty, Cowan and Thompson (1984) suggest such negative social evaluations may be forestalled if the actor's behaviour was influenced by mental or physical incapacity. Alicke (1990: 651) refers to the mental and physical abilities required to exert control of behaviour as 'capacity control'.[2] An actor may possess a degree of responsibility for the *development* of incapacity ('capacity-development responsibility'; CDR), and for the manner in which incapacity is *activated* in a situation ('capacity-activation responsibility'; CAR) (Alicke and Davis, 1990). CDR is particularly relevant to meta-responsibility (in terms of the generation or exacerbation of mental disorder). CAR is more relevant to traditional notions of criminal responsibility, which examine whether the mentally disordered offender can do otherwise with regard to *criminal acts*, rather than precipitant disorders. However, CAR may be relevant to meta-responsibility where, for example, 'epistemic duties' fall upon the mentally disordered to avoid activation of their incapacity (see Chapter 3).

The CDR/CAR may be applied to meta-responsibility thus. A person may be culpable for causing his disorder in the first instance (CDR; e.g. psychotic relapse through medication non-compliance). Although knowing he becomes paranoid around his ex-wife, he visits her whilst drunk and ends up assaulting her. The drinking episode and subsequent events constitute the CAR. However, in many cases the CDR/CAR distinction may be blurred, too simplified, or non-existent; it might be posited that medication non-compliance in fact represents the CAR. The meta-responsibility theory avoids such logical difficulties by providing for higher-order determinations involving *n*-level meta-responsibility determinations to reflect causal chains (see Chapter 3).

Finkel and Slobogin (1995) do not consider the CDR/CAR distinction in examining whether mock jurors assess culpability for bringing about mental disorder in insanity cases.[3] Their case vignettes included the following culpability

---

[1] Culpable causation in the sense that Alicke uses it here is not used in the same sense as the culpable causation of mental disorder, which simply refers to the notion that a person may cause (i.e. be culpable for) the genesis of mental disorder. However, Alicke's study would suggest that those exhibiting purposive meta-responsibility would be judged more harshly (or as having caused their disorder to a greater degree) than those exhibiting consensual meta-responsibility, as they are more morally blameworthy.

[2] Capacity control builds upon the notion of capacity responsibility (Hart, 1968; see SUPRA note 1, Ch. 1).

[3] Cirincione (1996) surveyed 7,299 insanity cases in seven U.S. states and found that only 14.4 per cent involved a jury trial (of which only 16.1 per cent led to an acquittal). It might thus be argued that mock juror experiments are largely irrelevant to insanity defence decision-making. However, this would be to ignore the special status of insanity cases tried before juries. For example, the 14.4 per cent are likely to include 'flagship' cases with greater contest of the defendant's mental condition, involve serious crimes (especially

manipulations: 1) refusing to seek therapy when it was strongly suggested; 2) refusing to take medication; 3) refusing to keep outpatient therapy appointments, even after the doctor strongly urges continuing them; 4) ignoring urgings to get help; 5) drinking before the criminal act; 6) drinking to calm down, and then drinking some more; and 7) taking some pills that were not prescribed. This *culpability* variable was a between-subjects variable with two levels (*with* or *without*). Each subject rendered a verdict on seven cases,[4] incorporating one of four insanity tests: QSJ (Quasisubjective insanity test based on justificatory defences of self-defence, provocation and duress); FINKEL (Finkel's Relative Culpability Schema [Finkel, 1988] which takes into account mental disability at the time of the act, degree of culpability for bringing about the mental disorder, and traditional *mens rea*); ALI (American Law Institute Model Penal Code test, with a volitional prong);[5] and IDRA (Insanity Defence Reform Act 1984, a restrictive version of the McNaughton Rules).[6] Some subjects received a *no instruction* condition in which no explicit insanity test instructions were given. Finkel's test (providing for reflection of culpability for disorder) was the only test to register the *culpability* variable (in the *with* condition, guilty verdicts of murder and manslaughter increase to the exclusion of not guilty and NGRI verdicts). The other tests failed to register an interaction effect with the *culpability* variable.

However, subjects in the *no instruction* condition *did* register culpability distinctions. It seems, therefore, that traditional insanity tests may distract jurors from considerations that they would otherwise introduce into their decision-making (culpability for disorder). Finkel (1991) shows that FINKEL (making provision for the consideration of culpability for disorder) produces verdicts more internally consistent with subjects' reasons for their verdicts and general culpability ratings. These results suggest that meta-responsibility is a commonsensical construct that

---

greatest potential for pretextual and sanist decisions). It is this small proportion of cases that perpetuates a large proportion of insanity defence myths and stereotypes of the mentally disordered due to, for example, selective reporting (Angermeyer and Matschinger, 1996). The judgments and attitudes of mock jurors thus represent a useful body of academic knowledge, subject to their methodological limitations and generalizability to the real world. These limitations will be discussed at greater length in Chapter 6.

[4] The following is an example of a case vignette used by Finkel and Slobogin (1995):

> Jacobs is a policeman, who killed a person he had just arrested. Three psychiatrists testify that he committed the crime as a result of an unconscious desire to be punished for his failure to be at home two years earlier, when his wife and small daughter were brutally murdered. There are a string of incidents to illustrate chronic depression, threats of suicide, bizarre behaviour, and bursts of anger. Jacobs, after the shooting, surrenders to his partner, saying 'I don't know why I did it' (p. 453).

[5] See *SUPRA* note 28, Ch. 2.

[6] See *SUPRA* note 28, Ch. 2.

jurors would address in insanity defence decision-making, were provision made for its consideration.

Finkel and Handel (1989) show the importance of a construct related to meta-responsibility in accounting for the variance in juror decisions. Jurors invoked 3.2 constructs per case for NGRI verdicts and 3.0 constructs for guilty verdicts. Two of these accounted for 62 per cent of the variance in the proportion of defendants found NGRI: capacity or incapacity to make choices, and culpability (relating to negligent or reckless actions before the crime). Finkel (1995: 292) indicates that this 'culpable-actions' factor is also 'common to situations that have little to do with insanity *per se*, indicating that this culpability judgment is commonplace and widespread'. Consideration of culpability for disorder might therefore 'spill over' into general attitudes toward the mentally disordered (with regard to stigma discussed in Chapter 4), as well as to other moral and causal judgments.

If experiments show that different insanity tests make little or no difference to the outcomes of jurors' decisions (e.g. Simon, 1967), then a reasonable explanation might be that such tests fail to register aspects of culpability that jurors find important, e.g. meta-responsibility. If a culpable actions factor is indeed widespread and commonplace to human moral and causal judgments, then its exclusion from insanity tests gives cause for concern, as 'responsibility ascription as the foundation of blaming gives us the robust social world in which we live' (French, 1991b: 15). If current insanity tests do not provide for proper responsibility ascription, covert punishment may assume such a role.

5.2 Legal Research

5.2.1 Fingarette and Hasse's Disability of Mind Doctrine

Finkel's investigations of culpability judgments stem from the socio-legal research of Fingarette, particularly the 'Disability of Mind' (DOM) doctrine (Fingarette and Hasse, 1979). DOM refers to a mental incapacity, for which there may be culpability. The doctrine is designed to deal with the following problem, central to this study.

> 'How can it be', the public may ask and the press may editorialize, 'that a defendant who should have and could have prevented his mental health deteriorating to the point of disability of mind, was found 'not guilty' for the subsequent crime that resulted?' (Finkel, 1988: 288).

The authors suggest that juries should be given the legal machinery to placate such concerns: after determining guilt or innocence to the charge, a determination of disability of mind and its culpability should be made. There are four DOM verdicts: non-culpable DOM, culpable DOM, non-culpable partial DOM, and culpable partial DOM. Finkel (1988) adds *partial culpability* for bringing about the DOM, making six verdicts (excluding a finding of no DOM, negating questions concerning culpability).

Table 5.1 Possible verdicts under Finkel's (1988) modification of Fingarette and Hasse's (1979) DOM doctrine with suggested levels of excuse or mitigation

DOM verdict	Culpability? (for DOM)	Final verdict	Suggested level of excuse/ mitigation*
Full DOM	Yes	Culpable full DOM	3
	Partial	Partially culpable full DOM	4
	No	Non-culpable full DOM	5
Partial DOM	Yes	Culpable partial DOM	1
	Partial	Partially culpable partial DOM	2
	No	Non-culpable partial DOM	3
No DOM	N/A	No DOM	0

*(0=none, 1=low, 4=high, 5=total)

Fingarette and Hasse (1979) suggest that culpability for the DOM may be established in three ways: 1) the defendant caused the disability or failed to take reasonable precautions to prevent it; 2) recklessness in the context of the DOM's origin; and 3) intent in the context of origin of the DOM.

Variants 1) and 2) are generally applicable to consensual meta-responsibility. Variant 3) is loosely referent to purposive meta-responsibility, e.g. where medication non-compliance is goal-directed towards the mentally disordered state. Variant 3) also provides for 'grand-schemer' defendants (e.g. 'Dutch courage').[7] Fingarette and Hasse (1979) propose extending the common law principle of criminal negligence to cover cases with less obvious intent: a defendant who is culpably mentally disordered (one who deviates from a reasonable standard of care) would be allowed an insanity defence but found guilty of a 'floor' offence of criminal negligence. Fingarette and Hasse see this as preferable to 'cheating' justice on the grounds of absence of *mens rea*.

Perhaps the major difficulty with the bifurcated trial process[8] that Fingarette and Hasse suggest is that presence or absence of a DOM (as well as consideration

[7] See *A-G for Northern Ireland v. Gallagher* [1963] AC 349.

[8] Finkel (1988) suggests a *trifurcation* of the trial (three distinct phases). The first phase (*actus reus* phase), adheres to a purely behavioural definition of *actus reus*. In the second phase (*mens* phase), the presence/absence of a DOM, and its gradation (partial/total) would be decided. If the DOM is deemed total, then the trial proceeds to a culpability phase, in

of any culpability for bringing about the DOM) cannot be considered independently of the issue of guilt or innocence; *actus reus* cannot equal guilt without *mens rea*.[9] In the insanity case of *People v. Hernandez* (2000),[10] it was stated that:

> Although guilt and sanity are separate issues, the evidence as to each may be overlapping. Thus, at the guilt phase, a defendant may present evidence to show that he or she lacked the mental state required to commit the charged crime.

Fingarette and Hasse's (1979) jury instructions do not adhere to such a principle:

> The defendant has entered a plea of disability of mind. Before you take up this issue at all, you should have completed your consideration of the proof as to each count, and you should have determined, in regard to each, whether the defendant is Guilty or Not Guilty (p. 264).

Even if the second phase found the defendant to have a non-culpable full DOM, the verdict would look very much like GBMI, in spite of the authors' caution that such a finding should be non-accusatory:

> Where a jury finds full Disability of Mind that is non-culpable in origin, this finding amounts to a finding of complete lack of criminal responsibility. It entails that even though the alleged act was proved, no criminal condemnation or punishment is warranted, and that the social problem posed should be resolved in a suitable nonaccusatory process (Fingarette and Hasse, 1979: 209).

Such non-accusatory processes are also inconsistent with guilt as to a 'floor' offence of criminal negligence for partially or fully culpable DOMs; a defendant might be found NGRI, but guilty of criminal negligence. This finding might be labelled Not Guilty by Reason of Insanity But Guilty of Being Not Guilty by Reason of Insanity.

That the DOM doctrine may be used to prove prior fault in cases of insanity is also excluded by Fingarette and Hasse (1979):

---

which culpability for the DOM is assessed. A finding of partial or no DOM elicits a *mens rea* phase (in which intent, etc. would be decided).

[9] Whilst disposal is of course likely to be of primary importance to the insanity acquittee (and perhaps foremost in his decision to plead NGRI in the first instance), one of the important consequences of being found insane by a criminal court of law should be the label 'not guilty'. Gibbons, Mulryan and O'Connor (1997), discussing the Irish 'Guilty but Insane' (GBI) verdict, incorrectly describe those receiving the verdict as 'insanity acquittees' (p. 467).

[10] *People v. Hernandez* (2000), 22 Cal. 4th 512.

> Verdicts reporting 'Nonculpable Disability of Mind' would appear in the types of cases where at present the defence successfully establishes either *Insanity*, or *Unconsciousness*, or *Automatism*, or *Involuntariness* (when due to mental derangement) (p. 252).

Through failing to consider culpability in verdicts currently reported as NGRI, the DOM doctrine itself becomes smothered under the very blanket exclusion of fault it wished to avoid. The authors see intoxication, substance abuse, etc. as falling under the remit of the culpability phase of the trial, but not major mental disorders, e.g. schizophrenia and depression (for which there may be meta-responsibility; see Chapter 3).

5.2.2 Robinson's Doctrine of Separate Liability

If the DOM doctrine's consideration of meta-responsibility is flawed, another method might be through the doctrine of transferred intent (Katz, 1987) that applies when a defendant has culpability with regard to a 'bad' event through attempting to bring about a different 'bad' event. However, developing mental disorder is not in itself an illegal ('bad') act. It is not therefore viable to transfer intent from the development of mental disorder (where there is purposive meta-responsibility) to a crime committed under its influence (as in an assassin killing a bystander mistaking him for his target, or in a conviction for felony-murder in US jurisdictions).[11] There is, quite simply, no *mens rea* to transfer. However, we *can* say that a person may have been reckless or negligent in developing his mental disorder, just as a person may have been reckless, negligent or intentional in getting drunk (Sherlock, 1984); being drunk, like mental disorder, is not in itself an illegal act. In neither case should the defendant be allowed to rely on their recklessly caused incapacity, as he has effectively caused the conditions of his own defence.

Robinson (1985) lists six ways with which causing the conditions of one's own defence is currently dealt: 1) withholding a defence upon any causal contribution; 2) withholding a defence upon a minimum culpability as to causing the defence conditions; 3) imposing reduced liability upon a minimum culpability as to causing the defence conditions; 4) imposing a degree of liability corresponding to the level of culpability as to causing the defence conditions; 5) inconsistent approaches within the same jurisdiction; and 6) no consideration of culpability with regard to the defence causing conditions. Such provisions cut across excusatory and justificatory defences, e.g. self-defence, intoxication, necessity, duress, etc.

Robinson's suggestion for reform permits the defence for the offence in question, but separately imposes liability for the defendant's earlier culpable

---

[11] See *INFRA* note 10, Ch. 9.

conduct. Such an analysis treats the defendant as an 'innocent actor' who was caused to engage in criminal conduct by the actor's prior, culpable actions.

The major problem with Robinson's suggestion, as with the DOM doctrine, is that through punishing the actor based on his initial conduct in causing his defence conditions, we are specifically punishing otherwise blameless conduct (undercutting the purpose and credibility of the criminal justice system). Is it right to punish an act that, *per se,* is not illegal? Would such liability require a culpable state of mind with regard to the eventual offence when developing the incapacity (e.g. 'Dutch courage')? Robinson's doctrine thus falls foul of the same hurdle as the DOM doctrine: conduct that is essentially nonculpable of itself (being mentally disordered) would be punished, and the verdict would essentially be one of 'Not Guilty by Reason of *x*, *y*, or *z* But Guilty of Being Not Guilty By Reason of *x*, *y* or *z*' (where, for example, *x*, *y* and *z* represent duress, self-defence and insanity). Applying the principle to intoxication would permit a voluntary intoxication defence, but punish the defendant for being drunk. The meta-responsibility theory does not fall foul of such inconsistencies through advocating the denial of the defence of which the defendant had culpably caused the conditions (as is the current legal situation with regard to voluntary intoxication; see Chapter 2).[12]

A further difficulty in operationalizing Robinson's doctrine is giving definition to 'earlier' conduct; how far should we look back in history to find prior fault? Immediately preceding the offence? To childhood? In many cases it may be impossible to delineate clearly a causal chain (as with Alicke's CDR/CAR distinctions). However, Finkel (1988) concludes that any time limit imposed upon such a 'historical search' would be 'arbitrary; worse, limits run counter to the spirit of scientific inquiry that demands free reign to pursue the causative thread no matter how far back it goes' (p. 302).

Such a search is illustrated in the case of *State v. Gooze* (1951).[13] The defendant ran over a pedestrian during a blackout from Ménière's Syndrome. The court reasoned 'while one cannot be liable for what one does during the unconsciousness of sleep, he is responsible for allowing himself to go to sleep'. The unconsciousness of sleep might be dubbed a *proximal cause*, whereas driving whilst knowing the potential outcome might be termed a *distal cause*. The distal cause constitutes the defendant's culpability in such a case, but exactly *how distal* a distal cause can be whilst still retaining a valid role in the causal chain (to say nothing of its *degree* of contribution to the proximal cause) has long been problematic for criminal and tort law (Katz, 1987).

Robinson's doctrine is difficult to operationalize for the mentally disordered offender. The person going to sleep at the wheel of his car seems to warrant punishment, as does the person who starts a fight and kills someone in self-defence. The mentally disordered offender seems less punishable (even if his mental disorder is culpable), especially if he is still substantially disordered at trial.

---

[12] See the meta-responsibility insanity test (MRIT) presented in Part II of this study.

[13] *State v. Gooze* (1951), 81 A.2d 811.

To punish him for the legal conduct of becoming mentally disordered *per se* (through a floor offence of criminal negligence) would prove an even greater conundrum. The possibilities for disposal of the meta-responsible offender will be discussed in Chapter 9, but suffice it to say meta-responsibility does not entail punishment; indeed, this study suggests that conceptions of meta-responsibility may *forestall* covert punishment.

There is clear need for a thorough appraisal of inconsistencies in the consideration of causing the conditions of one's own defence, cutting across defences such as provocation, duress, self-defence and insanity. However, the special conditions of insanity dictate that it should not be forced simply to 'fit in' with doctrines and statutory provisions that seem to make sense when applied to a variety of justificatory and excusatory defences, e.g. the doctrine of separate liability. Robinson (1985: 26) claims that 'a single general principle would assure a consistent approach to different defences'. Similarly, Peay (1997: 696) calls for a 'pluralistic model of the criminal justice system' and objects to 'piecemeal tinkering' in spite of placing particular emphasis on the fallacy of the mentally disordered as a homogenous group. The *special* verdict is so named for a reason: it is a flagship defence (a status unrelated to the frequency of its use) reflective of fundamental principles of the criminal justice system and morality more generally. Such status should be rewarded with special provision; it should not be lumped in with blanket judicial reform as an afterthought.[14] Whilst principles cutting across various defences might be applied to insanity (e.g. highlighting the inconsistency between the law's manner of dealing with voluntarily intoxicated and voluntarily mentally disordered offenders), it is clear that if good theory is to be translated into workable law (and if we are indeed inclined to show sympathy to the insane) then provision for meta-responsibility should not be sacrificed to convenience and an ill-judged desire for consistency. To this end, a meta-responsibility insanity test is presented in the next chapter.

5.3 Concluding Overview

This chapter has reviewed social psychological and legal research that has a bearing on meta-responsibility. Meta-responsibility may be an often-used construct in legal decision-making and other social situations more generally. This

[14] Indeed, the McNaughton Rules were originally designed to be consistent with the excuse of self-defence. When the 15 judges were asked by the House of Lords as to whether a person acting under an insane delusion could be excused, Tindal CJ's answer was 'We think he must be considered in the same situation to responsibility as if the facts were real. For example, if under the influence of his delusion he supposes another man to be in the act of taking away his life, and he kills that man, as he supposes, in self-defence, he would be exempt from punishment' (West and Walk, 1977: 79). The McNaughton Rules are a sure testament to the failure of a consistent approach to satisfy the needs of workable criminal law.

suggests the criminal law would do well to provide for meta-responsibility considerations in the insanity defence. However, the proposals for reform put forward by various authors suffer from problems of theory and implementation, most notably through their inappropriate imposition on a variety of mental condition and other legal defences. The punishment of mentally disordered offenders for criminal negligence or separate liability is a further limitation of such proposals, going against the humane treatment and disposal of mentally disordered offenders within the criminal justice system.

The second part of this book extends the socio-legal research examined in this chapter through experimental work that examines reactions of mock jurors to meta-responsibility information. The study presented in Part II uses a meta-responsibility insanity test (MRIT) that denies the defence of insanity to those being reckless with medication or knowingly contributing to their abnormal state of mind. It might be argued that such a test, by encouraging guilty verdicts for such defendants, also falls foul of the problem of punishing the mentally disordered. However, by avoiding a finding of 'Not Guilty by Reason of Insanity But Guilty of Being Not Guilty by Reason of Insanity', the MRIT imputes culpability only for the crime in question. Unlike the proposals for reform described in this chapter, the MRIT does not punish otherwise legal conduct, leaving sentencing or disposal to the court's discretion.

Chapter 6 details previous research in the mock juror research genre, and details the methodology of the present experimental research. Chapter 7 presents an analysis of the quantitative results of the study, and Chapter 8 discusses the results with reference to qualitative analysis of subjects' reasons for their insanity verdicts. Finally, Chapter 9 examines methodological limitations of the present research, examines potential directions for future research into the meta-responsibility theory, and concludes the study by examining whether the meta-responsibility theory is a viable birth.

PART II
AN EXPERIMENTAL INVESTIGATION INTO THE THEORY OF META-RESPONSIBILITY

Chapter 6

A Mock Juror Study of the Meta-responsibility Theory: Methodology

This chapter details the methodology of a study designed to investigate reactions of mock jurors to meta-responsibility information within insanity defence case vignettes.[1]

6.1 Previous Mock Juror and Attitudinal Research on the Insanity Defence

Trial by a jury composed of the defendant's peers has been a feature of the law at least since ancient Greek society; Hastie, Penrod and Pennington (1983) relate that over five hundred jurors sat at Socrates trial. Anglo-Saxon civil law made provision for a case to be settled by a group composed equally of the claimant's and defendant's friends. Aside from a few wayward attempts at reform (most notably the Norman system of trial by battle, the disputants usually hiring 'champions' to represent them on the battlefield), the system has remained a

---

[1] The possibilities for empirical research into aspects of the meta-responsibility theory were many-fold. Some areas considered were:

1) Examination of court transcripts or real cases in order to examine notions of meta-responsibility in medico-legal testimony and decision-making.
2) Examination of NGRI or other patient case-files to examine information concerning meta-responsibility (see SUPRA note 11, Ch. 3) e.g. relation of length of detention to the defendant's level of meta-responsibility.
3) Interview or questionnaire schedules administered to psychiatric staff/judges/criminal lawyers/magistrates, to determine inter-agency attitudes toward meta-responsibility.
4) Interviews with NGRIs or other forensic populations to examine self-reports of issues of concern to the meta-responsibility theory, e.g. subjective experience of benefit of being mentally disordered, medication non-compliance, etc.

It was felt, for reasons discussed below, that the meta-responsibility theory would best be served by a mock juror study, principally due to: 1) the need for a basic exploratory study; 2) comparability with previous insanity defence research; and 3) project constraints upon finances, time and space.

cornerstone of Anglo-American criminal law, alternately praised and berated by jurists, laypersons and academics. Juries have been described as both 'extraordinarily right in their conclusion[s]' (Nitzer, 1978: 359) and as composed of 'twelve men of average ignorance' (Williams, 1963: 271).

The jury trial has provided a pregnant research topic for social psychologists, due to 1) the empirical feasibility of jury research; 2) the applied nature of jury research; 3) the climate of constructive legal criticism through social science investigation; 4) the richness and relevance of material of psychological interest in the courts; and 5) the use of the jury paradigm as a 'test-bed' for psychological theories (Sealy, 1979).

However, since access by the public or researchers to jury deliberations remains illegal in the UK and US (Katz, 1972), and even the identity of jurors is protected in the UK, researchers have turned to *simulation experiments* to examine jury decision-making (e.g. Weld and Roff, 1938; Kalven and Zeisel, 1966; Simon, 1967). Experiments with the greatest external validity (i.e. most accurately simulate decision-making by real jurors and juries) are likely to be those conducted using representative samples of jury-eligible participants in natural settings (i.e. courtrooms), observing full-scale mock trials (Hans and Vidmar, 1986). However, constraints upon time and finances available for such experiments has resulted in the following methodological compromises: 1) the use of short video, audio or written trial materials (e.g. Simon, 1967; Finkel and Slobogin, 1995); 2) the use of student subjects (Bray and Kerr [1982] find that only 12.5 per cent of mock jury studies used jury pool participants); 3) the use of non-natural experimental settings (e.g. classrooms and laboratories); and 4) the abandonment of procedural elements (*voir dire*, opening statements, testimony, etc.). Researchers using the mock juror paradigm as a test-bed for psychological theories, whilst using trial case vignettes, have largely abandoned jury deliberation as a methodological component where individual responses provide the focus of study (e.g. Ellsworth *et al.*, 1984; Finkel, 1991, 1995; Finkel and Handel, 1989; Finkel and Slobogin, 1995; Hans, 1986; Poulson, Wuensch, Brown and Braithwaite, 1997; Poulson, Brondino, Brown and Braithwaite, 1998). Whilst Hastie *et al.* (1983) point out the tenuous external validity of such laboratory studies, they accept their utility:

> [as] the major goal of psychological researchers is to evaluate abstract theories and hypotheses concerning human behaviour…it is sensible to choose or create research settings to maximize the exploration of theoretical issues with little or no consideration of their application to important natural research settings (p. 41).

Such methodology (using the trial as a 'psychological stimulus') has particular relevance to insanity defence research, as only a small proportion of insanity cases are decided by a jury (Cirincione, 1996).[2] It is likely, therefore, to be *individual* opinions that determine the success of many insanity pleas and associated disposal, particularly those of judges, lawyers and psychiatrists. Whilst

---

[2] See *SUPRA* note 3, Ch. 5.

artificial mock juror studies tend only to be identified with more externally valid experiments due to their use of a legal case as stimulus material and the nature of response categories (guilty, not guilty, etc.), their object of research tends not to be real-life jury decision-making and few claims are made as their external validity. They do, however, allow for better control of: 1) experimenter effects (e.g. Rosenthal, 1966); 2) social contamination and desirability effects (which are particularly apparent in studies of attitudes toward the mentally disordered; Bord, 1971); 3) type and quality of response data (e.g. quantitative rather than qualitative); and 4) allocation of subjects to experimental conditions (thus maintaining internal validity). Laboratory studies are also economical in terms of time and finance. Such an 'unnatural' experiment was therefore felt to best serve the fledgling meta-responsibility theory.

Research using mock juror experiments has tended to focus on: 1) decision-making processes of mock jurors (e.g. algebraic, stochastic and narrative models of decision-making; Hastie, 1993); 2) optimal jury size and majority/unanimous requirements (e.g. Davis, Kerr, Atkins *et al.*, 1976); 3) the effect of manipulated trial variables on decision outcomes (e.g. type of insanity test [Simon, 1967], pretrial processes [Walker and Thibault, 1971]); and 4) demographic/attitudinal predictors of verdict (e.g. Ellsworth, 1993).

Of these areas of investigation, the latter two (manipulated trial variables and attitudinal predictors of verdict) are of particular interest to the meta-responsibility theory. Some of the studies which have focused on insanity defence decision-making have been described in the first part of this study (Chapter 5) where relevant to meta-responsibility; studies that are methodologically relevant are described in this chapter.

The seminal insanity defence study conducted by Simon (1967) involved over one thousand subjects drawn from jury pools. Subjects (in jury panels of twelve with full deliberation) listened to an audiotaped housebreaking or incest trial, and rendered a verdict using either *McNaughton* or *Durham* insanity tests, or no test at all. Jurors using the 'liberal' *Durham* criteria were only 12 per cent[3] more likely to find defendants NGRI than those using *McNaughton* (the *no instruction* condition elicited approximately the same proportion of NGRI verdicts as *Durham*).[4] Differences in expert testimony (actual expert testimony that had been presented at the real trials on which the scenarios were based, versus 'model' expert testimony composed in discussion with courtroom-experienced psychiatrists) did not have a significant impact on verdict. Jurors with lower levels of education rendered a greater proportion of NGRI verdicts, and jurors of black racial categorization were more likely to find the defendant NGRI.

However, no differences in proportions of verdict by gender were found, and attitudinal dimensions (attitudes towards the mentally ill, attitudes towards sexual

---

[3] Jury (rather than individual juror) decisions increased this proportion to 19 per cent.

[4] Similarly, Ogloff (1991) finds that McNaughton and ALI insanity test standards do not have an impact on verdict in his sample of 177 student mock jurors.

expression, and knowledge and attitudes concerning psychiatry) had no relationship to verdict. Saks and Hastie (1978: 70) cast such results as evidence that 'jurors are much more responsive to the evidence placed before them than to their own personalities and attitudes'. Similarly, the LSE Jury Project found that personality characteristics of jurors and their verdicts were almost completely uncorrelated, even under different methods of test scoring using factor scores across a diverse range of tests such as introversion-extraversion and measures of authoritarian, dogmatic and rigid personality structures (Sealy, 1975). However, if jurors really *were* objective fact finders influenced only by external evidentiary factors and immune to internal processes, we would expect unanimous panel decisions to be reached even before deliberation; in reality, this very rarely happens (Kalven and Zeisel, 1966). It would seem individual differences are at work in decision-making *somewhere.*

Other researchers have therefore attempted to investigate further the seemingly null relationship between attitudes and insanity verdicts. Ellsworth *et al.* (1984) presented written case vignettes to subjects (persons eligible for jury duty in California) involving an insanity plea in a homicide case. Subjects received a case detailing either a 'nonorganic' mental disability (schizophrenia) or an 'organic' disability (mental retardation or psychomotor epilepsy). Subjects were classified according to their views concerning the death penalty: those that were sufficiently opposed to the death penalty to void their participation as jurors in capital cases, or those who would be able to serve on such a jury due to their open views concerning the death penalty ('death-qualified' jurors). Death penalty attitudes have a powerful relationship with other crime control attitudes, appearing to be 'flagship' beliefs that are ideologically expressive of a person's self-image of his/her stance toward crime and corrections, and appear to be associated with a mistrust of the insanity defence (Vidmar and Ellsworth, 1974). Death-opposed jurors rendered a similar proportion of NGRI verdicts in each of the vignettes; type of mental disorder appeared unimportant to their verdicts. However, death-qualified jurors were much more likely to convict schizophrenic defendants than those with organic mental disabilities. They estimated that only 31 per cent of persons pleading NGRI are 'really' insane, contrasting with 56 per cent of death-opposed jurors. The authors concluded that death-qualified subjects were concerned that schizophrenic defendants might be faking their problems, whereas this concern did not generalize to organic defendants as there could be no doubt about malingering or the severity of their problems. In contrast, death-opposed jurors do not seem to differentiate between non-organic and organic mental disorders in this manner; the proportion of NGRI verdicts rendered did not differ significantly across conditions.

Other experimenters have also found death penalty attitudes to be predictive of insanity verdict outcome. Poulson *et al.* (1997) found that mock jurors (students) who favour the death penalty are more accepting of the prosecution's expert testimony, less prepared to endorse the crime as a result of the defendant's mental illness, and hold more negative attitudes to the insanity defence; moreover, they were significantly less likely to find a fictional defendant NGRI. Poulson *et al.* (1998), again using students, indicate that such verdict patterns are mediated by an interaction between these attitudes and the jurors' evaluations of the defendant's mental state, rather than being direct products of pre-existing attitudes *per se*.

Skeem and Golding (1999) stress the importance of individual prototypes of insanity in insanity defence decision-making. In 133 former venirepersons (former prospective jurors) they distinguished three exclusive prototypes of insanity using cluster analysis. A 'severe mental disability' prototype was held by 47 per cent of subjects, which entailed that the insane defendant should be afflicted with extreme, chronic, uncontrollable, mental disability that impairs ability to function in society (a prototype that seems to 'remain wed to the Wild Beast test of 1724'; Perlin, 1997: 1379). Thirty-two percent of subjects (and 65 per cent of women subjects) held a 'moral insanity' prototype, which 'conflates psychopathy and psychosis to represent a malevolent, detached, irrational, unpredictably violent offender' (Skeem and Golding, 1999; conference paper, p. 5). The third prototype, 'mental state centred', was held by 21 per cent of jurors (the majority of whom were male and highly educated) and conforms to legal notions of insanity: that insane defendants should be afflicted exclusively with impairments in mental state at the time of the offence that are supported by expert evidence. This group was significantly more likely to deem a fictional defendant NGRI than the severe mental disability and moral insanity groups, who did not differ significantly from each other in the proportion of NGRI verdicts rendered.

Attitudes toward the insanity defence and related issues have also provided the focus of descriptive studies (rather than experiments), and have therefore not been proved *predictive* of verdict. Hans and Slater (1984) delineated seven common lay definitions of legal insanity in a random sample of 434 Delaware residents asked about the Hinckley case and other issues. Only one subject gave a definition that closely approximated the Model Penal Code test for insanity in operation in Delaware at the time (which included the notions of product of mental disease or defect, lacking substantial capacity to appreciate the wrongfulness of conduct, or being unable to conform conduct to legal requirements). The seven most commonly offered definitions were: 1) *Don't know what you're doing* (23 per cent of respondents) involving constructs such as 'can't comprehend or think rationally', or 'someone who loses their mind, can't think at all'; 2) *Having no control* (12.8 per cent) – 'not being able to command faculties', 'out of control'; 3) *Cannot tell right from wrong* (12.3 per cent) – 'moral self loses it', 'don't know right from wrong'; 4) *Colloquial expressions* (6 per cent) – 'crazed', ' a real nut', 'misfits', 'doesn't have all his marbles'; 5) *Not responsible* (4.6 per cent) – 'not responsible for self', 'not responsible for actions'; 6) *Mental disease* (3.9 per cent) – 'something wrong with the mind', 'sick in the head', 'mental illness'; and 7) *Other* (18.8 per cent) – 'cannot cope with society's rules', 'anyone who commits such a crime is insane', 'no such thing as insanity', 'a gimmick to get away with your actions', 'dangerous to others'. In addition, two-thirds of the sample agreed with the statement 'the insanity defence is a loophole'.

Hans (1986) more closely investigated attitudes toward the insanity defence that relate to Perlin's (1996) myths about the insanity defence, using an Attitudes Towards the Insanity Defence scale. A survey among randomly selected residents of a Delaware county examined support for the insanity defence, attitudes toward the insanity defence, and estimates of insanity plea usage. The study also measured legal attitudes (using the Legal Attitudes Questionnaire; Brodsky and Smitherman, 1983), authoritarianism of subjects (using the Right Wing Authoritarianism scale; Altermeyer, 1981), fear of crime, and political liberalism.

The results of the survey showed the sample to be generally unsupportive of the insanity plea. Forty-nine per cent of subjects believed the insanity defence should be abolished, and 95 per cent believed that it needed a lot of reform. However, 77 per cent believed that the insanity defence is sometimes justified, and 64 per cent believed that it is a necessary part of the legal system. Regression analysis showed that higher levels of support for the defence were associated with lower levels of authoritarianism, higher levels of self-reported education, and lower self-reported income. However, these results accounted for only a small proportion of the variance of insanity defence support in spite of their statistical significance. Attitudes previously found to be associated with death penalty support, e.g. race and gender, did not predict support for the insanity defence.

Attitudes toward the insanity defence were also generally negative. Whilst 96 per cent endorsed the insane defendant's right to treatment, and 55 per cent said the insane should be punished just like everyone else who breaks the law, 91 per cent thought judges and juries have a hard time distinguishing sane from insane defendants, and only 21 per cent thought that most people found NGRI are *really* insane. Eighty-nine percent thought the insanity defence was a loophole allowing too many guilty people to be set free, and only 25 per cent were convinced that NGRIs are set free only when it is safe to do so. Eighty-eight percent thought that the insanity defence allows dangerous people out on the streets, and 61 per cent thought insanity was a rich person's defence. Seventy-eight percent thought the insanity defence sent a message to criminals that they can get away with crime, and 77 per cent thought it affected the crime rate. Whilst 91 per cent approved of psychiatric testimony at insanity trials, 55 per cent thought psychiatrists would say anything about a defendant's sanity if paid enough.

Factor analysis revealed five factors accounting for 60 per cent of the total variance in responses. 'Punishment', which accounted for 49 per cent of the variance of this five factor model, had strong positive loadings for items supporting punishment of the insane, and high negative loadings for items concerning the wrongness or ineffectiveness of punishment for the insane. 'Perceived danger' (25 per cent of the variance of the five factor model) had strong positive loadings for items that the insanity defence is a loophole, sends a message to criminals, and lets dangerous people onto the streets; and high negative loadings for NGRIs being *really* insane and released only when it is safe to do so. The final three factors accounted for 26 per cent of the variance of the five factor model between them. 'Perceived injustice' had strong positive loadings for psychiatrists saying anything if paid enough, insanity as a rich person's defence and insanity as a loophole. 'Belief in psychiatric treatment' had high loadings for the insane being entitled to treatment and support for psychiatric testimony. The final factor, 'belief in effectiveness of procedures' had positive loadings for punishment not working on the insane, that judges and juries have a hard time discriminating insane from sane defendants, and NGRIs being released only when safe to do so.

Estimates of insanity plea usage were perhaps the strongest indication of public misapprehension of the defence. Whilst, even in the United States, far less than one per cent of criminal defendants raise the insanity defence (Pasewark, 1981) subjects in Hans' sample thought an average of 38 per cent of criminal defendants pleaded insanity, of which 36 per cent were thought to be successful with the defence. By interpolation, subjects estimated 14 per cent of criminal defendants were found NGRI by the courts! Subjects estimated 25 per cent of NGRIs go free immediately, and that 50 per cent are sent to a mental hospital. This leaves a perplexing 25 per cent of NGRIs unaccounted for. Subjects estimated that NGRIs are detained in hospital for an average of 22 months.

6.2 Summary of Methodology

The present study combines an attitudinal research survey (e.g. Hans, 1986), with a mock juror experiment more typical of such research as that of Finkel and Slobogin (1995). A between-subjects 3 x 3 x 2 factorial case vignette 'treatment' design was embedded within a survey (designed to elicit a verdict on the case, opinions on aspects of the case, attitudes to related issues, and subject characteristics). The factors manipulated between vignettes were: diagnosis (schizophrenia, depression, or personality disorder), the defendant's meta-responsibility (none, consensual, or purposive), and the type of insanity test to be applied in reaching a verdict (McNaughton Rules or a meta-responsibility insanity test [MRIT]).

Subjects (students, n=334) received (via post) a covering letter (an invitation to take part in the study) and a questionnaire consisting of ten double-sided pages of which the first page detailed instructions and the case vignette (a fictional murder trial describing a defendant who raises an insanity plea). After reading the vignette and rendering a verdict (guilty or NGRI), subjects answered questions concerning reasons for the decision, recommended length of detention of the defendant, etc.

Further questions used Likert scales to measure meta-responsibility attitudes, insanity defence attitudes, attitudes towards other issues (e.g. left/right political attitudes, libertarianism/authoritarianism), and demographic characteristics.

6.3 Justification of the Experimental Design

The factorial experimental design allows issues of causality to be addressed (e.g. what is the effect of type of insanity test on verdict?), which a pure survey method does not allow. The factorial design allows randomization of subjects with regard to each of the experimental (treatment) conditions (i.e. the vignette factors), allowing for the control of extraneous external variables (e.g. subject characteristics) and maintenance of internal validity. In a randomized design, it may be assumed that any fluctuations in subject characteristics between treatment conditions are due to chance, as each subject has an equal chance of selection for any treatment condition. This avoids the need for statistical control of potentially confounding factors (e.g. Kenny, 1979), and establishes the factors as the true cause in a cause-effect (factors-verdict) relationship (Suppes, 1970), as all conditions are held constant except the independent variables (vignette factors). The current study may be described as an experiment embedded within a survey, utilizing open-ended and closed questions. Such a design, yielding qualitative as well as quantitative data, allows for greater richness and triangulation of data.

The postal administration of measuring instruments has several benefits in comparison to telephone or face-to-face interviews; most notably that interviews do not lend themselves well to experimental manipulation. Other benefits include economy (of time and finances), and standardization of administration procedures (decreasing experimenter-effect biases upon responses; Rosenthal, 1966). In particular, postal questionnaires appear to elicit 'truer' responses than interviews (responses more consistent with subjects' own opinions) by minimizing socially desirable responses through anonymity (Bord, 1971).

The other major methodology available was the use of panels of mock jurors (as in the study of Simon, 1967) with deliberation and group verdicts. Such methods are desirable in terms of external validity to the real courtroom setting, and analysis of tape- or video-recordings of deliberations yields rich qualitative data concerning decision-making processes (e.g. how does meta-responsibility information fare in the *social* context of a jury panel, where it may be inappropriate to express opinion that the defendant is 'the architect of his own downfall'?).

However, controlling for external variables (e.g. the influence of one particular juror on the panel) is difficult in such a design, unless a large number of such panels are held. Such a design was thus felt to be beyond the scope of the present study. Preliminary investigation of meta-responsibility was felt better served by a predominantly quantitative design, with greater 'richness' of data afforded by an open-ended question concerning decision-making processes.

Furthermore, the experiment was designed predominantly as a social psychological test of attitudes towards meta-responsibility information (designed to investigate basic research questions, e.g. whether subjects are indeed sensitive to meta-responsibility manipulations), rather than a legal study with maximal external validity to the courtroom setting. A panel design would better serve future research into meta-responsibility.

Keeping in mind such exploratory considerations, and the paucity of existing empirical research relating to culpability for incapacity, dimensions examined in previous insanity defence research were used in the present research in addition to factorial manipulations of meta-responsibility. The factors selected for the vignette were diagnosis, type of meta-responsibility and type of insanity test.

It was decided that the diagnoses of schizophrenia, depression and antisocial personality disorder would provide the most interesting diagnostic manipulations. These diagnoses are not only commonly raised in successful NGRI pleas (Mackay, 1990), but it was expected that a psychosis and a neurosis from DSM Axis I and an Axis II diagnosis would interact differentially with meta-responsibility information and type of insanity test (Finkel, personal communication). The meta-responsibility factor was represented by no meta-responsibility, consensual meta-responsibility, or purposive meta-responsibility. The insanity test factor was represented by either a McNaughton test or a meta-responsibility insanity test (MRIT), which gave subjects the opportunity to reflect their meta-responsibility determinations in their insanity verdicts.

It was expected that diagnosis, type of meta-responsibility, and insanity test would interact to produce different proportions of NGRI findings and variance in other responses, e.g. recommended length of detention. For example, consensual meta-responsibility may be 'forgivable' in a schizophrenic defendant even when using the meta-responsibility insanity test, but not for a personality disordered defendant (there would thus be a significant difference in the proportion of insanity verdicts rendered in the two conditions). Likewise, having the opportunity to reflect meta-responsibility determinations may reduce the proportion of NGRI findings across all conditions using the meta-responsibility insanity test, but might reduce the subjects' need to reflect the defendant's culpability in length of disposal (hence reducing covert punishment).

Questions following the vignette elicited verdict, reasons for verdict, recommended disposal, recommended length of detention in hospital or sentence in prison, evaluations of the defendant's meta-responsibility, level of ascription to different models of mental disorder, support for the insanity defence, attitudes towards the insanity defence, estimates of insanity defence usage, political attitudes, libertarianism/authoritarianism, legal attitudes, and finally demographic and other characteristics of the subjects (e.g. personal experience/knowledge of mental disorder). The review of mock juror and attitudinal research above showed these variables to be potentially important in insanity defence decision-making. They were therefore deemed to provide the most useful responses to investigate the meta-responsibility theory.

6.4 Sampling

The pre-attrition sample constituted the entire population of undergraduate and postgraduate students at a single college of Cambridge University (the university consists of 31 such colleges; each student of the university is also a member of a college, of which a few admit exclusively postgraduates). Subjects were offered £5 for answering the questionnaire, in the form of a cheque sent upon receipt of the completed questionnaire (identified by the subject writing his/her name on the covering letter to be returned with the questionnaire and immediately separated to ensure anonymity).

The sample clearly cannot be readily generalized to the wider population, from which a jury sitting on a real murder trial would be drawn (Foss, 1976). It has been suggested that students, especially those from an 'elite' university, differ from real jurors in terms of age, education, income, ethnic identity and ideology (Hastie *et al.*, 1983). Such characteristics might systematically affect their decision-making (Bray and Kerr, 1982; Simon and Mahan, 1971). There are, however, good reasons for selecting students for mock juror studies:

1. Dimensions upon which students may differ from real jurors (i.e. age, education, etc.) have not been proved of fundamental importance to insanity defence decision-making. However, it does appear that younger jurors may be more lenient (Sealy and Cornish, 1973). Simon (1967) found that college educated subjects in her sample were less likely to find the defendant NGRI than the non-college educated members, and also that black subjects were more likely to offer NGRI verdicts than white subjects. The current sample is likely to differ along these dimensions of age, education and ethnic identity compared to the wider population; however, any effect that such dimensions have upon decision-making is likely to remain constant between factorial conditions.
2. Previous mock juror studies have traditionally used student samples (e.g. Poulson *et al.*, 1997; 1998), particularly those studies examining culpability for incapacity (e.g. Finkel, 1988; Finkel and Slobogin, 1995). The use of any other sample population would therefore sacrifice comparability with previous studies. Furthermore, many pivotal studies of general attitudes toward the mentally disordered have used student samples (e.g. Furnham and Bower, 1992; Olmstead and Durham, 1976).
3. Students make obliging subjects, offering good quality responses and high return rates (especially for financial reward). The sample did not require prepaid envelopes; a cost saving enabled by questionnaire administration and return though college pigeonholes (mailboxes), and a return box placed in the Porter's Lodge (entrance hall) to college. It was also felt that the quality of responses and return rate observed in the pilot study conducted on a random sample of the Cambridge electoral register (see below) were inadequate for the purposes of this study.
4. Legal policy is generally dictated by those in the upper academic strata, the type of strata represented by those from an 'elite' university such as Cambridge. This is especially true of the present sample; the college has a strong legal tradition, with many students studying law and allied disciplines (e.g. criminology) who subsequently embark on legal careers. Although the results may not therefore be typical of the wider population, they are likely to be more typical of those with a significant role to play in criminal law and mental health law policy, thus providing an important 'testing ground' for the fledgling meta-responsibility theory.
5. The notion that students' attitudes and responses are particularly disparate to those of the general population is at least partly fallacious. Firstly, students *are* members of the general population (if less heterogeneous), dispersing more widely into this population after their education. Secondly, students' attitudes and responses do not appear to differ significantly from other social groups. Bord (1971) found that attitudes towards mental disorder of 350 college students were similar to those of a sample of the general population used by Phillips (1963). Although students may differ from the general

population in level of education, education appears unimportant as a predictor of attitudes towards the mentally disordered (Furnham and Bower, 1992; Nunnally, 1961). The heterogeneity of the present sample is increased by virtue of including postgraduate students as well as undergraduates, ranging in age from 18 years to 57 years. Colombo (1997) sampled *only* postgraduates at Cambridge colleges accepting predominately or exclusively postgraduates, who are likely to be limited in generalizability, even to the wider population of Cambridge University students.

6. Other samples may not offer considerably greater heterogeneity. The pilot study sampled subjects from the Cambridge electoral register. However, the considerable cost of purchasing sections of the electoral register means samples tend to be drawn from small sections of the register. Geographical distribution of subjects is likely to be inextricably linked with demographic variables such as social class, political affiliation, age and income. Demographic variables such as social class may be of greater heterogeneity in a student sample. Furthermore, Colombo (1997) estimates that in the early 1990s, the Cambridge electoral register listed only 69 per cent of the city's residents. Taking into account return-rate bias (those with greater amounts of free time such as the unemployed and elderly are more likely to return questionnaires), and generally low overall return rates (and response quality) from the general population, results from electoral samples may be far from representative of the general population.
7. Jurors themselves may not represent particularly heterogeneous populations. Jury selection, *voir dire*, and challenges to particular jurors in US cases, are explicitly designed to exclude population outliers (Hans and Vidmar, 1986). Males and persons of higher socio-economic status are traditionally over-represented on juries (Saks and Hastie, 1978).
8. Discussion with forensic and legal professionals elicited the opinion that there was something inherently edifying about sitting as a juror on a trial. By the end of the trial, jurors might be described as 'experts' on the various legal facets and phenomena they are there to consider. A person having performed jury service might give very different responses to issues concerning a real or fictional trial than a 'naïve' member of the general population who had not undergone such edification (a typical mock juror). It was felt that the present sample – educated students from a college with a legal tradition – might give responses more similar to those of 'real' jurors than 'naïve' members of the general population.

It is therefore contended that the external validity of results (i.e. generalizability of results to the wider population or a panel of jurors on a murder trial) from studies using student samples is unknown, rather than inherently weak (and quite possibly better than alternative samples often thought to offer greater external validity). It should be reiterated that this study wished to examine exploratory issues (rather than detailed decision-making processes) e.g. whether meta-responsibility information has *any* impact on decision-making. The present sample meets the requirements of such an exploratory study.

In terms of sample size, each cell in the table of factors (see Table 6.1) ideally requires a sufficient sample size so that the magnitude of factor interactions would be limited by effect size, not the size of the sample. Although Sudman (1983) states that 20 subjects per cell are required in a factorial study for statistical confidence, Finkel (personal communication) suggested that 15 subjects per cell would be adequate. Farrington (personal communication) comported with this view.

Colombo (personal communication) warned a greater number would be required for higher order interaction effects to crystallize under statistical analysis. However, it was decided that a greater number of subjects per cell would have been impractical for the purposes of this study, and thus statistical confidence in higher order interactions would have to be sacrificed, or else the number of factors would have to be reduced (e.g. 3 x 3 factorial design). The latter was seen as undesirable, due to the expected importance of each of diagnosis, type of meta-responsibility, and type of insanity test upon verdict.

The sample size required was thus 3 (diagnosis) x 3 (type of meta-responsibility) x 2 (type of insanity test) x 15 (subjects per cell) = 270, with no cell having less than 15 subjects. From the college's population of 594 subjects with pigeonholes, a return rate of at least 46 per cent was required. Colombo (1997) indicates this return rate is realistic for a postal questionnaire study, particularly one using the Total Design Method (TDM; Dillman, 1978). The TDM is a set of commonsensical procedures designed to increase response rates. It emphasizes the nature of exchange in the researcher-subject relationship, and that compliance/return rates may be increased through careful measuring instrument design, return envelopes, financial inducement, and informing the subjects about the importance of the research. All these factors were carefully attended to in the present study.

6.5 Ethical Issues

The measuring instrument was submitted (along with a detailed research proposal for general ethical and methodological scrutiny) to the British Society of Criminology (BSC) Professional Affairs Committee (c/o the Vice Chair) that acts as an ethics committee for the BSC. The potentially sensitive case vignette material (detailing a homicide and subsequent trial) drove the wish to pursue ethical approval (although such material is routinely administered to mock jurors). The Committee noted no ethical objections, and provided helpful methodological advice.

Informal ethical scrutiny was provided by college officers whose students would partake in the research. Their interest in the well-being of the sample in their charge was felt to offer a good test of the research design's ethical integrity.

No objections were noted by the college officers.[5] Subject anonymity was guaranteed through the immediate separation of name data from the rest of the questionnaire (name on the returned covering letter for payment tracking, and contact details for follow-up interview, if offered, on the final page of the questionnaire). Questionnaires were identified only by a code number (e.g. P>CMR>MN/132; see below) that could not be connected with any subject name.

The only question deemed to require particular sensitivity was the item concerning ethnic identity. It was decided to use the tried and tested UK census categories (Coleman and Salt, 1996), and precede the question with information that these were indeed census categories.

6.6 The Case Vignettes

6.6.1 Notation

The factors in the case-vignettes (i.e. treatment conditions) were referred to by the following system of notation:

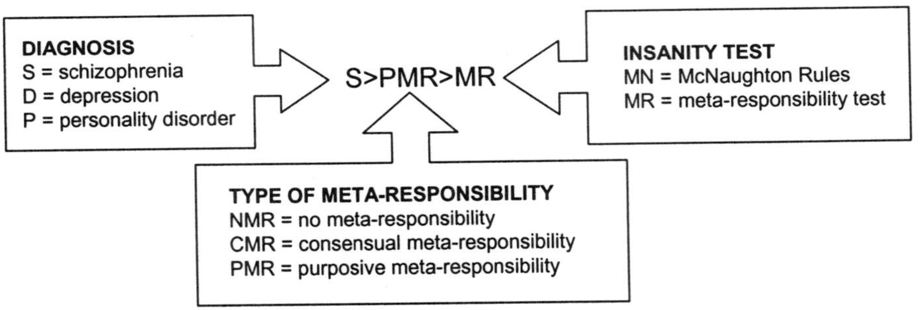

Figure 6.1 System of notation used to describe case vignettes

The notion has the general form of DIAGNOSIS>TYPE OF META-RESPONSIBILITY>TYPE OF INSANITY TEST. In the vignette represented by S>PMR>MR, Tom is therefore described as schizophrenic (S), having purposive meta-responsibility (PMR), and the subjects asked to render a verdict using the meta-responsibility insanity test (MR).

---

[5] These included the Master, Vice-Master, Senior Tutor, Bursar, and Tutor for Graduate Students of the college.

6.6.2 Instructions

Subjects were given the following instructions immediately preceding the vignette:

> Please read though the case study, and answer the questions that follow. Please take your time reading through the case study and questions, and consider your answers carefully. In particular, please read the Judge's instructions for being found 'Not Guilty by Reason of Insanity' carefully. You may feel you do not know the answer to a particular question as you do not have enough information, but PLEASE DO YOUR BEST WITH THE INFORMATION AVAILABLE RATHER THAN SAYING 'DON'T KNOW'. The questionnaire should not take much longer than 30 minutes.

The vignette described a clearly mentally disordered person, Tom, who killed his wife. Subjects were asked to place themselves in the role of a juror at his trial and decide whether Tom was guilty or NGRI based on information in the case-vignette and insanity test instructions. Aside from necessary differences in wording relating to factors, wording of the vignettes was identical, and wording was kept as consistent between the factorial manipulations as possible.

6.6.3 Gender of the Defendant

The use of a male defendant in the vignettes may be justified by a) the vast predominance of male-perpetrated murders, and b) the doubling of the sample size that would be needed to introduce another factor (i.e. gender) into the study. Gendered notions of meta-responsibility, however, would constitute an important future research area. It is possible that the vignette's description of Tom killing his wife might have introduced a 'battered-wife' schema into subjects' minds (perhaps especially for female subjects), affecting attitudes and verdicts.[6] A description of a wife killing her husband, however, may have introduced an even greater element of bias due to its atypical nature. A description of stranger violence may have circumvented such difficulties; however, stranger violence by mentally disordered persons is rare (Howlett, 1998) and would also have made the vignette atypical. The beginning of the vignette read thus:

---

[6] Only one subject explicitly mentioned a 'domestic violence' construct in giving reasons for their verdict: 'Far too many domestic murderers seem to get away with it lightly' (P>PMR>MR/188/guilty).

> Tom is in court on a charge of murdering his wife.
>
> Tom does not dispute that he killed his wife, but is claiming that he should be found 'Not Guilty by Reason of Insanity'. If found 'Guilty' Tom will be sent to Prison, whereas if his insanity plea is successful Tom will be sent to a special hospital and not punished for his crime (a successful insanity plea means the defendant was not responsible for his actions at the time of the crime). PLEASE IMAGINE YOU ARE A MEMBER OF THE JURY.

The instructions informed subjects about the consequences of an insanity acquittal (i.e. a hospital disposal). This was in order to remove the confounding variable of speculation from the experiment; jurors often make speculative (and erroneous) assumptions about the consequences of a NGRI finding (Bach, 1995).

6.6.4 Diagnosis and Background of the Defendant

It was felt necessary to 'ground' Tom in a social and familial environment, so the first line of the vignette contained information that Tom had a family and job. It gave Tom a premorbid history and context, combating the stereotype that the mentally disordered are somehow different to start with (Miles, 1987).

The description of behaviour given in the 'diagnosis' section of the vignette included all major DSM-IV diagnostic criteria for the relevant mental disorder. In the case of schizophrenia (undifferentiated type – DSM-IV code 295.90)[7] these are:

1. Delusions
2. Hallucinations
3. Disorganized speech
4. Catatonic behaviour
5. Negative symptoms
6. Social/occupational dysfunction.

This translated into the following vignette description (diagnosis: S):

---

[7] Although the delusion in the case of schizophrenia concerned the paranoid fear of his wife plotting against him, this would not be enough for a diagnosis of schizophrenia – paranoid type (code 295.30).

> Tom was married with two children and a job. However, about six months ago Tom started to become increasingly withdrawn and preoccupied. It seemed to both his family and friends as though he was in a world of his own. He became less interested in his work and his children. Most of the time Tom would sit upstairs on his own, though on occasion he would stand for hours, in a stiff upright position in the middle of the room. Tom's speech was often not clear as he would mutter very quickly and about things that just didn't make sense. Sometimes he would show sudden outbursts of anger, claiming his wife was plotting against him. He began to complain of hearing voices, fear of attack from his wife increased, and generally his whole behaviour became more bizarre.

In the case of a major depressive episode (severe, without psychotic features – code 296.23) diagnostic features are:

1. Depressed mood
2. Diminished interest and pleasure
3. Weight loss
4. Insomnia/hypersomnia
5. Psychomotor agitation (restlessness)
6. Fatigue/loss of energy
7. Feelings of worthlessness/guilt
8. Inability to concentrate, indecision
9. Suicidal ideation.

The vignette description given read thus (diagnosis: D):

> Tom was married with two children and a job. However, about six months ago Tom started to become depressed and restless. His family and friends noticed he was losing weight, had hardly any energy and could not concentrate properly. He became tearful and less interested in his work and his children. He was unable to sleep properly at night and wanted to sleep all day. Tom said he felt completely worthless and talked repeatedly of suicide. He also claimed that if he killed himself he would kill his wife too, to prevent her unhappiness.

In the case of antisocial personality disorder (code 301.7) diagnostic features are:

1. Failure to conform to social norms by repeatedly performing actions that are grounds for arrest
2. Deceitfulness – lying, use of aliases, or conning others for personal profit or pleasure
3. Impulsivity/failure to plan ahead
4. Irritability and aggressiveness
5. Reckless disregard for safety of self or others

6. Consistent irresponsibility, as indicated by repeated failure to sustain consistent work behaviour or honour financial obligations
7. Lack of remorse, e.g. indifference to or rationalizing having hurt, mistreated, or stolen from another.

The vignette description read thus (diagnosis: P):

Tom was married with two children and a job. Tom had always had problems of the sort described below but recently they became worse. He was often in trouble as both a child and as an adult. His family and friends noticed he was deceitful, manipulative, impulsive and aggressive. He got into fights on the spur of the moment and showed little remorse. He failed to pay back loans to people who subsequently threatened both Tom and his family: this did not seem to bother him. He showed signs of being depressed, and accused his wife (incorrectly) of having an affair.

6.6.5 Diagnosis and Medication Response by the Psychiatrist

The response of the psychiatrist to Tom's disorder was diagnosis-specific. Therefore, the psychiatrist prescribed anti-psychotic medication for schizophrenia (diagnosis: S):

His wife took him to a psychiatrist who said he was suffering from schizophrenia and prescribed anti-psychotic medication.

In the case of depression, the psychiatrist prescribed anti-depressants (diagnosis: D):

His wife took him to a psychiatrist who said he was suffering from depression and prescribed anti-depressant medication.

In the case of personality disorder, the psychiatrist also prescribed anti-depressants. Although personality disorders are often resistant to pharmacotherapy, anti-depressants are sometimes prescribed,[8] particularly for secondary symptoms (Garrido, Estaban and Molero, 1996). Tom's non-compliance provides the essential source of meta-responsibility that is needed within the vignette (diagnosis: P):

His wife took him to a psychiatrist who said he suffered from a personality disorder and prescribed anti-depressant medication.

---

[8] See *SUPRA* note 15, Ch. 4.

6.6.6 Medication Non-compliance as the Source of Meta-responsibility

Medication non-compliance provided the meta-responsibility component in the vignette. Either non-compliance did not occur (no meta-responsibility; NMR), occurred due to medication side-effects (consensual meta-responsibility; CMR), or occurred in the context of a preference for a mentally disordered existence (purposive meta-responsibility; PMR). No meta-responsibility was represented by the following vignette description (type of meta-responsibility: NMR):

> Tom accepted that he should take the advice of the psychiatrist and was careful to take his medication.

Consensual meta-responsibility was represented thus (type of meta-responsibility: CMR):

> Tom did not really seem to realise he was ill (probably due to the effects of his illness itself) but accepted that he should take the advice of the psychiatrist and was careful to take his medication. Soon however, his medication caused unpleasant side effects and because of this he stopped taking it.

Purposive meta-responsibility was represented by the following description (type of meta-responsibility: PMR):

> Tom seemed to realise he was ill but did not want to take the advice of the psychiatrist. He seemed to use his illness as an excuse to 'opt out' of normal responsibilities and stopped taking his medication.

6.6.7 The Criminal Episode

The reasoning behind the selection of homicide as the offence was the crime's seriousness and salience that were expected to polarize attitudes and opinions in subjects (allowing a greater degree of variance to emerge). Real insanity trials, especially one involving a homicide, would likely involve considerable expert testimony on each side. Whilst credibility of expert testimony has been shown to affect decisions on insanity defence case vignettes using mental healthcare personnel as subjects (Homant and Kennedy, 1986), the effect of expert testimony at trial is often, at least in the opinions of lawyers and experts themselves, to 'cancel out' the opinions of the two experts (Gutheil, personal communication). Expert testimony was not therefore described in the vignette for reasons of length/complication.

Motive for the murder was related to the type of mental disorder described. In the case of schizophrenia, the motive was delusional fear of being attacked (diagnosis: S):

> A few weeks later he stabbed and killed his wife with a kitchen knife, claiming that voices had told him she was about to kill him and his children.

In the case of depression, Tom killed his wife to prevent her unhappiness as he intended to kill himself (diagnosis: D):

> A few weeks later he stabbed his wife with a kitchen knife, claiming that he did so in order to prevent her unhappiness, as he intended to kill himself.

In the case of personality disorder, Tom lost control in a fight about his wife's alleged affair (diagnosis: P):

> A few weeks later he stabbed his wife with a kitchen knife, claiming that he had lost control during a fight about her alleged affair.

The relation of motive to the mental disorder is important; especially in the case of a 'product' test of insanity such as the McNaughton Rules or MRIT under which the crime must in some way be the product of the 'disease of the mind'.[9] If such a relationship between the mental disorder and the motive for the murder was lacking, then NGRI verdicts might fall to the extent that the effect of vignette factors upon verdict might be obscured.

6.6.8 Type of Insanity Test

The final vignette factor was the type of insanity test. This was either a McNaughton test, or a meta-responsibility insanity test (MRIT) which allowed the subject to deny the insanity defence if she/he was satisfied that Tom had been reckless with medication or knowingly contributed to his abnormal state of mind. These two provisions in the MRIT were designed respectively to deal with consensual and purposive meta-responsibility due to medication non-compliance. It was decided to avoid giving a definition of the term reckless to avoid increasing the length and complexity of the vignette.

The McNaughton Rules read thus (test: MN):

---

[9] The Butler Committee (1975) test is alone in *not* stipulating this 'product' element. The archetypal product test is the *Durham* test (see SUPRA note 28, Ch. 2): 'the accused is not criminally responsible if his unlawful act was the product of mental disease or mental defect'); see Chapter 2.

> The judge says *'Everyone is to be presumed sane and to possess a sufficient degree of reason to be responsible for their crimes until the contrary is proved...to establish a defence on the ground of insanity, it must be clearly proved that, at the time of committing the act, the party accused was labouring under such a defect of reason, from disease of the mind, as to not know the nature and quality of the act he was doing, or if he did know it, that he did not know what he was doing was wrong'.*

The meta-responsibility insanity test added a clause onto the end of the McNaughton test (test: MR):

> The judge says *'Everyone is to be presumed sane and to possess a sufficient degree of reason to be responsible for their crimes until the contrary is proved...to establish a defence on the ground of insanity, it must be clearly proved that, at the time of committing the act, the party accused was labouring under such a defect of reason, from disease of the mind, as to not know the nature and quality of the act he was doing, or if he did know it, that he did not know what he was doing was wrong'.* Furthermore, the judge adds that *'If you believe the defendant's behaviour with regard to treatment was reckless, or he knowingly contributed to his abnormal state of mind, then you should deny him the insanity defence, and find him guilty instead'.*

6.6.9 Summary of Vignette Factors

The vignette had 3 (diagnosis) x 3 (type of meta-responsibility) x 2 (insanity test) = 18 different versions, in a between-subjects design. These are displayed in Table 6.1.

Table 6.1 Table of vignette factors with shorthand reference codes

Diagnosis	*Type of meta-responsibility*	*Test*	*Ref:*	*Vignette number*
Schizophrenia	None	McNaughton	S>NMR>MN	1
		MR	S>NMR>MR	2
	Consensual	McNaughton	S>CMR>MN	3
		MR	S>CMR>MR	4
	Purposive	McNaughton	S>PMR>MN	5
		MR	S>PMR>MR	6
Depression	None	McNaughton	D>NMR>MN	7
		MR	D>NMR>MR	8
	Consensual	McNaughton	D>CMR>MN	9
		MR	D>CMR>MR	10
	Purposive	McNaughton	D>PMR>MN	11
		MR	D>PMR>MR	12
Personality Disorder	None	McNaughton	P>NMR>MN	13
		MR	P>NMR>MR	14
	Consensual	McNaughton	P>CMR>MN	15
		MR	P>CMR>MR	16
	Purposive	McNaughton	P>PMR>MN	17
		MR	P>PMR>MR	18

The vignette which described Tom as a schizophrenic with consensual meta-responsibility, in which the judge charged the jury with a meta-responsibility insanity test (denoted S>CMR>MR) was therefore composed thus:

Tom is in court on a charge of murdering his wife.

Tom does not dispute that he killed his wife, but is claiming that he should be found 'Not Guilty by Reason of Insanity'. If found 'Guilty' Tom will be sent to Prison, whereas if his insanity plea is successful Tom will be sent to a special hospital and not punished for his crime (a successful insanity plea means the defendant was not responsible for his actions at the time of the crime). PLEASE IMAGINE YOU ARE A MEMBER OF THE JURY.

Tom was married with two children and a job. However, about six months ago Tom started to become increasingly withdrawn and preoccupied. It seemed to both his family and friends as though he was in a world of his own. He became less interested in his work and his children. Most of the time Tom would sit upstairs on his own, though on occasion he would stand for hours, in a stiff upright position in the middle of the room. Tom's speech was often not clear as he would mutter very quickly and about things that just didn't make sense. Sometimes he would show sudden outbursts of anger, claiming his wife was plotting against him. He began to complain of hearing voices, fear of attack from his wife increased, and generally his whole behaviour became more bizarre.

His wife took him to a psychiatrist who said he was suffering from schizophrenia and prescribed anti-psychotic medication. Tom did not really seem to realise he was ill (probably due to the effects of his illness itself) but accepted that he should take the advice of the psychiatrist and was careful to take his medication. Soon however, his medication caused unpleasant side effects and because of this he stopped taking it. A few weeks later he stabbed and killed his wife with a kitchen knife, claiming that voices had told him she was about to kill him and his children.

The judge says *'Everyone is to be presumed sane and to possess a sufficient degree of reason to be responsible for their crimes until the contrary is proved…to establish a defence on the ground of insanity, it must be clearly proved that, at the time of committing the act, the party accused was labouring under such a defect of reason, from disease of the mind, as to not know the nature and quality of the act he was doing; or if he did know it, that he did not know what he was doing was wrong'.* Furthermore, the judge adds that *'If you believe the defendant's behaviour with regard to treatment was reckless, or he knowingly contributed to his abnormal state of mind, then you should deny him the insanity defence, and find him guilty instead'*.

6.7 Questions

Subjects were asked 68 questions on a variety of issues, using forced choice (categorical), numeric, open-ended, and Likert scale responses. A detailed list of questions is given in the Appendix.

6.7.1 Categorical Forced-choice Response

Questions requiring forced choice responses were used where response was required in a categorical dichotomized/trichotomized/etc. form. Subjects were asked to indicate their response by circling the appropriate answer. For example:

> 1) Given the information you have available, would you be inclined to find Tom 'Guilty' or 'Not Guilty by Reason of Insanity'? (Please circle your answer)
>
> Guilty Not Guilty by Reason of Insanity

6.7.2 Open-ended Response

Question 2, concerning reasons for the guilty/NGRI verdict, used an open-ended question designed to elicit qualitative data. A large text-box was given below the question in which to respond.

> 2) What are the reasons for your decision? (Please give as much detail as possible)

6.7.3 Numerical Response

Some questions, such as recommended length of detention, required a numerical response in a text box. For example:

4) Given the information you have available, how long do you think Tom should remain at the institution (prison or mental hospital)? (Please estimate a number even if you are not sure.)

years	months

Please write number(s) in boxes

6.7.4 *Attitudinal Response*

Most questions consisted of statements to which the subject indicated their agreement or disagreement on a Likert scale ranging from 1 to 7. The Likert style of unidimensional measurement (Likert, 1932) is commonly used to elicit attitudinal responses to statements in social science research (Sedlack and Stanley, 1992). For example:

12) Tom should have been more careful in taking his medication

1	2	3	4	5	6	7
Strongly disagree			Don't know			Strongly agree

The midpoint (Don't know) might not seem to be a 'true' midpoint between the polar responses; a more accurate midpoint might appear to be 'Do not agree or disagree', 'No opinion' or 'Indifferent'. It might be suggested that *no* midpoint is most suitable. However, literature on the matter suggests a midpoint is desirable where appropriate (Sudman and Bradburn, 1983). In a study where polarized opinions are sought (as in a courtroom setting), using the midpoint 'Don't know' will tend to avoid 'easy' repetitive midpoint responses and provoke the subject to give the statement careful consideration. Endorsement of the midpoint 'Don't know' is hopefully undesirable, especially for students for whom 'knowing' is important).[10] Of course, true indifference may always be reflected by endorsing the midpoint.

Other questions examining ordinal variables, such as the person's experience of mental disorder, also used Likert scales with various midpoints and endpoints. For example:

---

[10] Colombo (1997) also uses the midpoint 'Don't know' in Likert scale responses.

66) Please rate the amount of experience you think you have of mental disorder (e.g. personally suffered from it, friends/family suffered from it, etc.)

1	2	3	4	5	6	7
No experience			Some experience			Lots of experience

6.7.5 The Questions

The questions with their form of response were:

1. Verdict (categorical – guilty/NGRI).
2. Reasons for the subjects' decision (open-ended question).
3. Disposal recommendation (categorical – prison/hospital).[11]
4. Recommended time to spend at institution (numeric).
5. Nine items concerning meta-responsibility issues (Likert).
6. Two items concerning Tom's character before and after becoming mentally disordered (designed to test Reznek's [1998] hypothesis that evaluations of criminal responsibility rest on the degree of 'character change') (Likert).
7. Six items concerning subjects' subscription to three models of mental disorder derived from questions concerning aetiology and treatment used by Colombo (1997) that predicted subscription to the medical (organic) model, the moral (cognitive-behavioural) model, or the psychosocial model (Likert).
8. 25 questions comprising Hans' (1986) Attitudes Towards the Insanity Defence Scale (Likert and numeric).
9. Five items measuring left-right attitudes (comprising the left-right scale in the 1996 British Social Attitudes Survey; Jowell, Curtice, Park *et al.,* 1997) (Likert).

---

[11] Type and length of disposal in real-world decisions is, of course, not the province of jurors, so it might be argued that responses to such questions in a sample of mock jurors are irrelevant to real-world decision-making. However, such responses elicit a measure of attitudes towards the defendant in a similar manner to social distance scales frequently employed in studies of attitudes towards the mentally disordered (e.g. Crocetti *et al.*, 1971). Such responses may also not be significantly different to the decisions made by judges in courtrooms and psychiatrists in hospitals. Chapter 4 has suggested that decisions made by those with authority (i.e. covertly punitive, sanist, and pretextual) are representative (and perhaps expressive) of negative attitudes held by the general population. It is further apparent that members of the general population do partake in decision-making with regard to mentally disordered offenders, for example in MHRTs, as well as electing those with formal authority. It has also been argued above (see *SUPRA* section 6.1) that individual decisions are likely to play a large role in the fate of insanity acquittees, as only a small proportion of insanity pleas come to trial (Cirincione, 1996).

10. Six items measuring libertarianism/authoritarianism (comprising the libertarianism/authoritarianism scale in the 1996 British Social Attitudes Survey; Jowell et al., 1997) (Likert).
11. Three items measuring legal attitudes from the Legal Attitudes Questionnaire (Brodsky and Smitherman, 1983) used by Hans (1986) (Likert).
12. Five items concerning demographic characteristics (age, gender, ethnic identity, etc.) (categorical/numeric).
13. Two items concerning personal experience and knowledge of mental disorder and mentally disordered people (Likert).
14. One item requesting contact details if the subject was willing to be interviewed concerning the issues examined in the study.[12]

6.8 Operationalization of the Pilot Study

The vignettes and measuring instrument were subjected to a lengthy period of piloting and completed by over 100 subjects before embarking upon the main study. Many pilot subjects were criminology faculty/students who offered feedback on academic aspects of the study. Other subjects provided feedback on the 'look and feel' of the questionnaire, e.g. ease of use, time taken to complete the questionnaire, etc.

A formal pilot study was undertaken using subjects from the general population. The electoral register for Cherry Hinton (Ward D1) of Cambridge was purchased. Ward D1 consisted of 1987 registered electors, whose names and addresses were given in the register. A sample size of 100 was chosen, and a random number matrix was generated to select 100 random subjects in the ward. Each subject received, through the post, a covering letter, a copy of the pilot questionnaire (similar but not identical to the final questionnaire),[13] and a return envelope stamped first-class. Subjects did not receive follow-ups or re-mailings. A return rate of 37 per cent was achieved, not enough for statistical analysis, but yielding useful information concerning the operationalisation of the research, the quality of responses, and expected return rates. The most significant change to the final study in light of the pilot study was to use a student sample due to the poor response rate and the relatively low quality and brevity of responses of the electoral register sample.

---

[12] It was decided after reviewing the high quality of the responses (particularly subjects' reasons for their verdict) not to proceed with interviewing the subjects due to constraints on time and space available to report such extensive qualitative data. 35.3 per cent of subjects gave contact details on the questionnaire, indicating their agreement to be interviewed.

[13] The pilot questionnaire, tailored to the nature of the sample, included an item asking about employment category and level of education.

6.9 Operationalization of the Major Study

Seven hundred and twenty questionnaires were printed (40 of each of the 18 conditions in the study). A random sample of these, 594 questionnaires, were delivered to every student pigeonhole at the college, including a covering letter explaining the purpose of the study in general terms (so as not to introduce an element of bias), a compliments slip, and a labelled return envelope. The covering letter had a bottom tear-off section that the subject was asked to return (with the completed questionnaire) to claim the £5 offered for participation in the study (this slip was separated from the returned questionnaire to ensure anonymity, as were contact details on the last page, if completed). As a small number of students would be working away from Cambridge, it is a reasonable assumption that not all of the subjects received questionnaires, as with any type of postal research. Subjects were instructed to return their questionnaires to the clearly marked box placed by the pigeonholes in the Porter's Lodge. A full list of students at the college was obtained, which allowed tracking of which subjects returned their questionnaires for payment and re-mailing purposes.

Those subjects not returning their questionnaires after two weeks received a reminder letter. One in every three subjects who had not returned their questionnaire were re-mailed with the entire questionnaire a further week later (using a sampling interval of three on the list of those whose questionnaires had not been received). All subjects therefore received the initial mailing, those not returning their questionnaires two weeks later received a reminder letter, and a third of those who still had not replied a week later (three weeks after the initial mailing) received a complete re-mail.

6.10 Method of Data Input and Analysis

Responses (except Question Two requesting subjects' reasons for their verdicts) were coded by input into a quantitative data analysis computer program, SPSS for Windows (SPSS Inc., 1999; release 10.0.1). Each returned questionnaire was given a reference number, recorded as the first variable in the dataset and written on the questionnaire so any particular questionnaire could be easily located both physically and in the dataset. In addition, further variables were calculated from the existing data array to allow detailed analysis (these are detailed in the next chapter).

Question Two (subjects' reasons for their verdicts) was designed to 'flesh out' subjects' opinions to enrich the study's understanding of attitudes toward meta-responsibility and insanity defence decision-making and to offer a source of triangulation to the quantitative research method. This data was subjected to an informal thematic content analysis (Holsti, 1969). Thematic content analysis subjects the content of communication (such as responses to a survey question) to an analysis in terms of emergent or preset 'themes'. The procedure felt to be most appropriate to the present study was to examine each response and extract information pertinent to the meta-responsibility theory in order to illustrate the research findings.[14]

6.11 Concluding Overview

This chapter has described the methodology of a mock juror study using a 3 x 3 x 2 case vignette factorial experiment embedded within a postal questionnaire survey, designed to elicit information concerning insanity defence decision-making and attitudes towards meta-responsibility and related issues. Diagnosis, type of meta-responsibility, and insanity test were manipulated in an insanity defence case vignette, allowing investigation of the effect of factors on decision-making (as indexed by verdict, disposal, recommended length of detention, etc.). Chapter 7 presents quantitative analysis and results, and Chapter 8 discusses these results with reference to subjects' reasons for their verdicts.

---

[14] Simon (1967) also abandoned a formal content analysis of the insanity deliberations of mock juries:

> We could have done a more formal content analysis…but very quickly we began to see results from this less systematic technique that were much more useful…we think there is a latent representativeness in the excerpts we have included, but we can offer no scientific guarantee that someone else could not have studied the same deliberations and have come up with a different set of quotes. All we can say is that we are doubtful (p. 132).

Chapter 7

Quantitative Data Analysis and Presentation of Results

This chapter details the quantitative analysis of the data obtained from the research detailed in Chapter 6.

7.1 Data Analysis

Data analysis was composed of a search for relationships between the independent variables (vignette factors and attitudinal measures) and dependent variables (verdict, type of disposal, length of detention). The testing of rigid research hypotheses is incompatible with exploratory analysis, except where indicated by theory or previous research. The analyses of interest to the study (along with some tentative hypotheses) were:

1) The effect of vignette factors (diagnosis, type of meta-responsibility, insanity test)[1] upon verdict (guilty or NGRI), type of disposal (prison or hospital), and length of detention.
    i) Diagnosis.
        (1) Verdict. A diagnosis of schizophrenia (S) may be associated with a greater proportion of NGRI verdicts than depression (D), which in turn would elicit more NGRI verdicts than personality disorder (P). This would comport with 'real-world' data as to diagnoses of NGRIs (e.g. Mackay, 1990), as well as experimental data (Finkel and Slobogin, 1995).
        (2) Disposal. A hospital disposal might be preferred for schizophrenia due to its 'medical' features. Hospital disposals may also be more frequent for depression than personality disorder.
        (3) Length of detention. Length of detention might be longer for schizophrenia and personality disorder (due to their assumed impact on dangerousness) but depression may be seen as less severe, warranting a shorter period of detention.

---

[1] For details on the system of notation for vignette factors, see *SUPRA* section 6.6.1.

(a) For both disposals (prison and hospital)
(b) For prison only
(c) For hospital only.

ii) Type of meta-responsibility.

(1) Verdict. No meta-responsibility (NMR), in which Tom has no culpability for his disorder, may draw more NGRI verdicts than consensual meta-responsibility (CMR), which in turn may draw more NGRI verdicts than purposive meta-responsibility (PMR).

(2) Disposal. The culpability entailed by CMR and PMR may be 'punished' through a greater proportion of prison disposals than NMR, with PMR drawing the most prison disposals.

(3) Length of detention. CMR and PMR may be punished by longer periods of detention than NMR, with longest recommended length of detention for PMR.
(a) Across both disposals
(b) For prison only
(c) For hospital only.

iii) Insanity test.

(1) Verdict. Compared to the McNaughton test, the meta-responsibility test (MRIT) was expected to decrease NGRI verdicts for CMR and PMR conditions, due to Tom being respectively reckless with medication and contributing to his abnormal state of mind in the CMR and PMR conditions. The gravity of the PMR condition might lead to fewest NGRI verdicts. There should be no difference between the two insanity tests for the NMR condition in terms of proportion of NGRI verdicts as Tom has *no* overt culpability for disorder and hence there should be no meta-responsibility considerations to reflect.

(2) Disposal. The MRIT may increase prison disposals in the CMR and PMR conditions due to the hypothesized increase in guilty verdicts.

(3) Length of detention. Due to the hypothesized reduction in sanism, pretextuality, and concomitant covert punishment by the meta-responsibility test (by comporting with commonsense notions of justice and affording opportunity for proper ascription of culpability; see Chapter 4), it might decrease length of detention in comparison with the McNaughton test.
(a) Across both disposals
(b) For prison only
(c) For hospital only.

2) The effect of attitudes on verdict, disposal and length of detention.

(1) Verdict.
(2) Disposal.
(3) Length of detention.
(a) Across both disposals

(b) For prison only
(c) For hospital only.

3) The relative importance of attitudes and vignette factors in determining verdict.

7.2 Methods of Analysis

In each of 1) i) (1), 1) ii) (1), and 1) (iii) (1) above, binomial tests[2] were run to test for differences in the proportions of NGRI verdicts due to each vignette factor, using the appropriate reference category as the test proportion. In 1) i) (1) and 1) ii) (1), Kruskal-Wallis tests[3] were used to examine the overall effect of the vignette factor on verdict outcome; a Mann-Whitney test[4] was used for the same purpose in 1) (iii) (1). A 'dummy-coded'[5] univariate analysis of variance (ANOVA) was used to explore the effect of the vignette factors on verdict. Binomial logistic regression[6] was used to build a model of the predictive importance of vignette factors upon verdict.

---

[2] Binomial tests (essentially nonparametric *t*-tests) test differences between proportions rather than means. Binomial tests make no assumptions as to the underlying shape of the data (unlike *t*-tests), but sacrifice statistical power. If we are interested in the effect of the meta-responsibility insanity test in the SCHIZOPHRENIA>CONSENSUAL META-RESPONSIBILITY condition, a binomial test examines if there is a difference in the proportion of NGRI verdicts of this vignette (S>CMR>MR), compared to NGRI verdicts in the reference category (S>CMR>MN). The *p* value tells us whether the proportion of NGRI verdicts in the former vignette (with the meta-responsibility insanity test) differs significantly from the proportion of verdicts in the latter vignette (using the McNaughton test) i.e. whether the MRIT has a significant effect upon verdict in comparison to McNaughton.

[3] The Kruskal-Wallis test (a nonparametric equivalent of a one-way ANOVA), tests whether *k* independent samples come from the same population (required when the grouping variable has more than two values, e.g. DIAGNOSIS or TYPE OF META-RESPONSIBILITY).

[4] The Mann-Whitney test is equivalent to the Kruskal-Wallis test for a grouping variable with only two values (e.g. INSANITY TEST).

[5] 'Dummy-coding' (e.g. guilty=1, NGRI=2) is commonly used where a test requires data means. However, dummy-coding of *categorical variables* (which do not stand in quantitative relation to each other; what is 'the mean' of guilty and NGRI?) is not statistically valid for relationship prediction, which requires tests making provision for categorical response variables, e.g. logistic regression. Verdict means, however, provide a useful guide to the underlying pattern of the data.

[6] The binary logistic regression model used bifurcated categorical dependent variables (e.g. VERDICT = guilty/NGRI; DISPOSAL = prison/hospital) and independent factors (DIAGNOSIS, TYPE OF META-RESPONSIBILITY, TYPE OF INSANITY TEST) and their factorial combinations, entered stepwise into the regression model (Forward: LR) as categorical covariates and tested for significance. Rather than entering all the predictor variables into the regression equation in one block, the forward stepwise method begins with a model that contains only the regression constant and then enters each variable in

In each of 1) i) (2), 1) ii) (2) and 1) iii) (2) a binomial logistic regression model was used to examine the predictive importance of vignette factors upon type of disposal.

In each of 1) i) (3), 1) ii) (3), and 1) iii) (3) univariate analyses of variance were run for each of the disposals [across a) both disposals, b) for prison only, and c) for hospital only] using vignette factors as fixed factors and length of disposal as the dependent variable. *t*-tests examined whether the means of length of detention differed between disposals.

The analysis of 2) was driven by the need to reduce the large number of attitudinal responses to a set of variables representing particular attitudinal dimensions. Each of the particular subscales within the questionnaire (e.g. meta-responsibility attitudes, left-right attitudes, insanity defence attitudes) was subjected to a factor analysis[7] and factor scores calculated for each subject.[8] These

---

subsequent step. A likelihood-ratio (LR) statistic is calculated at each step, which estimates the model's fit to the observed data. Variables are retained if their LR statistic is 0.05 or less, and removed if the LR statistic is 0.10 or greater. Stepwise methods 'are defensible for when used in situations in which no previous research exists on which to base hypotheses for testing' (Field, 2000: 169), as in the present study. The reference category used for each factor is the first subset of each factor (i.e. DIAGNOSIS = S [schizophrenia], TYPE OF META-RESPONSIBILITY = NMR [no meta-responsibility], TYPE OF INSANITY TEST = MN [McNaughton]). Using deviation contrasts, each category of the predictor variable (except the reference category) is compared to the overall effect of the variable. Those factors that do not reach significance at each iteration of the model are discarded; leaving a model best explaining the observed data. A Hosmer and Lemeshow goodness of fit test divides observed results into deciles and computes a chi-square distribution of the model's fit from observed and expected frequencies. A *p* value of the statistic indicates whether the null hypothesis (H_0) that there is no difference between observed results and the model's predicted results can be rejected (a higher *p* value indicates a better fit of the model to the observed data). The -2 log likelihood statistic (analogous to the error sum of squares in multiple regression) gives an estimate of the amount of observed data that is unexplained by the model. The relative importance of the predictors in the model are revealed by the (exp)β statistic for each predictor, which indicates the change in odds of the dependent variable given a unit change in the predictor (the direction of change is indicated by the β statistic). The Wald statistic (and its corresponding significance level) test the significance of each of the independent variables (predictors) in the model. Those independent variables (DIAGNOSIS, TYPE OF META-RESPONSIBILITY, TYPE OF INSANITY TEST) that have a *p* value of 0.05 or less are deemed significant predictors of the dependent variable (e.g. VERDICT).

7 Scales were individually subjected to a principal component analysis (PCA). To confirm that each of the subscales warranted its own individual PCA, a Spearman's correlation matrix of all attitudinal items was inspected for significant correlations between a) each item in the subscale; and b) between each item in a particular scale and all other attitudinal measures. The presence of substantial numbers of significant large correlations in a) indicates the desired covariation between subscale variables; substantial numbers of significant large correlations in b) would indicate that the items in the subscale did not form a 'true' subscale and that a PCA of such items in isolation from other attitudinal measures

factor scores were then used in further analysis: logistic regression models of categorical response variables for 2) (1) (verdict) and 2) (2) (disposal); and univariate ANOVAs of continuous response variables 2) (3) (a), 2) (3) (b), and 2) (3) (c) (length of detention for both disposals, prison disposals, and hospital disposals respectively).

The analysis of 3) used a binomial logistic regression model with verdict as the dependent variable and vignette factors and attitudinal factor scores as predictor variables.

Before presenting the statistical analysis of the data, it is appropriate to examine a) the questionnaire return rate; and b) the characteristics of the sample.

---

would be inappropriate (as their covariance would be with items outside of the scale). This would be especially true where items were discarded from the PCA due to low communalities with other items within the subscale; it may be that to discard such variables would be inappropriate if they demonstrated communality with other items not in that subscale. Only a small number of significant correlations of positive/negative 0.3 or greater were noted outside of items within a particular subscale (such a low level of interrelationship between the factors is also represented by the relatively small size of significant correlations between the factor scores examined in *INFRA* section 7.9.2), validating individual PCAs of each subscale in isolation from items within other scales. Suitability for factor analysis of each scale was further confirmed by a) examining the distribution of Likert responses for each item within the scale for normality and multicolinearity (the graphs are plotted in each table of the percentage of responses for scale items); and b) subjecting each scale to a Bartlett's test of sphericity and Kaiser-Meyer-Olkin (KMO) test of sampling adequacy to check for common variance due to underlying factors. VARIMAX rotation was applied where the factor solution contained more than one component. The VARIMAX algorithm 'rotates' factor solutions to minimize the number of variables that have high loadings on each factor (thus assisting in the identification of the 'meaning' of each component). Items with low communalities (<0.5) were dropped from the final PCA; such items do not have much of their variance accounted for by the factor solution (<50 per cent).

[8] SPSS v.10.0 can create new variables – factor scores for each *individual case* (i.e. subject) in the analysis – in a factor analysis. This gives a measure of the degree to which that subject's responses match a particular factor (attitudinal dimension). The PCA computes factor scores for each subject via regression (which can be used in further analysis, e.g. in a logistic regression model of the degree to which newly calculated attitudinal factors predict verdict). For each subject k, the score for the jth factor is:

$$\hat{F}_{jk} = \sum_{i=1}^{p} w_{ji} x_{ik}$$

where x_{ik} is the standardized value of the ith variable for subject k, and w_{ji} is the factor score coefficient for the jth factor and the ith variable. The scores are linear combinations of the original variables, and the size of the coefficients corresponds to the size of the loadings on each factor.

7.3 Questionnaire Return Rate

Of the 594 mailed questionnaires, 334 (56.2 per cent) were completed and returned. Figure 7.1 displays the number returned by vignette type (combination of factors). The figure shows, for example, that 22 questionnaires were returned of the depression> consensual meta-responsibility>meta-responsibility test (D>CMR>MR) variety. No cell in the factors table (see Figure 7.1) had less than 15 subjects (the minimum estimated number required for sufficient statistical power in the analyses).

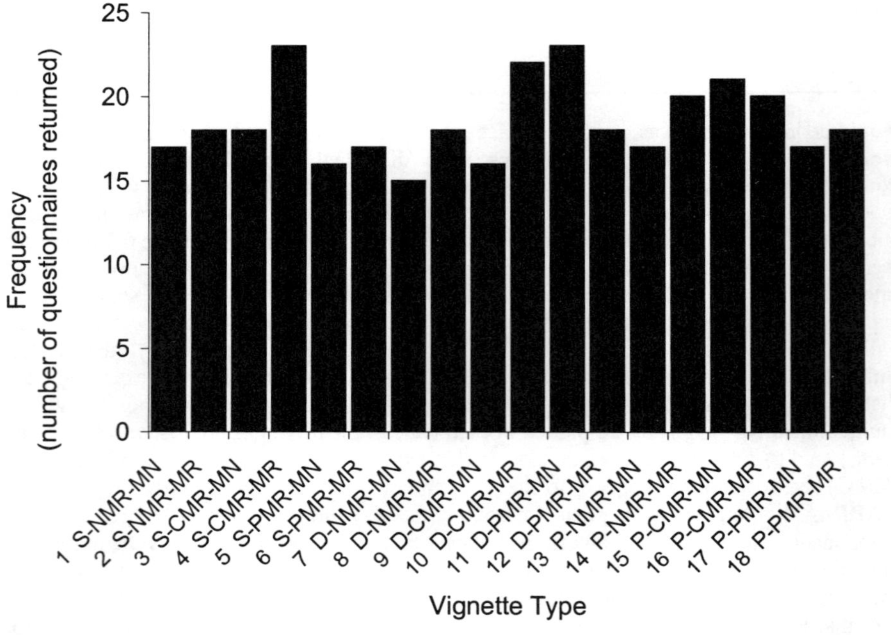

Figure 7.1 Return rate by vignette type

A chi-square statistic (x^2=5.305, df=17, p=0.997) shows the null hypothesis (H_0) may be accepted that there is no difference between observed and expected return rates for each vignette type (where expected return rates are equal across vignette types). The type of vignette the subject received therefore had no significant effect on participation in the study.

7.4 Sample Characteristics

7.4.1 Age

Subjects' ages ranged from 18 to 57, with a mean age of 22.5 (median=21.0, SD=4.65).

7.4.2 Gender

The sample consisted of 58.1 per cent males and 41.9 per cent females.

7.4.3 Ethnic Identity

Self-reported ethnic identities of the sample are displayed in Table 7.1.

Table 7.1 Ethnic identities of subjects (from UK Census 1991 categories)

Ethnic identity	Frequency	Per cent
White	281	84.1
Black (Caribbean)	2	0.6
Black (African)	3	0.9
Indian	13	3.9
Pakistani	4	1.2
Chinese	8	2.4
Other Asian	10	3.0
White Chinese	1	0.3
Other	10	3.0
Total*	332	99.4

* Less than 334 (total questionnaires returned) indicates missing values

Subjects' ethnic identities were: 84.1 per cent 'white', 12.3 per cent 'non-white', three per cent 'other', and 0.6 per cent missing values. Given the small numbers of respondents in each of the non-white ethnic origins, for further analysis subjects' ethnic identities were categorized as 'white' or 'other' (these two categories are, strictly, racial categorizations rather than ethnic identities).

7.4.4 Educational Background

63.2 per cent of the sample were undergraduates, and 32.6 per cent postgraduates (4.2 per cent missing values). Of the undergraduates, 34.1 per cent were in their first year of study, 33.2 per cent in their second year, 23.2 per cent in their third year, and 9.5 per cent in their fourth year. Of the postgraduates, 30.3 per cent were studying for Masters degrees, 38.5 per cent for PhDs, 8.3 per cent for LLMs (one year postgraduate law degrees), 0.9 per cent for an MBA, 0.9 per cent for a certificate in postgraduate study, and 0.9 per cent were engaging in post-doctoral work. 20.2 per cent of postgraduates did not indicate their degree.

7.8 per cent of the subjects were studying medicine, nine per cent law, 2.1 per cent criminology, and 1.2 per cent psychology (although psychology at Cambridge University is incorporated within Natural Sciences, so some of the 12.9 per cent of subjects studying Natural Sciences may have studied psychology) and 0.3 per cent philosophy (although some of the 4.5 per cent of subjects studying social and political sciences may also have studied philosophy). Therefore, approximately 21 per cent of the subjects were engaged in a discipline in which they might have learned about the issues with which the study dealt (i.e. psychiatry, law, criminology, philosophy, psychology). This is an approximate figure; for example, some law students may have been studying exclusively corporate law, some medical students may have not yet studied psychiatry, and some language PhDs (for example) may have a psychological background.

7.4.5 *Experience and Knowledge of Mental Disorder*

Table 7.2 displays proportions of subjects endorsing each Likert category in response to questions concerning experience of mental disorder in self or others (MDEXP), and how much the subject believed he/she was informed about mental disorder issues (MDINFORM). The items had means of 3.34 and 3.61 respectively, indicating that the sample generally felt they had some experience and were averagely informed concerning mental disorder.

Table 7.2 Percentage of Likert responses for experience and knowledge of mental disorder

Item[ab]	1	2	3	4	5	6	7	Total	Graph
Please rate the amount of experience you think you have of mental disorder (e.g. personally suffered from it, friends/family suffered from it, etc.) (MDEXP)	18.6	21.6	11.4	21.9	13.2	9.0	4.5	100.0	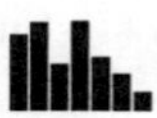
Do you think you are well informed about mental disorder and mental disorder issues? (MDINFORM)	12.6	20.4	12.9	20.4	20.1	9.0	4.8	100.0	

[a] For MDEXP: 1 = No experience, 4 = Some experience, 7 = Lots of experience
[b] For MDINFORM: 1 = Not well informed, 4 = Averagely informed, 7 = Well informed

A Spearman's rank test[9] shows the two variables have a significant positive correlation (r=0.489, α=0.671, p<0.001); those with more experience of mental disorder are thus likely to endorse themselves as being better informed. The measures were reduced to a single factor score using principal component analysis.[10] The factor produced by the analysis, 'Knowledge', had high positive loadings for both items (both 0.867), and explained 75.24 per cent of the variance between the variables. Factor scores were created for each subject;[11] the new variable was named FMDKNOW (factor-mental disorder-knowledge) and represents a general measure of subjects' self-reported knowledge and experience concerning mental disorder.

7.5 Effect of Vignette Factors on Verdict

Overall, across all 18 vignettes, Tom was found guilty by 204 subjects (61.3 per cent), and NGRI by 129 subjects (38.7 per cent).

Table 7.3 shows the observed frequencies and percentages of verdicts by vignette type. A chi-square test of vignette type and verdict shows the null hypothesis of no relationship between vignette type and verdict can be rejected (x^2=62.39, df=17, p<0.001) i.e. verdict is related to vignette type.

A cursory examination of the proportions of NGRI verdicts in Table 7.3 distinguishes several trends.

In terms of diagnosis, schizophrenia appears to result in the greatest proportion of NGRI verdicts, followed by depression and then personality disorder. NGRI verdicts are most common for schizophrenia when Tom displays consensual meta-responsibility and the McNaughton test is employed (S>CMR>MN; 83.3 per cent of verdicts are NGRI in this condition, compared with only 38.7 per cent overall). NGRI verdicts are least common for schizophrenia in the purposive meta-responsibility>McNaughton test condition (S>PMR>MN; only 50 per cent of verdicts are NGRI). NGRI verdicts are highest for depression (as with schizophrenia) in the consensual meta-responsibility>McNaughton test condition (D>CMR>MN; 43.8 per cent NGRI), and at their lowest in the no meta-responsibility>McNaughton condition (D>NMR>MN; 20 per cent NGRI). For personality disorder, Tom is most likely to be found NGRI when he has consensual meta-responsibility and the meta-responsibility test is used (P>CMR>MR; 33 per

---

9 A nonparametric test was chosen because the graphs in Table 7.2 show that the data does not appear to obey an unskewed normal distribution. MDEXP has a ratio of skewness (0.296) to standard error (0.133) of 2.22 (positive values above 2.0 indicate a long right tail; that is, subjects generally rate themselves as having low experience of mental disorder). MDINF has a ratio of skewness (0.105) to standard error (0.133) of 0.789, which indicates a slight left skewness, but conforming to a normal distribution.

10 The PCA is described in *SUPRA* note 7.

11 See *SUPRA* note 8.

cent NGRI), and least likely in the no meta-responsibility>meta-responsibility test condition (P>NMR>MR; only five per cent NGRI).

Table 7.3 Percentage of NGRI and guilty verdicts by type of vignette

Vignette	Guilty	NGRI	Total
S>NMR>MN	9 (52.9%)	8 (47.1%)	17
S>NMR>MR	8 (44.4%)	10 (55.6%)	18
S>CMR>MN	3 (16.7%)	15 (83.3%)	18
S>CMR>MR	8 (34.8%)	15 (65.2%)	23
S>PMR>MN	8 (50.0%)	8 (50.0%)	16
S>PMR>MR	4 (23.5%)	13 (76.5%)	17
D>NMR>MN	12 (80.0%)	3 (20.0%)	15
D>NMR>MR	13 (72.2%)	5 (27.8%)	18
D>CMR>MN	9 (56.3%)	7 (43.8%)	16
D>CMR>MR	15 (68.2%)	7 (31.8%)	22
D>PMR>MN	14 (63.6%)	8 (36.4%)	22
D>PMR>MR	14 (77.8%)	4 (22.2%)	18
P>NMR>MN	11 (64.7%)	6 (35.3%)	17
P>NMR>MR	19 (95.0%)	1 (5.0%)	20
P>CMR>MN	14 (66.7%)	7 (33.3%)	21
P>CMR>MR	12 (60.0%)	8 (40.0%)	20
P>PMR>MN	15 (88.2%)	2 (11.8%)	17
P>PMR>MR	16 (88.9%)	2 (11.1%)	18
Total*	204 (61.3%)	129 (38.7%)	333

* Less than 334 (total questionnaires returned) indicates missing values

In terms of type of meta-responsibility, it is perhaps surprising that consensual meta-responsibility (CMR) raises the proportion of NGRI verdicts over no meta-responsibility in five of the six consensual meta-responsibility (__>CMR>__) conditions, whereas the proportion of NGRI verdicts for the purposive meta-responsibility conditions (__>PMR>__) appears similar to the amount rendered in the no meta-responsibility conditions (__>NMR>__). Most NGRI verdicts for no meta-responsibility (NMR) are rendered in the schizophrenia>meta-responsibility test condition (S>NMR>MR; 55.6 per cent NGRI), and fewest in the personality disorder>meta-responsibility test condition (P>NMR>MR; five per cent NGRI). Most NGRI verdicts for CMR are rendered in the schizophrenia>McNaughton condition (S>CMR>MN; 83.3 per cent NGRI) and fewest in the depression>meta-responsibility insanity test condition (D>CMR>MR; 31.8 per cent NGRI). Most NGRI verdicts for PMR are rendered in the schizophrenia>meta-responsibility test condition (S>PMR>MR; 76.5 per cent NGRI), and fewest in the personality disorder>meta-responsibility test condition (P>PMR>MR; 11.1 per cent NGRI).

In terms of the type of insanity test used, there does not appear to be a clearly distinguishable trend in the proportions of NGRI verdicts for the two insanity tests. For the McNaughton test, NGRI verdicts are at their highest in the schizophrenia>purposive meta-responsibility condition (S>PMR>MN; 83.3. per cent NGRI). For the meta-responsibility test, NGRI verdicts are at their highest (76.5 per cent) in the schizophrenia>purposive meta-responsibility condition (S>PMR>MR; 76.5 per cent NGRI). The expected effect of the MRIT in decreasing NGRI verdicts (particularly when Tom showed consensual or purposive meta-responsibility) does not therefore seem to occur.

To examine in detail the effect of each of the factors (diagnosis, type of meta-responsibility, and insanity test) on verdict, graphs were produced of the effect of each factor on verdict (it may be noted that Figures 7.2, 7.3 and 7.4 are the same data plotted by each factor respectively), and binomial tests run on the proportion of NGRI verdicts of the vignette of interest against the reference category.[12] Finally, a regression model was fitted to the data that best explains observed verdicts in terms of the factors.

7.5.1 Effect of Diagnosis on Verdict

Figure 7.2 shows the proportion of NGRI verdicts for each vignette arranged by diagnosis.

A preliminary inspection of Figure 7.2 suggests that diagnosis has an effect on the proportion of NGRI verdicts rendered in each type of meta-responsibility>insanity test condition. A Kruskal-Wallis test confirms that diagnosis does have a significant effect on overall verdict outcome (x^2=42.442, df=2, p<0.001).

The general trend distinguished in Table 7.3 is made clearer in the graph: that Tom is generally less likely to be found NGRI when depressed than schizophrenic, and even less likely to be found NGRI in the personality disorder condition. Such trends may be confirmed by detailed analysis using binomial tests for differences between the respective NGRI verdict proportions.

Binomial tests for the effect of diagnosis on verdict Two sets of binomial tests were run for each group of vignettes along the *x*-axis of Figure 7.2, using the first and last categories of diagnosis (i.e. schizophrenia and personality disorder) as the reference categories. The tests measure the effect of changing the diagnosis on verdict (holding type of meta-responsibility and type of insanity test constant). In the first group of vignettes (the first row along the *x*-axis of Figure 7.2 below from back to front) we test whether the proportion of NGRI verdicts for D>NMR>MN and P>NMR>MN differ significantly from S>NMR>MN (whether NGRI verdicts for schizophrenia are significantly higher or lower than for depression and for

[12] See *SUPRA* note 2 for a description of the relationship between test proportion and the proportion in the reference category.

personality disorder). The second binomial test examines whether the proportions of NGRI verdicts differ between D>NMR>MN and P>NMR>MN (whether NGRI verdicts for depression are significantly higher or lower than for personality disorder). The binomial tests might show (when Tom had no meta-responsibility and the mock jurors applied a McNaughton test) that the proportion of NGRI verdicts rendered for depression is significantly lower than for schizophrenia. The first row of Table 7.4 below indeed shows this to be true (p=0.03).

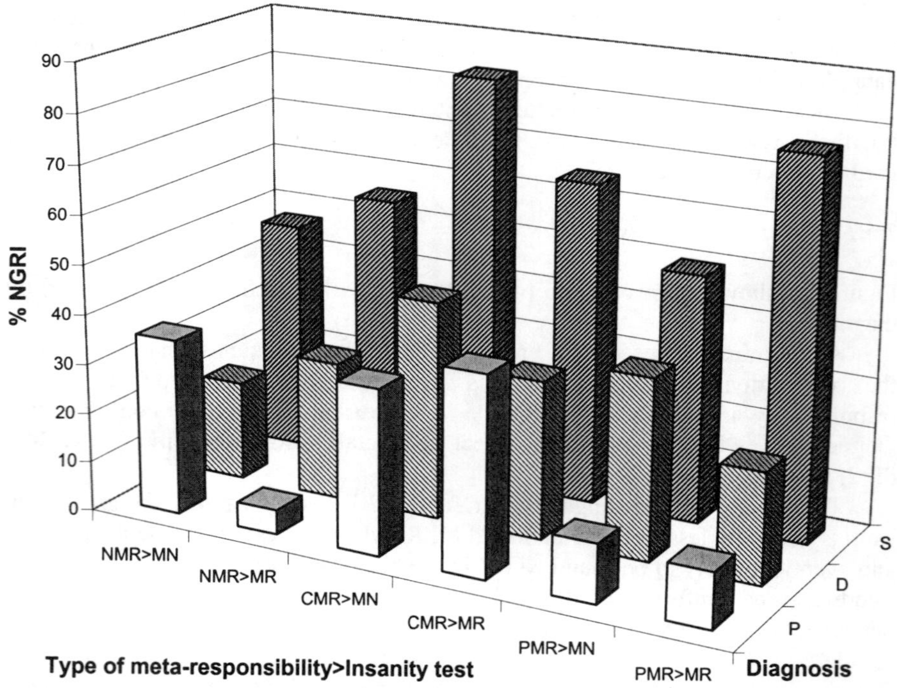

Figure 7.2 Percentage of Not Guilty by Reason of Insanity verdicts for each vignette, arranged using diagnosis as the contrast variable

The test proportions for each group are 1-(proportion of NGRI verdicts for the reference category) as the binomial test examines whether the proportion of the *first* category of the bifurcated response variable (i.e. proportion of *guilty* verdicts) differs from the test proportion.

Table 7.4 Binomial tests for the effect of diagnosis on verdict

Type/reference type	Category	N	Observed proportion	Test prop.	Sig.	Direction[a]
D>NMR>MN/S>NMR>MN	Guilty	12	0.800	0.529	0.030*	<
	NGRI	3	0.200			
P>NMR>MN/S>NMR>MN	Guilty	11	0.647	0.529	0.233	<
	NGRI	6	0.353			
D>NMR>MN/P>NMR>MN	Guilty	12	0.800	0.647	0.167	<
	NGRI	3	0.200			
D>NMR>MR/S>NMR>MR	Guilty	13	0.722	0.444	0.016*	<
	NGRI	5	0.278			
P>NMR>MR/S>NMR>MR	Guilty	19	0.950	0.444	0.000**	<
	NGRI	1	0.050			
D>NMR>MR/P>NMR>MR	Guilty	13	0.722	0.950	0.002**	>
	NGRI	5	0.278			
D>CMR>MN/S>CMR>MN	Guilty	9	0.563	0.177	0.001**	<
	NGRI	7	0.438			
P>CMR>MN/S>CMR>MN	Guilty	14	0.667	0.177	0.000**	<
	NGRI	7	0.333			
D>CMR>MN/P>CMR>MN	Guilty	9	0.563	0.667	0.262	>
	NGRI	7	0.438			
D>CMR>MR/S>CMR>MR	Guilty	15	0.682	0.348	0.001**	<
	NGRI	7	0.318			
P>CMR>MR/S>CMR>MR	Guilty	12	0.600	0.348	0.019*	<
	NGRI	8	0.400			
D>CMR>MR/P>CMR>MR	Guilty	15	0.682	0.600	0.290	<
	NGRI	7	0.318			
D>PMR>MN/S>PMR>MN	Guilty	14	0.636	0.500	0.286	<
	NGRI	8	0.364			
P>PMR>MN/S>PMR>MN	Guilty	15	0.882	0.500	0.002**	<
	NGRI	2	0.118			
D>PMR>MN/S>PMR>MN	Guilty	14	0.636	0.882	0.003**	>
	NGRI	8	0.364			
D>PMR>MR/S>PMR>MN	Guilty	14	0.778	0.235	0.000**	<
	NGRI	4	0.222			
P>PMR>MR/S>PMR>MN	Guilty	16	0.889	0.235	0.000**	<
	NGRI	2	0.111			
D>PMR>MR/P>PMR>MR	Guilty	14	0.778	0.889	0.131	>
	NGRI	4	0.222			

* $p < 0.05$ ** $p < 0.01$

[a] Direction refers to whether the observed NGRI proportion is greater (>) or less than (<) the proportion of NGRIs in the reference category

Examining Table 7.4 shows that varying the diagnosis in the vignette has a significant effect on verdict outcome in every group of *x*-axis (type of meta-responsibility>insanity test) conditions in Figure 7.2. This confirms the suspected trend that NGRI verdicts for schizophrenia are higher than for depression, which are in turn generally higher than for personality disorder.

For the no meta-responsibility>McNaughton condition (__>NMR>MN), in comparison to schizophrenia, NGRI verdicts were significantly less frequent for depression ($p=0.03$), but not for personality disorder ($p=0.167$). In the no meta-responsibility>MRIT condition (__>NMR>MR), the offer of NGRI significantly decreased for both depression ($p=0.016$) and personality disorder ($p<0.001$) compared to schizophrenia; furthermore, NGRI verdicts for personality disorder were significantly lower than for depression ($p=0.002$).

With consensual meta-responsibility and using the McNaughton test (__>CMR>MN), both depression ($p=0.001$) and personality disorder ($p<0.001$) elicited significantly fewer NGRI verdicts than schizophrenia, although the proportion of verdicts for depression and personality disorder did not differ from each other significantly. The same pattern also occurred when the MRIT was substituted for McNaughton (__>CMR>MR); NGRI verdicts for both depression ($p=0.001$) and personality disorder ($p=0.019$) were significantly less frequent than for schizophrenia, but not significantly different from each other.

For purposive meta-responsibility with the McNaughton test (__>PMR>MN), NGRI verdicts for depression were not significantly lower than for schizophrenia, although NGRI verdicts for personality disorder were significantly lower than both schizophrenia ($p=0.002$), and depression ($p=0.003$). Finally, for purposive meta-responsibility using the MRIT (__>PMR>MR), NGRI verdicts were significantly lower in both the depression ($p<0.001$) and personality disorder ($p<0.001$) conditions than for schizophrenia, but not significantly different from each other.

7.5.2 Effect of Type of Meta-responsibility on Verdict

Figure 7.3 shows the proportion of NGRI verdicts for each vignette arranged by type of meta-responsibility.

An inspection of Figure 7.3 shows that the type of meta-responsibility does not appear to have such a distinctive effect on verdict outcome as does diagnosis. However, a Kruskal-Wallis test shows that, overall, type of meta-responsibility does have a significant effect on verdict outcome ($x^2=8.750$, df=2, $p=0.013$).

The general trend distinguished from the inspection of Table 7.3 is more clear in Figure 7.3: consensual meta-responsibility draws NGRI verdicts with surprising frequency compared to no meta-responsibility and purposive meta-responsibility (*especially* when Tom is schizophrenic and the McNaughton test is applied). Purposive meta-responsibility is also more frequently associated with a NGRI verdict than expected (especially when Tom is schizophrenic and the MRIT is applied). The most clearly delineable trend, occurring in five of the six *x*-axis (diagnosis>insanity test) conditions, is that NGRI verdicts are more frequent for consensual meta-responsibility than no meta-responsibility, and tend to diminish in the purposive meta-responsibility condition to levels more comparable with the no meta-responsibility condition.

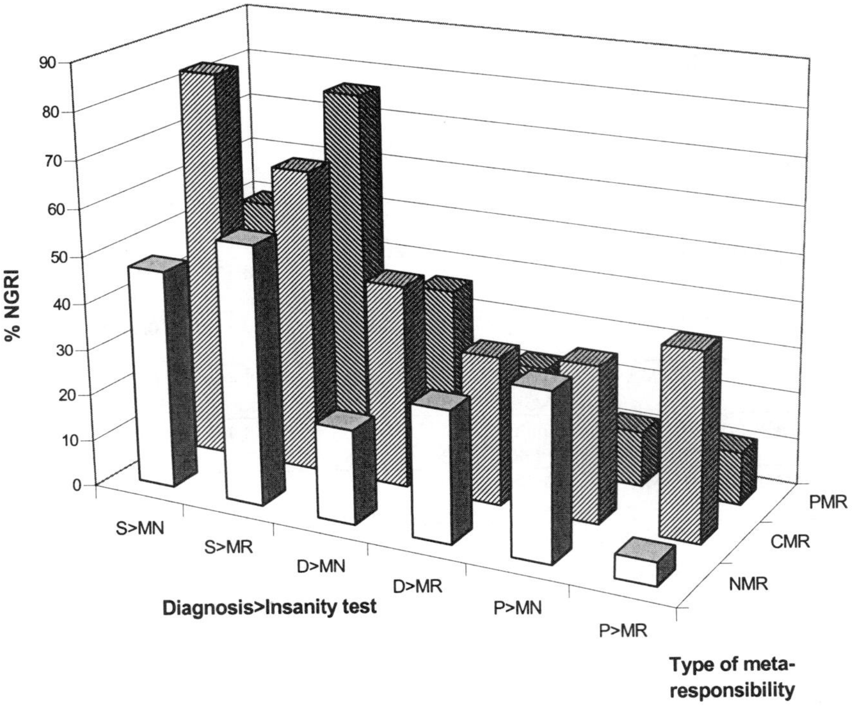

Figure 7.3 Percentage of Not Guilty by Reason of Insanity verdicts for each vignette, arranged using type of meta-responsibility as the contrast variable

Binomial tests for the effect of type of meta-responsibility on verdict Binomial tests, displayed in Table 7.5, indicate if the trends observed in Figure 7.3 are significant.

The binomial tests show that the suspected trend is significant (verdicts for consensual meta-responsibility are higher than for no meta-responsibility) in three of the six diagnosis>insanity test conditions (i.e. significant in three of the five conditions in which consensual meta-responsibility draws more NGRI verdicts than no meta-responsibility).

When Tom is schizophrenic and the McNaughton test is applied (S>__>MN), consensual meta-responsibility produces significantly more verdicts than both no meta-responsibility (p=0.002) and purposive meta-responsibility (p=0.008) (which do not differ significantly from each other). For the schizophrenia>meta-responsibility test condition (S>__>MR), NGRI verdicts for consensual meta-responsibility and purposive meta-responsibility do not differ significantly from the proportion rendered in the no meta-responsibility condition.

Table 7.5 Binomial tests for the effect of type of meta-responsibility on verdict

Type/reference type	Category	N	Observed proportion	Test prop.	Sig.	Direction[a]
S>CMR>MN/S>NMR>MN	Guilty	3	0.167	0.529	0.002**	>
	NGRI	15	0.833			
S>PMR>MN/S>NMR>MN	Guilty	8	0.500	0.529	0.505	>
	NGRI	8	0.500			
S>CMR>MN/S>PMR>MN	Guilty	3	0.167	0.500	0.008*	>
	NGRI	15	0.833			
S>CMR>MR/S>NMR>MR	Guilty	8	0.348	0.444	0.238	>
	NGRI	15	0.652			
S>PMR>MR/S>NMR>MR	Guilty	4	0.235	0.444	0.066	<
	NGRI	13	0.765			
S>CMR>MR/S>PMR>MR	Guilty	8	0.348	0.235	0.151	<
	NGRI	15	0.652			
D>CMR>MN/D>NMR>MN	Guilty	9	0.563	0.800	0.027*	>
	NGRI	7	0.438			
D>PMR>MN/D>NMR>MN	Guilty	14	0.636	0.800	0.560	>
	NGRI	8	0.364			
D>CMR>MN/D>PMR>MN	Guilty	9	0.563	0.636	0.355	>
	NGRI	7	0.438			
D>CMR>MR/D>NMR>MR	Guilty	15	0.682	0.722	0.414	>
	NGRI	7	0.318			
D>PMR>MR/D>NMR>MR	Guilty	14	0.778	0.722	0.411	<
	NGRI	4	0.222			
D>CMR>MR/D>PMR>MR	Guilty	15	0.682	0.778	0.199	>
	NGRI	7	0.318			
P>CMR>MN/P>NMR>MN	Guilty	14	0.667	0.647	0.525	<
	NGRI	7	0.333			
P>PMR>MN/P>NMR>MN	Guilty	15	0.882	0.647	0.031*	<
	NGRI	2	0.118			
P>CMR>MN/P>PMR>MN	Guilty	14	0.667	0.882	0.008**	>
	NGRI	7	0.333			
P>CMR>MR/P>NMR>MR	Guilty	12	0.600	0.950	0.000**	>
	NGRI	8	0.400			
P>PMR>MR/P>NMR>MR	Guilty	16	0.889	0.950	0.226	>
	NGRI	2	0.111			
P>CMR>MR/P>PMR>MR	Guilty	12	0.600	0.889	0.001**	>
	NGRI	8	0.400			

* $p < 0.05$ **$p < 0.01$

[a] Direction refers to whether the observed NGRI proportion is greater (>) or less than (<) the proportion of NGRIs in the reference category

For the depression>McNaughton condition (D>__>MN), NGRI verdicts are significantly higher for consensual meta-responsibility ($p=0.027$) than for no meta-responsibility (purposive meta-responsibility does not differ significantly in NGRI frequency from no meta-responsibility or consensual meta-responsibility). When the MRIT is substituted for the McNaughton test (the D>__>MR condition), verdicts do not differ significantly across types of meta-responsibility.

When Tom is personality disordered and the McNaughton test is applied (P>__>MN), verdicts do not differ between the no meta-responsibility and consensual meta-responsibility conditions, but purposive meta-responsibility produces significantly fewer NGRI verdicts than both no meta-responsibility ($p=0.031$) and consensual meta-responsibility ($p=0.008$). Substituting the MRIT in the personality disorder condition (P>__>MR) results in a significant increase in NGRI verdicts for consensual meta-responsibility ($p<0.001$) over both no meta-responsibility and purposive meta-responsibility ($p=0.001$) (the proportion of NGRI verdicts for no meta-responsibility and purposive meta-responsibility does not differ significantly).

7.5.3 Effect of Insanity Test on Verdict

Figure 7.4 below displays the proportion of NGRI verdicts for each vignette arranged by type of insanity test. A cursory examination of Figure 7.4 suggests that the effect of the meta-responsibility insanity test compared to the McNaughton test varies depending on the diagnosis and the type of meta-responsibility.

A Mann-Whitney test shows that, overall, type of insanity test does not have a significant effect on verdict outcome ($z=-0.541$, df=1, $p=0.589$). Mann-Whitney tests for the effect of insanity test by diagnosis and type of meta-responsibility also fail to reach significance, suggesting that no particular interaction effect of insanity test with either diagnosis or type of meta-responsibility predicts verdict.

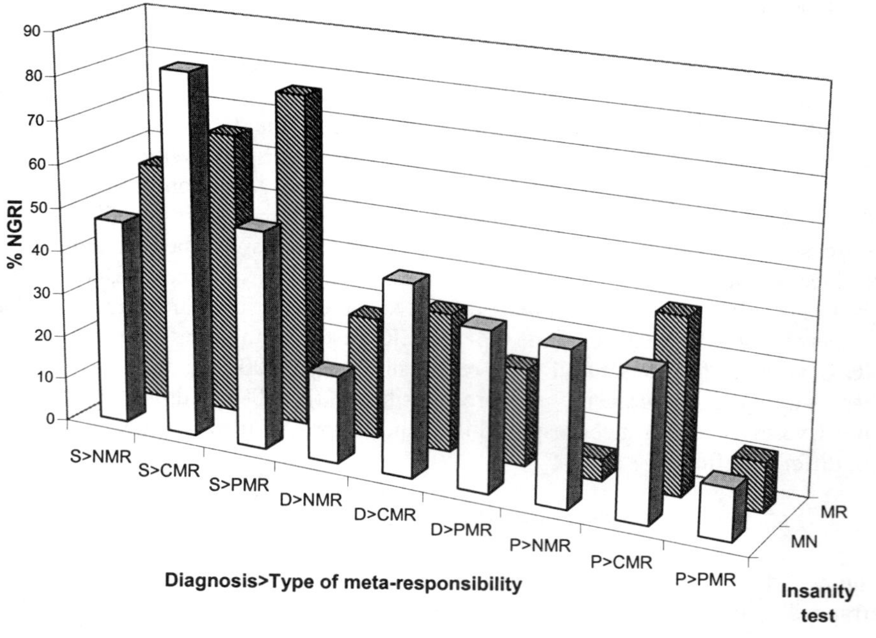

Figure 7.4 Percentage of Not Guilty by Reason of Insanity verdicts for each vignette, arranged using type of insanity test as the contrast variable

Binomial tests for the effect of type of insanity test on verdict These are presented in Table 7.6.

The binomial tests show that the meta-responsibility test significantly increases the percentage of NGRI verdicts for one condition (when Tom is schizophrenic and has purposive meta-responsibility [S>PMR>__; *p*=0.049]) and significantly decreases NGRI verdicts for two conditions (when Tom is schizophrenic and has consensual meta-responsibility [S>CMR>__; *p*=0.028], and when Tom is personality disordered and has no meta-responsibility [P>NMR>__; *p*=0.002]). The effect of the MRIT in *increasing* NGRI verdicts was unexpected, given that it is a 'more stringent' test than the McNaughton test (verdicts are increased in four out of the nine *x*-axis conditions in Figure 7.4, albeit not reaching significance in three). Its effect in the S>PMR>__ condition is particularly surprising, as in this condition Tom has purposive meta-responsibility which was expected to reduce NGRI verdicts, especially in the MRIT condition which allows culpable conduct to be reflected through a guilty verdict.

Table 7.6 Binomial tests for the effect of insanity test on verdict

Type/reference type	Category	N	Observed proportion	Test prop.	Sig.	Direction[a]
S>NMR>MR/S>NMR>MN	Guilty	8	0.444	0.529	0.314	>
	NGRI	10	0.556			
S>CMR>MR/S>CMR>MN	Guilty	8	0.345	0.167	0.028*	<
	NGRI	15	0.652			
S>PMR>MR/S>PMR>MN	Guilty	4	0.235	0.500	0.049*	>
	NGRI	13	0.765			
D>NMR>MR/D>NMR>MN	Guilty	13	0.722	0.800	0.284	>
	NGRI	5	0.278			
D>CMR>MR/D>CMR>MN	Guilty	15	0.682	0.563	0.182	<
	NGRI	7	0.318			
D>PMR>MR/D>PMR>MN	Guilty	14	0.778	0.636	0.157	<
	NGRI	4	0.222			
P>NMR>MR/P>NMR>MN	Guilty	19	0.950	0.647	0.002**	<
	NGRI	1	0.050			
P>CMR>MR/P>CMR>MN	Guilty	12	0.600	0.667	0.337	>
	NGRI	8	0.400			
P>PMR>MR/P>PMR>MN	Guilty	16	0.889	0.882	0.641	<
	NGRI	2	0.111			

* $p < 0.05$ **$p < 0.01$
[a] Direction refers to whether the observed NGRI proportion is greater (>) or less than (<) the proportion of NGRIs in the reference category

7.5.4 Models of the Effect of Vignette Factors on Verdict

The binomial tests indicate that there are differences between the proportions of guilty/NGRI verdicts for different 'treatment' combinations of factors, but it is appropriate to ask if any general model of factors or factor interactions can predict verdict outcome.

An exploratory ANOVA was performed using 'dummy-coded' categorical variables (guilty=1, NGRI=2).[13] Both diagnosis (f=24.362, df=2, p<0.001) and type of meta-responsibility (f=5.068, df=2, p=0.007) are important predictors of verdict in a saturated model of vignette factors.[14] Type of insanity test does not reach significance, and neither do any two or three way interaction effects between the three vignette factors.

The ANOVA estimated marginal means, plotted in Figure 7.5 confirm the general effect of depression and personality disorder to reduce the proportion of

[13] See *SUPRA* note 5 for a discussion of the problems of dummy-coding categorical data such as verdict.

[14] A saturated model includes main effects, two way (first order) and three way (second order) interactions.

NGRI verdicts, and the generally higher levels of NGRI verdicts for consensual meta-responsibility in comparison to no meta-responsibility and purposive meta-responsibility.

A binary logistic regression using categorical independent and dependent variables (rather than dummy-codings) confirms the predictive importance of diagnosis and type of meta-responsibility on verdict, and also excludes type of insanity test as a significant overall predictor. Running the model with the vignette factors in a saturated design produces a model that predicts verdict correctly in 70.0 per cent of cases with a -2 log likelihood (-2LL) of 392.66. A Hosmer and Lemeshow goodness of fit (H&L) test indicates that there is no significant difference between the observed verdict pattern and the model's predicted verdict pattern, indicating the model is a good predictor of verdict (x^2=2.997, df=7, p=0.887). Diagnosis (p<0.001) and type of meta-responsibility (p=0.01) are significant predictors of verdict. Insanity test does not reach a likelihood ratio statistic sufficient to be included in the final model (p=0.439), neither do any first or second order interaction terms. In terms of diagnosis contrasts to the reference category (schizophrenia), personality disorder has a significant effect on verdict (β=-0.714, exp(β)=0.489, p<0.001) but depression does not (β=-0.324, exp(β)=0.722, p=0.056). The negative β-values of the two contrasts indicate that both depression and personality disorder have a negative effect on verdict (i.e. increase the percentage of guilty findings) in comparison to schizophrenia (this difference just misses out on significance in the case of depression). The exp(β) value of personality disorder indicates that compared to schizophrenia, a diagnosis of personality disorder reduces the odds of an NGRI finding by 51.1 per cent ([1-0.489] x 100).

In terms of type of meta-responsibility contrasts, consensual meta-responsibility has a significant effect on verdict (β=0.502, exp(β)=1.653, p=0.003). This effect is a positive one: consensual meta-responsibility increases the odds of an NGRI verdict by 65.3 per cent in comparison to no meta-responsibility. Purposive meta-responsibility is not a significant predictor of verdict in the model (β=-0.159, exp(β)=0.853, p=0.365).

These results comport with the results of the binomial tests and the graphical plots of verdict patterns. Personality disorder significantly decreases the likelihood of an NGRI verdict in comparison to schizophrenia (depression also has the general effect of reducing NGRI verdicts, albeit non-significantly). Consensual meta-responsibility *increases* the likelihood of a NGRI finding in comparison to no meta-responsibility, but purposive meta-responsibility does not differ in verdict pattern from no meta-responsibility. Insanity test does not have a uniform effect on verdict pattern that can be accounted for by its inclusion in a regression model (confirming its failure to prove a significant predictor of verdict in the Mann-Whitney test). However, the binomial tests clearly indicate that it *can* significantly influence the proportion of NGRI verdicts under certain conditions of diagnosis and type of meta-responsibility.

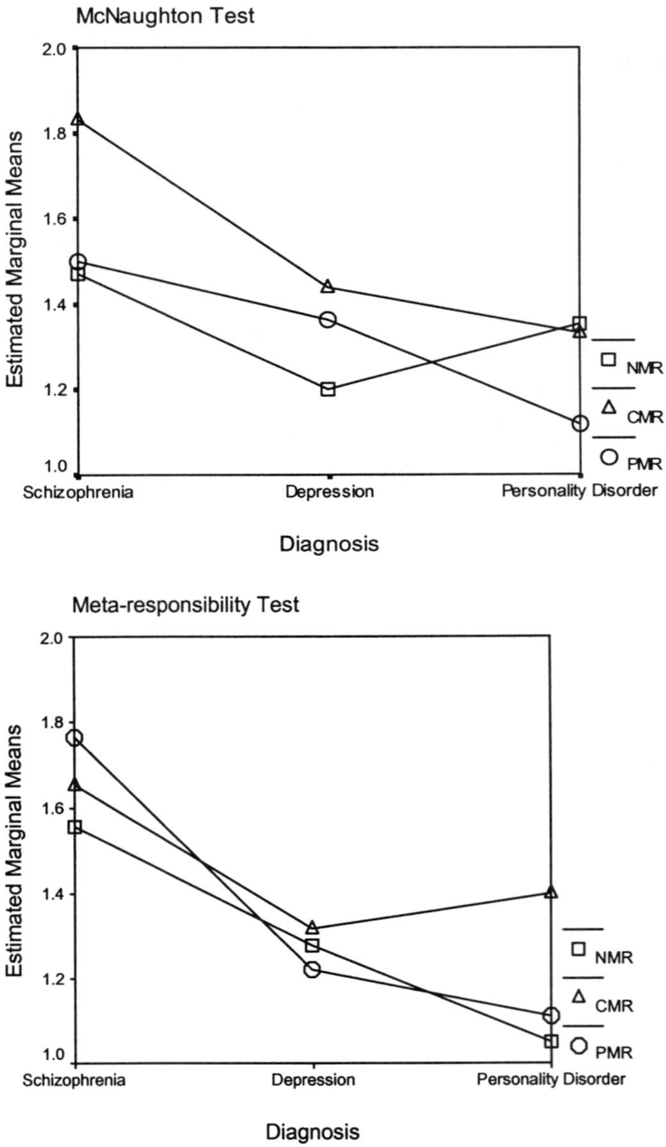

Figure 7.5 Estimated marginal means* from ANOVA for dummy-coded verdict by diagnosis, type of meta-responsibility and insanity test (as the panel variable)

* Higher marginal means indicate that a greater proportion of NGRI verdicts were rendered in that condition

7.6 Effect of Vignette Factors On Disposal Recommendation

A Spearman's test shows that verdict (guilty/NGRI) is closely related to disposal (prison/hospital) (r=0.635, p<0.001). This result is unsurprising, as the vignette instructed that 'If found "Guilty" Tom will be sent to prison, whereas if his insanity plea is successful Tom will be sent to a special hospital...'. Table 7.7 shows type of disposal by verdict.

Table 7.7 Frequencies and percentages of prison and hospital disposals by verdict

Verdict	Prison	Hospital	Total
Guilty	128 63.4%	74 36.6%	202
NGRI	0 0.0%	129 100.0%	129
Total	128 38.7%	203 61.3%	331*

* Less than 334 (total questionnaires returned) indicates missing values

A chi-square test shows we can reject the null hypothesis of independence between verdict and disposal (x^2=133.29, df=1, p<0.001). Not one subject who found Tom NGRI recommended a prison disposal. However, 74 subjects out of the 202 (36.6 per cent) who found Tom guilty recommended a 'hospital order'.

Table 7.8 shows the frequency and percentage of subjects opting for prison or hospital by vignette.

Table 7.8 Type of disposal by vignette type

Vignette	Prison	Hospital	Total
S>NMR>MN	5 (29.4%)	12 (70.6%)	17
S>NMR>MR	6 (33.3%)	12 (66.7%)	18
S>CMR>MN	1 (5.6%)	17 (94.4%)	18
S>CMR>MR	4 (17.4%)	19 (82.6%)	23
S>PMR>MN	1 (6.3%)	15 (93.7%)	16
S>PMR>MR	1 (6.3%)	15 (93.7%)	16
D>NMR>MN	9 (60.0%)	6 (40.0%)	15
D>NMR>MR	8 (44.4%)	10 (55.6%)	18
D>CMR>MN	5 (31.3%)	11 (68.7%)	16
D>CMR>MR	8 (36.4%)	14 (63.6%)	22
D>PMR>MN	9 (40.9%)	13 (59.1%)	22
D>PMR>MR	7 (38.9%)	11 (61.1%)	18
P>NMR>MN	9 (52.9%)	8 (47.1%)	17
P>NMR>MR	13 (65.0%)	7 (35.0%)	20
P>CMR>MN	10 (47.6%)	11 (52.4%)	21
P>CMR>MR	6 (30.0%)	14 (70.0%)	20
P>PMR>MN	11 (68.7%)	5 (31.3%)	16
P>PMR>MR	15 (83.3%)	3 (16.7%)	18
Total*	128 (38.7%)	203 (61.3%)	331

* Less than 334 (total questionnaires returned) indicates missing values

A logistic regression model shows whether the results depicted in Table 7.8 may be predicted by a pattern of vignette factors and/or their interactions.

7.6.1 A Regression Model of Vignette Factors on Disposal

A binary logistic regression (with the same parameters as for verdict but substituting type of disposal as the dependent variable), shows diagnosis ($p<0.001$) and type of meta-responsibility ($p=0.009$) to be important predictors of disposal. The model successfully predicts disposal in 61.3 per cent of cases, with a -2LL of 379. A H&L test ($x^2=3.0$, df=7, $p=1.00$) shows the model to have a good fit to the observed data. A diagnosis of personality disorder is a good predictor of a prison disposal (β=-0.966, exp(β)=0.381, $p<0.001$) in comparison to the reference category, schizophrenia (depression does not reach significance), reducing the odds of a hospital disposal by 61.9 per cent ([1-0.381] x 100).

Consensual meta-responsibility (β=0.431, exp(β)=1.539, $p=0.024$) significantly increases the odds of a hospital disposal in comparison to no meta-responsibility by 53.9 per cent (purposive meta-responsibility does not reach significance). A main interaction effect is observed between diagnosis and type of meta-responsibility ($p=0.046$). Contrasts for this interaction effect show that a combination of personality disorder with purposive meta-responsibility (in comparison to schizophrenia and no meta-responsibility) decreases the odds of a hospital disposal by 57.6 per cent (β=0.858, exp(β)=0.424, p=0.003). This interaction effect goes against the general tendency of purposive meta-responsibility to (albeit non-significantly) increase the odds of a hospital disposal over prison (by 5.2 per cent).

7.7 Effect of Vignette Factors on Length of Detention

Subjects did not always endorse a particular length of detention in the box provided. Subjects who simply stated 'life' were recoded as 25 years and subjects who stated 'until better' (or some variation) were coded as missing. The mean recommended prison sentence (15.75 years) was over twice as long as the recommended time for a hospital stay (7.15 years). This difference is significant (t=5.474, df=208.7, p<0.001). Those found guilty but still sent to hospital (those given a 'hospital order') spent over a year longer in hospital than those found NGRI (7.94 years vs. 6.69 years) although this difference is not significant.

Table 7.9 shows descriptive statistics for length of time at institution by disposal and vignette type.

Univariate ANOVAs of main effects of diagnosis, type of meta-responsibility, and insanity test (run separately for hospital, prison, and the two disposals combined) on length of disposal show only one significant result. This is the effect of insanity test on the length of hospital disposals (displayed in Figure 7.6).

Table 7.9 Descriptive statistics for type of disposal and length of disposal by vignette type

Vignette	Prison or hospital?	N	Minimum	Maximum	Mean
S>NMR>MN	Prison	5	10.00	15.00	12.00
	Hospital	12	1.00	100.00	14.70
S>NMR>MR	Prison	6	10.00	25.00	15.33
	Hospital	12	1.00	10.00	5.64
S>CMR>MN	Prison	1	25.00	25.00	25.00
	Hospital	17	1.00	97.00	13.88
S>CMR>MR	Prison	4	10.00	25.00	17.50
	Hospital	19	1.00	15.00	4.81
S>PMR>MN	Prison	1	10.00	10.00	10.00
	Hospital	15	0.50	25.00	5.96
S>PMR>MR	Prison	1	5.00	5.00	5.00
	Hospital	15	0.25	25.00	7.03
D>NMR>MN	Prison	9	3.00	25.00	13.78
	Hospital	6	0.50	25.00	7.25
D>NMR>MR	Prison	8	3.00	100.00	22.88
	Hospital	10	1.50	30.00	6.10
D>CMR>MN	Prison	5	6:00	10.00	8.40
	Hospital	11	1.00	15.00	5.35
D>CMR>MR	Prison	8	5.00	20.00	11.88
	Hospital	14	0.67	15.00	5.48
D>PMR>MN	Prison	9	5.00	15.00	9.00
	Hospital	13	0.50	25.00	7.71
D>PMR>MR	Prison	7	8.00	100.00	24.67
	Hospital	11	0.25	15.00	5.52
P>NMR>MN	Prison	9	10.00	30.00	16.44
	Hospital	8	3.00	20.00	8.13
P>NMR>MR	Prison	13	5.00	100.00	21.54
	Hospital	7	2.00	10.00	5.43
P>CMR>MN	Prison	10	4.50	25.00	11.55
	Hospital	11	2.00	15.00	6.95
P>CMR>MR	Prison	6	5.00	30.00	19.00
	Hospital	14	1.00	10.00	4.96
P>PMR>MN	Prison	11	8.00	50.00	17.95
	Hospital	5	2.00	10.00	5.38
P>PMR>MR	Prison	15	5.00	25.00	13.86
	Hospital	3	2.00	18.00	7.67

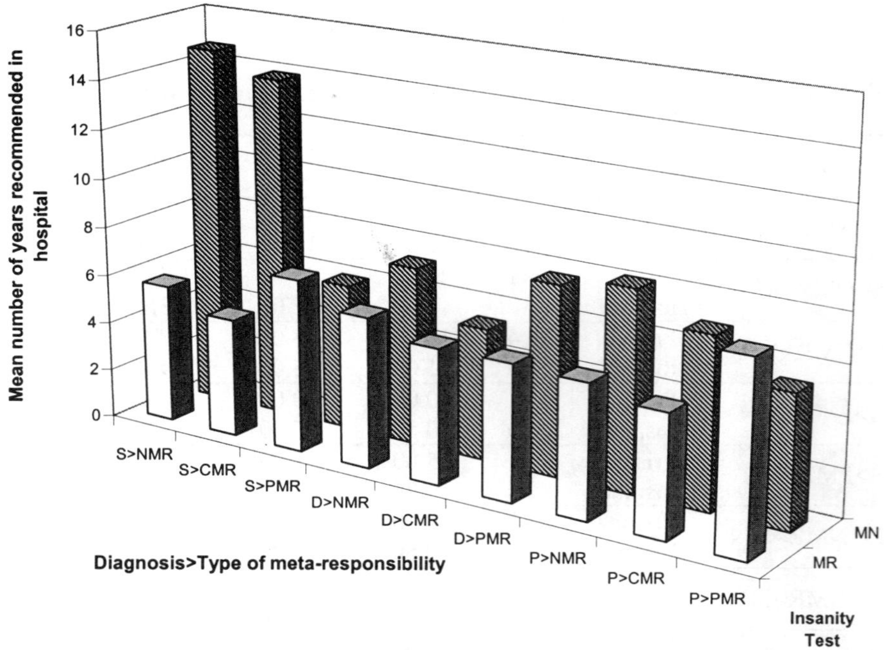

Figure 7.6 Mean number of years of recommended detention for hospital disposals, arranged using type of insanity test as the contrast variable

Figure 7.6 shows that length of hospital detention is reduced by the meta-responsibility test in six of the nine diagnosis>type of meta-responsibility (*x*-axis) conditions. The fall in length of detention is particularly dramatic for the schizophrenia conditions with no meta-responsibility (from 14.7 to 5.64 years) and consensual meta-responsibility (from 13.88 years to 4.81 years). Overall, the mean length of detention for the McNaughton test is 8.87 years, whereas if the MRIT is applied, the mean drops to 5.66 years. This difference is significant (f=4.168, df=1, p=0.043).

Insanity test does not, therefore, have an effect on verdict or type of disposal (in contrast to our expectations), but it *does* have an effect on the length of disposal (for hospital disposals). Ostensibly, insanity test should have nothing to do with a determination such as recommended length of disposal. A mechanism to explain this effect of the MRIT in significantly reducing recommended length of detention is the reduction of covert punishment discussed in Chapter 4. This will be discussed further in Chapter 8.

7.8 Data Reduction of Attitudinal Statements

This section of the analysis was driven by the need to reduce the attitudinal responses (questions 5-60 inclusive) to a smaller set of dimensions reflecting the central concerns of the subscales. The sub-scales measured: attitudes towards Tom's meta-responsibility; evaluations of the degree to which Tom's character changed due to disorder; ascription to various models of mental disorder; attitudes towards the insanity defence (including support for the insanity defence, general attitudes toward the insanity defence, and estimates of insanity defence usage); left/right political attitudes; libertarianism/authoritarianism; and legal attitudes (with regard to the harshness/leniency of the law). Data reduction was achieved using factor analysis and calculating factor scores for each subject to be used in further analysis.[15]

7.8.1 Meta-responsibility Attitude Statements

Questions five through 12 and question 15 measured subjects' opinions concerning various dimensions of Tom's meta-responsibility. These were expected to be dependent on vignette factors (i.e. diagnosis, type of meta-responsibility, and insanity test) in contrast to other scales reduced by factor analysis, which were expected to be independent of treatment variables by virtue of representing pre-existing attitudes (except evaluations of Tom's character change, which was expected to be similarly dependent on the vignette description). Table 7.10 shows the frequency of subjects' attitudinal responses to statements concerning Tom's meta-responsibility.

A principal component analysis (PCA) showed low communalities for DUTY, UNDSTOOD, CAUSED, and LIKED (less than 0.5) indicating these items had less than 50 per cent of their variance explained by the factor solution. They were dropped from the analysis. The PCA was repeated without these items. The pruned data satisfied both Bartlett's test of sphericity ($p<0.001$) and Kaiser-Meyer-Olkin test of sampling adequacy (KMO=0.670), indicating common variance due to underlying factors and hence the suitability of the data for a factor analysis. A PCA with VARIMAX rotation converged at a solution after three iterations, extracting two components accounting for 68.87 per cent of the variance. The components are displayed in Table 7.11.

The pruned items yielded two factors. The first component, named 'Meta-responsibility', explained 39.34 per cent of the variance; it had high positive factor loadings for *culpability for illness* items (Tom should have resisted his illness, been more careful with medication, and he made his illness worse through his own fault). This factor had a low negative loading for Tom killing his wife because of his illness, suggesting that appraisals of culpability for illness are linked with causal judgments of the effect of that illness on behaviour. The second component,

[15] See *SUPRA* note 8 for a description of how factor scores for each subject are calculated.

named ‘Product’ explained a further 29.53 per cent of the variance and had high positive loadings for items concerning Tom’s behaviour as a *product of his illness* (Tom killing his wife because of his illness and his illness affecting his ability to take medication).

Table 7.10 Percentage of responses endorsing Likert categories for meta-responsibility attitude items

Item [a]	1	2	3	4	5	6	7	Total [b]	Graph
Tom has a duty to take responsibility for his own illness (DUTY)	3.9	9.9	8.7	3.0	31.1	31.4	12.0	100.0	
Tom understood that he was ill (UNDSTOOD)	2.1	14.1	8.7	3.3	26.0	23.7	22.2	100.0	
Tom caused his own illness (CAUSED)	35.9	25.1	20.7	7.8	7.8	1.5	0.9	99.7	
Tom killed his wife because of his illness (KILLED)	3.0	6.0	12.9	10.2	26.6	26.6	14.7	100.0	
Tom’s illness affected his ability to look after himself (e.g. take medication) and resist getting more ill (AFFECTED)	5.1	15.0	12.0	5.1	26.0	21.3	15.5	100.0	
Tom liked being ill (LIKED)	28.7	17.3	15.9	16.8	13.5	6.6	1.2	100.0	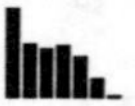
Tom should have resisted his illness more (RESISTED)	12.9	14.7	12.9	8.4	28.1	15.3	7.2	99.4	
Tom should have been more careful in taking his medication (CAREFUL)	6.0	9.9	8.4	8.4	27.8	19.8	19.5	99.7	
Tom made his illness worse through his own fault (FAULT)	12.3	20.7	15.6	6.0	24.3	15.3	6.0	100.0	

[a] 1 = Strongly disagree, 4= Don’t know, 7 = Strongly agree
[b] Where the total is less than 100% this indicates missing values – these are plotted as the first bar in the graph if applicable

Two new variables were computed for each subject using factor scores for each of the components: FMR (factor-meta-responsibility; of which higher values indicate increasing appraisal of Tom as meta-responsible) and FPROD (factor-product; of which higher values indicate increasing appraisal of Tom’s behaviour as a product of his illness).

Table 7.11 Principal component analysis for pruned meta-responsibility attitude items

Item	Component 1	Component 2
Tom killed his wife because of his illness (KILLED)	-0.220	0.782
Tom's illness affected his ability to look after himself (e.g. take medication) and resist getting more ill (AFFECTED)	1.59E-03	0.857
Tom should have resisted his illness more (RESISTED)	0.721	-0.258
Tom should have been more careful in taking his medication (CAREFUL)	0.860	0.129
Tom made his illness worse through his own fault (FAULT)	0.812	-0.216

7.8.2 Character Change

Questions 13 and 14 elicited attitudinal responses from subjects as to how good a person Tom was *before* he became ill and how good a person Tom was *after* he became ill. A new variable, which measured the degree to which subjects thought Tom's character was changed by illness, was computed by subtracting the Likert responses to Q14 from Q13. Higher values of this variable (named CCHANGE) indicated greater judgments of character change (negative values indicating Tom's character was assessed as better *after* he became ill). A univariate ANOVA of vignette factors on CCHANGE showed diagnosis (f=3.649, df=2, p=0.027) to be the only significant predictor of character change. The means of character change by diagnosis show subjects appraised Tom's character as changing most in the schizophrenia condition, less for depression, and even less for personality disorder.

Table 7.12 Descriptive statistics for CCHANGE (the difference between how good Tom's character was pre- and post-illness) by diagnosis

Diagnosis	N	Minimum	Maximum	Mean	Std. Deviation
Schizophrenia	107	0	6	1.019	1.317
Depression	112	-2	4	0.759	1.195
Personality Disorder	113	-3	4	0.584	1.140

7.8.3 Mental Disorder Models

Questions 16-21 measured ascription to three models of mental disorder: the medical (organic) model (questions 20 and 17), the moral (cognitive-behavioural) model (questions 18 and 19), and the psychosocial model (questions 16 and 21). The first question of each pair examined aetiology, the second examined treatment. Table 7.13 shows percentage of subjects' attitudinal responses to the questions.

A PCA showed the data satisfied both Bartlett's test of sphericity ($p<0.001$) and KMO test of sampling adequacy (0.50). High communalities (>0.636) for all items further indicated the suitability of factor analysis. A PCA with VARIMAX rotation converged at a solution after four iterations, extracting three factors accounting for 67.07 per cent of the variance.

Table 7.13 Percentage of responses endorsing Likert categories for mental disorder model items

Item [a]	1	2	3	4	5	6	7	Total [b]	Graph
Mental illness is caused by a number of social stresses such as money worries (PSYAET)	4.5	8.4	9.0	2.7	42.2	24.8	7.8	99.4	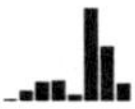
Mental illness should be treated through the use of medical drugs (MEDTREAT)	3.0	5.1	16.2	5.4	40.4	20.1	9.0	99.1	
Mental illness is caused by learning from others with similarly strange and bizarre behaviour (COGEAT)	38.9	29.0	18.3	3.3	8.1	2.4	0.0	100.0	
Mental illness should be treated by showing patients the proper way to act and think (COGTREAT)	12.0	14.7	16.4	5.4	31.1	11.7	8.1	99.4	
Mental illness is caused by medical problems such as chemical imbalance in the brain (MEDAET)	1.5	0.6	4.8	9.6	31.1	31.1	21.0	99.7	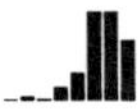
Mental illness should be treated by producing a more comfortable and less stressful society (PSYTREAT)	7.5	8.1	16.5	4.5	34.1	17.0	12.0	99.7	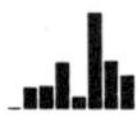

[a] 1 = Strongly disagree, 4= Don't know, 7 = Strongly agree
[b] Where the total is less than 100% this indicates missing values – these are plotted as the first bar in the graph if applicable

Table 7.14 shows the loadings of the items on the three factors. Component one, entitled 'Medical Model' explained 23.97 per cent of the variance. It had high positive loadings for both the medical model items. The second component, explaining 21.96 per cent of the variance, was termed 'Psychosocial Model'. It had high positive loadings for both the psychosocial items. The third component, 'Cognitive-behavioural Model', explained 21.14 per cent of the variance and had high loadings for the cognitive-behavioural items. Factor scores for each component were created, with higher values indicating greater ascription to that model; the three variables were termed FMED (factor-medical; ascription to the medical model), FPSY (factor-psychosocial; ascription to the psychosocial model), and FCOG (factor-cognitive-behavioural; ascription to the cognitive-behavioural model).

Table 7.14 Principal component analysis for mental disorder model items

Item	Component 1	Component 2	Component 3
Mental illness is caused by a number of social stresses such as money worries (PSYAET)	0.111	0.792	0.112
Mental illness should be treated through the use of medical drugs (MEDTREAT)	0.848	-1.56E-02	-6.84E-02
Mental illness is caused by learning from others with similarly strange and bizarre behaviour (COGEAT)	-0.146	-5.22E-03	0.798
Mental illness should be treated by showing patients the proper way to act and think (COGTREAT)	7.55E-02	0.132	0.783
Mental illness is caused by medical problems such as chemical imbalance in the brain (MEDAET)	0.816	6.12E-03	-1.05E-04
Mental illness should be treated by producing a more comfortable and less stressful society (PSYTREAT)	-0.120	0.820	1.53E-02

7.8.4 Attitudes Toward the Insanity Defence

Hans' (1986) Attitudes Toward the Insanity Defence questionnaire consists of three subscales: support for the insanity defence (Questions 22-25), insanity defence attitudes (Q26-41), and estimates of insanity defence usage (Q42-46).

Support for the insanity defence Table 7.15 shows the percentage of subjects endorsing Likert categories for Q22-25 – items measuring support for the insanity defence.

The responses show, in comparison to the sample of Hans (1986), a reasonably high level of support for the insanity defence, tempered by endorsement that the insanity defence needs a lot of reform. A PCA showed low communalities for REFORM (0.278) indicating it should be dropped from the analysis. The pruned data satisfied both Bartlett's test of sphericity (p<0.001) and KMO test of sampling adequacy (0.714).

Table 7.15 Percentage of responses endorsing Likert categories for insanity defence support items

Item[a]	1	2	3	4	5	6	7	Total[b]	Graph
The insanity defence should be abolished (ABOLISH)	51.5	26.9	13.2	0.9	3.6	1.8	2.1	100.0	
The insanity defence needs a lot of reform (REFORM)	3.3	6.3	8.1	27.5	20.6	19.5	14.4	99.7	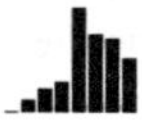
The insanity defence is sometimes justified (JUSTIFY)	1.2	0.6	2.7	0.3	12.6	27.5	54.8	99.7	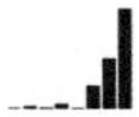
The insanity defence is a necessary part of our legal system (NECESSAR)	0.9	1.2	3.6	0.3	13.8	29.9	50.0	99.7	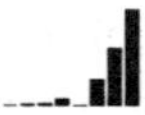

[a] 1 = Strongly disagree, 4= Don't know, 7 = Strongly agree
[b] Where the total is less than 100% this indicates missing values – these are plotted as the first bar in the graph if applicable

Table 7.16 Principal component analysis of pruned insanity defence support items

Item	Component 1
The insanity defence should be abolished (ABOLISH)	-0.857
The insanity defence is sometimes justified (JUSTIFY)	0.903
The insanity defence is a necessary part of our legal system (NECESSAR)	0.927

One component factored out, explaining 80.35 per cent of the variance. It was termed 'Support', with high positive loadings for items supportive of the insanity defence and a high negative loading for abolishing the insanity defence.

A new variable, FNGRISUP (factor-NGRI support) was created using factor scores for each subject. Higher values of this variable indicate greater support for the insanity defence.

Insanity defence attitudes Table 7.17 shows the percentage of Likert responses to questions 26-41, measures of general attitudes towards the insanity defence.

Table 7.17 Percentage of responses endorsing Likert categories for insanity defence attitudes items

Item[a]	1	2	3	4	5	6	7	Total[b]	Graph
It is wrong to punish insane people who break the law (WRONGPUN)	7.2	9.3	25.4	2.7	17.4	18.0	20.0	100.0	
Insane defendants are entitled to treatment (ENTTREAT)	0.6	0.0	0.6	0.3	10.5	25.4	62.6	100.0	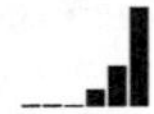
Most people found Not Guilty by Reason of Insanity are really insane (REALYMAD)	5.4	5.1	15.0	34.1	23.6	12.9	3.9	100.0	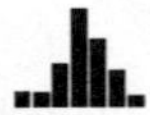
I'm confident that people found Not Guilty by Reason of Insanity are only released when it's safe to do so (RELSAFE)	18.6	31.1	25.1	9.3	10.2	4.2	1.5	100.0	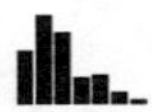
Psychiatrists should testify about a defendant's medical condition in insanity trials (MDTESTIF)	0.6	0.0	1.5	0.3	12.0	27.2	58.4	100.0	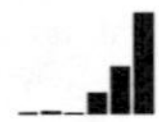
The insanity defence doesn't affect the crime rate (CRIMRATE)	3.6	6.6	12.9	30.8	14.3	18.0	13.8	100.0	
The insane should be treated rather than punished if they commit crime (TREATPUN)	1.2	2.1	12.0	1.5	22.5	29.3	31.1	99.7	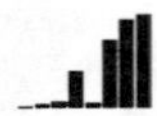
Punishment doesn't work on the insane (PUNWORK)	1.5	8.7	20.0	14.7	18.3	22.7	14.1	100.0	
The insanity plea is a loophole that allows too many guilty people to go free (LOOPHOLE)	11.4	13.8	23.6	12.3	24.2	9.6	4.8	99.7	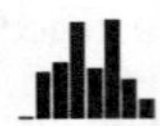
Even if people are insane, we should punish them if they break the law (INSAPUN)	18.9	19.7	19.2	4.2	27.2	6.9	3.3	99.4	
The insanity defence sends a message to criminals that they can get away with crime (MESSAGE)	21.2	19.2	21.5	4.5	21.6	7.5	4.2	99.7	

The insanity defence allows dangerous people out on the streets (DANGER)	9.9	17.7	19.4	7.8	26.6	12.0	6.3	99.7	
Judges and juries have a hard time telling whether defendants are really sane or insane (HARDTIME)	0.0	0.9	1.5	1.8	18.9	38.6	38.3	100.0	
If psychiatrists are paid enough, they will say anything about a defendant's sanity (PSYCH$$$)	14.4	16.5	18.5	10.5	23.9	10.2	5.7	99.7	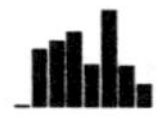
The insanity defence is mainly a rich person's defence (RICHDEF)	19.2	21.8	14.7	20.9	16.5	5.1	1.5	99.7	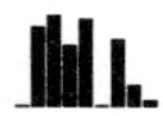
Insane people should be punished for their crimes just like everyone else (INSAPUN2)	24.2	21.9	24.8	2.1	20.1	4.8	2.1	100.0	

[a] 1 = Strongly disagree, 4= Don't know, 7 = Strongly agree
[b] Where the total is less than 100% this indicates missing values – these are plotted as the first bar in the graph if applicable

The items were subjected to a PCA with VARIMAX rotation, those items with communalities of less than 0.5 being dropped from the analysis (REALYMAD, RELSAFE, and PUNWORK). All remaining items had communalities of 0.61 or greater (i.e. had 61 per cent or more of their variance explained by the factor solution). The pruned data satisfied both a Bartlett's test of sphericity (p<0.001) and KMO test of sampling adequacy (0.857).

Four factors explaining 64.97 per cent of the variance converged after six iterations of the VARIMAX algorithm. Factor 1, named 'Punish', explained 22.76 per cent of the variance. It had high negative loadings for items supporting treatment and that punishment doesn't work on the insane, and high positive loadings for items favouring the punishment of the insane. Factor 2, explaining 18.42 per cent of the variance, was named 'Beat the Rap'. It had a high negative loading for the insanity defence not affecting the crime rate, and high positive loadings for the insanity defence as a loophole, sending a message to criminals, and allowing dangerous people out on the streets. The third factor, 'Legal Concern' explained 12.90 per cent of the variance and had high positive loadings for judges and juries having difficulty distinguishing sane from insane defendants, psychiatrists saying anything if paid enough, and the insanity defence as a rich person's defence. The fourth factor, 'Medical Approval', explained 10.88 per cent of the variance and had high positive loadings for the insane's entitlement to treatment and support for psychiatric testimony at insanity trials.

Table 7.18 Principal component analysis of pruned insanity defence attitude items

Item	Component 1	2	3	4
It is wrong to punish insane people who break the law (WRONGPUN)	-0.800	-0.120	-7.82E-02	0.122
Insane defendants are entitled to treatment (ENTTREAT)	-0.280	-6.71E-02	-3.75E-02	0.722
Psychiatrists should testify about a defendant's medical condition in insanity trials (MDTESTIF)	7.51E-03	1.56E-02	-9.47E-02	0.802
The insanity defence doesn't affect the crime rate (CRIMRATE)	-4.05E-02	-0.777	1.79E-02	7.65-02
The insane should be treated rather than punished if they commit crime (TREATPUN)	-0.729	-0.222	-7.25E-02	0.216
The insanity plea is a loophole that allows too many guilty people to go free (LOOPHOLE)	0.279	0.694	0.303	-4.03E-02
Even if people are insane, we should punish them if they break the law (INSAPUN)	0.845	0.255	0.146	-8.21E-03
The insanity defence sends a message to criminals that they can get away with crime (MESSAGE)	0.258	0.737	0.204	-4.09E-02
The insanity defence allows dangerous people out on the streets (DANGER)	0.346	0.707	0.179	8.44E-02
Judges and juries have a hard time telling whether defendants are really sane or insane (HARDTIME)	0.144	2.49E-02	0.692	0.240
If psychiatrists are paid enough, they will say anything about a defendant's sanity (PSYCH$$$)	5.98E-02	0.253	0.718	-0.266
The insanity defence is mainly a rich person's defence (RICHDEF)	9.26E-02	0.180	0.681	-0.205
Insane people should be punished for their crimes just like everyone else (INSAPUN2)	0.834	0.193	0.106	-1.70E-02

Factor scores for each component were created, named FPUNISH (factor-punish; higher values indicating support for punishing the insane), FBEATRAP (factor-beat the rap; higher values indicating support for the insane as 'beating the rap'), FLEGCONC (factor-legal concern; higher values indicating greater suspicion about legal aspects of the insanity defence), and FMEDCONC (factor-medical concern; higher values indicating support for medical involvement in the insanity defence and treatment of acquittees).

Estimates of insanity defence usage Table 7.19 displays descriptive statistics for questions 42-46: items pertaining to insanity defence usage and disposal.

Table 7.19 Descriptive statistics for insanity defence usage items

Item	Valid N	Missing N	Mean	Std. Deviation	Skewness	Range
Out of every 100 defendants who are charged with a crime, how many do you think plead Not Guilty by Reason of Insanity? (PLEAD#)	334	0	13.35	16.27	2.31	89.99
Out of every 100 defendants who plead insanity, how many are actually found Not Guilty by Reason of Insanity? (NGRI#)	333	1	28.34	22.77	0.58	94.90
Out of every 100 defendants found Not Guilty by Reason of Insanity, how many go free immediately? (FREE#)	332	2	14.95	19.69	1.72	97.00
How many are sent to mental hospital? (HOSP#)	331	3	56.32	35.48	-0.31	99.50
If defendants are sent to a mental hospital, how long do they stay there on average? (HOSPSTAY)	332	2	3.82	3.35	1.93	22.92

The table shows that subjects believe approximately 13 per cent of persons being charged with a crime plead insanity, and that approximately 28 per cent of these are successful with the defence. By interpolation, an average of 3.78 per cent of all criminal defendants are thought by the present sample to be found NGRI. Subjects estimate that approximately 15 per cent of NGRIs go free immediately, and approximately 56 per cent go to hospital. This leaves a perplexing 39 per cent of NGRIs unaccounted for. Average hospital stay for NGRIs is estimated as approximately three years and ten months.

7.8.5 Left/Right Attitudes

Table 7.20 displays percentages of subjects endorsing various Likert categories in response to questions 47-51: items measuring left/right attitudes.

Table 7.20 Percentage of responses endorsing Likert categories for left-right attitudes items

Item[a]	1	2	3	4	5	6	7	Total[b]	Graph
The Government should redistribute income from the better-off to those who are less well off (REDIST)	5.4	12.6	13.5	1.2	28.4	21.8	17.1	100.0	
Big business benefits owners at the expense of workers (BIGBUSIN)	3.6	8.7	19.8	2.7	28.4	21.5	15.3	100.0	
Ordinary people do not get their fair share of the nation's wealth (FAIRSHAR)	3.3	9.6	31.4	4.5	28.7	13.5	8.4	99.4	
There is one law for the rich and one for the poor (LAWRICH)	7.2	15.3	23.9	3.0	28.4	13.5	8.4	99.7	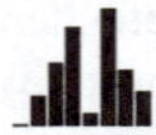
Management will always try to get the better of employees if it gets the chance (MANEMPL)	4.8	12.0	26.3	4.5	25.7	17.7	8.7	99.7	

[a] 1 = Strongly disagree, 4= Don't know, 7 = Strongly agree
[b] Where the total is less than 100% this indicates missing values – these are plotted as the first bar in the graph if applicable

REDIST, LAWRICH, and MANEMPL were dropped from a PCA due to low communalities (<0.5). A PCA showed the pruned data satisfied both Bartlett's test of sphericity (p<0.001) and KMO test of sampling adequacy (0.50).

Table 7.21 Principal component analysis of pruned left-right attitudes items

Item	Component 1
Big business benefits owners at the expense of workers (BIGBUSIN)	0.878
Ordinary people do not get their fair share of the nation's wealth (FAIRSHAR)	0.878

A PCA (unrotated) factored out one component (named 'Socialism') explaining 77.16 per cent of the variance of the two remaining items, with high positive factor loadings for both items: that big business benefits owners at the expense of workers and ordinary people do not receive their fair share of the nation's wealth. A new variable with factor scores for each item was created, named FLEFRIGH (factor-left-right attitudes; higher values indicate more left-wing attitudes).

7.8.6 Libertarianism/Authoritarianism

Table 7.22 displays Likert responses to questions 52-57: items measuring libertarianism/authoritarianism.

It is notable with regard to previous insanity defence research that the current sample was strongly anti-death penalty. RESPBRIT, LAWOBEY, and CENSOR were dropped from a factor analysis due to low communalities (<0.5). A PCA (unrotated) showed the pruned data satisfied both a Bartlett's test of sphericity ($p<0.001$) and KMO test of sampling adequacy (0.606).

A PCA factored out one component (named 'Authoritarianism') explaining 56.58 per cent of the variance, with high positive factor loadings for stiffer sentences, death penalty support, and support for children being taught to obey authority. A new variable, FLIBAUTH (factor-libertarianism/authoritarianism), was created with a factor score for each subject (higher values indicate greater authoritarianism).

Table 7.22 Percentage of responses endorsing Likert categories for libertarianism/authoritarianism items

Item [a]	1	2	3	4	5	6	7	Total [b]	Graph
Young people today don't have enough respect for traditional British values (RESPBRIT)	11.1	17.3	20.0	13.2	19.8	12.0	5.4	98.8	
People who break the law should be given stiffer sentences (STIFFER)	7.5	16.2	25.4	7.2	21.2	13.2	8.4	99.1	
For some crimes, the death penalty is the most appropriate sentence (DEATHPEN)	55.4	11.4	6.6	.9	6.9	6.3	12.2	99.7	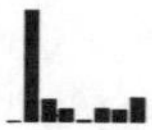
Schools should teach children to obey authority (OBEYAUTH)	7.5	7.8	10.8	2.1	31.4	18.9	20.3	98.8	
The law should always be obeyed, even if a particular law is wrong (LAWOBEY)	17.4	20.0	25.4	2.1	15.0	15.6	3.9	99.4	
Censorship of films and magazines is necessary to uphold moral standards (CENSOR)	20.9	16.2	15.3	1.2	23.9	12.6	9.6	99.7	

[a] 1 = Strongly disagree, 4= Don't know, 7 = Strongly agree
[b] Where the total is less than 100% this indicates missing values – these are plotted as the first bar in the graph if applicable

Table 7.23 Principal component analysis of pruned libertarianism/authoritarianism items

Item	Component
	1
People who break the law should be given stiffer sentences (STIFFER)	0.820
For some crimes, the death penalty is the most appropriate sentence (DEATHPEN)	0.755
Schools should teach children to obey authority (OBEYAUTH)	0.674

7.8.7 Legal Attitudes

Table 7.24 displays Likert responses to questions 58-60: items measuring legal attitudes.

Table 7.24 Percentage of responses endorsing Likert categories for legal attitudes items

Item [a]	1	2	3	4	5	6	7	Total [b]	Graph
Too many guilty persons escape punishment because of legal technicalities (LEGTECH)	3.3	5.4	10.5	8.1	32.9	23.0	16.5	99.7	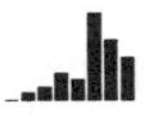
Illegally obtained evidence should not be admissible in court even if that evidence is the only way of obtaining a conviction (ILLEVID)	12.0	16.1	20.9	5.1	16.2	13.5	15.6	99.4	
In general, the courts deal too harshly with criminals (HARSH)	14.7	26.0	36.5	13.2	7.8	0.9	0.6	99.7	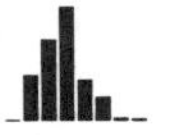

[a] 1 = Strongly disagree, 4= Don't know, 7 = Strongly agree

[b] Where the total is less than 100% this indicates missing values – these are plotted as the first bar in the graph if applicable

Low communalities were observed for all items (0.557, 0.494 and 0.451 for LEGTECH, ILLEVID and HARSH respectively) indicating that any factor solution did not account for much of the variance in each variable. A PCA (unrotated) on all items showed the pruned data satisfied both Bartlett's test of sphericity ($p<0.001$) and KMO test of sampling adequacy (0.602).

A PCA factored out one component explaining 50.1 per cent of the variance, with high positive loadings for support for the inadmissibility of illegally obtained evidence and that the courts deal too harshly with criminals, and a high negative loading for people escaping punishment due to legal technicalities. These items, when recoded to make higher values reflect harsher legal attitudes, had a Cronbach's α of 0.483, which together with the low communalities indicated that the creation of factor scores was not appropriate. This scale was dropped from further analysis.

Table 7.25 Principal component analysis for legal attitudes items

Item	Component 1
Too many guilty persons escape punishment because of legal technicalities (LEGTECH)	-0.746
Illegally obtained evidence should not be admissible in court even if that evidence is the only way of obtaining a conviction (ILLEVID)	0.703
In general, the courts deal too harshly with criminals (HARSH)	0.672

7.9 Relationships Between Vignette Factors, Attitudinal Variables and Demographic Characteristics

7.9.1 Vignette Factors and Attitudes

Are attitudes, rather than being subject characteristics *per se*, a product of the type of vignette that the subject received? It was expected that the degree to which subjects saw Tom as meta-responsible (FMR), the degree to which subjects saw Tom's behaviour as a product of his illness (FPROD) and the degree of character change attributed to Tom (CCHANGE) would be dependent on the vignette factors. This was not expected of other variables that were designed to measure pre-existing attitudes.

To test for independence of attitudinal items from the experimental design, a one way ANOVA was run using vignette factors as independent variables and attitudinal items as dependent variables, with Tukey's Honestly Significant Difference (HSD) post hoc tests for between-subjects effects. A p value of 0.05 entails that at least one in every 20 significant correlations will be due to chance rather than because of any underlying relationship between the variables. This danger, of incorrectly rejecting the null hypothesis of no relation (Type I error), increases with the number of tests run at any one time. Therefore, the significance level for reporting a difference in means was taken as $p \leq 0.01$ (only one in 100 comparisons or less should reach significance by chance).

Diagnosis had the expected effect on FPROD (the degree to which subjects saw Tom's behaviour as a product of his illness) (f=13.734, df=2, p<0.001), with Tom's illness seen as affecting his behaviour most for schizophrenia, then depression, and least for personality disorder. Diagnosis also had an unexpected effect on FPSY (the degree of ascription to the psychosocial model of mental disorder) (f=5.299, df=2, p=0.006) with ascription to the model lowest for the depression vignette, then schizophrenia, and highest for personality disorder.

Type of meta-responsibility had the expected effect on FMR (the degree to which subjects saw Tom as meta-responsible) (f=34.139, df=2, p<0.001); Tom was seen to be least meta-responsible in the no meta-responsibility condition. Consensual meta-responsibility and purposive meta-responsibility elicited respectively greater appraisals of Tom as meta-responsible. Type of meta-responsibility also affected subjects' appraisals of the degree to which Tom's behaviour was contingent upon his illness (FPROD) (f=26.199, df=2, p<0.001); his behaviour was seen as the product of his illness *most* for consensual meta-responsibility, then purposive meta-responsibility, and least for no meta-responsibility. This order of decreasing appraisals of Tom's behaviour as a product of his illness explains, at least in part, the unexpected excusatory power of consensual and purposive meta-responsibility observed above.[16]

Insanity test had no significant effects on attitudinal items apart from an interaction effect with type of meta-responsibility for FPROD (the degree to which subjects saw Tom's behaviour as a product of his illness) (f=4.927, df=2, p<0.008). This lends support to the notion of FPROD and FMR being functions of the vignette factors rather than pre-existing attitudes towards the criminally insane *per se*.

7.9.2 Attitudes and Other Dependent Variables

To inspect which of the newly created independent factor scores might be related (and have relationships with other dependent variables i.e. verdict, disposal and length of detention), Spearman's ranks were calculated between all variables. The large number of correlations meant a more stringent probability value was again required for reporting a significant relationship ($p \leq 0.01$). Only r values of 0.2 or greater (positive or negative) are reported, as lower values are indicative of only a weak relationship.

CCHANGE An appraisal of a greater pre- to post-illness change in Tom's character was associated with greater authoritarianism (FLIBAUTH; r=0.231).

DISPOSAL A hospital disposal was associated with endorsement of Tom's behaviour as a product of his illness (FPROD; r=0.544), less endorsement of Tom as meta-responsible (FMR; r=-0.222), fewer recommended years at the institution (DISYRREC; r=0.566), and a NGRI verdict (VERDICT; r=0.635).

DISYRREC Increased recommended time at an institution was associated with a belief that the insane should be punished (FPUNISH; r=0.204), a prison disposal (DISPOSAL; r=-0.566), a guilty verdict (VERDICT; r=-0.421), and a higher estimate of the time NGRI acquittees spend in hospital (HOSPSTAY; r=0.253).

---

[16] See SUPRA section 7.5.

FBEATRAP The attitude that NGRI acquittees 'beat the rap' was associated with increased authoritarianism (FLIBAUTH; r=0.424), and less support for the insanity defence (FNGRISUP; r=-0.287).

FCOG Ascription to the cognitive-behavioural model is associated with left-wing attitudes (FLEFRIGH; r=0.205).

FLEFRIGH Left-wing attitudes were associated with support for the cognitive-behavioural model of mental disorder (FCOG; r=0.205).

FLEGCONC Concern with legal aspects of the insanity defence was not associated with any other variables.

FLIBAUTH Authoritarianism was associated with a belief that NGRI acquittees 'beat the rap' (FBEATRAP; r=0.424), and an appraisal of greater character change pre- to post-illness (CCHANGE; r=0.231).

FMDKNOW Higher levels of experience and knowledge of mental disorder were not associated with any other variables.

FMED Ascription to the medical model of mental disorder is associated with support for the insanity defence (NGRISUPP; r=0.207), and approval of medical involvement with insanity defence/acquittees (FMEDCONC; r=0.296).

FMR A belief that Tom was meta-responsible was associated with ascription to the psychosocial model of mental disorder (FPSY; r=0.253), less support for the insanity defence (FNGRISUP; r=-0.235), support for punishing mentally disordered offenders (FPUNISH; r=0.239), a prison disposal (DISPOSAL; r=-0.222), and a guilty verdict (VERDICT; r=-0.320).

FNGRISUP Support for the insanity defence is associated with greater ascription to the medical model (FMED; r=0.207), less ascription to the psychosocial model (FPSY; r=-0.203), less support for punishing mentally disordered offenders (FPUNISH; r=-0.376), less endorsement of NGRI acquittees as 'beating the rap' (FBEATRAP; r=-0.287), approval of medical involvement with insanity defence/acquittees (FMEDCONC; r=0.317), endorsement of Tom's behaviour as a product of his illness (FPROD; r=0.237), and less endorsement of Tom as meta-responsible (FMR; r=-0.235).

FPROD Endorsement of Tom's behaviour as a product of his illness was associated with support for the insanity defence (FNGRISUP; r=0.237), a hospital disposal (DISPOSAL; r=0.544) and a NGRI verdict (VERDICT; r=0.594).

FPSY Support for the psychosocial model of mental disorder is associated with Tom being seen as meta-responsible (FMR; r=0.253), and less support for the insanity defence (FNGRISUP; r=-0.203).

FPUNISH Support for punishing mentally disordered offenders is associated with less support for the insanity defence (FNGRISUP; r=-0.376), endorsement of Tom as meta-responsible (FMR; r=0.239), and a guilty verdict (VERDICT; r=-0.281).

FREE# A higher estimate of the percentage of NGRIs set free immediately was associated with a higher estimate of the number of insanity pleas that are successful (NGRI#, r=0.283).

GENDER Gender is not associated with any other variables.

HOSP# A higher estimate of the percentage of NGRIs sent to hospital was associated with a lower estimate of the number of defendants pleading insanity (PLEAD#; r=-0.216), and a higher estimate of the percentage successful in their NGRI plea (NGRI#; r=0.353).

HOSPSTAY A higher estimate of length of stay by insanity acquittees is associated with an increased recommended period of detention (DISYRREC; r=0.253).

MEDCONC Approval of medical involvement in insanity trials and NGRIs was associated with ascription to the medical model of mental disorder (FMED; r=0.296) and support for the insanity defence (FNGRISUP; r=0.317).

NGRI# A higher estimate of the percentage of insanity pleas that are successful was associated with higher estimates of both the percentage of NGRIs being sent to hospital (HOSP#; r=0.353) and the percentage being set free immediately (FREE#; r=0.283).

PLEAD# A higher estimate of the percentage of criminal defendants who plead NGRI was associated with a lower estimate of the percentage of NGRIs being sent to hospital (HOSP#; r=-0.216), endorsement that insanity acquittees 'beat the rap' (FBEATRAP; r=0.339), and greater authoritarianism (FLIBAUTH; r=0.226).

VERDICT NGRI verdicts were associated with an appraisal of Tom's behaviour as a product of his illness (FPROD; r=0.594), less support for punishing mentally disordered offenders (FPUNISH; r=-0.281), less endorsement of Tom as meta-responsible (FMR; r=-0.320), fewer recommended years at the institution (DISYRREC; r=-0.421), and a hospital disposal (DISPOSAL; r=0.635).

7.9.3 Effect of Gender and Ethnic Identity on Dependent Variables

Independent sample t-tests were run for all dependent variables, grouping by gender (using a stringent p value of 0.01 or less). Gender did not have a significant effect upon any variable.

Ethnic identity, unlike gender, had an effect on a range of variables. In comparison to 'white' respondents, non-white respondents differed along a number of dimensions. They estimated a greater number of criminal defendants plead

NGRI (PLEAD#: t=-3.381, df=332, p=0.001), estimated a lower number of NGRIs go to hospital (HOSP#: t=3.50, df=329, p=0.001), were less endorsing of Tom's behaviour as a product of his illness (FPROD: t=3.305, df=329, p=0.001), were less supportive of the insanity defence (FNGRISUP: t=2.856, df=60.953, p=0.006), showed greater endorsement of NGRI acquittees 'beating the rap' (FBEATRAP: t=-2.892, df=328, p=0.004), showed greater concern about legal aspects of the insanity defence (FLEGCONC: t=-3.296, df=328, p=0.001), were less approving of medical involvement with insanity trials/NGRIs (FMEDCONC: t=2.236, df=328, p=0.026), and had higher levels of authoritarianism (FLIBAUTH: t=-4.492, df=327, p<0.001). A Mann-Whitney test shows that verdict does not vary significantly by ethnic identity (z=-0.777, df=1, p=0.437), however, non-white subjects were more likely to send Tom to prison than white subjects (z=-0.199, df=1, p=0.046). It appears that non-white subjects are less supportive of the insanity defence (particularly its legal aspects) and less likely to view illness as an excuse for behaviour; this has an effect on their recommended disposals.

7.10 The Effect of Attitudes On Verdict, Disposal and Length of Detention

7.10.1 Verdict

A forward stepwise logistic regression model was run using verdict as the dependent variable and the following variables entered as categorical or quantitative predictors: the number of criminal defendants estimated to plead insanity (PLEAD#), the number of such defendants estimated to be successful with their insanity plea (NGRI#), the number of NGRIs set free after a successful insanity plea (FREE#), the number of NGRIs going to hospital (HOSP#), the estimated length of time NGRIs spend in hospital (HOSPSTAY), the degree of Tom's character change pre- to post-illness (CCHANGE), the amount of meta-responsibility subjects attributed to Tom (FMR), the degree to which Tom's behaviour was judged as a product of his illness (FPROD), subjects' ascription to the medical model (FMED), subjects' ascription to the cognitive-behavioural model (FCOG), subjects' ascription to the psychosocial model (FPSY), the degree of support for the insanity defence (FNGRISUP), the degree of support for punishing the insane (FPUNISH), the degree to which insanity acquittees are viewed as 'beating the rap' (FBEATRAP), the degree of concern about legal aspects of the insanity defence (FLEGCONC), the degree of approval for medical involvement with insanity trials/acquittees (FMEDCONC), the degree of subjects' left-wing attitudes (FLEFRIGH), the degree of subjects' authoritarianism (FLIBAUTH), the degree of subjects' knowledge and experience of mental disorder (FMDKNOW), age (AGE), gender (GENDER), and finally ethnic identity (ETHNIC) (the latter two being entered as categorical variables).

The final model had a -2LL of 231.05. A H&L goodness of fit test showed no significant difference between the model's expected verdict pattern and the observed verdict pattern (x^2=8.706, df=8, p=0.368); the model predicted verdict correctly in 84.3 per cent of cases. It is clear that this model, incorporating attitudinal and demographic factors, predicts verdict even better than the model including only vignette factors described above.[17]

The significant variables included within the model were: the degree of meta-responsibility attributed to Tom (FMR) ($\beta=-1.210$, $p<0.001$), the degree to which Tom's behaviour was seen as a product of his illness (FPROD) ($\beta=2.238$, $p<0.001$), the degree of ascription to the psychosocial model of mental disorder (FPSY) ($\beta=0.518$, $p=0.006$), support for punishing the insane (FPUNISH) ($\beta=-0.428$, $p=0.017$), and the subjects' degree of authoritarianism (FLIBAUTH) ($\beta=0.462$, $p=0.009$). The β values show, in order, the most important predictors of verdict to be: the degree to which subjects saw Tom's behaviour as the product of his illness (FPROD), with greater values predicting a verdict of NGRI; the degree of meta-responsibility attributed to Tom (FMR), with higher levels predicting a guilty verdict; the degree of authoritarianism (FLIBAUTH), with higher levels unexpectedly associated with a NGRI verdict; the degree of ascription to the psychosocial model of mental disorder, with higher levels of ascription predicting a NGRI verdict; and finally, support for punishing mentally disordered offenders (FPUNISH), with higher levels of support associated with a guilty finding.

Running the same regression model for the no meta-responsibility>McNaughton test conditions (i.e. S>NMR>MN, D>NMR>MN, P>NMR>MN), where NO meta-responsibility information was given in the vignette (in the form of Tom's behaviour *or* insanity defence instructions) showed that the important predictors of verdict remain intact. These were: the degree to which subjects viewed Tom's behaviour as due to illness (FPROD) ($\beta=2.667$, $p=0.001$); the degree of meta-responsibility attributed to Tom (FMR) ($\beta=-1.564$, $p=0.021$); and the degree of ascription to the psychosocial model (FPSY) ($\beta=1.564$, $p=0.009$). This suggests that even when subjects receive no meta-responsibility information, and the insanity test does not draw their attention to the defendant's meta-responsibility, constructs related to meta-responsibility (i.e. FPROD and FMR) are *still* the best predictors of verdict out of all the attitudinal and demographic variables measured in the current study.

A regression model including the attitudinal/demographic items *and* the vignette factors showed FPROD ($\beta=2.108$, $p<0.001$) and FMR ($\beta=-1.094$, $p<0.001$) to be even better predictors of verdict than the vignette factor of diagnosis (contrast for depression: $\beta=-0.552$, $\exp(\beta)=0.576$, $p=0.028$; contrast for personality disorder: $\beta=-0.662$, $\exp(\beta)=0.516$, $p=0.015$). This model also included ascription to the psychosocial model (FPSY) ($\beta=0.619$, $p=0.002$), and support for punishing the insane (FPUNISH) ($\beta=-0.599$, $p=0.002$). Type of meta-responsibility and type of insanity test were not significant. This model fitted the data better than a model including *either* attitudinal variables *or* vignette factors, correctly predicting 86.2 per cent of verdicts with a -2LL of 213.49. There was no

---

[17] See *SUPRA* section 7.5.4.

significant difference between the model's predicted verdict pattern and the observed verdict pattern (H&L goodness of fit test; x^2=6.130, df=8, p=0.633).

In deference to previous insanity defence research, it was examined whether death penalty support (Question 54) was a predictor of verdict. Although death penalty support was lower for subjects finding Tom NGRI (mean of 2.43 for NGRI versus 2.71 for guilty), a Mann-Whitney test showed this difference was not significant (z=-0.851, df=1, p=0.395), and a discriminant analysis could not generate a significant function that predicted group membership (guilty or NGRI) (U=0.996, x^2=1.203, df=1, p=0.273). It is likely that the extremely low level of support for the death penalty in the current sample (see Table 7.22) obscured any relationship between death penalty support and verdict, whereas in US mock juror samples there is likely to be greater spread of death penalty support.

7.10.2 Disposal

As with the predictive importance of vignette factors on verdict and disposal, it was expected that attitudinal and demographic predictors of disposal would be similar to those that predict verdict. A logistic regression equation run with the same parameters as for verdict (but using disposal as the dependent variable) produced a model that correctly predicted 79.4 per cent of disposals correctly, with a -2LL of 290.74. The model's predicted verdict pattern was not significantly different from the observed verdict pattern (H&L goodness of fit test: x^2=4.358, df=8, p=0.823). The model shows the most important predictors of disposal to be: the degree to which Tom's behaviour was judged to be the product of his illness (FPROD) (β=1.619, p<0.001), the degree of meta-responsibility attributed to Tom (FMR) (β=-0.715, p<0.001), and the degree of ascription to the psychosocial model of mental disorder (FPSY) (β=0.375, p=0.021). Endorsing Tom as meta-responsible increases the likelihood of a prison disposal, whilst endorsing Tom's behaviour as a product of his illness increases the likelihood of a hospital disposal. Ascription to the psychosocial model of mental disorder is also associated with an increased likelihood of a hospital disposal. Also reaching significance in this model, however, is age (AGE) (β=-0.58, p=0.046). Older subjects are thus more likely to opt for a prison disposal.

7.10.3 Length of Detention

A stepwise linear regression model including all attitudinal variables shows that for both prison and hospital disposals combined the significant predictors of length of recommended institutional stay are: the degree to which Tom's behaviour was seen as the product of his illness (FPROD) (β=-0.350, t=-6.552, p<0.001), with greater illness-behaviour connection associated with a shorter length of stay; and the appraised degree of Tom's character change pre- to post-illness (CCHANGE) (β=0.161, t=3.007, p=0.003), with judgments of Tom as a 'badder' person after he became ill associated with a longer disposal.

For prison disposals only, FPROD (β=-0.298, t=-3.419, p=0.001), AGE (β=0.219, t=2.578, p=0.011) and FLIBAUTH (β=0.193, t=2.188, p=0.031) are significant predictors. Perceiving Tom's behaviour as due to his illness decreases the length of sentence. Older subjects impose longer sentences, as do subjects that are more authoritarian.

For hospital disposals only, the predictors of length of disposal are quite different. In this model, CCHANGE (β=0.238, t=3.324, p=0.001) and FPUNISH (β=0.148, t=2.063, p=0.041) are the significant predictors. Support for punishing mentally disordered offenders, and perceiving Tom being a 'badder' person after becoming ill are therefore associated with longer hospital disposals.

7.11 Concluding Overview

This chapter has presented the quantitative analysis of the results obtained from the experimental research detailed in Chapter 6. In particular, it has examined how diagnosis, type of meta-responsibility, type of insanity test, and various attitudinal and demographic dimensions (e.g. age, insanity defence support) affect insanity defence decision-making (as indexed by verdict, recommended disposal and recommended length of disposal). The next chapter discusses the results with reference to qualitative data concerning subjects' reasons for their verdicts.

Chapter 8

Discussion of Results with Reference to Subjects' Reasons for Their Verdicts

Refusal to take medication is both a symptom of his illness (his retreat and refuge in depression) and a cause of its continuance...insanity usually has its own internal logic.

Subject 284 (D>PMR>MN), finding Tom NGRI

This chapter discusses the results of the mock juror study with reference to subjects' responses to question two of the questionnaire: 'What are the reasons for your decision? (Please give as much detail as possible)'.[1]

Subjects' responses are identified by the type of vignette, followed by a code number used to identify the returned questionnaire. These numbers range from 047-380 (codes 001-046 were used to identify returns from the pilot study). S>CMR>MN/060/NGRI therefore refers to a subject in the schizophrenia>consensual meta-responsibility>McNaughton condition who found Tom NGRI, and whose questionnaire was given the reference number 060.[2]

8.1 Effect of Diagnosis on Verdict

Tom's diagnosis had a clear effect on verdict outcome, with the proportion of insanity verdicts being highest for schizophrenia in each of the type of meta-responsibility>insanity test conditions. The proportion of NGRI verdicts was always lower for depression; binomial tests show this difference is significant in five of the six types of meta-responsibility>insanity test conditions, although a diagnosis of depression just missed out on significance as a predictor of verdict in the regression model of vignette factors. A diagnosis of personality disorder significantly reduces the likelihood of being found NGRI in comparison with

---

[1] Of the 334 subjects, 329 offered reasons for their verdicts in the space provided (98.5 per cent). Presence or absence of such response did not vary by vignette type (x^2=20.26, df=17, p=0.261).

[2] See *SUPRA* section 6.6.1 for a detailed description of the notation used to denote vignette factors.

schizophrenia in the regression model, and NGRI verdicts for personality disorder were also less frequent than for depression for four of six types of meta-responsibility>insanity test conditions (significantly so in two of these conditions).

These verdict patterns mimic those found in real insanity defence decisions; Mackay and Kearns (1999) note that 52.3 per cent of insanity acquittals in England and Wales since 1992 have involved defendants with a primary diagnosis of schizophrenia. Only 6.8 per cent involved a diagnosis of depression and none involved a personality disorder diagnosis.

What is it about the individual diagnoses that characterizes their exculpatory power? Subjects' responses indicated that schizophrenia satisfied the cognitive requirements of the insanity tests better than other diagnoses: 'He was "labouring under a defect of reason" that made him act in self-defence' (S>PMR>MN/210/NGRI). The presence of delusions appeared particularly important in satisfying such cognitive requirements: 'He was no longer able to live by the logic of the world around him, but instead was concentrating on the deluded conclusions he had come to in his own mind...perhaps he saw the murder as essential to his own self' (S>NMR>MR/093/NGRI). The pervasive effect of schizophrenia on Tom's behaviour before the murder also appeared pertinent: 'There appears to be no reason why Tom should have killed his wife if he really were sane, and in the six months leading up to the killing his behaviour does not seem sane' (S>CMR>MR/241/NGRI). Schizophrenia's putative effect on Tom's identity was also exculpatory: '[he] cannot be acting voluntarily – it is as if he is not himself and this "other person" commits the crime' (S>CMR>MN/272/NGRI).

The lesser proportion of NGRI verdicts rendered in the depression and personality disorder conditions appeared largely due to their inability to satisfy the cognitive requirements of the insanity tests: 'I do not regard this as insanity – a significant proportion of people are clinically depressed and as far as I am aware, violence...and aggression are not listed among the clinical symptoms' (D>NMR>MR/348/guilty). This appeared particularly true for personality disorder: 'Long-term problems like depression or personality disorder and their expression in aggressive, deluded behaviour and attitudes are not necessarily ones I associate with a fundamental inability to judge right from wrong, or unawareness of one's own actions' (P>PMR>MN/298/guilty); 'Aggressive personality traits in themselves do not plausibly entail disturbed states of consciousness' (P>PMR>MN/145/guilty).[3]

---

[3] Such subjects may have felt more comfortable offering a verdict of diminished responsibility. This point was raised by a number of subjects (it should be remembered that the present sample was drawn from a college with a large proportion of law students): 'depression, while a mental illness, does not usually lead to a total breakdown of reason. Usually the person becomes withdrawn and suicidal, not homicidal...a more reasonable verdict would be diminished responsibility' (D>CMR>MN/296/NGRI); 'A Scottish verdict would probably be preferred if available – "insufficient evidence" with which to convict or release' (D>PMR>MN/250/guilty); 'It should be noted that following McNaughton's case, the defence of insanity is construed very strictly and would not be available unless Tom

Some subjects appeared to infer that Tom was legally insane because a diagnosis had been made: 'Psychiatrist had diagnosed personality disorder therefore it seems likely that this disorder would have affected his actions' (P>NMR>MN/153/NGRI); '...he did not know the nature and quality of the act...or it was wrong, but only because of the psychiatrist's diagnosis' (S>NMR>MN/377/NGRI).

8.2 Effect of Type of Meta-responsibility on Verdict

The most significant finding relating to type of meta-responsibility was the effect of consensual meta-responsibility to raise NGRI verdicts in comparison with no meta-responsibility. Indeed, NGRI verdicts were higher for consensual meta-responsibility than for no meta-responsibility in five of the six diagnosis>insanity test conditions (significantly so in three), and consensual meta-responsibility is a significant predictor of a NGRI verdict in the regression model of vignette factors. Purposive meta-responsibility generally reduces NGRI findings to a level similar to no meta-responsibility, except in one condition where Tom is schizophrenic and the meta-responsibility test is applied (S>__>MR), where the proportion of NGRI verdicts rendered in the purposive meta-responsibility condition is actually higher than for consensual meta-responsibility (though not significantly so).

This finding was unexpected – consensual meta-responsibility was expected to *reduce* NGRI verdicts due to Tom's greater culpability for causing the conditions of his own defence. This would have been especially true where the meta-responsibility test was applied (under which subjects are allowed to reflect such culpability through a guilty verdict). Whilst it does appear that there is a general effect of the meta-responsibility insanity test to reduce the degree to which consensual meta-responsibility draws NGRI verdicts in comparison with no meta-responsibility, NGRI verdicts for consensual meta-responsibility are still higher than for no meta-responsibility in all three diagnosis>type of insanity test conditions where the MRIT is applied.

In some of the subjects' decisions, it is clear that consensual meta-responsibility did provide a source of culpability, especially when the MRIT was applied: 'He stopped taking the prescribed medication of his own will and did not reconsult the doctor before stopping...he is responsible for the resulting behaviour as he was no longer on his medication' (S>CMR>MR/214/guilty); or 'It...appears that he didn't take any advice from a psychiatrist when he stopped. This was reckless' (S>CMR>MR/254/guilty). Some subjects wished for more information as to the reason for non-compliance, but convicted anyway: 'I'd examine what were side-effects of the drug' (D>CMR>MN/076/guilty); 'If he believed side-effects were worse than illness he was not wrong to stop taking it (if not then he

---

didn't understand the nature of the act...Tom would (at most) only succeed under provocation or diminished responsibility' (P>PMR>MR/193/guilty).

was responsible)' (S>CMR>MR/189/guilty). Although the consensual meta-responsibility case vignette (__>CMR>__) stated that Tom did not seem to realize that he was ill, some subjects still attributed insight: 'Tom was likely aware that this would cause a worsening of his condition' (D>CMR>MR/342/guilty).

Whilst consensual meta-responsibility could therefore provide a source of culpability as expected, the tables, graphs and statistical analysis showed a more significant characteristic of consensual meta-responsibility to be its apparent exculpatory power. How does this exculpatory power arise (or, more accurately, why does consensual meta-responsibility *fail* to provide the expected source of culpability)? It appears that both consensual meta-responsibility and purposive meta-responsibility entail *Tom not being on medication, and therefore more likely to have a 'defect of reason' or 'disease of the mind'.*

This schema was invoked by many subjects: 'He needed medication to control this depression, and without it he was not sane' (D>CMR>MN/207/NGRI); 'His behaviour when not taking medication certainly suggests he did not know the nature and quality of the act he was doing and that he was suffering from a disease of the mind' (S>CMR>MR/359/NGRI).

Whilst Tom may have been unmedicated (and thus more likely to qualify for an insanity defence), he would still be culpable for creating the conditions of his own insanity plea, which might be expected to reduce the proportion of NGRI verdicts in comparison to no meta-responsibility. This culpability seems to be forestalled by the lack of insight described in the consensual meta-responsibility vignette, i.e. *Tom could not be culpable for worsening his disorder, as he did not realize he had a disorder in the first instance.* Such reasoning has equivalence to the notion of disorder-mediated meta-responsibility discussed in Chapter 3:

> Tom did not knowingly contribute to his state of mind, as he did not know he was ill in the first place…for someone who does not accept they are ill, there is one easy solution to unpleasant side-effects caused by (in their eyes) unnecessary medication: stop taking it. Arguably, his illness was to blame for his failure to continue taking his medication' (P>CMR>MR/224/NGRI).

One subject alluded to this construct particularly eloquently: 'If one can be found "not guilty by reason of insanity" for a crime, it seems that one can also be found "not guilty by reason of insanity" for terminating treatment' (S>CMR>MR/085/NGRI). This schema might still be invoked even if Tom *was* medicated: '…to assume that he is capable of "recklessly" ending treatment is to assume that the treatment returned him to his sane state' (S>CMR>MR/085/NGRI).[4] Such a schema describes the class of patients whose

[4] This theme of lack of faith in drug treatments was common: 'His condition could well have been compounded by the anti-psychotic drugs' (S>NMR>MR/324/NGRI); 'Drugs aren't necessarily a good cure for psychiatric disorders' (S>NMR>MN/114/NGRI); 'The treatment does not appear to have included psychoanalysis/psychotherapy sessions, which are presumably essential if strong medication is prescribed' (P>CMR>MR/234/NGRI). This

'responsibility will be diminished but not eliminated by virtue of the fact that his medication only partially controls his illness' (Sherlock, 1984: 495).

Such schemas are complemented by the statistical relationship between FPROD (the degree to which Tom's behaviour was seen as the product of his illness), and the type of meta-responsibility described in the vignette.[5] It was found that the illness-behaviour connection was *greatest* for consensual meta-responsibility, followed by purposive meta-responsibility and finally no meta-responsibility. The failure of consensual and purposive meta-responsibility to provide a source of culpability (that would be reflected in more guilty verdicts) appears therefore to be mediated by their effect on the illness-behaviour connection; that both entail being off medication, which makes behaviour more vulnerable to the effects of illness.

The failure of consensual meta-responsibility to provide a source of culpability (in spite of its entailing a greater illness-behaviour connection) also appeared due to the reason for non-compliance: *side-effects*. This construct was apparent in both guilty and NGRI findings: 'The question becomes whether he was reckless with his medication. To stop taking one's medication because of side-effects is in no way reckless, much more likely it's responsible' (P>CMR>MR/205/guilty); 'There was an element of voluntariness [in non-compliance] due to dislike of unpleasant side-effects YET insufficient evidence of "recklessness" (subjective/objective)' (S>CMR>MR/135/NGRI).

However, side-effects were not referred to in the purposive meta-responsibility vignette, which suggests that purposive meta-responsibility's failure to provide a source of culpability was due, at least in part, to other reasons. In some cases, the apparent *irrationality* of not taking medication (especially for the purpose of courting mental disorder) could be considered *proof* of insanity (*res ipsa loquitur;* 'the thing speaks for itself'): 'The fact that he had not been taking prescribed medication for a mental illness diagnosed by a psychiatrist shows he was not behaving rationally' (D>PMR>MN/050/NGRI). Under such a schema, medication non-compliance is itself a 'crazy' act that therefore implies a 'crazy' defendant (i.e. a non-culpable one).

More remarkable is that the converse of this reasoning also seems true: that by having no meta-responsibility, Tom was medicated, and hence was not as eligible for an insanity defence as if he had consensual or purposive meta-responsibility. This schema is complemented by the no meta-responsibility condition entailing a low illness-behaviour connection (the mean of FPROD was lowest for no meta-responsibility; see above): 'He was sane enough to regularly take his medication'

---

tended to have the effect of transferring culpability for disorder away from Tom to the persons involved in his care: 'Maybe blame lies with the medical staff...didn't take sufficient action' (S>PMR>MR/061/NGRI); 'I'd draw the attention to the fact that this psychiatrist should've treated Tom's case much more seriously!' (S>PMR>MR/249/NGRI); 'The health services appear to have failed to spot that Tom had stopped taking his medication even over a period of 3+ weeks' (P>CMR>MR/234/NGRI).

[5] See *supra* section 7.9.1.

(S>NMR>MN/333/guilty); 'He had been sufficiently in charge of his senses to accept that he needed to take medication' (S>NMR>MN/118/guilty). Indeed, by accepting the psychiatrist's advice and medication '[he was] conscious of his problem and aware of how to control it [leading to] his responsibility to control his behaviour' (D>NMR>MR/130/guilty). That the act occurred several weeks after the initial appointment with the psychiatrist proved to some subjects, especially those receiving the no meta-responsibility condition, that the medication had been taken 'long enough for it to take effect' (S>NMR>MN/333/guilty). Thus Tom 'was on medication to reduce the schizophrenic behaviour and it should have helped him become more "normal"' (S>NMR>MN/180/guilty). Therefore, 'assuming the medication works, Tom's actions were by choice not as a consequence of insanity' (D>NMR>MR/197/guilty). If no meta-responsibility meant Tom was medicated and hence not mad, he must be bad.

In summary, these findings suggest that the different types of meta-responsibility have a much more complex effect on criminal responsibility determinations than originally envisaged. Having no meta-responsibility means there is no culpability for causing one's mental disorder, *but* provides a source of culpability for the criminal act as it entails being medicated and hence reduces eligibility for an insanity test that relies on a defect of reason or disease of the mind (such reasoning clearly relies on a degree of faith in the efficacy of psychiatric medication). Not only does consensual meta-responsibility entail that the defendant is unmedicated (and hence more likely to have a defect of reason or disease of the mind and hence not be culpable for the criminal act) *but* any culpability for causing one's own mental disorder is forestalled by non-compliance being due to lack of insight and medication side-effects (illness-behaviour connection is highest). Purposive meta-responsibility also entails being unmedicated, and whilst there is culpability for generating or exacerbating mental disorder, the reflection of such culpability may be forestalled through purposive meta-responsibility itself being indicative of 'craziness' (and hence eligibility for an insanity plea).

It might therefore be tendered that no meta-responsibility and purposive meta-responsibility are the 'abnormal' types of meta-responsibility that have an effect on culpability (increasing it); rather than some quality of consensual meta-responsibility being particularly exculpatory *per se*. The rate of insanity acquittals rendered in the consensual meta-responsibility conditions might represent the 'base-rate' of insanity acquittals, as the sort of behaviour exhibited in consensual meta-responsibility seems to conform to the subjects' 'prototypes' of insanity. No meta-responsibility and purposive meta-responsibility are less eligible for an insanity defence due to their entailment of culpability (for the *criminal act* in the case of no meta-responsibility, and for the *disorder of which it is a product* in the case of purposive meta-responsibility). The mock jurors seem to expect and tolerate mentally disordered persons not taking their medication due to side-effects or lack of insight (hence consensual meta-responsibility does not provide a source of culpability). Subjects do *not* expect or tolerate people stopping medication for the *purpose* of courting mental disorder (hence a drop in NGRI verdicts for purposive meta-responsibility in comparison to consensual meta-responsibility);

nor do they expect the *medicated* mentally disordered to commit murder (hence a drop in NGRI verdicts for no meta-responsibility in comparison to consensual meta-responsibility).

It does then appear, that the delineation of two different types of meta-responsibility (consensual and purposive) in Chapter 3 was justified; they do indeed appear to have differential effects on criminal responsibility, though in a manner more complex than originally envisaged. However, the results confirm the prediction by the 'culpable causation' model of Alicke (1992) that purposive meta-responsibility, by being morally more blameworthy than consensual meta-responsibility, results in fewer NGRI findings than consensual meta-responsibility.[6] The results raise the concern that the person who diligently takes his medication and follows psychiatric advice may, if he commits a crime, actually be *less* eligible for excuse or mitigation than those who have not been so diligent. This may reduce the motivation of mentally disordered persons to be compliant with treatment in the first instance. This finding may be important to a wide range of situations regarding the mentally disordered: are the medicated/treated mentally disordered afforded less sympathy in other situations if they perform negatively appraised acts (e.g. in the family environment or on psychiatric wards)? Might mentally disordered persons who commit a criminal offence whilst subject to a community treatment order receive more punitive disposals as they must be bad rather than mad?

8.3 Effect of Type of Insanity Test on Verdict

Although the type of insanity test is not a significant predictor of verdict across all vignette conditions, binomial tests show the MRIT to have a significant effect on verdict in some combinations of diagnosis and type of meta-responsibility in comparison to McNaughton. The effect of the MRIT is *generally* to lower the proportion of NGRI verdicts in comparison to McNaughton: this occurs in five of nine diagnosis>type of meta-responsibility conditions (significantly so in two of these conditions – when Tom is schizophrenic and has consensual meta-responsibility [S>CMR>__], and when Tom is personality disordered and has no meta-responsibility [P>NMR>__]). The MRIT *raises* NGRI verdicts in four conditions (but significantly so in only one – when Tom is schizophrenic and has purposive meta-responsibility [S>PMR>__]). It helps our exploration of the effect of the MRIT to examine these conditions in more detail.

The significant reduction in NGRI verdicts by the MRIT in the S>CMR>__ condition is not surprising; S>CMR>MN has the highest rate of NGRI verdicts (83.3 per cent) of any condition (schizophrenia and consensual meta-responsibility both being significant predictors of a NGRI verdict in the regression model). However, the significant reduction of NGRI verdicts by the meta-responsibility test

---

[6] See *SUPRA* note 1, Ch. 5.

in the P>NMR>__ condition is more perplexing, as this condition has no meta-responsibility in the first instance! It seems reasonable to suggest that this reduction is not therefore due to type of meta-responsibility, but rather to the remaining vignette factor: diagnosis.

Personality disorder might be viewed as an inherently 'meta-responsible' condition even in the absence of any specific consensual or purposive meta-responsibility. The personality disordered person, even one taking his medication faithfully, could be seen as responsible for his condition due to personality disorder not being an 'illness' in the same way as depression or schizophrenia ('There is a world of difference between depression and "personality disorder", even one requiring medication…' [P>NMR>MN/051/guilty]). Aside from preserved cognitive function and hence lack of eligibility for an insanity defence based on criteria of irrationality (Radden, 1985), Rudnick and Levy (1994: 416) state that 'personality disorders are regarded by some as a form of "mere" deviance and not "real" disease, and therefore as not excusable'.

This 'culpability' will be reflected through an insanity test that draws attention to responsibility for incapacity such as the MRIT, even when there is no responsibility for incapacity in terms of *specific* consensual or purposive meta-responsibility. Few personality disordered persons are successful with the insanity defence (none since 1992; Mackay and Kearns, 1999), and a more stringent insanity test such as the MRIT seems to reduce their eligibility even further. That this effect does not materialize for schizophrenia and depression suggests that these are seen as less 'meta-responsible' conditions; people with such disorders may be seen as less morally weak and therefore less 'the architects of their own downfall' than those with personality disorder. Hence, when attention is drawn to culpability in schizophrenia and depression by the MRIT (in the absence of any specific consensual or purposive meta-responsibility considerations) it makes no difference to NGRI verdicts.

This hypothesis is borne out by many of the subjects schemas' who received the personality disorder vignette: 'I feel the professionals often attribute wrong behaviour to "personality" disorders rather than an innate tendency towards wrongdoing' (P>CMR>MN/132/guilty); 'Personality disorder…may in fact refer to those characteristics of being "deceitful, manipulative, impulsive and aggressive" mentioned in the introduction' (P>CMR>MN/297/guilty); 'Tom's problems are not uncommon – many people are deceitful, aggressive and the like, this is not mental illness, but part of human nature' (P>NMR>MN/165/guilty).

If the meta-responsibility insanity test does indeed draw attention to culpability for a condition in the absence of specific meta-responsibility considerations, then conditions seen as 'nonculpable' or organic such as schizophrenia (Furnham and Bower, 1992) are unlikely to be particularly affected by a meta-responsibility insanity test if there is no specific meta-responsibility to consider. It appears that the covert feeling that mentally disordered persons may have responsibility for their condition is *not reflected in verdict*, except for personality disorder (but may be reflected by length of disposal through covert punishment).[7] This is a feature of the schizophrenia>no meta-responsibility and depression>no meta-responsibility conditions, for which the proportion of NGRI verdicts does not significantly vary when the MRIT is substituted for McNaughton (see Table 7.6).

Accounting for the increase in NGRI verdicts in the schizophrenia>purposive meta-responsibility condition when the MRIT is substituted for McNaughton is more difficult. It may be that schizophrenia is seen as so debilitating (that schizophrenics are 'crazy') that non-compliance for 'irrational' reasons such as wanting to be ill (a 'crazy' volition and act) is *seen by subjects as consistent with a 'crazy' diagnosis*. The MRIT (through 'requesting' subjects to analyse the condition in terms of its culpability, and through being a longer insanity test than McNaughton) engenders salience of such notions (*res ipsa loquitur*), as well as drawing attention to Tom's condition being unmedicated at the time of the murder and hence increasing his eligibility for an insanity plea. For example:

> Schizophrenics are often 'reckless' in their approach to taking medication due to the severe side effects it can cause. A cycle can occur when the sufferer takes the medication, feels better and then no longer wants to continue with the medication as they feel 'cured' and are suffering side effects (S>PMR>MR/213/NGRI).

Whilst the MRIT may therefore have engendered exculpation in some conditions, a more apparent characteristic of the MRIT was to draw attention to recklessness, resulting in conviction: 'The judge's final statement clinched it, ultimately. Knowing he was ill, he seemed reckless in his attitude to it and to his medication' (S>PMR>MR/056/guilty); 'The wording of the question hints at recklessness (in the everyday sense of the word – no legal technicalities if I'm on a jury!). This would override any other considerations, given the wording of the judges direction' (D>PMR>MR/172/guilty).

In summary, the MRIT appears to have disparate effects on verdict. It does not have the general expected effect of reducing the likelihood of NGRI verdicts across all conditions. The MRIT does, however, appear to have effects consonant with commonsense notions of justice and patterns of current insanity acquittals, through increasing the eligibility of schizophrenics for a defence of NGRI but reducing the eligibility of personality disordered persons. This eligibility is preserved for schizophrenics even if they have committed meta-responsible acts, but is waived for the personality disordered person committing such acts (indeed, personality disorder *itself* seems to be regarded as a 'meta-responsible condition').

What is perhaps more important is not the effect of the MRIT test on verdict *per se*, but its effect on the associated disposal. Whilst it seems that 'inviting' subjects to consider culpability for disorder does not have a significant overall effect upon their insanity verdicts, it is shown below that it has the beneficial effect

---

7 See *INFRA* section 8.5.

of reducing recommended length of disposal for hospital disposals (covert punishment).[8]

However, it is evident that the general effect of insanity test manipulation upon verdict was minor. This echoes previous studies on the effect of changing legal standards, both in the effect upon mock juror verdicts (e.g. Ogloff, 1991; Simon, 1967; Finkel and Slobogin, 1995) and in real-world changes in insanity defence legislature (e.g. Pasewark, Randolph and Bieber, 1984). Of such minimal effects on verdicts and rates of insanity pleas, Appelbaum (1994:198) states, 'the insight of the most recent round of reforms in the United States is that perceptions of moral culpability are not easily affected by legal rules'. Such a thesis bears resemblance to that of Eastman and Peay (1999) who deem tinkering legislative reforms of dubious worth in mental health law. However, if the failure of insanity defence reform to have an impact on verdicts 'should allow us to feel comfortable with the insanity defense as a genuine expression of our most profound moral principles' (Appelbaum, 1984: 198), then introducing concepts of meta-responsibility into the insanity defence may allow us to feel even more comfortable with the defence. Researchers into the effects of insanity defence change have generally not considered the effect of insanity defence reform on post-trial detention. The reduction in covert punishment engendered by the meta-responsibility test suggests that Appelbaum's 'almost a revolution' hypothesis for insanity defence usage and observed verdicts does not tell the whole story of the 'moral principles' of which the insanity defence is 'a profound expression'. Instead, this study does suggest that insanity defence reform designed towards satisfying commonsense notions of justice may have very significant consequences for the insanity acquittee, not in the form of verdict, but in the form of reduction in covert punishment through shorter terms of hospital detention.[9]

8.4 Effect of Vignette Factors on Type of Disposal

The Spearman's tests showed there was a significant positive correlation (0.635) between verdict and type of disposal. A guilty verdict is associated with a prison disposal, whereas a NGRI verdict is associated with a hospital disposal (in accordance with the vignette instructions). Whilst not one subject who found Tom NGRI sent him to prison, a perfect (+1.00) correlation between verdict and disposal was forestalled by the 74 subjects who found Tom guilty and opted for a hospital disposal.

Given the positive correlation between verdict and disposal, it is unsurprising that a regression analysis showed the most important predictors of disposal to be the same as those of verdict. A diagnosis of personality disorder significantly increases the odds of a prison disposal compared to schizophrenia, and this was

---

[8] See *INFRA* section 8.5.
[9] See *INFRA* section 8.5.

borne out in some subjects' responses: 'A personality disorder is a chronic condition and is not likely to benefit from a cure…the attitude of using prison "to protect society" seems reasonable to take' (P>CMR>MN/297/guilty). Consensual meta-responsibility significantly increases the likelihood of a hospital disposal. Having personality disorder and purposive meta-responsibility significantly increases the odds of being sent to prison.

This latter finding goes against the general effect of purposive meta-responsibility, which is slightly (albeit non-significantly) to raise the odds of a hospital disposal. It seems that whilst purposive meta-responsibility may be 'tolerated' in combination with schizophrenia or depression,[10] its interaction with personality disorder is to elicit a punitive response. Subjects receiving personality disorder>purposive meta-responsibility conditions often indicated an inherent mistrust of the defendant: 'It is likely that he is trying to deceive the jury' (P>PMR>MN/380/guilty); '[Tom] used his illness to his advantage – to claim diminished responsibility…poss. used as a cover for premeditated murder' (P>PMR>MR/238/guilty). Extending Rudnick and Levy's (1985) argument, if personality disorder is not seen as a medical illness, then a medical disposal cannot be justified: 'Tom's supposed "mental disorder" is the exact reason why people like him should be put in jail' (P>PMR>MR/285/guilty).

More generally, it was clear from subjects' responses across all vignette conditions that disposal considerations played a significant role in deciding the verdict. Such 'disposal-driven' NGRI verdicts were particularly common for schizophrenia, in which the primary concern was not exculpation *per se*, but treatment. Subjects stated that: 'It sounds like he is not well…therefore it would be better for him to be treated rather than locked away' (S>PMR>MR/152/NGRI), and that:

> While Tom is clearly a danger to others punishment in prison seems to me to be wrong…I believe a prison environment would upset and confuse him and be detrimental to his mental health…it seems more sensible and humane to me to try and treat the illness which makes him dangerous than make it worse and him therefore more dangerous (S>CMR>MN/126/NGRI).

Schizophrenia could, however, provide grounds for a *guilty* disposal-driven verdict if the defendant was seen as dangerous: 'He sounds dangerous – saying he is not guilty would mean he is free to repeat the crime' (S>NMR>MN/121/guilty). Such policy considerations were particularly evident for personality disorder: 'If I send him to mental hospital, how do I know that he'll not be back on the streets in a couple of years – a public danger?' (P>CMR>MR/220/guilty); 'If he were found not guilty, there would be many more killers on the loose…a killer is a dangerous person and should be treated accordingly' (P>CMR/MR/095/guilty).[11]

---

[10] See *SUPRA* sections 8.2 and 8.3.

[11] Such subjects may have felt more comfortable with a hybrid disposal order: 'He should be sent for mental care but he should still face some punishment for what he did after he is

Others, again invoking the construct of *res ipsa loquitur*, saw 'crazy' acts as indicating a disposal suitable for 'crazy' people, i.e. hospital: 'Arguably, any man who kills his wife needs urgent psychological help for a seriously disordered mind' (D>PMR>MN/102/NGRI). An ideological dislike of punishment led to a therapeutic response for one subject:

> I strongly believe that society is definitely more brutalised by the habitual employment of punishment than by the occasional occurrence of crime. Much mental illness is the result of a brutal, fractured society; why increase the sum of misery through further punishment? Care seems to be the answer (P>NMR>MN/184/NGRI).

Finally, a fascinating caveat: 'If ambiguous in any way – personally I would rather put a "sane" person into mental hospital than an insane one into a prison' (D>PMR>MN/102/NGRI).

8.5 Effect of Vignette Factors on Length of Detention

Recommended length of detention for prison disposals was significantly higher than that for hospital disposals. An ANOVA showed that diagnosis and type of meta-responsibility do not significantly affect the length of detention for both prison and hospital disposals combined, or individually. However, type of insanity test *does* have an effect on the recommended length of detention for hospital disposals. The meta-responsibility insanity test significantly reduces the length of detention in comparison with McNaughton, in spite of the notion that the insanity test should not be involved in considerations such as length of detention.

What is the mechanism by which the meta-responsibility insanity test shortens recommended hospital stay? Chapter 4 suggested that the hospital disposal may be imposed with covertly punitive considerations in mind, and that insanity acquittees (and those raising the insanity defence unsuccessfully) might be covertly punished by lengthy periods of post-acquittal detention. Such use of 'hospital as prison' has been suggested by some authors (e.g. Perlin, 1994) as due to a feeling that by invoking excuse, justification or mitigation, mentally disordered offenders (and particularly the insanity acquittee) are seen as 'cheating justice'. However, given that both law and medicine deem mental disorder as not of the afflicted person's own making (which should abate feelings of 'cheating justice'), sanist and pretextual decision-making was identified as the result of covert societal, legal and medical sentiment that the mentally disordered might be in some way responsible for their own disorder. It was suggested that covertly punitive medical disposals

---

"cured" at the mental institution' (P>CMR>MN/262/guilty); 'I feel he should be given treatment first and when he's well he should be made to pay (at least some punishment) for terminating an innocent life' (D>NMR>MR/328/guilty).

for the insanity acquittee are a result of a frustration at being unable to express such culpability through present insanity tests.

The results comport with such a hypothesis. The McNaughton test (which does not provide for the consideration of such culpability) resulted in a mean hospital stay of 8.87 years, whilst the MRIT (which made provision for consideration of such culpability, reducing covert punishment through not frustrating commonsensical notions of justice) resulted in a hospital stay of 5.66 years (over one third less).

Some subjects alluded to punitive elements of hospital disposals:

> A special hospital will:-
> a) remove him from society for treatment and rehabilitation.
> b) enable essential contact with his children, family and friends.
> c) place recommendation for an eventual return to society in the hands of specialists and the Probation Service.
> d) compulsory hospital placement will be seen by many in society as 'a punishment'. (P>PMR>MN/314/NGRI).

Other subjects did not appear so insightful into their aims of disposal. One subject stated 'He needs assistance in conquering and restraining his madness rather than simple punishment' (S>CMR>MN/336/NGRI), but recommended a 30 year hospital stay.

That the meta-responsibility insanity test did not have a significant overall effect on verdict (the expected fall in NGRI verdicts failed to materialize) seems to indicate that subjects are not generally willing to reflect determinations of culpability for disorder at the *verdict* level. Although the meta-responsibility insanity test 'invites' a greater proportion of guilty verdicts, this does not seem to occur (except in the case of personality disorder which appears to be viewed as an inherently 'meta-responsible' condition, inviting significantly more guilty verdicts under the MRIT even in the no meta-responsibility condition). If people hold a sentiment that schizophrenic and depressed persons are (to varying extents) responsible for their condition, they do not appear to reflect it at the verdict level but rather through length of disposal.[12] As suggested by previous mock jury studies, verdict appears almost invulnerable to differences in the wordings of insanity tests (e.g. Simon, 1967; Ogloff, 1991).

The potential of recommended length of detention to provide an index of attitudes towards mentally disordered offenders has not been exploited in previous

---

[12] Pre-existing attitudes sometimes appear to have quite counterintuitive effects on verdict. For example, the Spearman's rank tests (in *INFRA* section 7.9.1) show that ascription to the psychosocial model is associated with lower levels of support for the insanity defence. However, the logistic regression (in *INFRA* section 7.10.1) shows that level of ascription to the psychosocial model is associated with a verdict of NGRI. It is perhaps therefore unexpected that an attitude such as mentally disordered persons being responsible for their disorder, if it has an effect on decision-making at all, might not impact upon verdict but upon another dimension such as length of disposal.

studies, which have generally only examined verdict. However, it seems that verdict alone is not an adequate reflection of subjects' determinations of culpability towards mentally disordered offenders (for both the crime *and* the condition of which the crime is a putative product). The effect of the MRIT (on reducing recommended length of hospital detention) deserves more detailed analysis in future studies; in the meantime, however, the effect attests to the meta-responsibility theory's useful contribution to psychiatric and legal ethics.

8.6 Effect of Gender and Ethnic Identity on Dependent Variables

No effect of gender on verdict, disposal and attitudinal dimensions materialized. Although Simon (1967) found that female jurors were more sympathetic to the defendant (reflected in a slightly increased tendency to offer NGRI verdicts), both that study and the present one cannot confirm the folk wisdom of trial lawyers that male and female jurors differ along a multitude of dimensions.[13]

Ethnic identity has a more substantial effect on a range of variables than gender. Non-white respondents are more likely to recommend a prison disposal than white subjects, and show decreased overall support for the insanity defence (which is associated with concern about medical involvement in insanity trials and that NGRIs are 'beating the rap'). Non-white respondents are also less likely to endorse Tom's behaviour as a product of his illness. This latter finding has equivalence with the finding of Hall and Tucker (1985) that black respondents were more likely than white respondents to endorse the view that mental disturbances can be controlled by avoidance of morbid thoughts. Ethnic identity did not significantly affect verdict in the present study, in contrast to that of Simon (1967) who found that black subjects were more likely to find the defendant NGRI.

Whilst the influence of demographic variables on verdict and attitudinal dimensions is not a focus of the present study, such relationships can be useful in interpreting the other data. It should be remembered that the present sample was 84.1 per cent 'white', and therefore likely to differ along the dimensions mentioned above compared to a sample containing a greater diversity of ethnic identity.

[13] Hastie *et al.* (1983) offer the following folk wisdom of lawyers, which seems to be borne more from misogyny than empirical evidence: 'attorneys are instructed to avoid women in all defence cases', 'women are sympathetic and extraordinarily conscientious', 'with a woman as client, take all men', 'women are unpredictable and influenced by their husbands' experience', 'men are better jurors when counsel wants to avoid intuitive and sympathetic thinking', 'females are good for all defendants except attractive female defendants' (p. 122).

8.7 Effect of Attitudinal Dimensions on Verdict

The best predictors of verdict out of all the attitudinal dimensions measured in the current study are the degree to which subjects perceive Tom's behaviour (including his non-compliant behaviour) as a product of his illness, and their evaluations of the degree of Tom's meta-responsibility. These two dimensions have a greater predictive importance on verdict than any of the vignette factors (of which the most important was diagnosis). Endorsing Tom as meta-responsible increases the likelihood of a guilty verdict; endorsing Tom's behaviour as a product of his illness is associated with a finding of NGRI. Endorsement of Tom's meta-responsibility (or otherwise) is a predictor of verdict that remains intact even when NO meta-responsibility information is given within the vignette (i.e. in the __>NMR>MN condition for each of the diagnoses). Therefore, subjects appear to invoke the meta-responsibility construct in the absence of specific meta-responsibility information, and this has an effect on their verdict.

This phenomenon, of invoking a type of meta-responsibility test *in spite of not receiving that explicit test*, was evident in some subjects' responses. For example:

> ...most neurotic patients in fact do UNDERSTAND the concept of responsibility and know what they're doing is socially unacceptable, though they may not necessarily have CONTROL over their actions. This is why Tom should never have refused medication. In most cases neurotic patients also understand that medication will help them regain control (D>PMR>MN/144/guilty).

A related finding by Finkel and Slobogin (1995) showed that subjects register culpability distinctions in terms of blameworthiness for mental disorder even when they are given no explicit insanity test to apply.

An unexpected finding was that increased authoritarianism predicted a finding of NGRI. This might be explained by the discussion in Chapter 4 that hospital disposals (associated with a NGRI finding) can be used as a punitive measure. However, if this were the case (that those with high levels of authoritarianism were using hospital as prison), authoritarianism should also be a predictor of length of disposal for hospital disposals; this effect does not materialize.[14] It may be that the role of authoritarianism as a predictor of verdict is a statistical artefact. It disappears as a predictor if the regression model is rerun with a more stringent likelihood ratio (0.01 rather than 0.05) for stepwise entry.

Support for punishing mentally disordered offenders is also a significant predictor of a guilty finding, whereas endorsing the psychosocial model of mental disorder is a significant predictor of an NGRI verdict. This latter result is disparate with a finding from the Spearman's tests, that support for the psychosocial model is associated with *lower* levels of support for the insanity defence; it therefore appears that such attitudes do not map onto verdict.[15] The finding that support for

---

[14] See *INFRA* section 8.9.

[15] See *SUPRA* note 12.

the psychosocial model entails a greater generosity towards defendants in terms of the insanity plea has equivalence with that of Eker (1985), who found that subjects informed of a psychosocial aetiology to mental disorder were less stigmatizing of the mentally disordered in terms of desired social distance. Pam (1990) notes that social and psychological aetiological factors are considered by the liberal-scientific model only when biological factors partially or fully fail to account for a condition's aetiology. This failure to consider psychosocial factors as discrete aetiological hypotheses appears to affect the legal situation of the mentally disordered offender negatively (in terms of reducing likelihood of success of an insanity plea).

This finding has implications both for attempts to educate the population about mental disorder using the medical model to reduce stigma, and for expert witness testimony in the courtroom. As well as predicting an NGRI verdict, it was found that FPSY (degree of ascription to the psychosocial model) is influenced by diagnosis in the vignette.[16] This suggests that not only might courtroom testimony have an effect on people's ascription to various models of mental disorder, but that casting the defendant's mental disorder as 'biological' or 'medical' in the courtroom may not do the defendant's insanity plea any good, and may even do it harm.[17] More efficacious to the aims of defence teams and organizations attempting to reduce stigma and increase sympathy towards the mentally disordered may be education in terms of the psychosocial model. As Colombo (1997) states:

> ...the 'mental illness' explanation...may only serve to make the condition even more mysterious, unfathomable and 'spoilt'...a medical context may also be viewed as unhelpful in promoting a generally more tolerant approach...while the notion of an internal cause may benefit the schizophrenic in the sense that they are able to hold on to the 'sick' role and so not be viewed as morally responsible, perceptions of an inability to control one's actions inevitably provokes the detrimental feeling that the patient is unpredictable, the most salient hallmark of the mentally disordered...engendering the need to constrain and control those so identified...an approach which by implication could have a profound effect upon the liberty of the schizophrenic... (p.154).

It was expected that persons with greater knowledge or experience of mental disorder might be more sympathetic to the defendant (reflected in more NGRI verdicts), but this effect did not materialize (as indexed by its failure to provide a significant predictor of verdict in a regression model). However, such experience or knowledge clearly had an influence on some verdicts:

---

16 See *SUPRA* section 7.9.1.

17 For example, the attempt of 'Dr. Biological Psychiatry' (Stone, 1984: 86) to show Hinckley's widened sulci on a CAT scan at his trial.

> I know a family with a teenage son with a personality disorder that sounds similar to Tom's. He has been extremely difficult to deal with, and a major problem is the extent to which the authorities are prepared to accept a) that a problem exists; and b) that it is an illness, he is not just a 'bad' person, or the product of disadvantaged upbringing. Medication can help, but he cannot be trusted to take it all the time, and when he doesn't he can't control himself...Perhaps I'd be less likely to say not guilty though if I hadn't known a person in a similar situation (P>NMR>MN/208/NGRI).

Another subject stated that: 'I have suffered from depression, and I know what it's like. A person so severely depressed is incapable of being rational' (D>PMR>MR/167/NGRI).

Another case where knowledge concerning mental disorder clearly mapped on to verdict used a social constructivist argument (this subject, apparently familiar with both psychiatric debate and criminal law, was studying for a PhD in history and rated himself '7 – well informed' about mental disorder issues):

> 'Mental illness' is a term used by psychiatrists to describe abnormalities that are socially undesirable (e.g. reclusiveness, talking to oneself in public, etc.) as distinct from abnormalities which are socially desirable (exceptional facility in maths, wittiness, etc.). This distinguishes it from other genuine diminished capacity defenses (intoxication, head injury), which are clinically demonstrable conditions. That drugs can be used to alter the behaviour (or 'cure') a person who is mentally ill is not itself evidence of mental illness, since they can equally alter the behaviour of a putatively 'normal' person. Since it is impossible to demonstrate mental 'illness', it cannot be used as a defence (S>NMR>MR/334/guilty).

8.8 Effect of Attitudinal Dimensions on Type of Disposal

The best attitudinal predictors of disposal were those that best predicted verdict (reflecting the vignette instructions). Rating the defendant as meta-responsible predicted a prison disposal. A hospital disposal was predicted by endorsement of Tom's behaviour as the product of his illness, and increased levels of ascription to the psychosocial model of mental disorder. Being older also predicted a prison disposal, a surprising finding given the homogeneity of the present sample in terms of age (with two thirds of the sample under 23 years old). It appears that the stereotype of increasing conservatism and punitive attitudes with age is borne out in the present sample within a range of only a few years.

8.9 Effect of Attitudinal Dimensions on Length of Detention

Endorsement of Tom's behaviour as a product of his illness predicted a decreased recommended length of time for prison disposals, whilst an appraisal of Tom as meta-responsible predicted a longer sentence. This suggests that subjects are indeed reflecting culpability for the defendant creating the conditions of his own defence, and converting that culpability into punishment where a prison disposal is recommended.

Rating Tom as a 'badder' person after he became ill is a significant predictor of an increased length of detention for hospital disposals, as is support for punishing mentally disordered offenders. This latter finding indicates that recommended length of hospital disposal is not a purely therapeutic concern, but is better predicted by *punitive* and *retributive* dimensions (support for punishing mentally disordered offenders). This finding lends support to the analysis in Chapter 4; hospital may indeed serve a similar purpose to prison.

By what mechanism does character change influence length of detention? It might be expected that increasing appraisals of character change (i.e. being a 'badder' person after becoming ill) might be associated with a *decreased* length of hospital disposal as Tom's 'badness' would therefore be seen as due to his 'madness', and therefore retributive or punitive concerns should not play a part in length of disposal. On the other hand, a rating of Tom as a 'badder' person after he became ill may increase the recommended time in hospital, in order to restore Tom to a 'good' person. Higher ratings of character change might also increase length of detention due to dangerousness concerns: if Tom is a 'bad' person after he became ill, then he might be detained longer with incapacitation as a primary aim. How subjects construe the phrasing of the character change items may have an effect on their responses; does viewing Tom as a 'badder' person after becoming ill mean that his bad behaviour is attributed to his illness, or does it mean that Tom now has a genuinely poorer character?

In any case, the present results cannot support Reznek's (1997) hypothesis that we excuse the mentally ill due to their character change, as degree of character change was not a predictor of verdict; indeed, a greater appraisal of character change seems to have an adverse effect on Tom's liberty. However, Reznek's notion of character change as exculpatory (if not *mitigatory*, at least for length of hospital disposals) was borne out in some subjects' reasons for their decisions: 'Tom was a good man before' (S>PMR>MN/206/NGRI); 'Paranoid and aggressive behaviour had been characteristic of him since this change in his personality/behaviour. The implication is that these were not typical of him before the change' (S>NMR>MR/073/NGRI); 'He acted in a wholly out-of-character way indicating insanity' (S>PMR>MR/288/NGRI). In the same manner, a lower appraisal of the degree of Tom's character change could be used to convict, particularly in the personality disorder condition: 'His history of aggression indicates that his behaviour was not out of character therefore a plea of insanity does not seem appropriate' (P>CMR>MN/361/guilty); 'There is a suggestion of a long-term history of aggression suggesting that the crime was not entirely out of character' (P>NMR>MN/330/guilty).

However, lack of character change could also be a sign that Tom's problems were deep-seated, and thus used to acquit: 'Although I think that Tom has enormous depths of calculatingness "built into" him – it's not so much what he does as what he is' (P>CMR>MN/365/NGRI). Tom's background was of clear importance to the notion of character change, indicating that it was his 'illness' at work, rather than Tom *per se*: 'The fact that he had a wife and family suggests that he wasn't nasty all the time' (P>CMR>MN/313/NGRI); 'There is no reason why a rational person in Tom's situation would kill his wife when Tom's life up to then appears normal' (D>NMR>MN/164/NGRI). Others, however, used Tom's background to impute responsibility: 'Evidence that he had a job – sign of consciousness over his actions' (P>NMR>MR/090/guilty). It seems the role of character change in decision-making with regard to mentally disordered offenders is difficult to predict and depends largely upon the manner in which it is construed.

8.10 Estimates of Insanity Defence Parameters and Attitudes Towards the Insanity Defence

Subjects' estimates of insanity defence usage lend some credence to Perlin's (1996) myths being expressed by the current sample. Whilst the present sample did not overestimate insanity defence usage as much as that of Hans (1986), their estimates are still wildly inaccurate. Subjects believed the insanity defence to be raised by 13 per cent of persons charged with a criminal act,[18] of which 28 per cent were actually successful with their plea.[19] Subjects estimated that 15 per cent of those found NGRI were released immediately,[20] and that 56 per cent went to hospital.[21] This leaves 39 per cent of NGRIs unaccounted for by the subjects;[22] it is possible that many think that some insanity acquittees are sent to prison (a belief consonant with the punitive dimensions of the insanity disposal). Subjects estimate that the average hospital stay for insanity acquittees is just under four years[23] which, although data is not available for the UK, is an overestimate based on the US data of Steadman, Monahan, Hartstone *et al.* (1982).[24] It is not clear, however, of which types of crimes subjects are thinking when they estimate length of stay. Perlin (1994) suggests that most people think the insanity defence is raised disproportionately in murder cases; it would follow that people would think of most insanity acquittees as murderers.

There is clear evidence to show that a large minority of the present sample hold generally negative attitudes towards the insanity defence. Although 93.7 per cent agreed (to a varying extent) that the insanity plea is a necessary part of our legal system, 54.6 per cent of subjects agreed that the insanity defence needs a lot of reform, 38.7 per cent agreed that it was a loophole, 23.1 per cent agreed that it is a rich person's defence, and an overwhelming 95.8 per cent of subjects agreed with

---

[18] Compared with a mean of 38.16 per cent of defendants believed to invoke the insanity defence by Hans' (1986) sample of residents of a Delaware community conducted soon after the trial of John Hinckley.
[19] Compared with a mean of 36.33 per cent of defendants in Hans' (1986) study.
[20] Compared with a mean of 25.57 per cent of defendants in Hans' (1986) study.
[21] Compared with a mean of 50.60 per cent of defendants in Hans' (1986) study.
[22] Compared with a mean of 25 per cent of defendants in Hans' (1986) study.
[23] Compared with a mean of 21.82 months in Hans' (1986) study.
[24] See *SUPRA* note 13, Ch. 4.

the statement that judges and juries have a hard time telling whether defendants are sane or insane.

Such sentiments were prominent in some subjects' reasons for their verdicts, e.g. 'Not guilty by reason of insanity is just an excuse' (P>PMR>MN/350/guilty); 'A guy who has got a mind to plead "Not guilty by reason of insanity" is, I believe, relatively sane. An insane person would not give a damn whether he goes to jail, hospital or not. It's not as if he was born insane' (P>NMR>MN/131/guilty). This notion, that 'he who excuses himself, accuses himself' was invoked by other subjects: 'An insane person cannot claim his own insanity. Usually they rather deny it' (P>PMR>MR/140/guilty). To cast murder as an insane act would therefore extend such excuse to everyone: 'Tom is as guilty of this crime as anyone could be. Murder is an abnormal act, and one could therefore argue that all murderers are insane, abnormal' (P>PMR>MN/310/guilty); '[Tom] is probably using the insanity defense just to escape punishment' (P>NMR>MR/221/guilty). Another subject stated:

> I believe such a depressed person is still able to make conscious decisions with coherence, but more so that an amount of 'insanity' is involved in every such crime and to declare one man not guilty by reason of insanity would be inconsistent; for example multiple murderers or considered killers could also be described as insane, but they are in prison following a guilty verdict, in my opinion quite rightly (D>NMR>MN/183/guilty).

Following similar reasoning, another subject thought that 'Almost all of the people who murder could be described as clinically insane' (P>CMR/MR/095/guilty).

Perhaps one of the more interesting attitudes to the insanity defence was that over half the subjects thought that the insanity defence needed a lot of reform. It would have been interesting to find out exactly what sort of reform they had in mind, but the introduction of provision for the consideration of meta-responsibility in the insanity defence may represent the type of reform urged by the subjects in the present study.

8.11 Concluding Overview

The diversity of responses to a question concerning reasons for insanity verdicts suggests that mock jurors incorporate an extraordinary range of schemas, beliefs and attitudes into their decision-making concerning the insanity verdict. These responses triangulate, and assist in the interpretation of, the results obtained from the quantitative analysis. It might be argued that such schemas have a greater influence on results (verdicts, etc.) than vignette treatment factors or attitudes measured in the current study. However, the random allocation of subjects to vignette treatment conditions should mean that differences in schemas between groups of subjects (that are not directly due to such vignette factors) are due to chance.

One of the more significant results obtained from the analysis is the effect of the meta-responsibility insanity test in reducing the length of hospital disposals. This improvement in the legal situation of the mentally disordered helps allay the ethical concerns described in the preface concerning the introduction of the meta-responsibility theory, particularly as the meta-responsibility insanity test does not seem to reduce the overall frequency of NGRI verdicts. The finding also lends support to the notion that determinations of culpability for disorder are made covertly at the disposal stage rather than through verdict, which appears invulnerable to differences in the wording of insanity tests.

The final chapter of this book examines methodological limitations of the present study, future directions for research involving meta-responsibility, and asks whether the meta-responsibility theory is indeed a viable birth.

Chapter 9

The Meta-responsibility Theory: A Viable Birth?

Really what we want now, is not laws against crime, but a law against insanity. There is where the true evil lies.

Mark Twain, 'A New Crime'

This final chapter examines methodological limitations of the present study together with potential directions for future research related to meta-responsibility. The viability of the meta-responsibility theory in the light of the present research is discussed, as is the potential of the law and its fact-finders to consider meta-responsibility in insanity law.

This has been an exploratory study, by virtue of the paucity of previous research into culpability for incapacity and its effect on criminal responsibility. The results suggest that the blameworthiness for causing one's own mental disorder and the effect on concomitant criminal responsibility are worthwhile areas of research, if only because such notions do appear to impact upon decision-making in a sample of mock jurors. It is necessary to examine methodological limitations of the current research before making recommendations for future areas of investigation.

9.1 Limitations of the Mock Juror Study's Methodology

9.1.1 Sample Characteristics

The present sample consists of college students. Whilst (as discussed in Chapter 6) it cannot be substantiated that this sample has little external validity to the jury-eligible population, replication of the experiment in other groups would be desirable. Such groups might include: 1) stratified samples of the general population in accordance with eligibility for jury service; 2) samples actually selected for jury service (e.g. Simon, 1967); and 3) international and cross-cultural samples (meta-responsibility is likely to be most pertinent in the US where insanity defence usage is greater). A greater sample size would allow for more detailed analysis; for example, examining disposal recommendations of the P>PMR>MR condition for guilty verdicts, or division of each cell by ethnic identity (cell-size in the present study is too small to allow such micro-analysis). A larger sample also increases the efficacy of randomization, and the range of schemas uncovered by the qualitative analysis suggests that this is an important consideration. One 'outlier' subject who, for example, believes all persons should be punished irrespective of whether they are mentally ill or not, will affect the proportion of NGRI verdicts much less if he is included in a cell containing one hundred subjects rather than fifteen.

Micro-analysis might also be accomplished though limiting the number of factors in the experiment (e.g. a 2 x 3 [diagnosis x type of meta-responsibility] factorial design), and running a greater number of experiments with particular research hypotheses in mind. A reduced questionnaire length would be viable for such future research, making use of the results of the principal component analyses of attitudinal items to delineate 'flagship' items which are best predictive of more general attitudinal dimensions.

9.1.2 Methodological Characteristics

Triangulation and extension of the research findings using forms of methodology other than the experiment embedded within a survey would be desirable. Such experimental methodology might take the form of mock trials with panel deliberations, or structured or unstructured interviews (face-to-face or by telephone; Hans, 1986) to investigate attitudes towards meta-responsibility or general opinions concerning the insanity defence/mentally disordered offenders. Thirty-five percent of the present sample offered their contact details for a follow-up interview, but the time and resources available during the course of this study did not make such interviews viable.

The non-factorial within- or between-subjects design would be a further methodological direction in which subjects would each receive multiple case-vignettes (e.g. Finkel and Slobogin, 1995). Although vulnerable to cross-case contamination, within-subjects designs allow a greater number of cases to be examined in a particular sample size.

A larger qualitative component to the research would allow for better assessment of the degree to which the meta-responsibility insanity test produces verdicts consistent with subjects' reasons for their verdicts. This would require a more formal thematic content analysis using coding frames to identify constructs and schemas used in decision-making (e.g. Finkel, 1991); themes could then be tested for relation to independent and dependent variables. Such a study would also benefit from a large sample size.

9.1.3 Measuring Instrument and Analysis Characteristics

A continuous or interval dimension of verdict would, in hindsight, have been particularly desirable, as statistical power is sacrificed in analysing a categorical variable such as verdict with nonparametric tests, e.g. logistic regression or binomial tests, as opposed to a continuous variable with parametric methods, e.g. ANOVA or *t*-tests. As well as being asked to offer a guilty or NGRI verdict, subjects would be requested to indicate exactly 'how guilty' or 'how insane' they perceived the defendant. For example:

> 4) Please indicate on the following line with an 'X' exactly how Guilty or Not Guilty by Reason of Insanity you think Tom is.

Guilty ———————————————— Not Guilty by Reason of Insanity

This variable might show that, for example, type of insanity test does have an overall effect on the degree to which subjects deem the defendant culpable, but that the 'all or nothing' guilty/NGRI response category is not sensitive enough to distinguish such judgments.

Further items measuring attitudes towards the mentally disordered would have been appropriate in the present study. Whilst items investigating the degree of meta-responsibility attributed to Tom (and items concerning ascription to various models of mental disorder) were included, items eliciting attitudes towards culpability for incapacity *more generally* would have been useful. Examples of such attitudinal statements may have included: 'Mentally disordered persons are the architects of their own downfall'; 'Mentally disordered persons choose to act in the way they do'; 'Mentally disordered persons could help themselves to get better if they really tried'. Agreement with such items may, for example, be related to verdict, length of disposal, and attitudes such as authoritarianism or support for punishing mentally disordered offenders. Such items might play a central role in any future study.

9.2 Recommendations for Future Research

As well as studies designed to address the potential limitations of the present research outlined above, there are many possibilities for future research directions related to meta-responsibility.

9.2.1 Clinical Studies

The 'wish to be crazy', and the potential benefit of primary/secondary gains that mental disorder may provide to some mentally disordered persons and offenders would provide a rich avenue for future research (Chadwick, 1997). Such notions have been preliminarily examined by studies of medication non-compliance (e.g. Van Putten *et al.,* 1976), patient accounts of mentally disordered experiences (e.g. Chadwick, 1993), existential phenomenological models of mental disorder (e.g. Laing, 1969), and studies of the 'schizophrenic credit' (e.g. Claridge, 1985). However, the notion of gains in the mentally disordered state tends to represent only a peripheral research aim, at least in part because 'positive' perspectives on mental disorder tend towards dissonance with predominant liberal-scientific conceptions. No such investigations have been performed in forensic populations, a group of particular relevance to the present study.

A further clinical direction might be the development of scales related to meta-responsibility:

1. A scale to assess medication non-compliance (involving positive conceptions of mental disorder, side-effects, extra-pyramidal symptoms, forgetting, etc.). A trade off model between the benefits and costs associated with both compliance and non-compliance could be constructed using regression analysis in light of this scale (from offender case-files), which may have predictive power as to which patients are likely to become non-compliant. Taken in tandem with a meta-responsibility assessment scale (M-RAS; see below) for previous offences, these two scales could have significant implications for risk assessment. The scale and model together might, for example, show which patients would be high priority for a community treatment order after release to prevent non-compliance, or gauge suitability of NGRIs for release.
2. A scale to examine patient insight that does not rely on the patient's subscription to the medical model of mental disorder (model-independent insight assessment scale; MIIAS); a failure of current insight scales (Perkins and Moodley, 1993).
3. *A meta-responsibility assessment scale.* A scale to assess meta-responsibility (meta-responsibility assessment scale; M-RAS) in the same vein as Rogers Criminal Responsibility Assessment Scales (R-CRAS) (e.g. Rogers, Seman and Clarke, 1986; Rogers and Schuman, 2000) would provide for practical application of the meta-responsibility theory. Such a scale would complement the generation and testing of different types of meta-responsibility insanity tests.

9.2.2 Socio-legal Studies

Validation of a meta-responsibility assessment scale against various meta-responsibility assessment tests (including that used in the present study) would allow further research questions to be addressed. For example, do those scoring similarly on the M-RAS receive similar verdicts under different types of MRITs? What is inter-rater reliability on the M-RAS? Does the M-RAS have the ability to predict verdict in real insanity cases?

Further legal research into the effect of medication non-compliance on criminal responsibility is important, particularly with regard to whether non-compliance provides a source of recklessness or whether there has to be intent as to the end result of non-compliance to provide a source of culpability (e.g. Sherlock, 1984; C.N. Mitchell, 1986; Slodov, 1989; Weinstock, 1999; E.W. Mitchell, 1999b). Further investigation into purposive meta-responsibility is also crucial to the development of the meta-responsibility theory. Does purposive meta-responsibility differ from consensual meta-responsibility in terms of gravity and legal consequences? The present study suggests that it does not, at least as measured by verdict in the current sample. Further studies might examine the effect of consensual or purposive non-compliance in recommended length of a compulsory detention under a civil section, or its effect on perceived dangerousness (in a sample of psychiatrists or other mental health professionals). Do acts of consensual or purposive meta-responsibility have an effect in mock juror decision making on litigation cases? It might be expected that recommended awards in *Tarasoff*-type[1] cases are reduced if the patient shows consensual or purposive meta-responsibility, as the contributory negligence of the professional is reduced in proportion to the increase in the patient's negligence which consensual and purposive meta-responsibility entail.[2]

If Finkel (1995: 292) is right when he states that a 'culpable-actions' factor is 'common to situations that have little to do with insanity *per se*, indicating that this culpability judgment is commonplace and widespread' (see Chapter 5), then meta-responsibility (or variants of the notion of 'causing the conditions of one's own downfall') might be relevant to a wide range of social science research. For example, does management lay off more personnel in a troubled company they have just taken over, if that company's plight is evaluated as its own fault? Are persons who suffer an 'accident' due to carelessness likely to receive a longer waiting time in accident and emergency units than those whose accident was due to poor luck? Do teachers invest more effort with pupils who are behind in class due to family difficulties rather than those who are behind due to mere laziness? It will be seen from such diverse situations that where there are culpable actions leading to adverse consequences there are also possibilities for covert punishment of the culpable agent or agency.

9.3 Conclusion – The Meta-responsibility Theory: A Viable Birth?

Whilst this study formalizes the theory of meta-responsibility, it cannot be said to be a 'true birth', as notions of causing or avoiding one's own incapacity have long provided fruitful territory for writers, poets and others. When Ulysses' voyage took him near the island of the Sirens, he took action in order that he and his crew should not suffer a cruel end at their behest. He wished, however, to experience the Sirens' sweet but deadly song and lashed himself to the mast of his ship, so that whilst deprived of reason he might not direct his crew to shipwreck themselves on the island. He also plugged his crews' ears with wax to afford them protection from his directions that would result in shipwreck and from the volitional incapacity induced by the Sirens' song. Whilst still subject to reason, Ulysses thus took precautions which (however unpleasant at the time) prospectively saved him

---

[1] See *INFRA* note 9.

[2] See *SUPRA* note 33, Ch. 2.

from committing an act whilst deprived of reason and volition that would harm both himself and others.

This study has examined similar precautions against unreason relevant to mentally disordered offenders, and the effect of not taking such precautions upon excuse for their actions. In particular, it has been suggested that abdication of criminal responsibility on the grounds of incapacity should be associated with non-culpability for that incapacity.

Is the mentally disordered offender to be held to the same standard as Ulysses? Are Ulysses' actions particularly heroic, or are they merely what we would expect from someone in his situation? Not only did Ulysses have foreknowledge of danger (insight into his likely incapacity during a 'lucid' period), but also was sufficiently capacious to ward off such danger. Knowing this, if Ulysses had failed to take the precautions that he did, and shipwrecked himself and his crew, we might feel uneasy about affording him excuse. Ulysses' actions were not particularly heroic, *because to have omitted them would have resulted in culpability*. The mentally disordered offender, as capacious in his senses as Ulysses (and with similar foreknowledge of the likely consequences of inaction), seems to have a similar duty of care to ward off danger (and might therefore be held similarly culpable if failing to do so).

Whether mentally disordered offenders do have such capacity and ability is more contentious. Chapter 3 examined the fallacy of the automatic presumption that mentally disordered persons lack insight, and further examined cases in which there was ample foreknowledge of potential consequences (e.g. the NGRI burglar). Such persons, with knowledge about the likely outcome of their medication non-compliance, etc., effectively violate the Principle of Responsive Adjustment (PRA), thus attracting culpability. It may also be posited that the mentally disordered offender has a duty to acquire such foreknowledge in the absence of it being imparted by personal experience. In essence, Ulysses was simply obeying this PRA, although his foreknowledge did not come from his own experience.

Even if the mentally disordered *are* seen as lacking capacity and unable to gather the kinds of evidence required for responsive adjustment, it may be that mental disorder, and hence such incapacity, is to a certain extent autogenous (diminishing the excusatory power of the incapacity). Autogeny was discussed through the lens of the existential phenomenological and social constructivist models, which do not see mental disorder as a phenomenon beyond the bounds of personal responsibility in the same manner as the liberal-scientific (medical) model.

In summary, there are two (not necessarily exclusive) theoretical paths to meta-responsibility. The first does not necessarily contradict the predominant liberal-scientific conception of mental disorder, but holds the sensibilities and capacities of the mentally disordered person (e.g. insight) to the same standard as that of 'mentally healthy' persons. Mental disorder cannot, therefore, provide an excuse. This path might, therefore, not really be described as a true path to meta-responsibility – if mentally disordered persons are as capacious as others then the question of meta-responsibility becomes moot – they are simply always criminal responsible, as there is nothing in particular about their condition that would diminish or nullify criminal responsibility in the first instance. This path might be called the *autonomous* path, as the offender is presumed to have autonomy even if mentally disordered. This argument bears some resemblance to that used by some insanity defence abolitionists – there is nothing *per se* about mental disorder that provides excuse for actions, e.g. Szasz (1997). The argument does not, however, require subscription to the 'myth' of mental illness, but merely to posit that mental disorder is not incapacitating to the extent that it diminishes or negates criminal responsibility.

The second path to meta-responsibility is less straightforward and both complementary and antithetic to liberal-scientific model. It is complementary in that it presumes that the capacities and mental functions of the mentally disordered person are in fact impaired (as the liberal-scientific model holds them to be) and that such impairment would indeed give rise to a situation of diminished criminal responsibility. However, this path is antithetic to the liberal-scientific model, in that it posits that mental disorder may be generated or exacerbated by the person it 'afflicts' (through, for example, medication non-compliance or existential phenomenological conceptions of mental disorder which emphasize autogeny in such conditions). This path might be referred to as the *autogenous* path, as mental disorder is presumed to arise from processes of autogeny. This path to meta-responsibility does not require subscription to the notion that the mentally disordered are autonomous, capacious, insightful, etc.; the source of meta-responsibility is the generation or exacerbation of the condition (however ultimately incapacitating that condition may be). It is similar in terms of legal considerations to intoxication; few deny that alcohol severely impairs an individual's capacity, but drunkenness is held to be autogenous. Consensual and purposive meta-responsibility seem tied to this second, autogenous, path; they both assume that mental disorder is indeed a source of incapacity, but that the person has generated this source of incapacity (the mental disorder itself), either by *consent* or by *purpose*.

This study has not singled out particular diagnoses for attributions of meta-responsibility, nor made the blanket claim that all mental disorders engender meta-responsibility if invoked as an excuse. Mental disorder is a sufficiently heterogeneous phenomenon in terms of aetiology, symptomatology, therapy, etc. – as well as having differing effects upon capacity and insight in individual persons – that it would be impossible to state particular classes of mental disorder that would give rise to meta-responsibility. There are, of course, cases immediately attractive to voluntaristic analyses, e.g. drug-induced psychoses (Elliot, 1996), but not all persons who commit a crime whilst under the influence of such a condition could automatically be assumed to be meta-responsible. As courts inquire into the potential of an *individual* case of mental disorder to prove insanity (there is no blanket presumption that all mental disorder *equals* insanity), so each individual case of mental disorder has to be examined to see if it *features* meta-responsibility. Ostensibly meta-responsible acts such as medication non-compliance are not enough to ascribe meta-responsibility; one case may be disorder-mediated, another might be consensual in the pursuit of absence of side-effects, whereas still another may be purposive, being directed toward the goal of primary gains associated with mental disorder.[3]

This study has, however, offered a framework of culpability that may be considered in all cases of mental disorder leading to excuse, *but not necessarily proved*. The analysis has been driven by ethical concerns (that covert punishment may be due to tacit considerations of meta-responsibility), legal consistency (that some incapacitating conditions, e.g. intoxication and automatism, consider the aetiology of the incapacitating condition whereas insanity does not), and commonsense notions of justice (that those who cause the conditions of their own defence should not be eligible for excuse). The experimental research presented in this study suggests that our analysis is justified in terms of our ethical aims and commonsensical notions of justice (the former from the finding that mock jurors allowed to consider meta-responsibility are less punitive in terms of length of hospital disposal; the latter from the qualitative analysis of the mock jurors' responses); it also seems justified (from the examination in Chapter 2) in terms of legal consistency. Chapter 3 has attempted to justify the meta-responsibility theory in terms of clinical considerations; such notions are likely to be more contentious, especially for those allied to the liberal-scientific conception of mental disorder upon which purposive meta-responsibility does not rely.

Is meta-responsibility viable in the courtroom? To operationalize a meta-responsibility insanity test entails consideration of the defendant's state of mind not only at the time of the offence, but *also at the time he created his defence conditions*. For the law to find that a defendant is meta-responsible, a 'double product test' must be applied; the crime must be a product of mental disorder, and the mental disorder must be a product of prior fault. If only the former criterion is satisfied, then the defendant should be excused or offered mitigation through insanity or diminished responsibility. Where the defendant fits the latter criterion only, then traditional insanity or diminished responsibility tests would not be satisfied and the defendant would rightly receive no excuse, justification or mitigation. Where *both* limbs are satisfied then meta-responsibility may be attributed to the defendant. The meta-responsibility insanity test used in the present study denies the insanity defence to the defendant upon such a finding.

The court would also have to consider the merit of any 'defence' against a 'charge' of culpable mental disorder: that is, did the defendant have any justification or excuse that might reduce his culpability for culpable mental

---

[3] An example of the difficulties faced by such an inquiry is provided by the recent insanity acquittal of the assailant of George Harrison, former member of *'The Beatles'*. The defendant, Michael Abram, had been previously diagnosed as suffering from drug-induced psychosis, and might therefore be described as meta-responsible and therefore ineligible for an insanity acquittal. However, it is not clear whether his heroin abuse was an attempt at self-medication to ward off delusions and hallucinations in the absence of proper psychiatric care. In any case, no inquiry into the defendant's meta-responsibility was made. George Harrison's son, interviewed immediately after the verdict, described the insanity defence as 'a loophole' ('Beatles attacker is to be held indefinitely', *The Times*, 16 November 2000).

disorder? This entails fact-finders understanding and appraising disorder-mediated meta-responsibility, a complex legal determination. Jurors generally have a poor understanding of jury instructions (Robinson, 1985), and particularly insanity test instructions (Ogloff, 1991); however, it appears that the complexity of the legal concept under consideration is not responsible for such difficulties of comprehension. Robinson (1985) reviews factors responsible for juror confusion: 1) receipt of instructions only after presentation of evidence; 2) using verbal instructions only; 3) using jargon; 4) lengthy instructions; 5) illogical organization of instructions; and 6) reliance on abstract legal statements rather than focusing on specific inquiries and issues necessitated by the evidence.

These factors suggest that consideration of evidence of meta-responsibility may not provide jurors with significantly greater problems than those already faced. Whilst meta-responsibility instructions may be longer than existing instructions,[4] the only other dimension upon which they differ is the complexity of the legal concept under consideration (and this does not appear to be a factor influencing juror confusion). Indeed, considering meta-responsibility may make a jury's task easier, as it comports with commonsense notions of justice, focuses on specific enquiries and issues necessitated by the evidence, and appears to be an often used construct in jury decision-making anyway (Finkel and Handel, 1989). In any case, a legal system that expects its fact-finders to understand the distinction between crimes of specific or basic intent cannot reasonably object to meta-responsibility on the basis of complexity.

In order to be a viable birth, meta-responsibility must also be able to meet the requirements of effective law. Cotterrell (1992) deems these to be: 1) clear objectives expressed through clear maxims; 2) maxims which are adequately communicated, backed up by sufficient resources, and emanate from authoritative sources; 3) compatibility with society's prevailing conventions (i.e. do not contradict fundamental principles of commonsense justice); 4) clarity in respect of compliance and breach; 5) reward for compliance and punishment for breach; and 6) clarity in method of enforcement. Meta-responsibility does not appear to violate any of these principles, and appears to satisfy requirement 3) (consonance with commonsensical notions of justice) to a greater extent than current insanity law.

Robinson (1985) wonders if the doctrine of causing one's own defence is too complex to serve the general deterrence goal of the criminal law (i.e. if the population cannot understand a law, then how are they to abide by it?). He concludes, however, that complexity is less detrimental if it is based on sound principles of liability and exculpation concordant with notions of commonsense justice (a characteristic of the meta-responsibility theory). In the same way, difficulties faced by the prosecution and defence in proving or disproving culpable mental disorder are likely to suffer from no greater pitfalls in the courtroom than do inquiries into culpable states of mind at the time of the offence.

---

[4] However, Finkel (1991) found that an insanity test over four pages in length (Finkel's test) produced verdicts more consistent with jurors' ratings of the defendant's culpability.

What should happen to the meta-responsible mentally disordered offender? This study has not advocated their punishment, although it might be argued that through denial of the insanity defence (as a consequence of the MRIT) this may be an effect of a determination of meta-responsibility. This argument may be countered on at least two levels:

1. Although the MRIT may ostensibly sanction punishment of the meta-responsible offender (through a more stringent NGRI requirement), the mock juror study suggests that not only can the MRIT actually increase NGRI findings under certain conditions (particularly for the schizophrenic conditions), but that by reducing covert punishment, the consideration of meta-responsibility may have a beneficial impact upon the offender's liberty.
2. Punishment is not necessarily a corollary of conviction. In the same sense, responsibility does not negate treatment considerations (indeed, this study argues that treatment may actually be facilitated through greater ascription of responsibility, through avoiding covertly punitive disposals). Treatment considerations and restoration of control should, of course, take precedence over punishment where a defendant is substantially mentally disordered, no matter whether the mental disorder was autogenous in origin or beyond the defendant's control. Sympathy, mitigation and treatment considerations may therefore be reflected in, for example, the offer of a hospital order rather than imprisonment. If an ultimately punitive response is required, then treatment considerations can still take immediate priority over punitive aims through a hybrid disposal order.[5]

If the aim of the theory is not a punitive or retributive one, then what has been the point in introducing the consideration of meta-responsibility? This study has shown that considering meta-responsibility can actually benefit the socio-legal situation of the mentally disordered offender, through greater concordance with commonsense notions of justice. The putative mechanism of such benefit has been through allowing society and the legal system to consider more properly the defendant's blameworthiness and ward off concomitant covert punishment.[6]

---

[5] See *SUPRA* note 1, Ch. 2.

[6] Some conditions may be better suited to a punitive response than others. As Gerard (1999) states:

> If alcoholism and drug addiction were qualifying illnesses [for the insanity defence], when would acquittees be released? The answer would depend on whether one viewed the alcoholism/drug dependence as the illness or merely symptomatic of an underlying illness. Under the former view, acquittees would be released as soon as they were no longer addicted. The insanity defence would then become merely a detoxification procedure...the only known treatment for either addiction is withdrawal. This treatment can be administered as effectively, although perhaps not humanely, in a prison as in a hospital (p. 76).

This proper apportioning of blame is fundamental to the viability of meta-responsibility. It may seem that blaming is a relatively unimportant societal goal (compared to disposal, treatment, punishment, etc.). However, this study has argued that proper blaming (or *frustration* of proper blaming) may have very real consequences for the person who is the object of such blame (and indeed that the 'important issues' such as disposal, treatment, punishment, etc. *follow* from the proper assignment of blame). Blaming requires the correct ascription of responsibility, and 'responsibility ascription as the foundation of blaming gives us the robust social world in which we live' (French, 1991b: 15). If blaming is so important to our social world and requires proper responsibility ascription as its basis, then it comes as no surprise that its frustration (through the failure of the legal system to deal with meta-responsibility) may have serious effects on the socio-legal situation of mentally disordered offenders (outrage over insanity acquittals, the perpetuation of insanity defence myths, covertly punitive disposals, and stigma).

Compensation practices might also become better informed through consideration of meta-responsibility. In tort law, the proper ascription of responsibility is again paramount. A variant of the meta-responsibility theory might be applied to determinations of contributory negligence.[7] Mental health professionals should be particularly interested in the meta-responsibility theory's shift of some of the burden for the care and management of his condition onto the patient himself. The case of *Naidu v. Laird* (1988)[8] awarded $1.4 million in damages against a psychiatrist whose patient was found NGRI of manslaughter. The psychiatrist was found to be negligent in 'disregarding [the NGRI patient's] history...of a pattern of abandoning his medication and subsequent violent behaviour...[and] in failing to commit Mr. Putney involuntarily...in light of his condition and his failure to cooperate during his treatment'.[9] The meta-responsibility theory, whilst not forbidding such findings, suggests a greater level of responsibility to lie with the patient. This may paradoxically improve the patient's situation – mental health professionals may become increasingly reluctant to take on high-risk cases (and perhaps become more zealous in medicating and involuntarily detaining patients in the absence of treatment considerations) due to their liability for the patient's acts.

Perhaps the final goal of the meta-responsibility theory is deterrence. If Nissman *et al.* (1980) are correct in stating that the insanity defence affords the offender a 'free pass' (p. vii) to commit further crimes, then the meta-responsibility

---

In fact, it might be much more advantageous for the person to detoxify in prison rather than hospital due to the very real possibilities for indeterminate detention and covert punishment in the latter.

[7] See *SUPRA* note 33, Ch. 2.

[8] *Naidu v. Laird* (1988), 539 A. 2d 1064.

[9] Such a finding of liability for a patient's medication non-compliance acknowledges the duty of certain mental health professionals to third parties, found in *Tarasoff v. Board of Regents of Univ. of California* (1976), 551 P.2d 334.

theory places clear restrictions on eligibility for such a free pass.[10] This situation may again benefit the mentally disordered offender. Would restricted patients be released sooner if release was contingent upon a strict liability for similar acts in the future? Would the introduction of community treatment orders be so zealously pursued by the UK government if mentally disordered persons had more of a stake in their own management, and were not seen as 'outside the law' upon commission of an offence? Would the insanity defence be so much maligned and under threat of restriction and/or abolition if it actually *contributed to* deterrence?[11]

The non-offending patient may also benefit by being held more responsible for medication compliance. Sherlock (1984: 499) states that that the mentally disordered often view themselves as 'helpless cripples' and 'use the sick role to avoid responsibility for their own situation'. Sherlock concludes:

> ...anything less than the stringent justification for non-compliance...will only feed this pattern of avoidance that is seen especially among patients with long histories of minor scrapes with the law (p. 499).

Similarly, Halleck (1988) sees ascription of responsibility in clinical practice as having important consequences for patients in terms of treatment and therapeutic outcome:

> In the course of medical practice, physicians encounter many situations in which they must either excuse or hold patients responsible for symptoms or behaviour associated with symptoms. Examination of the process of excusing or ascribing responsibility clarifies a number of complex issues in psychiatry such as the determination of disability, the meaning of psychiatric diagnosis, and the stigmatization of the mentally ill. In so far as the patient's own assessment of his responsibility for his symptoms influences the manner in which he deals with symptoms, this process also has important implications for the treatment of patients with both physical and mental disorders (p.352).

A final purpose of this study was simply to provoke debate concerning the level of autonomy of mentally disordered persons and the amount of autogeny involved in mental disorder. If the claim of Szasz (1990) is correct – that there can

---

[10] The felony murder provision in US jurisdictions is intended to have such a deterrent effect ; see *Victory v. Bombard* (1977), 432 F. Supp. 1240. Whilst there is no *mens rea* to transfer in medication non-compliance (becoming medication non-compliant with its inherent risks differs fundamentally in its legality to the risks involved in bank robbery; see Chapter 5), a system of liability for mental disorder (meta-responsibility) pursuant to that in felony-murder may have a similar aim of deterrence (see D. Robinson, 1984). However, also see P. Robinson (1985): 'Punishing blameless conduct undercuts the condemnation and credibility of the criminal justice system' (p. 29).

[11] This threat is most notable in the US. See SUPRA note 8, Ch. 1.

be no liberty without responsibility – then an increase in the standard of responsibility required from the mentally disordered should have proportional and beneficial effects on their liberty. The theories of authors working within social constructivist or existential phenomenological paradigms are often dismissed due to their radical anti-psychiatric and political connotations. It is hoped that their careful consideration in theses such as this indicates that there is useful material to extract from such theories and apply to clinical psychiatry, mental health law, and criminal law. Through understanding meta-responsibility, we may also understand more about mentally disordered states and mentally disordered persons, whether they are offenders or not. Such a goal, even by itself, would surely justify the present research into the meta-responsibility theory and perhaps provide a stimulus for future research.

POSTSCRIPT: THE CLOSING ARGUMENTS OF THE PROSECUTION IN *R V. JEKYLL* (1886)

Let us be fanciful and imagine that in Robert Louis Stevenson's classic 1886 tale *Dr. Jekyll and Mr. Hyde*, Edward Hyde never committed suicide, but was captured alive and restored to the persona of Dr. Jekyll who is placed on trial for the murder of Sir Danvers Carew. After a protracted trial in which the defendant offers a plea of insanity, the counsel for the prosecution, Mr. Kernel, stands before us and addresses the court for the final time.

> 'Ladies and Gentlemen of the Jury, your task of incomprehensible peculiarity is almost at an end. During the last few weeks, you have heard tales the like of which no courtroom has ever heard and, Lord willing, hopes never to hear again.'
>
> 'It is not, however, simply the behest of the divine that a case like this does not again trouble a court of law. That particular matter will be decided by your finding today. For if you do your duty and convict, you will be sending a message to beware those who have the knowledge and aforethought to induce a state of personhood or identity in which they commit crimes for which they will subsequently abdicate responsibility.'
>
> 'You have been charged with finding the defendant guilty or not guilty by reason of insanity under the rules stated by The Lords during the furore over the acquittal of Mr. McNaughton some forty years ago. Your case shares with that one the likelihood of public outcry if a conviction is not secured.'

'Why such outcry, you ask? Because a guilty man is acquitted? That may have been true of Mr. McNaughton's acquittal, but in this case, *two* guilty persons would be set free. Although we have heard testimony from expert chemists and physicians that Dr. Jekyll is firmly restored to his original persona and that Mr. Hyde will be bringing forth his countenance no longer, does it not remain that it was Mr. Hyde who murdered Sir Danvers? So surely the defendant standing before you today is innocent! After all, it was not *he* who plunged his cane into the heart of the deceased.'

'Whilst that conjecture, Ladies and Gentlemen, is an attractive one, the truth is that the defendant standing before you today is guilty of some crucial and heinous misdeeds. Was it not he who, in the full knowledge of what he was doing, voluntarily induced the persona of Mr. Hyde through that terrible concoction, the recipe of which has thankfully been deleted from the record? That he did not again *voluntarily* induce the persona of Mr. Hyde after the murder of Sir Danvers was, by his own admission, merely a ploy to evade capture. The defendant has stated that "Jekyll was now my city of refuge; let but Hyde peep out in instant, and the hands of all would be raised to take and slay him"'.[12]

'Dr. Jekyll thus knew what he was doing both when he decided to induce the persona of Mr. Hyde, and indeed, when he decided *not* to do so. Both were instrumental: one in the commission of terrible acts, the other in evading retribution for those acts. If you are persuaded by the arguments of the defence – that Dr. Jekyll cannot be found guilty for the crime of murder as he was truly "not himself" at the time – I grant that you might instead see Dr. Jekyll as a conspirator in the crime, of felonious intent in procuring the services of Mr. Hyde to commit unspeakable acts. I quote once more from the defendant's statement:

> Men have before hired bravoes to transact their crimes, while their own person and reputation sat under shelter. I was the first that ever did so for his pleasures. I was the first that could thus plod in the public eye with a load of genial respectability, and in a moment, like a schoolboy, strip off these lendings and spring headlong into the sea of liberty.'

[12] All quotes attributed to the defendant come from the final chapter of the novel, 'Henry Jekyll's Full Statement on the Case'.

'Did not Dr. Jekyll by his own implication secure a bravo to commit heinous acts that he could only perform in the guise of Mr. Hyde? It matters not that his intentions were, to his mind, beneficent; so he could then separate the evil side of his self that he, Dr. Jekyll, might concentrate on the good. Every time Dr. Jekyll sipped that draught he wilfully and with aforethought induced a state during which he was at risk for the most terrible violence. He did so purposively, and, moreover, appeared to derive some sort of revelation whilst as Mr. Hyde; he himself has attested to his satisfaction whilst in this condition:

> There was something strange in my sensations, something incredibly new and, from its very novelty, incredibly sweet. I felt younger, lighter, happier in body; within I was conscious of a heady recklessness, a current of disordered sensual images running like a mill race in my fancy, a dissolution of the bonds of obligation, an unknown but not an innocent freedom of the soul...the constellations looked down upon me, I could have thought, with wonder, the first creature of that sort that their unsleeping vigilance had disclosed to them.'[13]

'Whilst he may have derived happiness from his transformation of persona, others most certainly did not, foremost among them Sir Danvers. What is worse, Dr. Jekyll had intact memory of his acts committed as Mr. Hyde. Yet again and again he so induced a state of utter depravity. Dr. Jekyll, and only Dr. Jekyll, sipped that draught; for when he did so, Mr. Hyde was nowhere to be seen (and would have remained so but for Dr. Jekyll's repeated ingestion of that foul broth).'

'So is the man before us insane? No, by the defendant's own words it was Mr. Hyde that had the monopoly on insanity, on evil, on irrationality. Dr. Jekyll continued to live a life as near as normal as anyone could given his knowledge of the acts of his alter-ego. If it was Mr. Hyde that stood before you today, then I confess your duty to convict might be a difficult one; for how can a being composed of pure evil meet the requirement of knowing right from wrong?'

'Dr. Jekyll, unfortunately for his insanity plea, was never thus deprived of reason. His abdication of criminal responsibility now, through charging himself insane, is tantamount to admission that he committed the crime. That he was, quite literally, not *him-self* when these crimes were committed has little bearing on the issue of insanity

---

[13] Stevenson's description of Dr. Jekyll's revelations is arrestingly similar to the accounts given by some schizophrenic patients such as that related in Chapter 3, e.g. Chadwick (1997).

for it was Dr. Jekyll who autogenously brought about that insane state. How he lived with the knowledge of his crimes may indeed have driven him insane, but by that time it was too late, the murder of Sir Danvers was already passed. We are not interested in his mental state after that murder, or indeed at the present time; we must leave that for the legion of alienists, alchemists, philosophers and physicians who will no doubt beat a path to Dr. Jekyll's door in the hope of furthering their careers through studying this most peculiar and compelling case. It is your duty to see that the door to which they beat that path should be the door of a prison cell. I agree that *Mr. Hyde* would perhaps not be criminally responsible, but as it was *Dr. Jekyll* who brought about that person, he has, as it were, responsibility for his criminal responsibility. In the defendant's own words:

> I was conscious, even when I took the draught, of a more unbridled, more furious propensity to ill...I had voluntarily stripped myself of all those balancing instincts, by which even the worst of us continues to walk with some degree of steadiness.'

'Whether a drunkard is oblivious to the risks he runs, the law is quite clear on this point – *voluntarily* stripping oneself of balancing instincts through drunkenness provides no defence to committing an ill upon a fellow man whilst intoxicated.'

'The defendant's refuge in his current persona will be a successful one if you fail to do your duty and convict in this sad case. The murder of Sir Danvers will go unpunished. More terrifying is the prospect of many other evils going unpunished, if you send a message to those with knowledge of chemistry and alchemy that they may replicate the foul acts of Dr. Jekyll and induce a persona, the acts of which the possibility of punishment is waived. No, Ladies and Gentlemen, I do not relish your task in this case, for you have heard unspeakable acts the like of with which good citizens such as yourselves should not have to deal. A master of literature could not concoct a more twisted tale. If you do otherwise than convict, you will open the sluices to a rash of such claims. And that would be a terrible harm inflicted upon society. Your duty today is clear, Ladies and Gentlemen – you must secure a conviction for the evils of the defendant.'

'Your Honour, Ladies and Gentlemen of the court, the prosecution in this case rests'.

Bibliography

Alicke, M.D. (1990). 'Incapacitating conditions and alteration of blame'. *Journal of Social Behaviour and Personality* 5: 651-664.

Alicke, M.D. (1992). 'Culpable causation'. *Journal of Personality and Social Psychology* 63: 368-378.

Alicke, M.D. and Davis, T.L. (1990). 'Capacity responsibility in social evaluation'. *Personality and Social Psychology Bulletin* 16: 465-474.

Allen, M.J. (1991). *Textbook on Criminal Law*. London: Blackstone Press.

Altermeyer, R. (1981). *Right-wing Authoritarianism*. Winnipeg: University of Manitoba Press.

American Law Institute (1962). *Model Penal Code (proposed official draft)*. Philadelphia: American Law Institute.

American Psychiatric Association (1982). *Statement on the Insanity Defense*. Washington DC: American Psychiatric Association.

American Psychiatric Association (1994). *Diagnostic and Statistical Manual of Mental Disorders (DSM-IV)*. Washington DC: American Psychiatric Association.

Angermeyer, M.C. and Matschinger, H. (1996). 'The effect of violent attacks by schizophrenic persons on the attitude of the public towards the mentally ill'. *Social Science and Medicine*, 43(12): 1721-1728.

Appelbaum, P.S. (1994). *Almost a Revolution: Mental Health Law and the Limits of Change*. New York: Oxford University Press.

Appelbaum, P.S., Jick, R.Z., Grisso, T., Givelber, D., Silver, E. and Steadman, H.J. (1993). 'Use of posttraumatic stress disorder to support an insanity defense'. *American Journal of Psychiatry* 150: 229-234.

Aristotle (1955). *Nichomachean Ethics*. Harmondsworth: Penguin.

Ashworth, A. (1975). 'Reason, logic and criminal liability'. *Law Quarterly Review*: 91-130.

Bach, M. (1995). 'The Not Guilty by Reason of Insanity Verdict: Should juries be informed of its consequences?', *Whittier Law Review*: 645-674.

Barham, P. and Barnes, M. (1999). 'The Citizen Mental Patient' in Eastman, N. and Peay, J. (eds.) *Law Without Enforcement*. Oxford: Hart Publishing.

Barney, K. (1994). 'Limitations of the critique of the medical model'. *The Journal of Mind and Behaviour* 15: 19-34.

Bateson, G., Jackson, D., Haley, J. and Weakland, J. (1968). 'Toward a theory of schizophrenia' in Jackson, D. (ed.) *Communication, Family and Marriage*. Palo Alto: Science and Behaviour Books.

Baumeister, R.F., Heatherton, T.F. and Tice, D.M. (1994). *Losing Control: How and why people fail at self-regulation*. San Diego: Academic Press.

Beaudoin, M.N., Hodgins, S. and Lavoie, F. (1993). 'Homicide, schizophrenia and substance-abuse or dependancy'. *Canadian Journal of Psychiatry* 38: 541-546.

Beck-Sander, A. (1998). 'Is insight into psychosis meaningful?'. *Journal of Mental Health* 7: 25-35.

Bentall, R. (1990). *Reconstructing Schizophrenia*. London: Routledge.

Berglas, S. and Jones, E.E. (1978). 'Drug choice as a self-handicapping strategy in response to non-contingent success'. *Journal of Personality and Social Psychology* 36: 405-417.

Blackwell, B. (1976). 'Treatment adherence'. *British Journal of Psychiatry* 129: 513-531.

Blom-Cooper, L., Hally, H. and Murphy, E. (1995). *The Falling Shadow: One Patient's Mental Health Care 1978-1993*. London: Duckworth.

Bloom, J.D. and Williams, M.H. (1994). *Management and Treatment of Insanity Acquittees: A Model for the 1990s*. Washington DC: American Psychiatric Association.

Bolton, D. and Hill, J. (1996). *Mind, Meaning, and Mental Disorder: The nature of causal explanation in psychology and psychiatry*. Oxford: Oxford University Press.

Bonnie, R. (1983). 'The moral basis of the insanity defense'. *American Bar Association Journal* 69: 194-197.

Bonta, J., Law, M. and Hanson, K. (1998). 'The prediction of criminal and violent recidivism among mentally disordered offenders: A meta-analysis'. *Psychological Bulletin* 123: 123-142.

Boorse, C. (1976). 'What a theory of mental health should be'. *Journal for the Theory of Social Behaviour* 6: 61-84.

Bord, R.J. (1971). 'Rejection of the mentally ill: Continuities and further developments'. *Social Problems* 18: 496-509.

Boyle, M. (1990). *Schizophrenia: A Scientific Delusion*. London: Routledge.

Bracton, H. (1210-1268/1968). *De Legibus et Consuetudinibus Angliae*. Cambridge: Belknap Press and Selden Society.

Bray, R.M. and Kerr, N.L. (1982). 'Methodological considerations in the study of the psychology of the courtroom' in Kerr, N.L. and Bray, R.M. (eds.) *The Psychology of the Courtroom*. New York: Academic Press.

Breggin, P. (1991). *Toxic Psychiatry*. New York: St. Martin's Press.

Brodsky, S.L. and Smitherman, H.O. (1983). *Handbook of Scales for Research in Crime and Delinquency*. New York: Plenum.

Brown, P. (1990). 'The name game: Toward a sociology of diagnosis'. *The Journal of Mind and Behaviour* 11: 385-406.

Buchanan, A.W. (1996). *Compliance with Treatment in Schizophrenia*. London: Psychology Press.

Buchanan, A.W. (2000). *Psychiatric Aspects of Justification, Excuse, and Mitigation in Anglo-American Criminal Law*. London: Jessica Kingsley.

Burroughs, W. (1959/1992). *The Naked Lunch*. New York: Grove Weidenfeld.

Burston, D. (1996). *The Wing of Madness: The Life and Work of R.D. Laing*. Cambridge: Harvard University Press.

Busfield, J. (1986). *Managing Madness: Changing Ideas and Practice*. London: Unwin Hyman.

Butler, Lord (1975). 'Report of the Committee on Mentally Abnormal Offenders'. London: HMSO.

Butler, S. (1872/1970). *Erewhon*. Harmondsworth: Penguin.

Caldicott, F., Conlan, E. and Zigmond, A. (1999). 'Client and clinician – law as an intrusion' in Eastman, N. and Peay, J. (eds.) *Law Without Enforcement*. Oxford: Hart Publishing.

Callahan, L.A., McGreevy, M.A., Cirincione, C. and Steadman, H.J. (1992). 'Measuring the effects of the Guilty but Mentally-Ill (GBMI) verdict – Georgia 1982 GBMI reform'. *Law and Human Behaviour* 16: 447-462.

Chadwick, P.K. (1993). 'The stepladder to the impossible: A first hand phenomenological account of a schizoaffective psychotic crisis'. *Journal of Mental Health* 2: 239-250.

Chadwick, P.K. (1997). *Schizophrenia: The Positive Perspective*. London: Routledge.

Cirincione, C. (1996). 'Revisiting the insanity defense – contested or consensus?', *Bulletin of the American Academy of Psychiatry and the Law* 24: 165-176.

Cirincione, C., Steadman, H.J. and McGreevy, M.A. (1995). 'Rates of insanity acquittals and the factors associated with successful insanity pleas'. *Bulletin of the American Academy of Psychiatry and the Law* 23: 399-409.

Claridge, G. (1985). *Origins of Mental Illness*. Oxford: Basil Blackwell.

Cohen, M.R. (1940). 'Moral aspects of the criminal law'. *Yale Law Journal* 49: 987-1026.

Coke, E. (1719). *Institutes of the Laws of England*. London: R. Gosling and H. Lintit.

Coleman, D. and Salt, J. (1996). *Ethnicity in the 1991 Census, Volume 1: Demographic Characteristics of the Ethnic Minority Populations*. London: HMSO.

Colombo, A. (1997). *Understanding Mentally Disordered Offenders: A Multi-agency Perspective*. Aldershot: Ashgate.

Comings, D.E., Rosenthal, R.J., Lesieur, H.R., Rugle, L.J., Muhleman, D., Chiu, C., Dietz, G. and Gade, R. (1996). 'A study of the Dopamine D2 receptor gene in pathological gambling'. *Pharmacogenetics* 6: 223-234.

Conolly, J. (1830). *The Indications of Insanity*. London: Dawsons of Pall Mall.

Cooper, A.E., Garside, R.F. and Kay, D.W. (1976). 'A comparison of deaf and non-deaf patients with paranoid and affective psychoses'. *British Journal of Psychiatry* 129: 532-538.

Cotterrell, R. (1992). *The Sociology of Law*. London: Butterworths.

Crocetti, G., Spiro, H. and Siassi, I. (1971). 'Are the ranks closed? Attitudinal social distance and mental illness'. *American Journal of Psychiatry* 127: 1121-1127.

Crumbaugh, J.C. (1968). 'Cross-validation of Purpose-in-Life test based on Frankyl's concepts'. *Journal of Individual Psychology* 24: 74-81.

Crow, T.J. (1980). 'Molecular pathology of schizophrenia: More than one disease process?'. *British Medical Journal* 280: 66-68.

Cumming, E. and Cumming, J. (1957). *Closed Ranks: An Experiment in Mental Health Education*. Cambridge: Harvard University Press.

D'Arcy, C. and Brockman, J. (1977). 'Public rejection of the ex-mental patient: Are attitudes changing?'. *Canadian Review of Sociology and Anthropology* 14: 68-80.

Davis, J.H., Kerr, N.L., Atkin, R.S., Holt, R. and Meek, D. (1975). 'The decision processes of 6- and 12-person juries assigned unanimous and two-thirds majority rules'. *Journal of Personality and Social Psychology* 32: 1-14.

Dell, S. (1983). 'Wanted: An insanity defence that can be used'. *Criminal Law Review*: 431-437.

Dell, S. and Robertson, G. (1988). *Sentenced to Hospital: Offenders in Broadmoor*. London: Institute of Psychiatry.

Dillman, D.A. (1978). *Mail and Telephone Surveys: The Total Design Method*. New York: Wiley-Interscience.

Dressler, J. (1982). 'Rethinking heat of passion: A defense in search of a rationale'. *Journal of Criminal Law and Criminology* 73: 421-462.

Eastman, N. and Peay, J. (1999). *Law Without Enforcement: Integrating Mental Health and Justice*. Oxford: Hart Publishing.

Eisendrath, S.J. (1996). 'When Munchausen becomes malingering: Factitious disorders that penetrate the legal system'. *Bulletin of the American Academy of Psychiatry and the Law* 24: 471-481.

Eker, D. (1985). 'Effect of type of cause on attitudes towards mental illness and relationships between the attitudes'. *International Journal of Social Psychiatry* 31: 243-251.

Elliot, C. (1996). *The Rules of Insanity*. New York: State University of New York Press.

Ellsworth, P.C. (1993). 'Some steps between attitudes and verdicts' in Hastie, R. (ed.) *Inside the Juror*. Cambridge: Cambridge University Press.

Ellsworth, P.C., Bukaty, R.M., Cowan, C.L. and Thompson, W.C. (1984). 'The death qualified jury and the defence of insanity'. *Law and Human Behaviour* 8: 81-93.

Erasmus, D. (1509/1993). *In Praise of Folly*. London: Penguin.

Eskey, A. (1958). 'Insight and prognosis'. *Journal of Clinical Psychology* 14: 426-429.

Fein, R.A. (1984). 'How the insanity acquittal retards treatment'. *Law and Human Behaviour* 8: 283-292.

Feinberg, J. (1970). 'Sua Culpa' in Feinberg, J. (ed.) *Doing and Deserving: Essays in the Theory of Responsibility*. Princeton: Princeton University Press.

Fenwick, P. (1993). 'Brain, mind and behaviour: some medicolegal aspects'. *British Journal of Psychiatry* 163: 565-573.

Field, A. (2000). *Discovering Statistics using SPSS for Windows*. London: Sage.

Fingarette, H. (1972). *The Meaning of Criminal Insanity*. Berkeley: University of California Press.

Fingarette, H. (1988). *Heavy Drinking – The Myth of Alcoholism as a Disease*. Berkeley: University of California Press.

Fingarette, H. and Hasse, A.F. (1979). *Mental Disabilities and Criminal Responsibility*. Berkeley: University of California Press.

Finkel, N.J. (1988). *Insanity on Trial*. New York: Plenum Press.

Finkel, N.J. (1989). 'The Insanity Defense Reform Act of 1984: Much ado about nothing'. *Behavioural Sciences and the Law* 8: 403-419.

Finkel, N.J. (1991). 'The insanity defense: a comparison of verdict schemas'. *Law and Human Behaviour* 15: 533-555.

Finkel, N.J. (1995). *Commonsense Justice: Jurors' Notions of the Law*. Cambridge: Harvard University Press.

Finkel, N.J. and Handel, S.F. (1989). 'How jurors construe insanity'. *Law and Human Behaviour* 13: 41-59.

Finkel, N.J. and Slobogin, C. (1995). 'Insanity, justification and culpability: Toward a unifying schema'. *Law and Human Behaviour* 19: 447-464.

Fisher, J.D. and Farina, A. (1979). 'Consequences of beliefs about the nature of mental disorders'. *Journal of Abnormal Psychology* 88: 320-327.

Fitzgerald, F.S. (1965). *This Side of Paradise, The Crack-Up, and Other Autobiographical Pieces*. London: Bodley Head.

Flew, A. (1985). 'Mental health, mental illness, mental disease: The medical model' in Bean, P. (ed.) *Mental Illness: Changes and Trends*. Chichester: Wiley and Sons.

Foss, R.D. (1976). 'Group decision processes in the simulated trial jury'. *Sociometry* 39: 305-316.

Foucault, M. (1967). *Madness and Civilisation: A History of Insanity in the Age of Reason*. London: Tavistock.

French, P.A. (1991a). 'Fishing the red herrings out of the sea of moral responsibility' in French, P.A. (ed.) *The Spectrum of Responsibility*. New York: St. Martin's Press.

French, P.A. (1991b). 'A world without responsibility' in French, P.A. (ed.) *The Spectrum of Responsibility*. New York: St. Martin's Press.

Freud, S. (1926/1991). 'The question of lay analysis' in Freud, A. (ed.) *The Essentials of Psychoanalysis: The Definitive Collection of Sigmund Freud's Writings*. London: Penguin.

Frith, C.D. (1992). *The Cognitive Neuropsychology of Schizophrenia*. Hove: Lawrence Erlbaum Associates.

Furnham, A. and Bower, P. (1992). 'A comparison of academic and lay theories of schizophrenia'. *British Journal of Clinical Psychiatry* 26: 25-34.

Gacono, C.B., Meloy, J.R., Sheppard, K., Speth, E. and Roske, A. (1995). 'A clinical investigation of malingering and psychopathy in hospitalized insanity acquittees'. *Bulletin of the American Academy of Psychiatry and the Law* 23: 387-397.

Garety, P.A. (1992). 'Making sense of delusions'. *Psychiatry* 55: 282-291.

Garrido, V., Esteban, C. and Molero, C. (1996). 'The effectiveness of the treatment of psychopathy: A meta-analysis' in Cooke, D.J., Forth, A.E., Newman, J. and Hare, R.D. (eds.) *International Perspectives on Psychopathy*. Leicester: British Psychological Society.

Gerard, J.B. (1999). 'The medical model of mental illness: Its application to the insanity defence'. *International Journal of Law and Psychiatry* 22: 65-78.

Gibb, F. (2001). 'Insanity defence set to be scrapped' *The Times, 4*, February 14th. London, UK.

Gibbons, P., Mulryan, N. and O'Connor, A. (1997). 'Guilty but Insane: The insanity defence in Ireland, 1850-1995'. *British Journal of Psychiatry* 170: 467-472.

Goffman, E. (1963). *Stigma: Notes on the Management of Spoiled Identity*. New York: Prentice Hall.

Goldstein, J. and Katz, J. (1963). 'Abolish the "Insanity defense" – Why not?'. *Yale Law Journal* 72: 853-870.

Gomes M. and Maia F.H. (1998) 'Medication-taking behavior and drug self regulation in people with epilepsy'. *Arquivos de Neuro-Psiquiatria*, 56: 714–719.

Gottfedson, M.R. and Hirschi, T. (1990). *A General Theory of Crime*. Stanford: Stanford University Press.

Grounds, A.T. (1987). Talk to annual meeting of the Forensic Section of the Royal College of Psychiatrists. Stratford, UK.

Grounds, A.T. (1990). 'Transfers of sentenced prisoners to hospital'. *Criminal Law Review*: 544-551.

Gustafson, S.B. (1996). 'Aberrant self-promotion: The dark side of normal' in Cooke, D.J., Forth, A.E., Newman, J. and Hare, R.D. (eds.) *International Perspectives on Psychopathy*. Leicester: British Psychological Society.

Hale, M. (1736). *The History of Pleas of the Crown*. London: E. R. Nutt and R. Gosling.

Hall, L. and Tucker, C. (1985). 'Relationships between ethnicity, conceptions of mental illness, and attitudes associated with seeking psychological help'. *Psychological Report* 57: 907-916.

Halleck, S.L. (1986). 'Responsibility and excuse in medicine and law: A utilitarian perspective'. *Law and Contemporary Problems* 49: 127-146.

Halleck, S.L. (1988). 'Which patients are responsible for their illnesses?' *American Journal of Psychotherapy* 42: 338-353.

Halpern, A. (1977). 'The insanity defense: a judicial anachronism'. *Psychiatric Annals* 7: 41-63.

Hans, V.P. (1986). 'An analysis of public attitudes toward the insanity defense'. *Criminology* 24: 393-414.

Hans, V.P. and Slater, D. (1984). 'Plain crazy: Lay definitions of legal insanity'. *International Journal of Law and Psychiatry* 7: 105-114.

Hans, V.P. and Vidmar, N. (1986). *Judging the Jury*. New York: Plenum Press.

Hart, H.L.A. (1968). *Punishment and Responsibility: Essays in the Philosophy of Law*. Oxford: Clarendon Press.

Hart, H.L.A. and Honore, A.M. (1959). *Causation in the Law*. Oxford: Clarendon Press.

Hastie, R. (1993). *Inside the Juror*. Cambridge: Cambridge University Press.

Hastie, R., Penrod, S. and Pennington, N. (1983). *Inside the Jury*. Cambridge: Harvard University Press.

Heginbotham, C. and Elson, T. (1999). 'Public policy via law: Practitioner's sword and politician's shield' in Eastman, N. and Peay, J. (eds.) *Law Without Enforcement*. Oxford: Hart Publishing.

Heider, F. (1958). *The Psychology of Interpersonal Relations*. New York: Wiley.

Hermann, D.H.J. (1983). *The Insanity Defense: Philosophical, Historical and Legal Perspectives*. Springfield: Charles C. Thomas.

Hogarty, G.E., Goldberg, S.C. and The Collaborative Study Group (1973). 'Drug and sociotherapy in the aftercare of schizophrenic patients'. *Archives of General Psychiatry* 28: 54-63.

Holsti, O.R. (1969). *Content Analysis for the Social Sciences and Humanities*. Reading: Addison-Wesley.

Homant, R.J. and Kennedy, D.B. (1986). 'Judgment of legal insanity as a function of attitude toward the insanity defence'. *International Journal of Law and Psychiatry* 8: 67-81.

Howlett, M. (1998). *Medication, Non-compliance and Mentally Disordered Offenders: A Study of Independent Inquiry Reports*. London: The Zito Trust.

Hume, D. (1739/1978). *A Treatise of Human Nature*. Oxford: Oxford University Press.

Ingleby, D. (1980). *Critical Psychiatry: The Politics of Mental Health*. New York: Pantheon Books.

Jaspers, K. (1963). *General Psychopathology*. Chicago: University of Chicago Press.

Jeffery, C.R., del Carmen, R.V. and White, J.D. (1985). *Attacks on the Insanity Defence: Biological Psychiatry and New Perspectives on Criminal Behaviour*. Springfield: Charles C. Thomas.

Jellinek, E. (1960). *The Disease Concept of Alcoholism*. New Haven: Hillhouse Press.

Johnson, D.A.W. (1984). 'Observations on the use of long-acting depot neuroleptic injections in the maintenance therapy of schizophrenia'. *Journal of Clinical Psychiatry* 5: 13-21.

Joint Commission on Mental Illness and Health (1961). 'Action for Mental Health'. New York: Basic Books.

Jones, A.H. (1999). 'Moral capacity examined in three autobiographical narratives of patients with manic depressive illness'. *XXIVth International Congress on Law and Mental Health*. Toronto, Canada.

Jones, D.W. (1996). 'Families and the experience of mental distress' in Heller, T., Reynolds, J., Gomm, R., Muston, R. and Pattison, S. (eds.) *Mental Health Matters*. Basingstoke: MacMillan/The Open University.

Jowell, R., Curtice, J., Park, A., Brook, L., Thomson, K. and Bryson, C. (1997). *British Social Attitudes, the 14th Report: The End of Conservative Values?* Aldershot: Ashgate.

Kalven, H. and Zeisel, H. (1966). *The American Jury*. Boston: Little Brown.

Kandel, E.R. (1991). 'Disorders of thought: Schizophrenia' in Kandel, E.R., Schwartz, J.H. and Jessell, T.M. (eds.) *Principles of Neural Science*. East Norwalk: Appleton and Lange.

Kandel, E.R., Schwartz, J.H. and Jessell, T.M. (1991). *Principles of Neural Science*. East Norwalk: Appleton and Lange.

Karlsson, J.L. (1972). 'An Icelandic family study of schizophrenia' in Kaplan, A.R. (ed.) *Genetic Factors in Schizophrenia*. Springfield: Charles C. Thomas.

Katz, J. (1972). *Experimentation with Human Beings*. New York: Russel Sage.

Katz, L. (1987). *Bad Acts and Guilty Minds: Conundrums of the Criminal Law*. Chicago: University of Chicago Press.

Kelley, H.H. (1967). 'Attribution theory in social psychology' in Levine, D. (ed.) *Nebraska Symposium on Motivation*. Lincoln: University of Nebraska Press.

Kenny, A. (1978). *Freewill and Responsibility*. London: Routledge and Kegan Paul.

Kenny, D.A. (1979). *Correlation and Causality*. New York: Wiley.

Kermani, E.J. & Castaneda, R. (1996). 'Psychoactive substance abuse in forensic psychiatry'. *American Journal of Drug and Alcohol Abuse* 22: 1-27.

Kittrie, N.N. (1971). *The Right to be Different: Deviance and Enforced Therapy*. Baltimore: Johns Hopkins University Press.

Kovel, J. (1988). 'A critique of DSM-III'. *Research in Law, Deviance and Social Control* 9: 127-146.

La Russo, L. (1978). 'Sensitivity of paranoid patients to non-verbal cues'. *Journal of Abnormal Psychology* 87: 463-471.

LaFond, J.Q. and Durham, M.L. (1992). *Back to the Asylum: The Future of Mental Health Law and Policy in the United States*. New York: Oxford University Press.

Laing, R. (1965). *The Divided Self*. Harmondsworth: Penguin.

Laing, R.D. (1964). *Sanity, Madness and the Family, Vol I: Families of Schizophrenics*. London: Tavistock.

Laing, R.D. (1967). *The Politics of Experience and the Bird of Paradise*. Harmondsworth: Penguin.

Laing, R.D. (1969). *The Self and Others*. London: Tavistock.

Laing, R.D. and Cooper, D. (1964). *Reason and Violence: A Decade of Sartre's Philosophy, 1950-1960*. London: Tavistock.

Laor, N. (1984). 'Hobbesian principles in Szasz's writings'. *Clio Medica* 19: 32-39.

Laub, J.H. and Sampson, R.L. (1994). 'Unemployment, marital discord and deviant behaviour: The long term correlates of childhood misbehaviour' in Hirschi, T. and Gottfredson, M.R. (eds.) *The Generality of Deviance*. New Brunswick: Transaction Publishers.

Lehrman, N.S. (1994). 'Review of J. D. Bloom and M. H. Williams (1994) "Management and Treatment of Insanity Acquittees: A Model for the 1990s". Washington DC: American Psychiatric Press'. *The New England Journal of Medicine* 330: 1765-1766.

Leng, R. (1990). 'Mens rea and the defences to a criminal charge' in Blugrass, R. and Bowden, P. (eds.) *Principles and Practice of Forensic Psychiatry*. London: Churchill Livingstone.

Leonard, M. (1999). 'Outings for Hinckley: Wellness vs. safety'. *Boston Globe, A1, August 7th*. Boston, USA.

Lewis, A.J. (1955). 'Health as a social concept'. *British Journal of Sociology* 4: 109-124.

Likert, R. (1932). 'A technique for the measurement of attitudes'. *Archives of Psychology* 140: 1-55.

Lindqvist, P. (1986). 'Criminal homicide in northern Sweden 1970-1981: Alcohol intoxication, alcohol abuse and mental disease'. *International Journal of Law and Psychiatry* 8, 19-37.

Linhorst, D.M. and Dirks-Linhorst, P.A. (1997). 'The impact of insanity acquittees on Missouri's public mental health system'. *Law and Human Behaviour* 21: 327-338.

Lord, J.R. (1927). *Mental Hospitals and the Public*. London: Adlard and Son.

Ludwig, A. (1971). *Treating the Treatment Failures: The Challenge of Chronic Schizophrenia*. New York: Grune and Stratton.

Lysaker, P., Bell, M., Milstein, R., Bryson, G. and Beam-Goulet, J. (1994). 'Insight and psychosocial treatment compliance in schizophrenia'. *Psychiatry* 57: 307-315.

MacDonald, M. (1981). *Mystical Bedlam: Madness, Anxiety, and Healing in Seventeenth Century England*. Cambridge: Cambridge University Press.

Mackay, R.D. (1990). 'Fact and fiction about the insanity defence'. *Criminal Law Review*: 247-255.

Mackay, R.D. (1995). *Mental Condition Defences and the Criminal Law*. Oxford: Clarendon Press.

Mackay, R.D. and Kearns, G. (1999). 'More fact(s) about the insanity defence'. *Criminal Law Review*: 714-725.

Mackay, R.D. and Kearns, G. (2000). 'An upturn in unfitness to plead? Disability in relation to the trial under the 1991 act'. *Criminal Law Review*: 532-546.

Mackie, J.L. (1985). *Persons and Values*. Oxford: Clarendon Press.

MacLean, U. (1969). 'Community attitudes to mental illness in Edinburgh'. *British Journal of Preventative Social Medicine* 23: 45-52.

MacPherson, R., Alexander, M. and Jerrom, W. (1998). 'Medication refusal among patients treated in a community mental health rehabilitation service'. *Psychiatric Bulletin* 22: 744-748.

Maeder, T. (1985). *Crime and Madness*. New York: Harper and Row.

Matthews, E. (1999). 'Mental and physical illness – An unsustainable separation?' in Eastman, N. and Peay, J. (eds.) *Law Without Enforcement*. Oxford: Hart Publishing.

McSherry, B. (1999). 'Criminal responsibility and voluntary conduct: Legal versus psychological concepts'. *American Psychology-Law Society (APLS) and European Association of Psychology and Law (EAPL) International Conference*. Dublin, Ireland.

Menninger, K.A. (1930). *The Human Mind*. New York: Kopf.

Mickenberg, I. (1987). 'A pleasant surprise: the Guilty But Mentally Ill verdict has both succeeded in its own right and successfully preserved the traditional role of the insanity defence'. *University of Cincinnati Law Review* 55: 943-996.

Miles, A. (1987). *The Mentally Ill in Contemporary Society*. Oxford: Basil Blackwell.

Mill, J.S. (1843/1967). *A System of Logic Ratiocinative and Inductive*. London: Longmans.

Miller, K.S. and Radelet, M.L. (1993). *Executing the Mentally Ill: The Criminal Justice System and the Case of Alvin Ford*. Newbury Park: Sage.

Miller, R.D., Olin, J., Johnson, D., Doidge, J., Iverson, D. and Fantone, E. (1996). 'Forcing the insanity defence on unwilling defendants: Best interests and the dignity of the law'. *The Journal of Psychiatry and Law* 24: 487-509.

Mishler, E. (1973). 'Man, morality and madness: Critical perspectives on the work of R.D. Laing' in Rubenstein, B. (ed.) *Psychoanalysis and Contemporary Science*. New York: MacMillan.

Mitchell, C.N. (1986). 'Culpable mental disorder and criminal liability'. *International Journal of Law and Psychiatry* 8: 273-299.

Mitchell, E.W. (1999a). 'Does psychiatric disorder affect the likelihood of violent offending? A review and critique of the major findings'. *Medicine, Science, and the Law* 39: 23-30.

Mitchell, E.W. (1999b). 'Meta-responsibility and mental disorder: Causing the conditions of one's own insanity plea'. *Journal of Forensic Psychiatry* 10: 597-622.

Monahan, J. (1997). 'Clinical and actuarial predictions of violence' in Faigman, D., Kaye, D., Saks, M. and Sanders, J. (eds.) *Modern Scientific Evidence: The Law and Science of Expert Testimony*. St. Paul: West Publishing Company.

Moore, M. (1975). 'Some myths about mental illness'. *Archives of General Psychiatry* 32: 1483-1497.

Moore, M. (1984). *Law and Psychiatry: Rethinking the Relationship*. Cambridge: Cambridge University Press.

Moore, M. (1985). 'Causation and the excuses'. *California Law Review* 73: 1091-1149.

Moore, M. (1993). *Act and Crime*. Oxford: Clarendon Press.

Moran, R. (1981). *Knowing Right from Wrong: The Insanity Defense of Daniel McNaughtan*. New York: Macmillan.

Moran, R. (1986). 'The punitive uses of the insanity defence: The trial for treason of Oxford, Edward (1840)'. *International Journal of Law and Psychiatry* 9: 171-190.

Morris, G.H. (1975). *The Insanity Defense: A Blueprint for Legislative Reform*. Toronto: Lexington.

Morris, G.H. (1997). 'Wickedness, mental disorder and law'. *Psychiatric Annals* 27: 638-641.

Morris, N. (1982). 'The criminal responsibility of the mentally ill'. *Syracuse Law Review* 33: 477-531.

Morse, S.J. (1994). 'Causation, compulsion, and involuntariness'. *Bulletin of the American Academy of Psychiatry and Law* 22: 159-180.

Mossman, D. (1994). 'Predictions of violence: Being accurate about accuracy'. *Journal of Consulting and Clinical Psychology* 62: 783-790.

Mullan, B. (1995). *Mad to be Normal: Conversations with R. D. Laing*. London: Free Association Books.

Nasar, S. (1998). *A Beautiful Mind: A Biography Of John Forbes Nash, Jr., Winner Of The Nobel Prize In Economics, 1994*. New York: Simon and Schuster.

Neaman, J. (1975). *Suggestion of the Devil: The Origins of Madness*. New York: Doubleday.

Neumann, C.S., Walker, E.F., Weinstein, J. and Cutshaw, C. (1997). 'Psychotic patients' awareness of mental illness: Implications for legal defense proceedings'. *The Journal of Psychiatry and Law* 24: 421-442.

Nissman, D.M., Barnes, B.R. and Albert, G.P. (1980). *Beating the Insanity Defense: Denying the License to Kill*. Toronto: Lexington.

Nitzer, L. (1978). *My Life in Court*. New York: Jove.

Nunnally, J.C. (1961). *Popular Conceptions of Mental Health: Their Development and Change*. New York: Holt, Rinehart and Wilson.

Ogloff, J.R.P. (1991). 'A comparison of insanity defense standards on juror decision making'. *Law and Human Behaviour* 15: 509-531.

Ogloff, J.R.P. (1996). 'Legal issues associated with the concept of psychopathy' in Cooke, D.J., Forth, A.E., Newman, J. and Hare, R.D. (eds.) *International Perspectives on Psychopathy*. Leicester: British Psychological Society.

Olmstead, D.W. and Durham, K. (1976). 'Stability of mental health attitudes: A semantic differential study'. *Journal of Health and Social Behaviour* 17: 35-44.

Pam, A. (1990). 'A critique of the scientific status of biological psychiatry'. *Acta Psychiatrica Scandinavica* 82: 1-35.

Parsons, T. (1951). *The Social System*. New York: The Free Press.

Pasewark, R.A. (1981). 'Insanity plea: A review of the research literature'. *Journal of Psychiatry and Law* 9: 357-401.

Pasewark, R.A., Bieber, S., Bosten, K.J., Kiser, M. and Steadman, H.J. (1982). 'Criminal recidivism among insanity acquittees'. *International Journal of Law and Psychiatry* 5: 365-374.

Pasewark, R.A. and McGinley, H. (1985). 'Insanity plea: National survey of frequency and success'. *Journal of Psychiatry and Law* 13: 101-108.

Pasewark, R.A., Randolph, R., and Beiber, S. (1984). 'Insanity plea: Statutory language and trial procedures'. *Journal of Psychiatry and Law* 12: 399-422.

Peay, J. (1997). 'Mentally disordered offenders' in Maguire, M., Morgan, R. and Reiner, R. (eds.) *The Oxford Handbook of Criminology*. Oxford: Clarendon Press.

Peele, S. (1989). *The Diseasing of America*. Boston: Houghton Mifflin.

Perkins, R. and Moodley, P. (1993). 'The arrogance of insight'. *Psychiatric Bulletin* 17: 233-234.

Perlin, M.L. (1985). '"The things we do for love": John Hinckley's trial and the future of the insanity defense in federal courts'. *New York Law School Law Review* 30: 857-863.

Perlin, M.L. (1989). *Mental Disability Law: Civil and Criminal*. Charlottesville: Michie Co.

Perlin, M.L. (1994). *The Jurisprudence of the Insanity Defense.* Durham: Carolina Academic Press.

Perlin, M.L. (1996). 'Myths, realities and the political world: The anthropology of insanity defense attitudes'. *Bulletin of the American Academy of Psychiatry and the Law* 24: 5-26.

Perlin, M.L. (1997). '"The borderline which separated you from me": The insanity defense, the authoritarian spirit, the fear of faking, and the culture of punishment'. *Iowa Law Review* 82: 1375-1426.

Perlin, M.L. and Dorfman, D.A. (1993). 'Sanism, social science, and the development of mental-disability law jurisprudence'. *Behavioural Sciences and the Law* 11: 47-66.

Phillips, D.L. (1963). 'Rejection: A possible consequence of seeking help for mental disorders'. *American Sociological Review* 18: 963-972.

Pinel, P. (1806/1962). *A Treatise on Insanity.* New York: Hafner.

Platt, A.M. and Diamond, B. (1965). 'The origins and development of the 'Wild Beast' concept of mental illness and its relation to theories of criminal responsibility'. *Journal of the History of Behavioural Sciences* 1: 355-367.

Potas, I. (1982). *Just Deserts for the Mad.* Canberra: Australian Institute of Criminology.

Poulson, R.L., Brondino, M.J., Brown, M.B. and Braithwaite, R.L. (1998). 'Relations among mock jurors' attitudes, trial evidence, and their selections of an insanity defense verdict: A path analytic approach'. *Psychological Reports* 82: 3-16.

Poulson, R.L., Wuensch, K.L., Brown, M.B. and Braithwaite, R.L. (1997). 'Mock jurors' evaluations of insanity defence verdict selection: The role of death penalty attitudes'. *Journal of Social Behaviour and Personality* 12: 1065-1078.

Rabkin, J. (1974). 'Public attitudes toward mental illness: A review of the literature'. *Schizophrenia Bulletin* 10: 8-33.

Radden, J. (1985). *Madness and Reason.* London: George Allen and Unwin.

Raine, A. (1993). *The Psychopathology of Crime.* San Diego: Academic Press.

Raine, A., Lencz, T. and Mednick, S.A. (1995). *Schizotypal Personality.* Cambridge: Cambridge University Press.

Reverley, M.A. and Deakin, J.F.W. (1999). *The Psychopharmacology of Schizophrenia.* London: Arnold.

Reznek, L. (1991). *The Philosophical Defense of Psychiatry.* London: Routledge.

Reznek, L. (1997). *Evil or Ill: Justifying the Insanity Defense.* London: Routledge.

Roberts, G. (1991). 'Delusional belief systems and meaning in life: A preferred reality?'. *British Journal of Psychiatry* 159 (Suppl. 14): 19-28.

Robinson, D.N. (1980). *Psychology and Law: Can Justice Survive the Social Sciences?* New York: Oxford University Press.

Robinson, D.N. (1996). *Wild Beasts and Idle Humors: The Insanity Defense from Antiquity to Present.* Cambridge: Harvard University Press.

Robinson, P.H. (1984). 'Imputed criminal liability'. *Yale Law Journal* 93: 609-665.

Robinson, P. H. (1985). 'Causing the conditions of one's own defense'. *Virginia Law Review* 71: 1-63.

Rogers, R. (1988). *Clinical Assessment of Malingering and Deception.* New York: Guilford.

Rogers, R. and Schuman, D. (2000). *Conducting Insanity Evaluations.* New York: Guilford.

Rogers, R., Seman, W. and Clark, C.R. (1986). 'Assessment of criminal responsibility: Initial validation of the R-CRAS with the M'Naghten and GBMI standards'. *International Journal of Law and Psychiatry* 9: 67-75.

Rosenthal, R. (1966). *Experimental Effects in Behavioural Research.* New York: Appleton-Century Crofts.

Rudnick, A. and Levy, A. (1994). 'Personality disorders and criminal responsibility: A second opinion'. *International Journal of Law and Psychiatry* 17: 409-420.

Sacks, O. (1985). *The Man Who Mistook His Wife for a Hat*. New York: Simon and Schuster.

Saks, M.J. and Hastie, R. (1978). *Social Psychology in Court*. New York: Van Nostrand Reinhold.

Sarbin, T. (1991). 'The social construction of schizophrenia' in Flack, W., Miller, D. and Wiener, M. (eds.) *What is Schizophrenia?* New York: Springer-Verlag.

Sarbin, T.R. and Mancusco, J.C. (1970). 'Failure of a moral enterprise: Attitudes of the public toward mental illness'. *Journal of Consulting and Clinical Psychology* 35: 159-172.

Sarbin, T.R. and Mancusco, J.C. (1972). 'Paradigms and moral judgment: Improper conduct is not disease'. *Journal of Consulting and Clinical Psychology* 39: 1-5.

Sartre, J.-P. (1943/1969). *Being and Nothingness*. London: Methuen.

Scadding, J.G. (1967). 'Diagnosis: The clinician and the computer'. *Lancet* 2: 877-882.

Schaler, J.A. (1997). 'Smoking right and responsibility'. *Psychnews International* 2 *(Internet journal)*. Available at http://mentalhelp.net/pni/pni22b.htm.

Schanda, H., Felsberger, C., Topf, R., Grunberger, J. and Linzmayer, L. (1993). 'Aggression, psychiatric disorder, and offense – the Freiburger Aggressionfragebogen (FAF) (Frieburg Agression Inventory) in mentally disordered offenders'. *Neuropsychiatrie* 7: 176-182.

Scheff, T.J. (1966). *Being Mentally Ill*. London: Weidenfeld and Nicholson.

Schopp, R. (1991). *Automatism, Insanity, and the Psychology of Criminal Responsibility*. New York: Cambridge University Press.

Sealy, A.P. (1975). 'The jury: Decision-making in a small group' in Brown, H. and Stevens, R. (eds.) *Social Behaviour and Experience*. London: Hodder and Stoughton.

Sealy, A.P. (1979). 'The contribution of psychology to legal processes: An analysis of jury studies' in Farrington, D.P., Hawkins, K. and Lloyd-Bostock, S. (eds.) *Psychology, Law and Legal Processes*. London: MacMillan.

Sealy, A.P. and Cornish, W.R. (1973). 'Jurors and their verdicts'. *Modern Law Review* 36: 496-508.

Sedgwick, P. (1973). 'Illness – mental and otherwise'. *The Hastings Center* 1: 19-40.

Sedlack, G. and Stanley, J. (1992). *Social Research: Theory and Methods*. Boston: Allyn and Bacon.

Shah, P.J., Greenberg, W.M. and Convit, A. (1994). 'Hospitalized insanity acquittees level of functioning'. *Bulletin of the American Academy of Psychiatry and Law* 22: 85-93.

Shelford, L. (1833). *A Practical Treatise on the Law Concerning Lunatics, Idiots, and Persons of Unsound Mind*. Philadelphia: J. S. Little.

Sherlock, R. (1984). 'Compliance and responsibility: New issues for the insanity defense'. *Journal of Psychiatry and Law* 12: 483-505.

Silver, E. (1995). 'Punishment or treatment – comparing the lengths of confinement of successful and unsuccessful insanity defendants'. *Law and Human Behaviour* 19: 375-388.

Simon, R.J. (1967). *The Jury and the Defense of Insanity*. Boston: Little Brown and Company.

Simon, R.J. and Mahan, L. (1971). 'Quantifying burdens of proof'. *Law and Society Review* 5: 319-330.

Skeem, J.L. and Golding, S.L. (1999). 'Understanding juror decision-making in insanity defense cases: The nature and variability of jurors' intuitive prototypes of insanity and their relationship to verdict selection'. *American Psychology-Law Society (APLS) and*

European Association of Psychology and Law (EAPL) International Conference. Dublin, Ireland.

Slodov, M.D. (1989). 'Criminal responsibility and the noncompliant psychiatric offender: Risking madness'. *Case Western Reserve Law Review*: 271-330.

Slovenko, R. (1995). *Psychiatry and Criminal Culpability*. New York: John Wiley and Sons.

Solomka, B. (1996). 'The role of psychiatric evidence in passing "longer than normal" sentences'. *Journal of Forensic Psychiatry* 7: 239-55.

Spackman, M.P., Belcher, J.C. and Sauls, A. (1999). 'Effects of perceived emotional intensity on attributions of responsibility for emotions'. *American Psychology-Law Society (APLS) and European Association of Psychology and Law (EAPL) International Conference*. Dublin, Ireland.

Spring, R.L. (1998). 'The return to *mens rea*: Salvaging a reasonable perspective on mental disorder in criminal trials'. *International Journal of Law and Psychiatry* 21: 187-196.

SPSS Inc. (1999). 'SPSS for Windows'. Chicago: SPSS Inc.

Star, S. (1952). 'What the public thinks about mental health and mental illness'. *Annual Meeting of the National Association for Mental Health*. Chicago: University of Chicago Microfilms.

Star, S. (1955). 'The public's idea about mental illness' *Annual Meeting of the National Association for Mental Health*. Chicago: National Opinion Research Center (NORC) Library.

Steadman, H.J. and Cocozza, J. (1977). 'Selective reporting and the public's misconceptions of the criminally insane'. *Public Opinion Quarterly* 41: 523-533.

Steadman, H.J., Monahan, J., Hartstone, E., Davis, S.K. and Robbins, P.C. (1982). 'Mentally disordered offenders: A national survey of patients and facilities'. *Law and Human Behaviour* 6: 31-38.

Stephen, J. (1883). *A History of the Criminal Law of England*. London: Macmillan.

Stevens, A. and Price, J. (1996). *Evolutionary Psychiatry*. London: Routledge.

Stone, W.A. (1984). *Law, Psychiatry, and Morality*. Washington DC: American Psychiatric Press.

Storr, A. (1972). *The Dynamics of Creation*. London: Secker and Warburg.

Sudman, S. (1983). 'Applied sampling' in Rossi, P.H., Wright, J.D. and Anderson, A.B. (eds.) *Handbook of Survey Research*. London: Academic Press.

Sudman, S. and Bradburn, N.M. (1983). *Asking Questions: A Practical Guide to Questionnaire Design*. San Francisco: Jossey-Bass.

Suppes, P. (1970). *A Probabilistic Theory of Causality*. Amsterdam: North-Holland.

Sutherland, P.J. and Gearty, C.A. (1992). 'Insanity and the European Court of Human Rights'. *Criminal Law Review*: 417.

Svensson, T. (1995). *On the Notion of Mental Illness*. Aldershot: Ashgate.

Swanson, J.W., Holzer, C.E., Ganju, V.K. and Jono, R.T. (1991). 'Violence and psychiatric disorder in the community: evidence from the Epidemiologic Catchment Area surveys'. *Hospital and Community Psychiatry* 41: 761-770.

Swartz, M.S., Swanson, J.W., Hiday, V.A., Borum, R., Wagner, H.R. and Burns, B.J. (1998). 'Violence and severe mental illness: The effects of substance abuse and nonadherence to medication'. *American Journal of Psychiatry* 155: 226-231.

Syre, F.B. (1932). '"*Mens Rea*"'. *Harvard Law Review* 45: 974-1026.Szasz, T.S. (1960). 'The myth of mental illness'. *American Psychologist* 15: 113-118.

Szasz, T.S. (1961). *The Myth of Mental Illness: Foundations For a Theory of Personal Conduct*. New York: Hoeber-Harper.

Szasz, T.S. (1963). *Law, Liberty and Psychiatry*. New York: Macmillan.

Szasz, T.S. (1973). *The Second Sin*. London: Routledge and Kegan Paul.

Szasz, T.S. (1974). *The Myth of Mental Illness: Foundations For a Theory of Personal Conduct*, Revised ed. New York: Harper and Row.

Szasz, T.S. (1990). *The Untamed Tongue: A Dissenting Dictionary*. La Salle: Open Court.

Szasz, T.S. (1997). *Insanity: The Idea and its Consequences*. New York: Syracuse University Press.

Teubner, G. (1993). *Law as an Autopoietic System*. Oxford: Blackwell.

The Law Commission (1989). *Criminal Law, A Criminal Code for England and Wales, Volume I: Report and Draft Criminal Code Bill*. London: HMSO.

Thomas, P. (1997). *The Dialectics of Schizophrenia*. London: Free Association Books.

Tiffany, L.P. and Tiffany, M. (1990). *The Legal Defense of Pathological Intoxication – With Related Issues of Temporary and Self-inflicted Insanity*. New York: Quorum Books.

Tuke, S. (1813). *Description of the Retreat*. York: W. Alexander.

Turnbull, A. (1964). *The Letters of F. Scott Fitzgerald*. London: Bodley Head.

Turner-Warwick, M. (1994). 'The marvel of the lung and human responsibility – a great contempt of God's good gifts: The Harveian Oration of 1994'. *Journal of the Royal College of Physicians of London* 28: 530-537.

Van Putten, T., Crumpton, E. and Yale, C. (1976). 'Drug refusal in schizophrenics and the wish to be crazy'. *Archives of General Psychiatry* 33: 1443-1446.

Veatch, R.M. (1997). 'The medical model: Its nature and problems' in Edwards, R.B. (ed.) *Ethics of Psychiatry: Insanity, Rational Autonomy, and Mental Health Care*. Amherst: Prometheus Books.

Verdun-Jones, S. (1989). 'Sentencing the partly mad and partly bad: The case of the hospital order in England and Wales'. *International Journal of Law and Psychiatry* 12: 1-27.

Vidmar, N. and Ellsworth, P.C. (1974). 'Public opinion and the death penalty'. *Stanford Law Review* 26: 1245-1270.

Walker, L. and Thibaut, J. (1971). 'An experimental examination of pre-trial conference techniques'. *Minnesota Law Review* 60: 1113-1129.

Walker, N. (1968). *Crime and Insanity in England*. Edinburgh: University of Edinburgh Press.

Walker, N. (1985). 'Psychiatric explanations as excuses' in Roth, M. and Blugrass, R. (eds.) *Psychiatry, Human Rights, and the Law*. Cambridge: Cambridge University Press.

Ward, M. and Applin, C. (1998). *The Unlearned Lesson: The Role of Alcohol and Drug Misuse in Homicides Perpetrated by People With Mental Health Problems*. London: Wynne Howard Books.

Weibe, R.P. (1997). 'Psychopathy as a sexual strategy'. *American Society of Criminology 49th Annual Meeting*. San Diego, USA.

Weibe, R.P. and Hirschi, T. (1997). 'Lack of diligence and the development of the delinquent personality' *American Society of Criminology 49th Annual Meeting*. San Diego, USA.

Weinstock, R. (1999). 'Comparison of moral capacities of psychotic and addicted individuals'. *XXIVth International Congress on Law and Mental Health*. Toronto, Canada.

Weld, H.P. and Roff, M. (1938). 'A study in the formation of opinion based upon legal evidence'. *American Journal of Psychology* 51: 609-628.

West, D. J., and Walk, A. (Eds.). (1977). *Daniel McNaughton – His Trial and the Aftermath*. London: Gaskell Books.

Williams, G. (1963). *The Proof of Guilt*. London: Stevens.

Willis, T. (1680). *Opera Omnia*. Geneva: Apud Samuelem de Tournes.

Wing, J.K., Monck, E., Brown, G.W. and Carstairs, G.M. (1964). 'Morbidity in the community of schizophrenic patients discharged from London mental hospitals in 1959'. *British Journal of Psychiatry* 110: 10-21.

Young, J.L., Zonana, H.V. and Shepler, L. (1986). 'Medication noncompliance in schizophrenia: Codification and update'. *Journal of the American Academy of Psychiatry and the Law* 14: 105-122.

Zilboorg, G. (1935). *The Medical Men and the Witch During the Renaissance: The Hideyo Nogushi Lectures*. Baltimore: Johns Hopkins Press.

Legal Cases

A-G for Northern Ireland v. Gallagher [1963] AC 349
A-G v. Prior (2001), (Unreported, Royal Court of Jersey Judgment No. 2001/035, 9th February)
Ahluwalia [1992] 4 All ER 889
Bailey [1983] 1 WLR 760
Bowen [1996] Crim. LR 577
Bratty v. A-G for Northern Ireland [1963] AC 386
Brawner v. United States (1972), 471 F.2d 969
Caldwell [1982] AC 341
Cunningham [1957] 2 QB 396
Daniel McNaughton's Case (1843), 10 C. & F. 200
Davies [1983] Crim. LR 741
Davis (1881), 14 Cox CC 563
DPP v. Majewski [1977] AC 443
Durham v. United States (1954), 214 F.2d 862
Elliot v. C (a minor) [1983] WLR 939
Fain v. Commonwealth (1879), 78 Ky. 183
Fleming (1993), 14 Cr. App. R(s) 151
Ford v. Wainwright (1986), 477 U.S. 699
Hennessey [1989] 2 All ER 9
Hill v. State (1978), 358 So.2d 190
Hobart v. Shin (1998), Ill. Sup. Ct., WL 884567
Howell (1985), 7 Cr. App. R.(s) 360
In re Noel (1979), 601 P.2d 1152
Jackson v. Indiana (1971), 406 U.S. 715
Jones v. United States (1983), 463 U.S. 354
Kay v. Butterworth (1945), 173 LT 191
Kingston (1994), 99 Cr. App. R. 286
L v. Bournewood Community NHS Trust, ex parte L (Secretary of State and Others Intervening) [1998] 3 All ER 289 (HL).
Naidu v. Laird (1988), 539 A.2d 1064
Parsons v. Alabama (1886), 2 So. 854
Pate [1987] Crim L. R. 645
People v. Chavez (1981), 629 P.2d 1040
People v. Hernandez (2000), 22 Cal. 4th 512
Quick [1973] Q.B. 910
R v. Byrne [1960] 2 Q.B. 396
R v. Hardie [1984] 3 All ER 848
R v. Kemp [1957] 1 Q.B. 399
R v. Merseyside MHRT and Another ex p. K [1990] 1 All ER 694

R v. MHRT for South Thames Region, ex parte Smith (1998), (unreported QBD)
R v. Podola [1959] 3 All ER 418
R v. Sullivan [1984] A.C. 156
R v. Tandy [1989] 1 WLR 350
R v. Thomas (1996), 2 BMLR 120
Reg. v. Oxford (1840), 9 C. & P. 525
Rex v. Arnold (1723), 16 How St. Tr. 684
Rex v. Hadfield (1800), 27 How. St. Tr. 1281
Robinson v. California (1962), 370 U.S 660
Salzman v. United States (1968), 405 F.2d 358
State of New Hampshire v. Pike (1869), 49 NH 399
State v. Gooze (1951), 81 A.2d 811
State v. Johnson (1988), 753 P.2d 154
State v. Krol (1975), 344 A. 2d 289
State v. Maik (1972), 60 N.J. 203
State v. McLeary, No. CR49471 (C.P. Cuyahoga City, Ohio Nov. 19, 1979), reversed No. CR42116 (Ohio Ct. App. 8th Dist. Nov 20 1980)
Sullivan [1984] AC 156
Tarasoff v. Board of Regents of Univ. of California (1976), 551 P.2d 334
Thomas [1995] Crim LR 314
United States v. Burnim (1978), 576 F.2d 236
United States v. Henderson (1982), 680 F.2d 659
United States v. Lyons (1984), 739 F.2d 994
United States v. Samuels (1986), 810 F.2d 1052
Victory v. Bombard (1977), 432 F. Supp. 1240
Winterwerp v. The Netherlands [1979] 2 EHRR 387

Appendix: The Measuring Instrument Questions

The following questions followed the preliminary instructions and case vignette.[1]

1) Given the information you have available, would you be inclined to find Tom 'Guilty' or 'Not Guilty by Reason of Insanity'? (Please circle your answer)
2) What are the reasons for your decision? (Please give as much detail as possible)
3) Given the information you have available, do you think Tom should be sent to prison (to be punished) or mental hospital (to be cared for as a patient)?
4) Given the information you have available, how long do you think Tom should remain at the institution (prison or mental hospital)? (Please estimate a number even if you are not sure)
5) Tom has a duty to take responsibility for his own illness
6) Tom understood that he was ill
7) Tom caused his own illness
8) Tom killed his wife because of his illness
9) Tom's illness affected his ability to look after himself (e.g. take medication) and resist getting more ill
10) Tom liked being ill
11) Tom should have resisted his illness more
12) Tom should have been more careful in taking his medication
13) Tom was a good person before he became ill
14) Tom was a good person after he became ill
15) Tom made his illness worse through his own fault
16) Mental illness is caused by a number of social stresses such as money worries
17) Mental illness should be treated through the use of medical drugs
18) Mental illness is caused by learning from others with similarly strange and bizarre behaviour
19) Mental illness should be treated by showing patients the proper way to act and think
20) Mental illness is caused by medical problems such as chemical imbalance in the brain
21) Mental illness should be treated by producing a more comfortable and less stressful society
22) The insanity defence should be abolished

---

[1] See *SUPRA* section 6.7 response methods available to the subjects for various questions.

23) The insanity defence needs a lot of reform
24) The insanity defence is sometimes justified
25) The insanity defence is a necessary part of our legal system
26) It is wrong to punish insane people who break the law
27) Insane defendants are entitled to treatment
28) Most people found Not Guilty By Reason of Insanity are really insane
29) I'm confident that people found Not Guilty by Reason of Insanity are only released when it's safe to do so
30) Psychiatrists should testify about a defendant's mental condition in insanity trials
31) The insanity defence doesn't affect the crime rate
32) The insane should be treated rather than punished if they commit crime
33) Punishment doesn't work on the insane
34) The insanity plea is a loophole that allows too many guilty people to go free
35) Even if people are insane, we should punish them if they break the law
36) The insanity defence sends a message to criminals that they can get away with crime
37) The insanity defence allows dangerous people out on the streets
38) Judges and juries have a hard time telling whether defendants are really sane or insane
39) If psychiatrists are paid enough, they will say anything about a defendant's sanity
40) The insanity plea is mainly a rich person's defence
41) Insane people should be punished for their crimes just like everyone else
42) First of all, when defendants are charged with a crime, they can decide to plead Not Guilty By Reason of Insanity. Out of 100 defendants who are charged with a crime, how many do you think plead Not Guilty By Reason of Insanity? (Again, please estimate if you do not 'know')
43) Now, when defendants plead Not Guilty By Reason of Insanity at their trials, a judge or a jury has to decide whether or not the defendants are indeed Not Guilty By Reason of Insanity. Out of every 100 defendants who plead insanity, how many are actually found Not Guilty By Reason of Insanity by judges or juries?
44) Out of every 100 defendants found Not Guilty by Reason of Insanity, how many go free immediately?
45) How many are sent to mental hospital?
46) If defendants are sent to a mental hospital, how long do they stay there, on average?
47) The Government should redistribute income from the better-off to those who are less well off.
48) Big business benefits owners at the expense of workers
49) Ordinary people do not get their fair share of the nation's wealth
50) There is one law for the rich and one for the poor
51) Management will always try to get the better of employees if it gets the chance
52) Young people today don't have enough respect for traditional British values

53) People who break the law should be given stiffer sentences
54) For some crimes, the death penalty is the most appropriate sentence
55) Schools should teach children to obey authority
56) The law should always be obeyed, even if a particular law is wrong
57) Censorship of films and magazines is necessary to uphold moral standards
58) Too many guilty persons escape punishment because of legal technicalities
59) Illegally obtained evidence should not be admissible in court even if that evidence is the only way of obtaining a conviction
60) In general, the courts deal too harshly with criminals
61) Age:
62) Gender:
63) The 1991 Census uses the following ethnic categories. Which would you use to best describe yourself? Ethnic origin:
64) Occupation (if student, then please write subject and year):
65) At what age did you finish full time education? (If still in full-time education, then please write in the age at which you EXPECT to finish).
66) Please rate the amount of experience you think you have of mental disorder (e.g. personally suffered from it, friends/family suffered from it etc.)
67) Do you think you are well informed about mental disorder and mental disorder issues?
68) Would you be willing for us to contact you to arrange an interview about your opinions on the insanity defence? If so, then please fill out contact details (your answers to this questionnaire will still be treated anonymously).

Index

DATE DUE
